13649
6.95

DI204989

THE CANADIAN WORKER
IN THE TWENTIETH CENTURY

THE CANADIAN WORKER IN THE TWENTIETH CENTURY

Edited by

Irving Abella

and

David Millar

TORONTO
Oxford University Press
1978

Canadian Cataloguing in Publication Data
Main entry under title:
The Canadian worker in the twentieth century
Bibliography: p.
ISBN 0-19-540250-2

1. Labor and laboring classes—Canada—History—
Addresses, essays, lectures. I. Abella, Irving
Martin, 1940-   II. Millar, David, 1936-

HD8106.C35   301.44'42'0971   C78-001154-6

© Oxford University Press (Canada) 1978
Cover photograph courtesy of the United Church Archives
ISBN-0-19-540250-2
1 2 3 4—1 0 9 8
Printed in Canada by Webcom Limited

Contents

Introduction

The Canadian Worker in the Twentieth Century is a documentary anthology of the twentieth-century Canadian worker—man, woman, and child. Despite its title the book clearly cannot encompass the whole of this century, and in fact covers only the period from 1900 to 1940, although a few selections have been included to show how earlier social problems have resurfaced in the present. We have not attempted to put together a documentary history of the union movement and its bitter struggle for legal status. Nor is this simply an anecdotal social history of Canada. Rather it is an attempt, largely through first-hand accounts, to reconstruct the daily lives of the men, women, and children who helped build this nation.

In selecting these documents our guiding principle has been to prefer eyewitness views of the activities of work, home, and leisure rather than the manifestoes and monuments of labour history. Where possible we have chosen material that is not readily available in print, but not at the expense of sources that show significant patterns of life and work. It is implicit in this book that we believe the crucial developments in Canada since 1900 to be the growth of immigration, industrialism and urbanization, and as a corollary to these, the advent of social democracy, national minimum standards of welfare, and the organization of workers in mechanized industry. We hope, however, that the materials and stories we have chosen will provide a much greater range of themes.

We have tried to make the whole collection representative of the experiences of large groups of workers, and to that extent of the condition of the Canadian working class in this period. To accomplish this we have attempted to provide as large a variety of physical settings as possible: home and workplace, bush camp and homestead, outport, farm, small town and city. We have sought to explore some of the diversity of popular culture in various regions, as well as to portray some of the unrecognized similarities among ethnic groups, and among different industries and occupations.

Who, then, was the Canadian wage-earner in this period? He or she was typically a blue-collar labourer (manual or industrial) who began paid work at about fourteen. British ancestry or its equivalents (property, primary education, some skill or literacy) might lift a workingman's income above the subsistence level. There were other strategies of 'making it' as well: setting the whole family to work, exploiting them or fellow immigrants, crowding lodgers into the home, leaving wife and children behind while working for a 'stake'. Few workers had control of the means of production or distribution, skills, tools, credit or (with the important exception of homesteaders) land. Their power to determine their working conditions was severely—if not completely—limited.

In the last ten years, labour history in Canada has had a sort of industrial take-off. Despite gaps still to be filled by further research, we were pleasantly surprised to find that a treasure-house of material awaits the researcher, professional or amateur. Archivists have recognized the value of tape-recordings, but much work still needs to be done with interviews, local records, court documents, and the files of charitable institutions. Nevertheless, there is an immense range of testimony on work, home, and leisure—so immense that it would be impossible in one volume to cover every significant industry, region and ethnic group, or even to mark the major developments in each period. And we have had to omit some aspects of working-class life—for example, the impact of religion and education. We have also been forced regretfully to leave out some explosive unpublished documents on government repression during the First World War, secret alliances between unions and bosses in the early 1920s, and the union-busting tactics used by employers in the 1930s. There have been some hard choices: for every document included, two or three at least as intriguing have been reluctantly omitted.

Naturally many of these documents have a built-in bias, but this is an inevitable corollary of the attempt to present experience at first hand. Although we have taken care to identify the group or viewpoint of each eyewitness, the reader should be on guard against self-justification in oral or written memoirs, and against special pleading or one-sided presentation of a case in briefs to government bodies. What may be lost in objectivity is more than compensated for, we feel, by the intensity of the experience being described. It is precisely because these statements are rooted in individual lives, rather than a picture of Mr Average derived from a statistical composite, that we get some idea of the human side of the process. This book is not a substitute for political analysis or union history. These deal with the anatomy of the working class; we have tried to show the living bodies.

1
Working Conditions
1900 – 1918

The first two decades of this century in Canada have been described as the great boom, a time of swelling immigration that peopled the West, filled the factories of the East, and put new sparkle in the Canadian mosaic. But what is not well known is that it was also a time of periodic economic collapse that brought in its wake much unemployment, widespread deprivation, and a pervading sense of hopelessness.

In both East and West, in city and country, immigrants drove up land values and drove down wages. They were good for business, and quick to learn its ruthlessness. The peasant of today hoped to be the contractor, landlord, or farmer of tomorrow. There were internal migrants as well: Canadian boys from the bush farms became 'skilled workers' and lorded it over those of lesser abilities. In the rush to the new camps, boomtowns, and factories they could become in rapid succession a foreman, a clerk, a boss. Those who spoke and wrote English hoped to get riches, or the status of a white collar, or both. But when the boom failed, these tens of thousands whom it had pulled across the seas and off the farm were left stranded in the cities. They were now mere wage slaves at the mercy of the market.

Working conditions were brutal. In good times there was the ever-present hope of 'success'; in bad times the worker had no choice but to labour from dawn to dusk. In North America especially, the traditions of the artisan were thrust aside: there was a continent to conquer, vast new markets to satisfy. Mass production meant speed, not quality, and in industry after industry the craft skills were diluted or replaced by repetitive machine work. The change came at different times in different places, sometimes quickly, sometimes slowly, but it had already been evident in the factory system of the 1880s. Treatment of the worker had changed little since then: new faces and accents might be found at the machine, but the harsh discipline, danger and dirt remained. A few skilled, essential men, with strong unions, won 8-to-10-hour days, and some women and children were partly protected by inadequate legislation. Seniority was unknown, and the best the broken-down labourer could expect at the end of his service was 'light work' as a favour from the boss. The employer fired and hired at will, though he occasionally had a fatherly concern for his 'hands' or 'boys'. And there were many child labourers. It was usual to be at work in the factory by 13, and even at half that age in some trades. Fatal accidents and maiming were common. Many workers' earliest memories of their jobs were of some dreadful accident to a young chum, badly mangled by belts, saw-teeth, or gears, or horribly burned by bursts of steam.

As the new century dawned, none of this changed. Wages rose slightly but somehow they often bought less. Why did workers appear to accept these desperate conditions?

The answer is surprising. First of all, most of them judged the conditions of factory, mill, and mine by the standards of rural poverty, which were even worse. The vast majority of Canadian workers seldom dared to strike, especially if they were married—they might be risking the starvation of their family. Most were deferential to their bosses and 'betters', voted the party line of their fathers, and remained outside the unions. Sheer force and terror by the owners of industry account for some of their timidity. Part of the answer may also lie in the Canadian mosaic itself: the fragmentation of languages, traditions, race, religion, and region. Workers were scattered thinly across 3,000 miles of geography. Few could afford to travel about, to meet face to face. Family men had their children's and relations' jobs to worry about—could they risk them? Immigrants who joined a strike could be deported as 'criminals'. Most men had something to lose, part of a house or property. They wanted to be 'respectable'. Others sold out, spied, scabbed, or even skipped town with union funds. Above all, there was what one historian calls the 'success psychology' that made so many workers unwilling to risk their position until they could be reasonably sure of ending up on the winning side. And even those who joined unions and took part in strikes were subjected to anti-labour laws, to strike-breaking by company thugs or government troops, or to threats of dismissal, arrest, and deportation. Unions of the time were more likely to be conservative than radical, their leaders more craft conscious than class conscious, and their concerns more immediate 'bread-and-butter' issues than long-range reforms.

It has become a commonplace to blame the weakness of working-class action in these years on Samuel Gompers' American Federation of Labor. The AFL was an exclusive group of craft unions. They opposed radical politics, compulsory arbitration, and industrial unionism. They refused to organize the unskilled and the non-white races, and urged that their Canadian affiliates in the Trades and Labor Congress, adopt a non-partisan political policy. Thus labour's political clout in Canada was severely weakened.

Yet industrial unions and radical politics were thwarted at least as much by the attitudes of ordinary Canadians as by the ideology of Sam Gompers. With few exceptions, it was an era of racism, individualism, and uncertainty. Unions were new and opposed not only by politicians and businessmen but by farmers, consumers, and conservative churchmen as well. Many labourers put more faith in their own strong backs and the patronage of gang boss or ward heeler, than in their fellow worker. Few could afford to take the long view. And from 1900 to 1920, the AFL itself was still a young and expanding movement in Canada, wary of political entaglements and engaged in major drives for recognition. The crafts had their own battles to fight. Most employers were bitterly opposed to unions of any kind; only as a last resort would they recognize TLC unions to fend off the more radical industrial unions. Furthermore, Canadian politicians had little time for labour questions. They were more concerned with 'industrial peace', that is, stopping strikes, than with workers' rights. Canada is a counter-revolutionary country. Only the fact that so many trade-union leaders in Canada spoke with British accents, appealed to British rights, and (when avowed socialists) took as their model the respectable British Independent Labour Party, saved them from ruthless repression.

At the bottom of the social scale, workers voted with their feet. Migration took the place of militancy—whether it was the rural-born moving to camp or city; or the peasant fleeing the Old World's wars and misery; or the native Canadian seeking the big money south of the border; or the pioneer trek to the 'last best West'; or the great swings of the tramps and hobos along the railways to seek summer harvests on the Prairies, 'mechanic's' jobs in construction or logging camps or the rising cities of the Midwest, then south to California for the winter and back north with the spring. The poor of Quebec and the Maritimes fled to the mills and cities of New England, or moved out to log drive and fishery. Settlers invaded the North, only to find that poor land made them (like the Prairie homesteader) seek seasonal wages out of sheer necessity. British Columbia's traditional pattern had always been the goldrush and the salmon run, with their ebbs and flows of men; and in its logging camps there were always three gangs, 'one away getting drunk, one working, and one coming', as a lumberman put it. Only in the coal towns was there a stable population: and here there was class war, the blacklist, and the imported strikebreaker. And yet few of the miners had been in the region long enough to have their own home. And curiously, among all the migrants, that was the great dream: a home, a small garden, a little security in old age.

The lure to migration might be simply food. It might be land, or status ('Here you need not bow the head', one immigrant told his Ukrainian compatriots), a cash stake to go back home with, education for the children, or escape from persecution and overcrowding. Almost all these were linked to land, in an age when almost no countries provided welfare, and land was free in Canada.

Even in North America, however, there were landless labourers. The depressions of the late-nineteenth century had sent armies of dispossessed tenant farmers and craftsmen 'on the tramp'. The old hobo life of adventurous youth, beggars, and journeymen took on a new dimension. But midway between the age of the horse and the car, this migration took to the railways. Riding the rods remained a staple theme of the folk-life of the continent until the 1940s. And so the youth of the small town and the backroads drained away: to bushcamp, city, mine and mill, to success—or the hobo jungle.

TRAMPING AND CONTRACTING:
AN ITALIAN GANG BOSS OF 1901

'Tramp' originally meant a migrant worker, not a bum. Thomas Cozzolino worked his way up to a fortune, but lost his construction company in poorly engineered projects in the 1920s and the crash of 1930. Born in Italy in 1867, he lost his mother and sisters in a cholera epidemic and at age 13, assisted by a 'patronage' loan from relatives, came to labour in America. He quickly learned English as well as construction skills, becoming an interpreter and employment agent for fellow Italians. He was an exceptionally honest gang boss, backing his men in disputes with crooked contractors; by contrast, exploitation of contract labourers by other padrones *was serious enough to warrant a Royal Commission in 1904. The story below begins when at 19 he began contracting for his own gang.*

Diary of Thomas Cozzolino, c.1940. Courtesy of Dr John Burke, Sydney, N.S., and Professor A. A. MacKenzie, Saint Francis Xavier University.

When I left Lennoxville in September of 1885 I went to Girard, Ohio near Youngstown. There was a new steel plant under construction where I worked for three months. In March 1886 I went to Pittsburgh, Pennsylvania, as a foreman on the city sewer and water works until the month of May when I came to Canada as the C.P.R. was building a branch from Montreal to Smiths Falls, Ontario. I landed first in Toronto by railway, then took the boat to Prescott and stopped at Cornwall where they were building a canal. I had a crew of men and asked the Superintendent if he could place us. He did so and we began working the next day.... The men were working 10¾ hours a day instead of 10 and getting paid for only 10. I left there the next day with my crew and went to Apple Hill, Ontario to work on the new railway the C.P.R. was building. The names of the contractors were MacKenzie, Mann and O'Neill. They had a section of five miles grading. I worked with them all summer as a foreman and then to St. Anne de Bellevue at the big bridge, making the fill. At its termination I went to Sherbrooke, Quebec; hired by Luke Madigan all winter. We had over eight feet of snow and every morning we had to shovel for over an hour before we could begin to work as the cut was full of snow. In the spring the same contractor wanted me to do the next section. Over half the road was through woods and the mosquitoes were terrible so we decided to go to Ottawa instead. While we were there someone was hiring men to go to Cape Breton, where the government was building a railway ... we arrived at Mulgrave and were supposed to take a boat to St. Peter's Canal but it was blocked with ice so the manager directed us to West Bay Road, where the boat would pick us up. I inquired how far it was and was told ten or eleven miles so we hired some teams to carry our baggage and walked behind them, arriving at West Bay Road in the late afternoon. The weather was extremely cold and as we stayed on the wharf waiting for the boat we nearly perished. We built a big fire but it didn't help much. There were no accommodations in the little town for so many and the people were afraid of strangers and would not allow us near their places. The next night came and still no boat. We decided that we could not stay outside and freeze to death so we broke into the school house, lit the stove and thus, kept ourselves warm .... It is very cold at night along the seashore even in the summer. The next day about 9 a.m. we were glad to continue our journey, arriving at Grand Narrows that evening with the same problem of seeking quarters for the night. Finally we found a barn where we spent the night. There still remained twenty more miles to reach Boisdale so we started out the next morning with three teams to carry our luggage and we men walking along side. The same evening in Boisdale we rented a large house for the men and gathered straw to make all the beds. The men all felt comfortable and enjoyed a well earned good night's rest. I boarded at a place called MacIntyres near the Post Office. They were very nice people. As no one seemed aware that such a large number of men were coming, they had no preparations for extra food, etc. As it was impossible to buy bread, we lived on potatoes and eggs. I went to Sydney riding horseback without a saddle to bring some provisions for my men. I couldn't buy bread anywhere so I bought many barrels of hard crackers and also purchased bricks enough to build an oven. All arrived the next day and we started to build an oven. At that time we baked bread; eggs were very cheap, 8 cents a dozen. We actually lived on them for a while. I was in charge of a gang for over a month. Then the contractor gave me full charge of a 5 mile section. I realized I was pretty young to have the responsibility but I managed with God's help. While we worked there the people only earned 90 cents a day. My men being under contract for six months were paid $1.25. The natives were equally good but when they discovered this, they went on strike for more money. But since all the contractors were paying 90 cents a day they lost two days' work and no increase. After our six months expired the contractor wanted our men to work on and finish for 90 cents an hour. I was sorry as he had been good to me, but we all left at the end of October. We took the train for Riviere du Loup knowing they were building the Temiscouata Railway from there to Edmundston where men were needed. When we reached Temiscouata we found that Malcolm and Ross had a section of 30 miles just started and had agents hiring men for them. I saw one of them and he said we would be placed if we went on the job about 70 miles away. Some of the men objected saying it was far and they might not like it. But when we discovered that we could take the train to Montreal, if we didn't like the place all agreed to try. That afternoon we walked fifteen miles behind the wagons again, stopping at a farm house in vain as they hadn't any room. All slept in the barn but I was lucky and had a bed in the house. . . .

We had three miles to walk to work and had to be there at 7:00. We worked until the end of December and remained in that house all winter. There was a rock cut not completed and to obtain the government subsidy, they laid the steel on the top of the rock cut and ran over. The government inspector never noticed this as there was so much snow on the ground and the company ran their trains all winter. The next Spring in 1888 I went to Notre Dame where that rock cut was and worked there until we finished. With two gangs going night and day the cut was completed in June. Then I was given charge of a gravel pit at Cabano for a few months and afterward transferred to another pit called Daigle Pit, three miles from Edmundston. From there we graveled and blasted the whole of the Edmundston Yard and finished it about the end of December, when we packed our tools and went home for winter, awaiting our pay. A telegram arrived saying that we had to go to Riviere du Loup for our pay so we boarded the train . . . . When we arrived at Riviere du Loup we saw 300 men still waiting for their pay and every man short of one hour a day and they had taken their tools to the company's office. I left mine in Edmundston under lock and key. When the men began to kick I went to investigate and discovered they were all being paid forty-five hours short so I saw the president, MacDonald, and told him. He said my men could not have worked ten hours a day in November and December as the days were short. I told him we did, the men hardly had time to eat their dinner and I started them working early in the morning and he could check with the engineer. He said he was at fault as he should have warned them to work only nine hours a day. I told him all the men worked hard and earned their money and if he did not pay them in full none would accept the pay. The men said I was a good boss because I protected them from being cheated out of $4.00 each....

In January, 1900 I was in Sydney, Nova Scotia,... I tried to land a contract on the steel plant. But the company would not give any work to the Canadians whom they thought too slow. As I was leaving, the Chief Engineer, Mr. Waterman, told me they needed many men and if I could find a few hundred he was interested. I asked what was in it for me and he gave me charge of some construction in the Excavation part and paid well. I was also permitted to again supply my men with their necessary needs and was given free camps and room for my store to keep the provisions. This sounded good to me. I received an excellent salary and all my expenses, including hotel, laundry and transportation to and from the work, were paid. After Christmas I journeyed to New York and returned with 200 men and also some from Montreal under the same conditions. The company even built me a large oven to bake bread, all this free of charge. Then the company gave me some excavation at the coke ovens with a small branch of railway where a steam shovel was also working. This was in January 1901. The excavation all over the plant was badly handled as the ground was frozen and they were digging it with picks. This was very hard on the men who were not accomplishing anything. Their supervisor was unacquainted with that kind of work being a bricklayer. I was supposed to take orders from him so when I suggested how the work should be done he told me to mind my own business. But I felt terrible as we were paid and being foreman and not allowed to say anything I was getting fed up. One day a young man came on the job and asked me how I was getting along. I informed him I wasn't making any headway and that the superintendent would not even listen to what I had to say so I intended to leave. I didn't know that I was talking to the general manager's son as I showed him if a trestle were erected where there were 80 men on the dump the same work could be done by 8 and the steam shovel could do at least 3 times as much work as it wouldn't have to wait for cars to be dumped. Also where the men were digging with picks could be blown out with dynamite and the men could accomplish 3 times more work. He went to his father and repeated all I had said. The next day the General Manager sent for me to convince him that I could cut expenses. I reassured him as I was dissatisfied to see so much waste of money. He said, "From now on you will have full charge of the excavation at the coke ovens and do as you see fit." I returned to the job and made immediate changes. I had now only 8 men on the dump instead of 80 and the whole train could be unloaded in a few minutes. The first week I took out 4 times more material. I blasted with dynamite and that cut the cost. The superintendent tried to buck me in every imaginable way. One day a little piece of frozen earth fell on his office roof after a blast. He, at once, reported me to the head office claiming I was trying to kill all his staff. But they knew he was jealous so disregarded his comment.... At first all the men were against me thinking I intended firing them but it was not very long before they changed their minds and did everything I wanted. Of course I fired a few of the foremen and some of the leaders for they did not do their work. Then I had trouble with one foreman who was doing the shooting for all the gangs on the work where he kept 6 men. I did not like to discharge him as he had a family so I called him aside and told him in future he would do the shooting alone as it was not necessary to have anybody. "I will keep the 6 men on, and place them with one of the gangs here." He became furious and told me I could not fire him nor my men and got very nasty. He went to the Chief Engineer claiming that he had a license which the law of the country exacted. He frightened the Chief Engineer who called me up and asked to see me at once. But I explained the man was trying to bluff him so I fired him and his crew and I wired for a powder man in Montreal that would fill his place. It was costing the company $10.00 a day as he was giving himself overtime. The next man from Montreal cost $15.00 a week. After he was there a few days he asked me for extra work as he said he was doing nothing and wasn't used to being idle. So in the day time he went out to the dump helping the men through his own initiative. After the first week the cost was 45% lower than the other company. The engineer in making out his cost sheet could not believe it. He thought he had made a mistake in figuring or measuring the work. I assured him the figures were correct, it should not cost any more. The cut that was costing 80 cents averaged on the whole 20 cents per cu. yard and the Open Hearth and Blooming Mills formerly costing $1.00 per cu. yard now was done for 42 cents.

RIDING THE RODS: PUNKS, TRAMPS, AND BINDLESTIFFS,
1890-1930

When Jack London wrote these stories of tramp life in the 1890s, a depression had left armies of unemployed and landless. Some of these tramps were youths in search of adventure, some were hardened bums, and many were desperate men in search of work. They learned to ride freight trains across North America, from the industrial East to the Prairies, and down to California following jobs and harvests every year. Their unceasing trek on the transcontinental railways went on to the early 1930s.

Jack London, *The Road* (London, 1967), pp. 24-6, 59-60, 62-7, 74-6.

Drunken men are the especial prey of the road-kids. Robbing a drunken man they call 'rolling a stiff'; and wherever they are, they are on the constant lookout for drunks. . . .

. . . It is a dark night. My push [gang] is coming along the sidewalk in the suburbs. Ahead of us, under an electric light, a man crosses the street diagonally. There is something tentative and desultory in his walk. The kids scent the game on the instant. The man is drunk. He blunders across the opposite sidewalk and is lost in the darkness as he takes a short-cut through a vacant lot. No hunting cry is raised, but the pack flings itself forward in quick pursuit. In the middle of the vacant lot it comes upon him. But what is this—? Snarling and strange forms, small and dim and menacing, are between the pack and its prey. It is another pack of road-kids, and in the hostile pause we learn that it is their meat, that they have been trailing it a dozen blocks and more and that we are butting in. But it is the world primeval. These wolves are baby wolves. (As a matter of fact, I don't think one of them was over twelve or thirteen years of age.) . . . Our pack flings forward. The baby wolves squeal and screech and fight like little demons. All about the drunken man rages the struggle for possession of him. Down he goes in the thick of it, and the combat rages over his body after the fashion of the Greeks and Trojans over the body and armour of a fallen hero. Amid cries and tears and wailings the baby wolves are dispossessed, and my pack rolls the stiff. But always I remember the poor stiff and . . . the really hurt expression on his face when he, unoffending he, was clutched at by many hands and dragged down in the thick of the press.

'Bindle-stiffs' are favourite prey of the road-kids. A bindle-stiff is a working tramp. He takes his name from the roll of blankets he carries, which is known as a 'bindle'. Because he does work, a bindle-stiff is expected usually to have some small change about him, and it is after the small change that the road-kids go. The best hunting-ground for bindle-stiffs is in the sheds, barns, lumber-yards, railroad-yards, etc., on the edges of a city, and the time for hunting is the night, when the bindle-stiff seeks these places to roll up in his blankets and sleep.

'Gay-cats' also come to grief at the hands of the road-kids. In a more familiar parlance, gay-cats are short-horns, *chechaquos,* new chums, or tenderfeet. A gay-cat is a newcomer on The Road who is man-grown, or, at least, youth-grown. A boy on The Road, on the other hand, no matter how green he is, is never a gay-cat; he is a road-kid or a 'punk', and if he travels with a 'profesh', he is known possessively as 'prushun'... And be it known, here and now, that the profesh are the aristocracy of The Road. They are the lords and masters, the aggressive men, the primordial noblemen, the *blond beasts* so beloved of Nietzsche.

Barring accidents, a good hobo, with youth and agility, can hold a train down despite all the efforts of the train-crew to 'ditch' him—given, of course, night-time as an essential condition. When such a hobo, under such conditions, makes up his mind that he is going to hold her down, either he does hold her down, or chance trips him up. There is no legitimate way, short of murder, whereby the train-crew can ditch him. That train-crews have not stopped short of murder is a current belief in the tramp world. Not having had that particular experience in my tramp days I cannot vouch for it personally.

But this I have heard of the 'bad' roads. When a tramp has 'gone underneath', on the rods, and the train is in motion, there is apparently no way of dislodging him until the train stops. The tramp, snugly ensconced inside the truck, with four wheels and all the framework around him, has the 'cinch' on the crew—or so he thinks, until someday he rides the rods on a bad road. A bad road is usually one on which a short time previously one or several trainmen have been killed by tramps. Heaven pity the tramp who is caught 'underneath' on such a road—for caught he is, though the train be going sixty miles an hour.

The 'shack' (brakeman) takes a coupling-pin and a length of bell-cord to the platform in front of the truck in which the tramp is riding. The shack fastens the coupling-pin to the bell-cord, drops the former down between the platforms and pays out the latter. The coupling-pin strikes the ties between the rails, rebounds against the bottom of the car, and again strikes the ties. The shack plays it back and forth, now to this side, now to the other, lets it out a bit and hauls it in a bit, giving his weapon opportunity for every variety of impact and rebound. Every blow of that flying coupling-pin is freighted with death, and at sixty miles an hour it beats a veritable tattoo of death. The next day the remains of that tramp are gathered up along the right of way, and a line in the local papers mentions the unknown man, undoubtedly a tramp, assumably drunk, who had probably fallen asleep on the track.

As a characteristic illustration of how a capable hobo can hold her down, I am minded to give the following experience. I was in Ottawa, bound west over the Canadian Pacific. Three thousand miles of that road stretched before me; it was the fall of the year, and I had to cross Manitoba and the Rocky Mountains. I could expect 'crimpy' weather, and every moment of delay increased the frigid hardships of the journey. Furthermore, I was disgusted. The distance between Montreal and Ottawa is one hundred and twenty miles. I ought to know, for I had just come over it and it had taken me six days. By mistake I had missed the main line and had come over a small 'jerk' with only two locals a day on it. And during these six days I had lived on dry crusts, and not enough of them, begged from the French peasants.

Furthermore, my disgust had been heightened by the one day I had spent in Ottawa trying to get an outfit of clothing for my long journey. Let me put it on record right here that Ottawa, with one exception, is the hardest town in the United States and Canada to beg clothes in; the one exception is Washington, D.C. . . .

When I arrived at the depot, I found, much to my disgust, a bunch of at least twenty tramps that were waiting to ride out the blind baggages of the overland. Now two or three tramps on the blind baggage are all right. They are inconspicuous. But a score! That meant trouble. No train-crew would ever let all of us ride.

I may as well explain here what a blind baggage is. Some mail-cars are built without doors in the ends; hence, such a car is 'blind'. The mail-cars that possess end doors, have those doors always locked. Suppose, after the train has started, that a tramp gets on to the platform of one of these blind cars. There is no door, or the door is locked. No conductor or brakeman can get to him to collect fare or throw him off. It is clear that the tramp is safe until the next time the train stops. Then he must get off, run ahead in the darkness, and when the train pulls by, jump on to the blind again. But there are ways and ways, as you shall see.

When the train pulled out, those twenty tramps swarmed upon the three blinds. Some climbed on before the train had run a car-length. They were awkward dubs, and I saw their speedy finish. Of course, the train-crew was 'on', and at the first stop the trouble began. I jumped off and ran forward along the track. I noticed that I was accompanied by a number of the tramps. They evidently knew their business. When one is beating an overland, he must always keep well ahead of the train at the stops. I ran ahead, and as I ran, one by one those that accompanied me dropped out. This dropping out was the measure of their skill and nerve in boarding a train.

For this is the way it works. When the train starts, the shack rides out the blind. There is no way for him to get back into the train proper except by jumping off the blind and catching a platform where the car-ends are not 'blind'. When the train is going as fast as the shack cares to risk, he therefore jumps off the blind, lets several cars go by, and gets onto the train. So it is up to the tramp to run so far ahead that before the blind is opposite him the shack will have already vacated it.

I dropped the last tramp by about fifty feet, and waited. The train started. I saw the lantern of the shack on the first blind. He was riding her out. And I saw the dubs stand forlornly by the track as the blind went by. They made no attempt to get on. They were beaten by their own inefficiency at the very start. After them, in the line-up, came the tramps that knew a little something about the game. They let the first blind, occupied by the shack, go by, and jumped on the second and third blinds. Of course, the shack jumped off the first and on to the second as it went by, and scrambled around there, throwing off the men who had boarded it. But the point is that I was so far ahead that when the first blind came opposite me, the shack had already left it and was tangled up with the tramps on the second blind. A half-dozen of the more skilful tramps, who had run far enough ahead, made the first blind, too.

At the next stop, as we ran forward along the track, I counted but fifteen of us. Five had been ditched. The weeding-out process had begun nobly, and it continued station by station. Now we were fourteen, now twelve, now eleven, now nine, now eight. It reminded me of the ten little niggers of the nursery rhyme. I was resolved that I should be the last little nigger of all. And why not? Was I not blessed with strength, agility, and youth? (I was eighteen, and in perfect condition.) And didn't I have my 'nerve' with me? And furthermore, was I not a tramp-royal? Were not these other tramps mere dubs and 'gay-cats' and amateurs alongside of me? If I weren't the last little nigger, I might as well quit the game and get a job on an alfalfa farm somewhere.

By the time our number had been reduced to four, the whole train-crew had become interested. From then on it was a contest of skill and wits, with the odds in favour of the crew. One by one the three other survivors turned up missing, until I alone remained. My, but I was proud of myself! No Croesus was ever prouder of his first million. I was holding her down in spite of two brakemen, a conductor, a fireman, and an engineer.

And here are a few samples of the way I held her down. Out ahead, in the darkness—so far ahead that the shack riding out the blind must perforce get off before it reaches me—I get on. Very well. I am good for another station. When that station is reached, I dart ahead again to repeat the manoeuvre. The train pulls out. I watch her coming. There is no light of a lantern on the blind. Has the crew abandoned the fight? I do not know? One never knows, and one must be prepared every moment for anything. . . .

Again I see the lantern come forward to the engine. But this time it comes conspicuously. A bit too conspicuously to suit me, and I wonder what is up. At any rate I have something else to be afraid of than the shack on the engine. The train pulls by. Just in time, before I make my spring, I see the dark form of a shack, without a lantern, on the first blind. I let it go by, and prepare to board the second blind. But the shack on the first blind has jumped off and is at my heels. Also, I have a fleeting glimpse of the lantern of the shack who rode out the engine. He has jumped off, and now both shacks are on the ground on the same side with me. The next moment the second blind comes by and I am aboard it. But I do not linger. I have figured out my countermove. As I dash across the platform I hear the impact of the shack's feet against the steps as he boards. I jump off the other side and run forward with the train. My plan is to run forward and get on the first blind. It is nip and tuck, for the train is gathering speed. Also, the shack is behind me and running after me. I stand on the steps and watch my pursuer. He is only about ten feet back and running hard; but now the train has approximated his own speed, and, relative to me, he is standing still. I encourage him, hold out my hand to him; but he explodes in a mighty oath, gives up and makes the train several cars back.

The train is speeding along, and I am still chuckling to myself, when, without warning, a spray of water strikes me. The fireman is playing the hose on me from the engine. I step forward from the car-platform to the rear of the tender, where I am sheltered under the overhang. The water flies harmlessly over my head. My fingers itch to climb up on the tender and lam that fireman with a chunk of coal; but I know if I do that, I'll be massacred by him and the engineer, and I refrain.

At the next stop I am off and ahead in the darkness. This time, when the train pulls out, both shacks are on the first blind. I divine their game. They have blocked the repetition of my previous play. I cannot again take the second blind, cross over, and run forward to the first. As soon as the first blind passes and I do not get on, they swing off, one on each side of the train. I board the third blind, and as I do so I know that a moment later, simultaneously, those two shacks will arrive on both sides of me. It is like a trap. Both ways are blocked. Yet there is another way out, and that way is up.

So I do not wait for my pursuers to arrive. I climb upon the upright ironwork of the platform and stand upon the wheel of the hand-brake. This has taken up the moment of grace and I hear the shacks strike the steps on either side. I don't stop to look. I raise my arms overhead until my hands rest against the down-curving ends of the roofs of the two cars. One hand, of course, is on the curved roof of one car, the other hand on the curved roof of the other car. By this time both shacks are coming up the steps. I know it, though I am too busy to see them. All this is happening in the space of several seconds. I make a spring with my legs and 'muscle' myself up with my arms. As I draw up my legs, both shacks reach for me and clutch empty air. I know that, for I look down and see them. Also I hear them swear.

I am now in a precarious position, riding the ends of the down-curving roofs of two cars at the same time. With a quick, tense movement, I transfer both legs to the curve of one roof and both hands to the curve of the other roof. Then, gripping the edge of that curving roof, I climb over the curve to the level roof above, where I sit down to catch my breath, holding on the while to a ventilator that projects above the surface. I am top of the train—on the 'decks', as the tramps call it, and this process I have described is by them called 'decking her'. And let me say right here that only a young and vigorous tramp is able to deck a passenger train, and also, that the young and vigorous tramp must have his nerve with him as well.

The train goes on gathering speed, and I know I am safe until the next stop—but only until the next stop. . . .

Registering a fervent hope that there are no tunnels in the next half mile, I rise to my feet and walk down the train half a dozen cars. And let me say that one must leave timidity behind him on such a passage. The roofs of passenger coaches are not made for midnight promenades. And if anyone thinks they are, let me advise him to try it. . . .

In conclusion, I want to tell of what happened when I reached the end of a division. On single-track, transcontinental lines, the freight trains wait at the divisions and follow out after the passenger trains. When the division was reached, I left my train, and looked for the freight that would pull out behind it. I found the freight, made up on a side-track and waiting. I climbed into a box-car half-full of coal and lay down. In no time I was asleep.

I was awakened by the sliding open of the door. Day was just dawning, cold and grey, and the freight had not yet started. A 'con' (conductor) was poking his head inside the door.

'Get out of that, you blankety-blank-blank!' he roared at me.

I got, and outside I watched him go down the line inspecting every car in the train. When he got out of sight I thought to myself that he would never think I'd have the nerve to climb back into the very car out of which he had fired me. So back I climbed and lay down again.

Now that con's mental processes must have been paralleling mine, for he reasoned that it was the very thing I would do. For back he came and fired me out.

Now, surely, I reasoned, he will never dream that I'd do it a third time. Back I went, into the very same car. But I decided to make sure. Only one side-door could be opened. The other side-door was nailed up. Beginning at the top of the coal I dug a hole alongside of that door and lay down in it. I heard the other door open. The con climbed up and looked in over the top of the coal. He couldn't see me. He called to me to get out. I tried to fool him by remaining quiet. But when he began tossing chunks of coal into the hole on top of me, I gave up and for the third time was fired out. Also, he informed me in warm terms of what would happen to me if he caught me in there again.

I changed my tactics. When a man is paralleling your mental processes, ditch him. Abruptly break off your line of reasoning, and go off on a new line. This I did. I hid between some cars on an adjacent sidetrack, and watched. Sure enough, that con came back again to the car. He opened the door, he climbed up, he called, he threw coal into the hole I had made. He even crawled over the coal and looked into the hole. That satisfied him. Five minutes later the freight was pulling out, and he was not in sight. I ran alongside the car, pulled the door open and climbed in. He never looked for me again, and I rode that coal-car precisely one thousand and twenty-two miles, sleeping most of the time and getting out at divisions (where the freights always stop for an hour or so) to beg my food. And at the end of the thousand and twenty-two miles I lost that car through a happy incident. I got a 'set-down' [meal], and the tramp doesn't live who won't miss a train for a set-down any time.

STANDING UP TO THE BOSS: THE CRAFT UNIONIST, c.1900-1910

Skilled British immigrants with socialist ideas, and organizing drives by craft unions of the American Federation of Labor, brought a new militancy to Canada in the boom of the early 1900s. Young advocates of the 'international' defied the bosses, older Grit and Tory leaders, and perhaps logic: they combined Labour Party ideology with 'pure and simple' trades unionism. Bruce typifies the new spirit. For 50 years he was one of the chief AFL organizers in Canada.

Excerpts from John Bruce Interview by Don Montgomery, at Toronto, Feb. 1963.

[I was born in Australia,] thirteen brothers and sisters. All the boys lived in one room and all the girls in another. We had a shortage of beds... and we all handed our clothes down, one to the other, you see, they were all worn out. I was 15 when I went to work. They used to have to set up soup kitchens. You had to go over with a bucket and get some soup for the family and a few loaves of bread. Enough to keep you, just....

I got my [journeyman plumber's] book in 1897, my first blue book. I'd been in as an apprentice, and got married; my first daughter was born in '98 and the other, two years after. And then I left in 1902 to go to Africa ... took the side of the Matabeles in the Rebellion in South Africa, and of course the Police were searching for me.... I put my wife and three children on the boat—and here's me watching for a chance to slip aboard.... Well then I went to England. I could have stayed in England to work but didn't like the conditions or anything like that. They were pretty hostile. Then I came here [to Toronto] in June 1906.... I landed here on a Sunday, and Monday morning I went up and reported to the office and I showed the business agent my book ... and he said, "That's no good here, we don't accept—travellers from other countries." He said, "You'll have to join over afresh." However, we talked it over and he said, "Well, you know there's a lot of hostility here to Englishmen." "Who says I'm an Englishmen," I said, "I'm an Australian; I've just come here from Africa," and I explained the situation ... of course, you could see plenty of ads in the paper, "NO ENGLISHMEN NEED APPLY"— them days, very pronounced. So I went down and went to this shop and said, "Any need of plumbing?" and he said, "Yeah, I need a bloody plumber but I don't need any bloody Englishman." I was pretty quick with my tongue then as always:

"Well no doubt you couldn't be wrong, is there?"

"No godammit there can be no doubt, a bloody Englishman and no damn good."

"Well that might be your experience but I just come from a place where I found a lot of Englishmen pretty good guys." (I didn't tell him where. I had one fellow who was a really good guy, a Boer, a mixture of Dutch and British.)

"Where the hell did you come from?"

"I don't know that that is any of your business ...," and everyone in there, their ears pricked, they thought nobody would talk back to this guy.... I said, "You wanted a plumber, I can do any goddamn thing that any of them can do and perhaps do it better."

"Oh, you've got a bloody fine opinion of yourself."

"Well, I've travelled a long way." (And it's a long time since I've worked at the tools of the trade, because I was superintendent even in South Africa.)

So after a bit of badgering back and forth he said, "Well, goddammit, I need one bad, come in on Monday morning."

"Oh," I said, "that's something I never do ... "

He looked at me, says "What?" "Something I never do ... I don't need a job that bad and if I did you'd be the last man in the world I'd want to work for. I've never in all my experience bumped into an employer of labour so brutal and callous. You never waited for me to tell my story, where I come from or what I could do. You prejudged me, and therefore I wouldn't work for you under any circumstances." And say, it took him right off his feet, he went white, he didn't know whether to fly back at me. "Well," he says, "you're the first sonofabitch that dared to talk back to me...." I went back to the Labour Temple and I went to our business agent, but in the meantime he'd got him and "What bloody tiger did you send down here?"

[I tried another shop,] the foreman there was a Yorkshireman with a burr.... When I went in he said, "We don't want any Englishmen." I looked him square in the eye, I said, "Well it would take a goddamn good file to take that burr off your tongue ... how long is it since you left Yorkshire? I didn't think a Britisher would disown another Britisher in a new country like this." And with that he burst out laughing: "I heard about the story—and I give you credit for standing up, but—we haven't any work unless you want to wait a week." I said, "Don't have to, there's work right round, don't have to wait." Things were good in them days. [He sent me] over to another Yorkshireman. I said, "I've been in Africa and I came here to see what my chances were in this country." "Oh well," he says, "you can start." ... It wasn't long before, right in the midst of it, we had just completed a one-year agreement and they were laying for us and we went out in 1907 and we were out on strike a year! I was secretary of the strike committee.... In fact I was out two weeks longer because when the boss tried to get me back, I said, "I want 2½¢ more...." They made me president of the building trades in 1907, then I got active on the Toronto Trades Council.

We had a number of fellows there who were prominent in the Conservative party, John Armstrong, one of the men that was arrested in the [1872] Printers' Strike. He was quite closely associated with old Dan O'Donoghue [first Ontario labour MPP, in 1873]. We lined up the Council, Liberals on one side, Conservatives on the other, and us, those who were in the opposition, the Socialist bunch.... In 1908 I was a labour candidate in East Toronto, just east of the Don River.... And in the 1910 election. Right after that we started the campaign for workmen's compensation. It was labour's biggest step forward, secured through our own efforts, in every province....

UNDERGROUND: HARDROCK MINERS, c. 1905

The miners of East and West were to lead the development of industrial unionism; here we see some reasons why. Ross has put flesh on the dry bones of the Mine Inspectors' Reports, the standard primary source, by using taped interviews, newspaper articles, etc. This was a world where lung disease, maiming, and sudden death were traditionally blamed on miners' carelessness rather than on working conditions, which remained largely unchanged, sordid though they were, until recent times.

W. Gillies Ross, *Three Eastern Townships Mining Villages Since 1863: Albert Mines, Capelton and Eustis, Quebec* (Lennoxville, Quebec, Bishop's University, Department of Geography, 1975), pp. 52-6. Reprinted by permission of W. Gillies Ross.

UNDERGROUND IN THE EUSTIS MINE

The day shift arrives at the mine entrance a little before seven in the morning. After changing into their work clothes they take up their lunch pails and drinking water, walk 1,000 feet along the horizontal adit to the hoist room, and board the riding car, which accommodates about 30 miners sitting on steps. The men wear a variety of bowlers and soft hats and light their way by carbide lamps. A few old-timers still use candles stuck into metal holders on their hats. Descending on the riding car the men disembark at various levels and walk into the drifts to their respective jobs. Originally hand methods were employed for drilling, one man holding and rotating a 15-inch steel drill while another tried his best to hit it with a four-pound hammer. But modern science has effected wonders in technique and the miners now employ machine drills operated by compressed air. A disadvantage is that they create a fine dust at the working face which the men cannot avoid breathing. It is said to be the primary cause of "miners' T.B." or silicosis, which has caused the premature death of many. The men affectionately call the dry drills "widow-makers".

The men work continuously until lunch, and then the Company generously allows them thirty minutes to eat. Their wives provide them with home-made bread, sliced meats or stew, hot tea, and perhaps a custard or piece of pie. Crumbs and left-overs are thrown to the rats which inhabit all levels of this subterranean world. The rats keep the mine clean and provide amusement. Furthermore, they can save lives. It is well known that just before a rock fall they begin to howl and then run up the shaft. When the rats display this peculiar behaviour the men do not hesitate; they follow the animals to the surface in a curious reversal of the Pied Piper routine.

Walking up the shaft is far from being a Sunday stroll however. The shaft is inclined, on the average, at about 40° to the horizontal and at places is close to 70°. It is now almost 4,000 feet in depth along the dip. Several hours are required to climb up from the bottom.

However, one group descends the shaft on foot every day. This is the timber gang, looking for fallen rock or "loose" and checking the hoisting cables, rollers, and tracks. Men's lives depend on the thoroughness of their inspection.

It is hot working underground. Air temperatures increase with depth and remain high even in winter, when doors are closed at the mine entrance to bar the entry of cold air. Men work stripped to the waist and consume two gallons of water each during the course of a day, plus a lunchtime beverage. Yet many of them grow to love the underground life and come to regard sunshine and fresh air as alien. One miner tells us:

> You get up on surface and get up in the sun and, I don't know, I used to feel half dead when I got in the sun. I didn't want to *see* the sun. You get used to working underground and what you do is you go home and to bed and have your sleep and first thing you know it was time to go back underground. And that was it. I didn't mind the night shift, but day shift, boy, you come up there, you know and the sun was shining—that wasn't natural.

After their shift underground, the men ascend on the riding car, wash side by side in a long trough, and make their way home.

Accidents

Accidents are a fact of life in the mines where men descend several thousands of feet in a steep shaft and make their living hewing out solid rock with air drills and blasting powder, and sending it to the surface in ore cars and skips. One of the miners, with experience in Ontario, considers safety precautions far less stringent in the Eustis mine; in particular, the detection and removal of loose rock by scaling is not thorough enough; pieces are often overlooked, only to fall later upon some unsuspecting victim. Individual carelessness often makes matters worse. The terse summaries of mining accidents in the Quebec Bureau of Mines Annual Reports express some of the illogical, not always avoidable, causes of accidents and remind us that man is only human.

One account reads as follows: "While handling a tie, he stumbled and put his hand on another tie just as a fellow workman drove his axe into it." Another refers to a man who "was holding a wedge when another man striking it with hammer missed it and struck his wrist." There is something pathetic in the following account: "in a blast at the mine some loose stones were thrown high in the air and deceased fearing lest he should be struck by the falling stones, in stepping aside to escape them, fell over an embankment and received injuries from the fall which caused his death." It is harder to sympathize with the miner who "was playing around the chute at the mill and jumped over the side and fell on his back," or the man at Asbestos who "kept hold of a loaded box of rock after signal had been given to hoist by the cable derrick. He was raised to a height of about 75 feet...." Man's capacity for misjudgment is best exemplified by the terse account of an accident at the Eustis mine which reads, "Stepped into chute he was discharging car into."

At Eustis, the most common cause of accidents is falling rock. If the victims can be moved they are taken to the surface, cleaned up and given a hot drink, while a doctor is summoned. The company doctor is Dr. Colquhoun, a McGill graduate, who fell in love with the Eastern Townships while working his way through college and took up practice at Waterville seven years ago. He visits Eustis regularily to treat patients and comes on call for emergencies at five dollars an accident. The doctor's voyages to Eustis are made either on horseback or by horse and sled. Although the distance by way of the covered bridge across the Massawippi is but a few miles the trip can be uncomfortable and even hazardous in winter. Sometimes he has to travel in blizzards, huddling beneath buffalo robes, and he has lost his way more than once in driving snow.

Dr. Colquhoun must have confronted many grisly accidents, but the one that is said to have bothered him most was a small one. A man demonstrating to his wife how she should really cut up the squash was both overbearing and overhasty; he removed the top of his finger. According to an eyewitness:

> the doctor come over there and when he see the blood he passed out. So we just took him and turned him over the chair and left him there and put the piece (of the finger) on and bandaged; took the first aid kit and picked up his finger and when Doctor Colquhoun came to we had his finger all fixed up ...

The miners seem to accept accidents as part of the job; it is really their women who bear the greater burden of anxiety:

> and if we saw him (Dr. Colquhoun) going up the hill fast we knew there was an accident, because he never drove fast otherwise. And every woman would be out waiting for him to come back ... And sometimes we'd see him fly up the hill and the next thing would come the ambulance. And you'd stand there with your heart in your mouth wondering who it was ...

DEATH ON THE GRAND BANKS: FISHERMEN, c.1907

The conditions described here were those of the entire Atlantic coast. Like miners, fishermen looked on accidents and death as part of their trade, taking a fierce pride in survival. But even these rugged individualists could organize against starvation prices. The Fishermen's Protective Union of 1908-9 under William Coaker was a revolt of Protestant outports against St John merchants. The FPU was the first fishermen's co-operative in the Empire, one of the earliest successful attempts to organize primary producers; it won a short-lived majority in the legislature.

J. G. Millais, *Newfoundland and Its Untrodden Ways* (London, 1907), pp. 151, 152, 154-8.

Cod-fishing being the principal industry of Newfoundland, it may be as well to briefly survey the various methods of taking this fish. The men of the outports begin to fish about the 1st of May, for it is at this season that the cod move in from the ocean. The usual method is to fish from "bankers," small ocean-going schooners, carrying little boats with trawls. A "trawl" is not such as we understand it in England, but five dozen cod-lines, each 30 fathoms long, and baited in spring with herring. This method goes on till about the 15th of June. Then a large number of men desert the "bankers" and employ "cod-traps," seine-nets, or nets, hand-lines, and trawls all together. At this season the fish are at their best quality, as the caplin are in, and on these the cod largely feed. Caplin strike on to the south coast about the 10th of June, and last till 1st August, dying in myriads on the shore after spawning amongst the seaweed. . . .

As soon as the cod are brought ashore they are treated as follows. One man cuts the throat, another cuts the head off, a third splits and cleans the fish, and a fourth salts it. These "green" fish are then arranged in piles for a week or a fortnight. They are then taken out and washed in salt by boys and girls, and again packed in bulk for twenty-four hours. After this they are spread out to dry in the sun on the fir-branched trestles or flakes. It takes about five fine days to dry a cod. The dried fish is then packed in bulk and stored in the house, ready for removal. A usual price for outport curers is five dollars a quintal. (A quintal is 112 lbs., and it takes about fifty trawl fish, or a hundred trap fish, to realise this weight.)

The cod-fishing has for centuries been the mainstay of the island, and when all other things fail, this (and the caribou) will last, if taken care of. Of course seasons fluctuate owing to the irregular movements of the fish, but it may be taken as a general rule that if the season is bad off Newfoundland it is good on "The Labrador," or "Down North" as it is always called, where a large percentage of the Newfoundlanders go to fish. . . .

The Grand Banks extend from Labrador southwards past Newfoundland to the Massachusetts coast, a distance of over 1000 miles, and every year some 1200 vessels, carrying crews of 20,000 fishermen, go out to battle with the surges as they have done for the past four hundred years. The fishermen of all lands have to encounter the perils of the deep, but none have to face the risks that the "bankers" do. Their special dangers are swift liners, that steam full speed through the fog, ice-bergs, ice-floes, chilling frosts, and furious storms. The fishing zone lies right in the track of great liners plying between Europe and America, and many a poor fisherman has lived to curse

> "Some damned liner's lights go by
> Like a great hotel";

whilst nearly all have some heartrending tale to tell of the destruction of fishing craft of which he has been an eye-witness. There is an ever-increasing record of sunken ships, of frosts which overpower, and of dory crews driven from their schooners by sudden tempests, and, during the fishing season, hardly a week goes by without some tale of misfortune. Of the method of fishing and the disasters which overtake the ship I must quote a passage from one of Mr. P.T. M'Grath's articles, which are full of interest and accurate information.

"When fishing is actually in progress, the smacks always anchor, for the shoals carry only thirty to sixty fathoms of water, and hempen cables are used instead of iron chains to moor them, as the latter would saw their bows out from the lively pitching they do in these choppy seas. The fishing itself is done from dories, light but strong flat-bottomed boats, each carrying two men, who set their lines or trawls overnight, and examine them next day, removing the fish impaled on the hooks with which the trawl is furnished, and then rebaiting them for another night's service. The ship is therefore like a hen with a flock of chickens, the dories standing in this relation to her, while the trawls radiate from her as spokes from a wheel-hub, being laid outward from her at a distance of one or two miles, the ship serving as a depôt for feeding and housing the men and for cleaning and storing their catch. In setting and cleaning his trawls and cleaning his catch the doryman finds abundant occupation, and rarely gets more than a few hours' sleep in a night, sometimes none at all.

"Thus it is that when fogs obscure the water, vigilance is relaxed by the toil-worn look-out, to whom is entrusted the lives of a score of comrades, tiredly sleeping below. Though the fog-horn each vessel carries is sounded regularly, still many a horror is enacted amid this curtain of gloom, when a mighty steamship splits a hapless fisher-boat and, like a marine juggernaut, rushes on over the wreckage and bodies she sends to the bottom by the stroke of her steel-clad prow. Often at night a sudden crash rends the stillness, and a shriek of despair rises from the stricken schooner's crew, a swirl of splintered wood in her wake to mark the eddies for a while, and then vanish, a tomb for fifteen or twenty men.

"Last summer one of the German liners cut down a trawler on the banks, but it was in the daytime, and the crew fortunately escaped. The previous year two similar occurrences took place with equally harmless results. The freighter *Endymion*, however, bound to Montreal, crashed into the smack *Albatross* off Cape Race last July, and of the nineteen on the latter only one was saved. In September 1902 the collier *Warspite* sank the smack *Bonavista* on one of the banks, three only surviving out of twenty-two on board. In 1898 the *City of Rome* ripped the stem off the smack *Victor* of St. Pierre Miquelon, but she kept afloat, and a relief party from the liner got her safely to land after three days of trying endeavour, as she was leaking badly from the shock. This humane action on the liner's part is agreeably remembered yet among the fishing fleets, for, if the bankmen are to be believed, steamers usually keep on as if nothing had happened, and tell the passengers who may have felt the shock that it was caused by striking loose ice or suddenly changing the course. It is, indeed, alleged among the bankmen, that crews of foreign steamers will beat off with belaying pins the wretches from the founder-ing vessels who try to swarm on board, that the name of the destroyer may not be known, and local complications be thus avoided.

"How many of the missing bankmen meet their end in this way can only be conjectured, but certain it is that far more are sunk than are reported to the world. Frequently the steamer's people scarcely know what has happened when such a catastrophe occurs to the accompani-ment of a midnight storm, so slight is the shock of impact on her huge hull, and with spectators few at these times, and look-outs and watch-officers having every reason to escape inquiry and possible punishment, the temptation to hurry on and make no alarm is usually yielded to. Many lives are certainly sacrificed every year because of this which could otherwise be saved, for the fishing schooners are all wooden-built and, unless mortally smitten, will float for some time. Even at the worst the men can cling to planks or spars long enough to be rescued if the steamer would stop to launch a boat, which, of course, is always done when the collision occurs while passengers are on deck or in daylight....

"So frequent are these collisions, that the recent comic papers had a rather ghastly joke about a tourist returning to America and bemoaning the uneventful passage, as the ship 'ran down only one fishing smack, don't you know.' All steamers are supposed to slow down to half-speed during a fog, but this rule is rarely observed, and it is to its ignoring that most of the fatalities are due.

"Equally terrible destruction is often wrought by the gales which sweep the banks in the fishing time. Chief among these, in its appalling fatality list, was the 'Seventh of June Breeze' of 1896. The day was fine and fair for fishing, when the tempest broke and caught hundreds of dories far from their ships, imperilling not alone the skiffs and occupants, but also the vessels themselves, because only the captain and cook remain aboard while trawling is on. Scores of boats and several vessels sank, and over 300 lives were lost. Three Newfoundland, two Canadian, and three Americans were sunk at their moorings, and all hands were lost." . . .

WEST COAST SALMON FISHERMEN:
THE NEWCOMERS, c.1900-1907

There are three major salmon runs a year up the Fraser River and the Gulf of Georgia. From the earliest days they provided a source of quick riches for a few weeks' work by Coast Indians and a mixture of Europeans. By the late 1890s cutthroat competition among the canneries, over-fishing of the salmon, and the threat of unions led the bosses to form the British Columbia Packers combine and import Japanese contract labour. The Japanese were regarded as strikebreakers, and the failure of early union attempts led to a bitter heritage of race prejudice. This is the Japanese side of the story.

Jane Irwin and Maya Koizumi, 'Steveston: The Japanese-Canadian Experience', *Sound Heritage*, vol. III, no. 3 (1974). Reprinted by permission of Aural History, Provincial Archives of British Columbia.

The first Japanese fisherman arrived in Steveston in 1887. He must have been overwhelmed by the size of the salmon run in the Fraser because he returned to Japan to encourage his friends and family to come to Canada. By 1899, there were more than 2,000 Japanese in British Columbia.

Most of the early Japanese immigrants were males in their twenties and most of them came to Steveston to fish. What had begun as Manoah Steves' 400 acre farm [on Lulu Island, south of Vancouver], and had gradually attracted a small population of white and Indian fishermen, became home to a large and lively population of single young men. When they first arrived fishermen lived in shoreline bunkhouses provided for them by the same canneries which equipped them and bought their fish. It was only after 1907 when many had married or were joined by their families that they moved into small homes of their own. Gradually a

Japanese village developed and by 1927, there was a community of 3,000 Japanese in Steveston.... They established their own stores and Japanese-language school, a Japanese hospital and a Buddhist Temple, Sumo games [Japanese wrestling], judo and kendo were the popular sports. The Japanese maintained alliances with their native villages in Japan and people from the same village or province in Japan helped one another in Canada, especially with events such as marriages and funerals. ...In a move for greater independence from the canneries, they organized a fishermen's co-op to market the fish....

Asamatsu Murakami was among the first of the Japanese fishermen to come into Steveston. He lives and fishes there still:... "They did not have wives, they were only single men. They had a boss—a boss who hired a cook. They paid board monthly. There were only men—they were wild. With a drink, they started a fight, I was scared. I saw fighting often. Some killed each other, some were put in jail. There were no women so no wonder the men became wild. Later the wives began arriving from Japan. Men's lives were improved but they started to have their own houses. When the wives came, they could not live in a bunk house together with the others so the cannery gave them small houses. They married late, a picture marriage. There were no Japanese girls in this country. I was also married by picture with my old woman. I lived my life with her without a quarrel. Before I was married, nobody was married.... Yet, a lot of women came. They thought America must be a good place. They came here to find such a hard life. 'I wish I hadn't come,' they said. Too late."

Moto Suzuki came to Canada in 1925, a young woman of 23. Her husband had preceded her. "There was a deck around the house and the grass so long it was swaying left to right. It looked like a deserted place where foxes might be living. I am from farm country but even near my village, I had never seen a place like this.... When I came, I was almost six months pregnant. It was in July, fishing season, so I started to work in the cannery even before the harvest came.... It was small, small, very small.... The fish were cut by machine. The Chinese men brought the cans and I packed each can with fish. It started from about June and went until the middle of November, then we went to the Chinese men's mess house where they counted the tickets when finally we could get some money. Nowadays, we are paid every two weeks. In those days, those who washed the fish were paid by the hour, like 15 cents an hour. ...In those days, there were not enough fish for a whole day's work. Whenever the fish came in, they let us know by whistle, no time limit, night or day. Sometimes we worked one hour a day, sometimes five hours, sometimes ten hours a day. There was a day care house. Mothers looked after the kids in turn when we went to work. We took turns baby sitting. I was one of them the year after we arrived."

While women found summer employment in the canneries or some-times in the fields harvesting strawberries, the men were fishing salmon. They went out in groups of two, a boss who fished and a helper who guided the boat.

Omanosuke Suzuki, now 80 years of age: "When I went to the Skeena, we fished by sailboat, no engine boats there yet. There were engine boats around here.... I could take just a suitcase with me to go to Skeena. There was a house boss who hired a cook, ten or fifteen fishermen went to him. He gave us bed and board. He rented us a net and boat. When we caught fish, we paid him back for the nets and so on and we received the balance. June 20 was the opening day there and the season lasted about two months and then the canneries were closed. There were whites, Indians and Japanese.... If you do it for a year, you get used to it. It's not a job where you're hired by somebody. It's not a job where you work under a white man. A fisherman is his own boss so he feels easy. If he works hard using his brain to find a good place to work, he can catch a lot of fish."

Hideo Kokubo is a second generation Japanese Canadian, born in Stev-eston in 1912: "When I think about them now, I think that the people in the old days were worth more respect than now. Everything is ready-made for today's fishermen, everything mechanized, very easy. They work fewer hours. In the old days, the fishermen didn't know the language and they were tougher too. They started fishing on Sunday evening at 6 o'clock until Friday evening at 6. On top of that, during the week ends if the nets were not damaged, we got wood to burn in the winter, collected driftwood, chopped it into even logs.... The Japanese had Gyosha Kumiai [the Fishermen's Co-op] something like a union. Since we lived in a cannery house, we gave the cannery sockeye as rent; as for the fall fish, Kumiai sold them for us and Kumiai had a store. We bought things at the Kumiai as much as possible. The profits were divided among the members in the form of stocks...."

Mr. Morakami: "The Japanese worked so hard. If he was a fisherman, he would catch a lot of fish. The Japanese were more efficient than the white people so they were jealous. I think that they had the idea that they didn't want the Japanese because they would lose their position. It wasn't just the Englishmen that thought so, other nationalities like the Italians, Norwegians, Germans, Russians, etc., not well-educated Europe-ans. The well-educated men wouldn't have done such a thing. We went through a time when third class Europeans would do such a thing to us.

Whatever jobs, fishing or farming, since the Japanese had a little better brains, they thought that without the Japanese they wouldn't lose in the competition . . . didn't want to have us. This was the basis of the discrimination. For example, the Japanese fishermen caught fish better or in the cannery they like us better and said, 'Come on, come on,' those guys thought it would be better without the Japs. Throw them out . . . "

Anti-Japanese sentiment climaxed in the evacuation of all Japanese during the second World War. They lost most of their possessions which were either confiscated or stolen by vandals who ransacked the vacated homes. . . .

COMPETING STANDARDS: ASIAN IMMIGRANTS TO B.C., c.1908

White racism in B.C. was fed by importation of Asian 'contract' immigrants, used as cheap labour by the coal, rail, fish, and lumber barons of British Columbia, and often used as strikebreakers as well. During the depression of September 1907 anti-Asiatic riots broke out in Vancouver. Federal investigator Mackenzie King referred to the fear of workers and small businessmen (threatened by the low wages and consequent low standards of living of coolie workers) as the 'Law of Competing Standards' in his post-riot negotiations with the Japanese, Chinese, and Indian governments. Their 'gentlemen's agreement' to cut immigration is here seen from the Chinese point of view. King became Minister of Labour a year later.

Public Archives of Canada [PAC], King Papers, MG26, J4, vol.13.

Translation of Circular Letter issued by Chinese Board of Trade, thirty thousand copies of which were sent from Port of Vancouver on June 3rd, 1908, per SS. Empress of Japan to Tung Wah Hospital, Hong Kong, for distribution at all Treaty Ports of China:

At present business of all kinds is dull all over Canada, and employment in any kind of labor is hard to obtain. Only about one-third of the Canneries are in operation. The Shingle Mills, Factories of every industry, and Working Mines industry have shut down to more than one-half of their usual activity. Besides, Japanese and Hindu laborers have come in large numbers, hence wages have been reduced. White laborers look upon these with ill feeling, and are organizing to force out our people from all kinds of works.

On September last White laborers gathered in large numbers, marched through the streets, and smashed the doors and windows of our people. We were forced to stop business for several days. Besides all this, owing to the stringency of the money market in the States, business in Canada is greatly affected. At present many of our people are out of employment. Those of us who speak English and are skilled workmen have a hard time to find work. What can a new comer, who cannot speak the language and knows nothing about the ways and customs of the country, expect in the way of finding work on their arrival here?

As all immigrants have to pay a head tax of $500 gold, which is more than a $1000 in our money, and that money, many of them, may have to borrow or sell their property to obtain the same, thinking that they can easily earn it back and many times over on their arrival here, will be sorely disappointed. They will find that the conditions here are very hard, without work, and perhaps much harder than in China. It is doubly so, because the cost of living, here is about 5 times more than in our own country. If he should be without work for a single month he will find his savings will soon be gone.

Now, in spending so much money to come here, even if he should find work with ordinary wages, it would be several years before he could regain what he paid as head tax, so why not take that money and go into some business in our own country and earn a living. We would suggest that our countrymen think over the matter carefully.

We are informed that there are false rumors circulating about in the interior of China to the effect that Canada is about to increase the head tax of Chinese immigrants to $1000 gold a head. On that account many of our people rush to reach here to avoid the said tax. We assure you that such is not the case. Our Countrymen, why should you spend a thousand dollars in order to exile yourself from your home with but little prospect to get it back again? Let us examine into those Hindus who recently arrived here. What employment have they? All they do is to walk the streets. They have not even a place to rest their tired bodies at night. Indeed they suffer greatly. When we see their condition we pity them, as they are now begging the authorities of the City to feed them, and we hear that the authorities are about to ship them back to their own Country.

Although our Countrymen have not as yet reached that stage, but we fear that that will come, and therefore take the precaution to warn you that unless you have a position provided for you before you come, do not come here to take any chance. If you should not heed this warning you should at least bring sufficient money to support yourself for some time and not to suffer cold and hunger after you reached here, as otherwise you will surely regret.

AN IMMIGRANT'S FIRST JOBS: IN THE WEST, 1906-1908

Unlike most other immigrants, Louis Kon had a classical education. The letters from which these excerpts are taken are thus an untypically literate account of the experiences undergone by thousands of unlettered newcomers who had neither the opportunity nor the inclination to tell of their experience. A radical student during the Russian revolts of 1905, Kon had led a strike in his father's printing plant in Moscow, and escaped into Austro-Hungarian territory (he claimed) only one step ahead of the Czarist secret police. The pidgin English he affects, with too much verve and humour not to indicate that he was possessed of real command of the language, conceals a keen intelligence.

This is a view from the inside. Kon's letters put in print what many Slavs could only feel about the rough-hewn North American lifestyle, its political freedom, harsh conditions, and high hopes, and—for he assimilated this too —its 'white' men's prejudice against Asiatic immigrants in the West. Like many Slavs of his generation, Kon was to become a sympathizer of the Bolshevik revolution in 1917, and in the 1920s he simultaneously aided the Soviet 'trade Delegation' to Canada, while acting as confidential secretary to the arch-capitalist Sir Herbert Holt, a Montreal utilities tycoon.

Louis Kon, 'The Letters of Louis', *Canada West*, vol. VI (April 1909), 402-4 and (May 1909), 44-6.

The time I want to describe my experience in Canada was unfortunately a leap year, that means a year, when average human being has to think, if can not take, three hundred sixty and six times, instead of 365 about breakfast, dinner and supper; also in the period of very strong financial crysis in the States; immense profits of different trust corporations; great fights between Hackenshmidt and Gotch, Taft and Bryan; in the time of overflow of Canada with Salvation Army emigrants (as it was expected a war between the humanity and devils) . . .

I was born in a beautiful country, very similar to the Canada, regarding the greatness of occupied area, vegetation, climate, soil and mineral richness, but where a man, who do not have the same opinion as the government, or his officials, about anything at all, what strikes his mind in daily life, or do not belong to the governement church (church and government in my country is the same meaning, but different prononciation) is called and fined as a most dangerous murderer or is sent to a very, very cold country, which in geography figures under the name of Siberia.

It is quite simple and easy to understand, that some people becomes desperate in such conditions, and not withstanding great love and attachment to his mother-country, customs, habits, folk and friends, looks in the large world after any new and more free fatherland, where he can freely talk even about reduction of liquor licenses, or compulsory education and choose together with his fellow-citizens his own governement; free think and talk and push ahead the civilization. . . .

Our steamer approached to Halifax in the late afternoon hour, and all I could see on the coast were the many lights and white snow spots, all I could hear it was indistinct whistles and noise.

How great thing is imagination. In the white snow spots and the many lights, I have see Indian wigwams and tents, in the railroad whistles and bells and factories noise, I have heard the dancing and singing of Indians.

My disappointment in the next early morning was awfull. Forts and fortresses of Halifax with sticking out heavy guns of different sizes, masses of smoke, hanging from factory chimneys, sound of railroad engine bells, towers of churches, lighted with rising sun rays, were before my sight—but not one Indian, not one Wigwam.

However, I consolated myself, that farther from the coast in the heart of the Canadian prairies my expectations will be not disappointed.

I inhabited in the Capitol of the golden North-West [Winnipeg].

Broad streets and sidewalks, electric street-cars and light, fancy carriages and autos, very nice and big sensible hight buildings, up to date cafes, restaurants and hotels, most fashionable goods in lovely trimmed store-windows, a few theatres and every comfort charm and luxury of an modern city. Is this really Canada? Canada about which I read so many romances in my young years?

Fortunately I made acquaintance with some gentleman, who spoke one of the languages I knew, and he was good enough to be my guide in the strange place. . . .

"You see," said Mr. X., "the Indians in this country sing God Save the King and My Old Centucky Home; read magazines and subscribe matrimonial newspapers from Chicago; play cricket, hockey and diabolo; ride in street cars and automobiles. They eat plum-pudding and oysters cocktail; they purchase phonographs and sweet caporals; they very often say: 'Come on, have a drink,' but they never got it. Why? probably white people is too afraid he short himself on liquor." . . .

. . . came to me one of my countrymen, who was living in this country for some years and was interested in political affairs.

He proposed to me to go on the country and held political meetings among foreigner farmers. . . .

All of the present at the meeting farmers were at least living in Canada three years, and very many six, eight and more, but none had the slightest idea about importance, even signification of politic. They were sure that political parties are some business companys, doing as butcher or second-hand dealer some kind of large business, but how, who and what kind of business it is, they did not know and were not very anxious to learn.

In their own country, they were not allowed to get in politics. That part of progress belongs there to the rich people. In this country, they do not understand the language and they can not read the papers....

Certainly I could not take any country without knowledge of English a man can be just a common laborer. But I was anxious to work among English speaking peoples, to learn the language. Here began the experience.

I found a place as a porter in some hardware store. As a green man, whose knowledge of English was equal to zero, my occupation was to clean store, offices and windows, carry barrels and different cases.

After few days we received a lot of eighty barrels of tiles for stove-mantles and I had the honour to be appointed to pile all this stuff on the shelfs in basement.

During fortnight from early in the morning, till six o'clock pile the tiles! I suppose, that even most patient and bloodless man could be mad, would the tiles not be of different colors and size....

My progress in English was awful slow and when I was talking to some English speaking man, he certainly listened to me, for Britishers are gentlemen as a rule, but he said usually "yes," when doubtless it should be "no," and "no" when it should be "yes," or was laughing in the most sad parts of my talk and was very grief in the most gay....

I felt a strong want for some steady and hard work, as idling during few months shaked yet more my nerves, disturbed during three years of Russian revolution.

I took "job" on the railroad grading in Saskatchewan and paying my last dollar bill to the employment-agent. After few days I was in the railroad camp on the prairies, about 85 miles away from the next railway station.

It happened first time in my life to be so far from civilization, to see how rapid, progressive and solid the railways are build in Canada, to see such an immense space untouched by humanity, and prove the life of a manual labor.

The living in tents, sleeping on self-made bunks, covered with hay and blankets, eating soup, meat, vegetables, fruit-sauce, pudding and pie on one and the same tin plate, drinking coffee or tea from a tin cup and to be always on the open air, was strange and very pleasant to me.

I was surprised how the Canadian laborers are well fed. I will not talk about my country, or Italy, where the chief nutriment of labor class are potatoes and buttermilk or fruit, and meat for Christmas and Easter, but even in Germany or France the middle class don't eat so many and different dishes. Porridge, tea or coffee and milk, pancakes or toast, potatoes, warm and cold meat and cakes for breakfast. Soup, two kinds of meat, two or three kinds of vegetables, pudding, two kinds of pie and few kinds of cakes and tarts, tea, coffee, for dinner, and the same menu for supper, probably can and should satisfy the most particular people.

My first work was using of pick and shovel, and as I was not accustomed to the manual work my hands were all in blisters, my back did awful pain, the fingers during the night became so stiff that in the morning I could hardly wash myself, but such a sleep and appetite I never knew before.

After short time lifting of very heavy rocks, working during ten hours a day seemed to me the most pleasant game I ever had before. My nerves very rapidly started to mend, and muscles and bones become more elastic and enduring to the hard work.

I struck happily a camp, where nearly all laborers were English speaking people and I started pretty soon talk English, having as teachers Scotchmen, Welshmen, Irishmen, Yankees and Canadians.

After short time came along the promotion to a dumpsman. It means a gentleman, whose duties are to stand all day in sand, dirt, or clay and direct the approaching teamsters "gee" or "ha," and when they reach the proper point yell "dump" in two tones higher as the high C, which make so famous Caruso.

I liked this work very well, because the dump was the best observation spot to look at the beauty of sunrise and sunset. . . .

The different works I had to perform during my stay in the railroad camp were very amusing and interesting for short time, as they gave exercise only to the physical strength, leaving the brains in deepest sleep. Therefore the days spendet on the sand started to seem to me too uniform. . . .

The heads of the firm I was working for in the construction camp belonged to the geographical society, the chief object of which was to make acquainted the largest number of people, without difference of confession, age or nationality, with the Canadian Prairies—and therefore they did pay the laborers in time checks, which are changed for bank check in the head office, about 87 miles from the camp.

It was a very smart idea from the geographical and sport point of view, but did not agree very well with my pockets, from which a vacuum pump could pump out plenty of air, containing all kinds crumbs of tobacco, broken matches, buttons, dirt and sand, but not a piece of noble metal in the form of coin.

I packed together my propertie, which the sheriff would not probably find sufficient to cover the laundry bill for two collars and one handkerchief. Having fastened on the back the blankets, I started to walk to some town in the Saskatchewan Valley, where according to our present financial system I could exchange my performed work for a piece of paper, the possession of which would open for me the hearts of bartenders, grocers, clothiers, restaurant-keepers and such.

To walk the distance of 87 miles may be a trifle for a Russian army's officer, who hearing the Japanese "banzai" is able to run away few thousand miles, but it seemed pretty hard to me.

As it was a new railroad line, the settlements were very scarce, and the only sleeping accommodations for travellers was the largest-in-the-world-hotel, "Open Prairies".

It was the most proper hotel for my fashionable clothes and financial situation. However, it did not protect from moskitos, grass hoppers, which runs races on my face, gophers, which tried to find out the taste of my hair or moustache, and from the rain. . . .

After few days I was looking for work on the streets of Edmonton. Proud of the knowledge of English language achieved in railroad camp I started dispute with some Canadian.

"You better don't talk so loud on the streets in English, because anybody of the police force can take you in the court."

"How is that?" I asked very surprised.

"May be you don't know," said the gentleman, "that for improper and strong language as you use the countrys law foresees a fine. . . .

Hearing such an judgment about my English I bought the largest edition of Webster's dictionary and during two days was looking for the words I knew, but alas! neither in Webster's, nor in Collins I could find it.

I understood that they were, may be, pure English words, but *behind* the printing limit.

Shortly I had a job in the brick yard, performing all kinds of work for pretty good wages.

Few days afterwards the agricultural department of Nature's management decided to pour some rain, to make the grain better grow. The business of brickmakers do not always agree with those of farmers.

In result the work was stopped for long time and I went back to the railroad camp. . . .

Some place in Alberta I met on the trail a farmer driving a very nice teams. He was polite enough to propose to me take a ride on his wagon.

From the first glance I recognized his Slavonian destraction, and after short talk learned that about ten years ago he came from the same place I was living. . . .

He told me how he was hard working during ten years in some paper factory as a foreman and all he could save was a sum of money just sufficient to pay his and families passage to Canada.

There, however, working few years as in a factory he saved money enough to start the farming in proper way. Now beside a valuable property he has got few thousand dollars in bank.

"Yes, my boy," said the farmer, "in my own country I would never be secure of my life. My children and grandchildren would be always poor laborers, uneducated people, living from day to the day without a prospect for better days and quiet hours." . . .

I left Calgary for a nice little town of Revelstoke in the British Columbia, where-from I had the nearest way to the place of my employment as "experienced bushman".

Next morning I awakened just at the time when conductor entered our coach, announcing Revelstoke next.

The station was overcrowded with Japanese, Chinese and Hindoos. In the first moment I wanted go to the agent to request him take me back to Canada, because it was not my intention to stay neither in Japan or China, nor India. Where I was in the fact I did not know, but sure not in the white peoples' country.

The coolness of a November morning sobered me soon and I remembered very well that to get to the Celestial Kingdom, or to the kingdom of the Sun or White Elephant, one has to cross the ocean. I could not be asleep during three weeks. It was absurd to suppose for a second, that C.P.R. would carry me to China or Japan on a ticket paid just to Revelstoke.

Leaving luggage on the station I went in the town; seeing on every step crowds of yellow faced people, fear to be in Asia returned again. . . .

Trade, industrie and commerce were awful slack and secure job was the next to impossibility. Saved money was pretty fast disappearing. The prospects were approaching for living in a type-of-charge-hotel, runned by government or city, where the rooms are given for special merits, called vagrancy.

Lucky enough I found work on the C.P. as mason helper, carrying stones, cement, mixed concrete, learning again more English words and experiencing new kind of life in "box-car."

Would somebody tell to me a couple of years ago, that I'll live in box-car, which suppose to serve for transporting cattle and freight, I would call him for duel. But now I blessed the hour I could get it.

It was my first New Year eve spent on the American continent, far away from my people and friends.

By the slight light of an small coal oil lamp, which burned in the middle of our car, the masons and their helpers, in clothes bearing signs of cement and clay, were sitting on the bench, reading old magazines and smoking pipes. It was the most sad picture of welcoming New Year, I ever saw before. . . .

Sharp at midnight whistles of few engines and shops, lasting few minutes, but eternity for me, replaced the clink of champagne glasses and the noise of usual "Happy New Year," announced to the railroadmen the beginning of New Year's reign.

Next day, instead of the usual New Year's visits, again mixing of concrete and carrying of stones.

It was a happy beginning of a New Year, as next day we were all discharged. . . .

Here the sports have quite a different object and give different results.

An average European is effeminated, which word does not exist in this country in the sense I mean, for here even a girl of sixteen can far better face a hard-life proposition and is more fitted for every day struggles in our present life conditions as an average full grown man in the European cities. . . .

Great many European adventurers of the class I am describing here, come down to Canada with the plan to settle down, but have not the courage to go through the hard but wholesome and profitable experience, every one has to put, to be sure of success of his career and to receive the degree of B.C.L.B. (Bachelor of Canadian Life Experience). . . .

They talk different stories about the country, notwithstanding their knowledge of it is equal to letters of a tourist printed then and again in different newspapers. Such a tourist usually buys a first class ticket in Montreal or Halifax and after six days safely reaches Vancouver, to start next morning or evening for Japan. His studies of the country made through the window of a passenger coach and by looking over the postcards and views sold in the train by the news-agent, are sufficient to write an article about "Canada from ethnological, geographical, economical, social, religious, sport and artistical point of view."

I came personally across such creatures and all informations I could get out of him was the following:

"Every Canadian has in his wardrobe at least one blue serge suit and a pair of patent leather shoes. In Manitoba on every schoolhouse are Union Jack flags, but not everybody is taught to reade and write. The Premier of Manitoba, Roblin, is a very broad man, for he wares collars size 22 and is weighing 289 lbs. (before elections campaign, after only 225). A druggist in Canada does sell in his shop tailor made suits and ice cream, and bookstores use to keep patent medicines and Merry Widow handkerchieves, (those are the best sellers on the western book markets.)"

Very surprised I asked if it is all he knows about Canada, and he said: "Why, no. I can give you a lot of informations about this country. They call every foreigner John and do eat too much meat. They have nearly in every hotel a very nice dining room in which you can see very tasteful furniture, and very often on the sideboards nice silver jardiniers and cups or odd pieces of nice china, but do not look at walls, for you mostly will strike framed pictures, which you would steale and tore to pieces. . . .

The most interesting part of my experience in Canada I have to postpone for some time and first learn correct the English, for this part is not a material to make the reader laugh of bad language and style or cry of inexperience of some people in every day' life.

I mean the psychology, ethics habits and life of lumber-jacks, miners and men working on the railroad grading. The modern scholar of psychology cannot fancy any better and more interesting types for his studies as are among this part of Canadian citizens. It could be volumes printed about those men. . . .

Yours for Canada,

LOUIS KON.

THE GOVERNMENT INTERVENES: THE I.D.I. ACT OF 1907

No piece of legislation was more important than the Industrial Disputes Investigation Act (the 'Lemieux Act') to the Canadian worker in the period before the Second World War. Even though its application was severely restricted by the courts in 1925, it nevertheless established the pattern for federal labour legislation to the present day. What is significant about this act and subsequent federal legislation is that it is 'consumerist'—concerned more with the maintenance of industrial peace than with union recognition or bargaining in good faith. It was the brainchild of the young Mackenzie King, and like most of his labour legislation it put many restrictions (such as the 'cooling-off period') on the rights of unions, and few on the rights of management.

H. J. Walker, 'Prairie Assignment', *Labour Gazette*, vol. L (Sept. 1950), 1488-93. Reprinted by permission of the Canada Department of Labour, Ottawa.

On a bleak day in November, 1906, a young Canadian Deputy Minister stepped briskly down the gang-plank from the red-funnelled Cunarder "Caronia" to its pier at New York. . . .

. . . [H]e had just been handed a telegram from the Prime Minister of Canada, Sir Wilfrid Laurier, assigning him to an urgent mission to the prairies. . . .

The telegram informed him of a critical situation in the Canadian West where an eight months' coal strike in the Lethbridge area had resulted in a desperate situation. Farmers were burning fence posts and straw stacks. Two provincial governments and municipal committees, backed by health officers, were appealing to the Federal Government to do something quickly to avert disaster as zero temperatures and blizzards swept the prairies, bringing dangerously close to many people the imminence of death by freezing.

Within 24 hours of his return to Ottawa, he was on his way, via the Canadian Pacific Railway....

At Winnipeg he had been handed a sheaf of material on the developing crisis. Included was an open letter to Sir Wilfrid—an appeal so compelling that it had made headlines across the country. The district of Ramsay, from its headquarters in the hamlet of Bladworth, Saskatchewan, faced deadly peril. Its chairman, William Ramsay—after pointing out that the settlers were burning bramble, twisted hay and grain; that the schools were closed; that the Saskatchewan Hotel (a thirty-roomed structure) had only one stove going, and that a blizzard was blowing in sub-zero temperature—lashed out in these words:

We are informed that those persons operating the mines of the people are disputing over their rights—regardless of the right of the people to live.

I would respectfully ask that you, sir, put an end to a dispute that is intolerable, and the maintenance of which endangers the life and happiness (inalienable rights of all free people) of all settlers.

I ask you, sir, on behalf of a suffering people, that by the powers vested in you the right of eminent domain be exercised.

I can assure you, sir, without exaggeration, that this matter is one of life and death to the settlers here, one requiring immediate action.

Your obedient humble servant,
Wm. L. RAMSAY
Chairman of Committee....

This last outburst from a community, frightened and suffering acutely, confirmed his own belief in two fundamentals:

(1) That, under certain circumstances, the rights, real or fictitious, of two parties to an industrial conflict must be subordinated to the right of a third—the Community, or even the Nation.
(2) That if some machinery could be established it could be a medium, with effective publicity, of exposing and remedying the underlying causes and injustices in industrial disputes.

These two principles—with their variants and concomitants of collective bargaining and a "cooling-off" period—are inherent in arbitration and conciliation procedures of today. But in those days, with our pioneering concepts of "rugged individualism" and "the public-be-damned" attitude, it was too new and much too heretical for general acceptance as sound labour economics, or sociology....

Shortly after he stepped off the train at Lethbridge he realized that the long-standing dispute had hardened into defiant unyielding attitudes on both sides without any interest in the consequences to suffering fellow citizens, not even remotely concerned in the causes, but vitally affected by the results.

Straight Talk

He had to break down the resistance of the recalcitrants in union halls and behind the doors of company offices. They were not even talking to each other except out of the corners of their mouths. But King talked straight at them. They were still sullen and time was running out.

More frantic appeals had come to him but the appeals now were edged with sharpness on the part of responsible Saskatchewan officials. These men began to talk rough....

The major point at issue revolved about the question of full recognition of the mine workers' union and the concession of the check-off. It was the then familiar story—which still has a faintly reminiscent ring—of a Company who would meet only its own employees or a committee of them, and of employees equally determined to meet the Company through representatives of the Union, some of whom were not in the employ of the Company.

A complicating factor was the absence, at considerable distance from the scene, of the managing director of the company and the reluctance of the workers (in the last stages of the dispute) to accept settlement without consultation with the International president of the Union at Indianapolis.

Then, there were shades of interpretation to reduce to terms that meant the same thing to both parties.

Finally the young conciliator wrote the clauses concerning union recognition. His clear-cut presentation, impartiality, and his insistence on a speedy settlement in the face of an imminent death toll for the guilt of which the Canadian public would be the judge—turned the tide and brought about a resumption of work and coal production.

Even in the final stages, the miners were dubious about a matter of union protocol—whether International headquarters in Indianapolis would accept the new clauses pertaining to union security. Harassed by all the other considerations in the snarled case, King now had to decide whether he should remain on the scene or go to Indianapolis with a committee of miners.

Misunderstanding, either at Lethbridge or Indianapolis, could still bog down the negotiations he had almost brought to fruition. His immediate presence and counsel were required at all points of contact. In his own mind he was uneasy as to storms delaying communications and he was tortured by the approaching spectre of tragedy in all those prairie homesteads. Balancing all the factors, he boarded the first train for Indianapolis. He had no sooner arrived when he received the managing director's acceptance of his formula. King showed it to the miners' committee, who also approved. The strike was over.

Disaster Averted

Production was immediately stepped up to meet the emergency and Western Canada was saved. . . .

Sir Wilfrid summoned him to offer congratulations. King offered suggestions for the machinery of compulsory investigation.

"Well, then, draft such a law", said Laurier. . . .

The result was the adoption by the Canadian Parliament in 1907 of the Industrial Disputes Investigation Act. In it he did not take away from Labour any right—not even the right to strike. And he gained for Labour a right which it never had—the right of investigation, at public expense, and with the full light of publicity, into any deleterious situation likely to develop into a strike or lockout. The only compulsory feature was to place in abeyance, by law, the right to strike or lockout (and this affected employers as well) until the dispute had been the subject of investigation and conciliation.

It was the first legislation to impose what is popularly known as "the cooling-off" period. The main principles of the Act have since been incorporated in the laws of several countries. The Transvaal (now a part of the Union of South Africa) saw its merit in 1909, and Norway adopted it in 1915. Its major principles were written also into the United States Railway Labour Disputes Act, 1926. . . .

Its principles have been amplified in the [1948] Industrial Relations and Disputes Investigation Act. While the new measure is stream-lined to include such features as compulsory collective bargaining, certification of bargaining representatives, compulsory arbitration of misinterpretations or violations of existing agreements, maintenance of the status quo in terms of employment during reference to conciliation—the machinery is geared to the motive power provided in the original formula drafted by a young man of vision 43 years ago.

LABOUR RELATIONS, CAPE BRETON STYLE

In few areas of Canada have strikes been as frequent and as bloody as in Cape Breton Island. Steel mills and coal pits were controlled by absentee capitalists with close links to the provincial government. The Dominion Steel and Coal Companies were in a continual state of financial crisis, and managers were told to squeeze out the last cent of wages rather than cut dividends. Fillmore, a Socialist, and MacLachlan, later to become the legendary leader of the Cape Breton miners, present a labour viewpoint, while the bosses' Canadian Mining Journal emphasizes the strong conservative attitudes among older workers.

R. A. Fillmore, 'Strikes and Socialism in Eastern Canada', *International Socialist Review*, Vol. X (April 1910), 891-3.

In Nova Scotia there has existed for about thirty years a labor organization known as the Provincial Workmen's Association. Its adherents have been mostly miners (or ground hogs) but a few other crafts have affiliated with it. Its stronghold has, until recently, been in the mining communities of Cape Breton. A few years ago a corporation known as the Dominion Coal Company came upon the scene. Until its appearance the P.W.A. had, in its dealings with individual employers, attained quite a measure of success. But when the coal merger appeared a change was wrought. The P.W.A., a mere sectional organization, found itself powerless to cope with so large an organization of capital.

About five years ago the coal company, true to its traditions as an astute business corporation, decided to "recognize" the P.W.A. This of course was granted only because it did not injure the company and would have a tendency to pacify the workers. After many flowery promises and pledges had been made by the company the workers came to a working (be it noted these are always "working" agreements. Work is all that wage earners are good for) agreement with their masters. And since that the edifying sight has been presented of the lion and the lamb lying down together (the lamb within the lion as usual).

None of the master's pledges have, as yet, been redeemed and the tyrannical rule of the Dominion Coal Company has steadily become more hateful to the workers as was natural. A three-year contract had been signed by the P.W.A. officials and Brother Capital and Brother Labor were locked in each others arms in a loving embrace. And it might be noted in passing that the latter has been unable to extricate himself from the bear-hug up to date.

The men, being unable to do otherwise and being under the domination of the master's moral teachers who expatiate upon honor (whatever that may be) and such like, lived up to the letter of the agreement with

Brother Capital, as usual, flagrantly disregarding it. At the expiration of the first contract the workers were forced by economic necessity to sign a second and even more enslaving "working" agreement. The men became dissatisfied with their union officials suspecting them, with a very large degree of truth as later developments prove, of being merely tools of the masters. They tried to oust Moffat the grand secretary and the other tools of Dominion Coal but without success. Then a number of P.W.A. men invited the U.M.W.A. to come into the provinces. This the U.M.W.A. refused to do until a majority of the miners should declare for it. The P.W.A. officials, Moffat and his gang, submitted the question to the membership and a referendum was taken. The officials—no doubt expecting the proposition to be turned down—pledged themselves to abide by the result of the vote.

The vote was taken. About 75 per cent of the P.W.A. membership voted for affiliation with the U.M.W.A. and organizers were invited to visit the province and came. But Moffat, labor dictator, refused to vacate. He, and those who had voted against affiliation, still supported the obsolete organization. Those who had voted in favor of the proposition joined the U.M.W.A. Then the fun began. Members of the new organization were discharged—over a thousand of them. The P.W.A.-Brother Capital agreement had not yet expired. The U.M.W.A. demanded recognition and a new contract, also a cessation of discrimination against their members.

The company held up its hands in holy horror. Recognition! What! To a "foreign" organization! Ye Gods! Treason! Sedition! etc., etc., *ad nauseum.* A new contract! Some more spasms of righteous indignation over the terrible depravity of men who would break the unexpired contract, made by the P.W.A., and demand a new one. Finally the U.M.W.A. called a strike about July 1st, 1909, and about 6000 men dropped their tools. But Brother Labor, represented by Moffat and the remnants of the P.W.A. considered themselves bound by "honor" to stay on the job. So a labor (?) organization becomes a scab agency.

The second day of the strike some women, wives of strikers, clawed the face of General Manager Duggan of the Coal Company and pulled his hair. This was made a pretext for calling out the soldiery. The mayor and a majority of the councillors of Glace Bay were opposed to the calling of the military (as they know another civic election would be held within a few months.) But the red coated thugs were sent for nevertheless and came—500 officers and men from the Halifax garrisons armed with machine guns. It later developed that even before the requisition papers were signed the machine guns were entrained and the men under arms.

For some time after the arrival of the thugs everything was peaceful. But this did not suit the purpose of the masters. So Pinkertons were hired; a series of bomb outrages planned and carried out and then a number of workers were arrested for conspiracy. Meantime the lickspittle press of the company spread the news far and near that Cape Breton was in a state closely bordering upon anarchy. It was reported that the residence of Mine-Manager Simpson had been completely wrecked by a bomb presumably the work of the U.M.W.A. Later we learned from authoritative sources that $1.25 repaired the damage done. And so it went on.

On July 31st several thousand strikers, carrying their master's flag "the glorious Union Jack," formed in procession for the purpose of demonstrating the strength of their organization to the public. They were met by the military armed with machine guns. In spite of the flag of "their" country which the strikers carried the military ordered them to disperse upon pain of being blown full of lead if they refused. They dispersed. Men were arrested for calling "scab" at those who were at work and this still continues. Pickets are arrested almost daily. A few days ago a picket was shot by a company thug who had been sworn in special as constable. The fight is still on and likely to continue for some time. The company claims it has plenty of men and is getting out as much coal as before the strike. Whether this be true or not the strikers will probably lose the fight. Within the past few weeks a merger has been effected by the Dominion Steel Company another Cape Breton corporation. This, of course, has strengthened the masters.

R. A. Fillmore, 'Strike Situation in Eastern Canada', *International Socialist Review*, vol. X (May 1910), 1007-8.

I met several members of the strike committee, several of them being comrades, and learned something of the conditions leading to the strike. The men had been steadily victimized by a system of docks and fines. The following table will perhaps make this clear:

	1906		1907		1908	
	Docks	Fines	Docks	Fines	Docks	Fines
No. 2 slope	1738	1028	1827	1260	4219	3561
No. 3 slope	5079	1101	5631	831	14297	2582
Grand Totals	6817	2129	7458	2091	18516	6143

Note the enormous increase in docks and fines between 1906 and 1908. A dock means that the entire box of coal is taken from the miner if 60 pounds of stone is found. A fine means twenty cents off the price if 40 pounds of stone is found. Docks and fines for 1908 represent approximately 21,000 tons of coal, and, after making liberal allowance for the actual weight of stone found in the boxes, the company has appropriated some 20,000 tons of coal which, if paid for, would represent at least $8,500.00 additional wages to the miners.

From the foregoing it will be seen that the burdens of the men were steadily increased until the climax came just before the strike, when the company tried to enforce a general reduction of fifteen per cent. The Lemieux conciliation act, (which serves the purpose of warning the masters of an impending strike and is therefore a very useful list of labor(?) legislation—for the masters) was called into use. But all attempts at hoodwinking the men were vain, as they were thoroughly aroused. After several boards of conciliation had droned for weeks (at $10 per day) over quibbles and the crooked bookkeeping of the company the decisions were against the men. And quite naturally. Then came the strike.

The U.M.W.A. has paid strike benefits since the beginning of the struggle. It has also bought wood land and the men are thus supplied with fuel free of charge. At almost any hour of the day or night strikers may be seen hauling wood home, many of them using hand-sleds.

Lately an effort has been made to scab the mines, numbers of men having been brought in from Montreal, Cape Bulow, Halifax and other places, but the scabs leave as fast as others arrive. Only about 100 are at present at work and very few of these are experienced miners. The company claims it raised 3500 tons of coal during February, but probably one half of this amount would be more nearly correct. The men claim that cars of coal have been hauled back and forth over the railroad so many times (in order to lead the public to the belief that they are raising an enormous quantity) that the coal begins to look gray and weather-beaten. Whether this is true or not, the fact remains that Springhill coal has become conspicuous by its absence in the coal markets of the country.

Pinkerton and Thiel thugs are as plentiful as pretty girls at a husking. On the evening of February 26th one of the Thiel spies succeeded in raising a row and he and his pals got soundly mauled at the hands (and feet) of a body of strikers. The detective fired a revolver and was then passed over to the town police. He was fined $10. Had he been a striker he would doubtless have received a year in jail.

J. B. MacLachlan, 'Still Fighting at Glace Bay', *International Socialist Review*, vol. 10 (Sept. 1910), 1102-3.

... As soon as navigation closed in November, 1908, the Dominion Coal Company locked out one thousand men, and expected that zero weather and starvation would crush the spirit of revolt, that Moffat's silly, pious platitudes about patriotism had failed to stay. Failure again was the result. The men stuck to the organization of their choice, and March, 1909, at length arrived. Navigation was again about to open and coal could be shipped up the St. Lawrence. The Dominion Coal Company was in a dilemma. Greed and fear filled their hearts. Greed said, "Take back the men and make profits right now." Fear pointed to a strong, virile, aggressive organization that would assuredly, if it got a foot hold, make a large inroad on the dividends in the future. A hurried meeting of all the coal operators of the province was called, and met in the town of Truro, N.S., and a compromise between fear and greed was reached. Each was sworn, "not to deal in any way whatever with the U.M.W. of A. but to sustain and 'do business' with the P.W.A." The locked out men were taken back, but they realized that the cessation of hostilities was only temporary, and on July 1, 1909, over two-thirds of the employees of the Dominion Coal Company walked out on strike. The remainder staying with the P.W.A. and giving the glad hand of welcome to every strike-breaker and thug imported by the Dominion Coal Company.

The fight was now on in dead earnest. A month previous to the strike the coal company had 625 special police sworn in. Many of the "loyal" P.W.A. members, including John Moffatt, donned the tin badge of the corporation thug, which gave them the right to swagger around town with a gun on their hip. 600 soldiers and three machine guns were rushed into the mining towns about Glace Bay. During the summer months, specially on Saturday nights, these gun men without reason, or warning would swoop down on the town of Glace Bay flaunting their naked knives in the air, and hustle peaceable strikers from the side-walk into the street. The strikers were arrested in scores on frivolous and trumped-up charges and thrown into jail. Two continents were ransacked and everybody that could be induced to take a free trip to Glace Bay, was given one, in the hope that he would remain there a strike-breaker. Scabs and thugs were expected to break the strike. They failed. One month after another sped away and the men still stuck to each other. Meantime the coal company with its "loyal" P.W.A. men and imported scabs had managed to raise their daily output a few thousand tons. Winter again arrived; enraged at its inability to break the strike with jails, thugs, and scabs the Dominion Coal Company like another Nero or Nana Sahib turned its ferocity against tender women and little children. During the past winter months hundreds of mothers with crying, clinging, trembling little children hanging to their dresses, have been evicted from their homes, and thrown on to the streets in blinding snow storms, with the glass ranging from zero to 18 below. Neither youth, age, sex nor sickness appealed successfully to these pitiless iron-hearted ruffians. An old and obsolete law was resurrected and the peoples' belongings taken for back rent, and some families were left with nothing but what they stood up in.

The strikers have weathered the rigours of another Canadian winter imbued with the spirit that it would be better to fill a freeman's grave than a coward's job.

Some weeks ago the old management resigned, which means that they had conferred on them the ancient and honorable Order of the Sack. A new superintendent and general manager were appointed. Press and pulpit rang with the praises of the new men. For a few weeks all evictions were stopped. Men were let out on suspended sentences, honeyed words were now tried where brutality had failed. The men had been fighting for ten months for something substantial, and refused to go back to work on promises which appeared to them pretty little airy nothings. The mask was then dropped and seventeen families thrown on to the street. Men out on suspended sentences were arrested and placed in jail, One fellow, who had the hardihood to leave the employ of these good, God fearing men and join the strikers, had his home entered at midnight by a band of thugs and he and his family driven off the "company's property" four hours after he had joined the U.M.W. of A. . . .

It has been a grand time for socialist propaganda. Hundreds of the men imported were the discontented of the capitalist countries of Europe. They thought they saw an escape from capitalist oppression by taking the free passes handed out by the Dominion Coal Company. The coal company thought it was importing scabs when it was really bringing men who shall be its grave diggers. The writer visited a shack where sixteen of these men were; a U.M.W. of A. interpreter told them I was an officer of the U.M.W. They grinned and nodded; not one of them speaking a word of English. He then said, I was a member of Glace Bay socialist local. That did the trick, in a moment they were round me shaking my hand and the grins gave place to beaming faces.

'The Glace Bay Strike', *Canadian Mining Journal*, 1 Aug. 1909, 473-4.

. . . It is scarcely a correct use of words to refer to the present labour troubles at Glace Bay as a "strike." The cessation of work by the adherents of the United Mine Workers, and the intimidation of hundreds of other men who wish to work, has not arisen out of the struggle of legitimate trade unionism against oppressive capitalism. It is not one incident out of the many that daily occur in the never-ending struggle of the proletariat against plutocratism that is as old as time and will still be waging when our civilization and our race is but a memory. Many of the deluded men who have gone on strike believe otherwise, and are honest in their belief, not realizing that they are the miserable victims of men whose mouths are filled with lies. . . .

Probably there never was a strike in Canada that had less justification. The Dominion Coal Company are now dealing with the first strike in their history, and, in fact, there has only been one strike of any consequence in the coal mines of Cape Breton since 1868. The Canadian press, with the exception of one ephemeral and intermittent broadsheet that has made its appearance on perhaps a dozen occasions, has with one voice condemned the action of the United Mine Workers. Some provincial newspapers that have assiduously fanned the agitation for months past are now trying to lay the fire they have caused, much to the bewilderment of those simple people who believe what they read in the newspapers. All shades of public opinion, religious, political, and commercial, unite in deploring this strike as a national calamity. Nevertheless, a very large amount of misapprehension exists as to the true magnitude of the trouble. The vastness of the Dominion Coal Company's enterprise has so impressed itself on the public that it is assumed that any labour trouble that seriously affects its operations must have behind it the support of a large and determined body of men. This, however, is not the case. The United Mine Workers are in a decided minority of the Coal Company's employees, and their determination is a mixture of desperation and American money. At the end of the second week of the strike two-thirds of the Coal Company's employees are working, and many of them have risked and are risking their lives, voluntarily, to protect what they conceive to be their company's interests and their own. Before the strike the U.M.W.A. publicly announced in the newspapers that they were about to call out 95 per cent of the Coal Company's employees. On the first day of the strike the output of the company's mines was just about half a normal output, and the number of men that absented themselves was well under two thousand. Taking into consideration the number of men who were waiting to see how things would develop, it is safe to assume that the actual number of strikers did not exceed 1,700, which is generally supposed to be approximately the number of U.M.W.A. men in the Coal Company's employ. The day following was marked by disgraceful and riotous scenes. Men were beaten, stripped naked, assailed by the most opprobrious epithets imaginable, and things were said and done that deserve the most emphatic and sternest condemnation. As a result men were intimidated from coming to work, and we in Glace Bay witnessed the terrorizing of a community of ten or twelve thousand people by a body of persons who did not represent ten per cent of the population.

The situation was not improved by the Mayor of Glace Bay, who applied a very extraordinary remedy for the amelioration of such intolerable conditions. This gentleman accepted the offer of the U.M.W.A.

leaders to furnish him with a number of special constables to be sworn in to keep the peace, and a considerable number of the strikers were sworn in as special constables, in which position they played the dual role of pickets and policemen, a condition of affairs that has surely never been paralleled in any British municipality. The result of this peculiar civic action was such as might have been expected. These U.M.W.A. constables proceeded to arrest the special constables of the Coal Company, and the singular scene was several times witnessed of the Coal Company's officials being arrested and haled before a magistrate by some half-grown hobbledehoy clothed with a brief authority by the Chief Magistrate of the municipality. It was well that the populace saw the undoubted humour of the situation, otherwise it would have been intolerable. These appointments were after several days revoked by the Police Committee, upon which the Deputy Mayor and another councillor took upon themselves to re-make the appointments, which were speedily cancelled once more by the Police Committee. By this time no one knew how things stood, and the townspeople ceased to take any serious interest in the farce....

The United Mine Workers have evidently a keen desire to control the mines of the Dominion Coal Company. At the Glace Bay Hotel, which during the past fortnight has provided rest and refreshments for the leaders of the opposing forces, and a horde of newspaper reporters, the U.M.W.A. have five of their officers from the United States, assisted by a clerical force of two female clerks and a male clerk. The business of these gentlemen in Cape Breton is to lead and supervise the campaign of an American labour union in its attack on one of the most important industries of Canada, in the attempt of a foreign union to usurp and destroy a Canadian union, which was in existence and was doing a good work many years before the U.M.W.A. had emerged from the womb of time. A gentleman prominent in American governmental circles, who has made a special study of industrial conditions on this continent, recently stated that the U.M.W.A. were very anxious to control the eastern mines of Canada in order to be able to neutralize them whenever a strike was considered necessary in the bituminous coal fields of the United States. This, and this only, is the reason for the presence of these U.M.W.A. gentlemen in Glace Bay. Their efforts will fail; must fail, in fact, because American domination in any shape is something that Canada will not tolerate. Annexation was once a live issue in the Dominion. It is now dead as Moses. Labour legislation and labour organization always lags a decade or two behind the general progress of our race, but when the time comes—and it is not far distant—when Canada chooses between international trade unionism, or, in other words, domination of Canadian unionism by that of the United States, and national trade unionism—when that time comes, the national spirit will assert itself....

One interesting result of the past two weeks' events has been to prove how thoroughly unreliable the statements of the U.M.W.A. leaders are, and have been. For a long time past the local newspapers have given a wide license to the U.M.W.A. and have published their claims in good faith. During the two weeks that have just gone, however, even the most indulgent newspaper men have had to confess that they were unable to place any reliance on the statements given to them by the U.M.W.A. For example, Mr. Harry Bousfield, a gentleman 'whose accomplishments in the gentle art of stuffing newspaper men are not excelled by any of his colleagues, stated that the Coal Company could not possibly have produced more than 1,600 tons of coal on a certain day, unless they had transported it by aviation. As a matter of fact the Coal Company's output on that day was over 6,000 tons. No. 1 Colliery has so far been operated on a quite normal basis since the strike. The workmen there are P.W.A. men almost entirely, and the strike does not exist at No. 1 Colliery. Nevertheless the U.M.W.A. declared to all and sundry that the number of workmen employed there was not over 145 men. However that may be the mine that produced over 1800 tons of coal as a daily output, which would mean that so small a force as mentioned by the U.M.W. would have to "hustle some." To be exact, No. 1 had over 600 men. After a little more of this it was felt that in whatever else the U.M.W. was lacking, its capacity for prevarication was unstinted.

The result of the strike has never been in doubt. At the time of writing men are returning to work in greater numbers every day, and new men are coming in from the outside. One interesting feature has been that many of the younger men whose homes are in the country districts of Cape Breton, and who went home when the strike was called, speedily came back. In many instances the "old man" failed to understand why his son should have quit a lucrative employment at the beck of American agitators, and in more than one instance these young men have come back to work with a flea in the ear. Exactly two weeks after the commencement of the strike the Coal Company put on cars the not inconsiderable tonnage of 9,000 tons, to which total Dominion No. 1 contributed over 2,000 tons and Reserve over 1,100 tons. As we have previously had occasion to remark, the older mines, where the population is even yet largely composed of native born Canadians, have shown very little falling off in output, and the disaffection is chiefly confined to the newer mines such as No. 2 and No. 6, where the workmen are of all nationalities.

The pinch of need has not yet been felt, as the pay which was disbursed on the 17th was one of the largest in the Company's history. There are many poor wives and children, however, in homes across the water who will feel the pangs of hunger, for their husbands have been grossly ill-treated and deceived by the American leaders. These men have been prevented from working by the direst threats, the true significance of which their imperfect understanding of English does not enable them to perceive, and dread prevents them from giving the information which would enable the law to deal with these cowardly blackguards. These men have been told that if they work they will be remembered hereafter. They are told that things may be all right so long as the militia is here, "but you wait till afterwards." Many of them are going in mortal fear of their lives, and their plight is a piteous one. Never at any rate in Nova Scotia has such shameful and wholesale intimidation been resorted to. The U.M.W.A. have imported interpreters from the mining districts of the States, who for months past have been instilling into the minds of these unlettered foreigners the awful consequences of thwarting the will of the U.M.W.A.

IWW BOOMERS AND RAILWAY ARISTOCRATS

Bob Russell was to become one of Western Canada's leading labour militants, and to play an important role in both the Winnipeg General Strike and in the One Big Union. He contrasts the radical outlook of British, native-born, and immigrant workers in the West with the 'gold-braid' mentality of the labour aristocrats, 'running trades' unions, which included railway engineers, firemen, brakemen, and conductors, and refused even to join the Trades and Labor Congress. This is an example of the serious split in the labour movement, which later was to doom the Winnipeg Strike.

R. B. Russell Interview by Lionel Orlikow, c.1958. Public Archives of Manitoba.

The reason I became a socialist? . . . Two of my father's brothers were ministers of the gospel and they used to land in the house every night and my father was a socialist. Of course he was always arguing with his brothers and I suppose I imbibed all of that . . . . [When I came to Canada] it was a very strong movement in Britain at that time and here you had an agricultural country back in 1910-1911 and the only place around Winnipeg was the Railway shops. Outside of that, it was just a little 2 by 4 place. There was a big immigration of Scotch and English and there were immigrants from Poland, immigrants from Germany, immigrants from Romania. We had them from all over. We used to get together and of course the first thing we knew, we formed a political organization. I joined up with the Socialist Party of Canada because I was always inclined to Marxian economics. John Queen [a Winnipeg strike leader in

1919] and a bunch of them belonged to the old Social Democratic Party here, which was Social Democrats. Most of the German boys were Social Democrats....

...[The Socialist Party of Canada] were more or less armchair philosophers. It wasn't a question of putting a soap box out in the Market Square you know, and giving a speech and gathering a crowd around. This fellow Love, he used to go out there. He was a strong fellow, he was a physical culturalist you know and well muscled, chest and everything. To get a crowd around the Queen's Hotel there, around the Market Square where the public talking used to be done, he would strip off, show his fine muscles, then he would get somebody to tie a rope around him and bust the rope with his chest you know. He'd do this to attract a crowd. You were competing against the Salvation Army, Brass Bands, Silver Band, and you were competing against other crowds, Seventh Day Adventists and everything else and this was to get the crowd around and then they'd get old George Armstrong. He'd be carrying coals to Newcastle, shovelling the class struggle over his shoulder like this, and half of the audience didn't know what they were talking about you understand. But this is where they produced their platform then.... And then when the younger element came out here from Britain and the other parts and joined up, they very soon changed the Socialist Party's attitude... The everyday struggle on the job you understand, was part of the class struggle....

...The railways were expanding and we were looking for redress under the conditions to which we were working,... we were working on Saturday, we were working six days a week. Well, you come from Britain there where you quit at 12 o'clock on Saturday and go to football games and there was a lot of enjoyment. We couldn't understand this working all those long hours, seven o'clock in the morning until five o'clock in the evening, working on a Saturday, so we decided that we were going to ...remedy that situation and get the shorter work week and have some fun and some sports. So we made approaches in the formation of organization and we approached the management and they said no. So then we adopted a tactic, we just, all of the old country fellows just refused to come to work on a Saturday and we done much like what the old IWW used to do, we blew the whistle for a stop and we stopped and we [refused] to go back again and that's how we established the half day on a Saturday here in Western Canada....

...[W]hen we went into negotiations even with the CPR alone and the CNR alone, it was always the Grand Trunk Pacific that was held up to you.... Well we organized it and we struck it. Of course their main shop was at Rivers, Manitoba. Well they set up a bull-pen there and they brought immigrants from the old country from Scotland and from England and they run them right off the boat onto the trains, and the trains right in here and they put them right into the roundhouses and slept them there ... We won the strike when they went out to get jobs elsewhere ... in the CP or in the CNR. I never saw a bunch of men got rid of so quick in your life. Things would just fall off the engines. A bolt would be loose here, sabotage of the worst kind you see ... A fellow would be working up at the top of the locomotive, maybe they'd take a long iron spanner and of course, the belly of the boiler you know, like that. You'd lay it down and of course he'd kick it and it fell off. Of course nobody knocked it off. Things would fall off the running board, cross-rods would fall, everything would fall and things would happen like that ... They were just the same days as the woolly west that you read about down in the United States. There were pretty rough days there....

The CPR ... adopted a paternal attitude of social clubs, recreation. They provided recreational activities, baseball teams, football teams. The Royal Alexandra Hotel was used Saturday night. They had a social club and the common staff from the jobs would go down there and dance with the foreman or the foreman's wife, you understand, and the manager would look in. It was all paternalism you understand. Well of course, the rebels that were out from Europe, they were having none of this kind of stuff you know. This was just soothing syrup to them and they'd buck those things, but you'd always have a bunch that were always willing to hob-nob with the boss you see. It was a better thing ... little gold striping or that, and the CPR developed that kind of system the same as they did in amongst their locomotive engineers. Instead of giving an increase of wages, they'd paint their name on the side of the car the same as you'll see when you go on to your train. You'll see those conductors and brakemen with their silver stripes or their gold stripes. Five years of servitude for every one of them you understand. Well, they worship those things just the same as the old soldier worships his medals you see. They think that this is a great honour. With seven of those bars across him, he thinks he's a real hero and that's the kind of stuff the CPR played on all the time and of course we'd been through that experience in the old country, you see. First of all, it started off with paternalism, and then it developed into a piece-work system and from the piece-work system, then came the necessity of organizing to defeat those things....

The American influence in the years Canada was developing in the west and these fellows were moving around, that influence was good. The Yankees coming in here, they were internationally broad in their outlook you understand and of course, in the early days, ... you used to look upon them as 'American blowhards' you know and all that. The old American, the Big Man you know, he didn't care for the boss, he didn't care for him and they were 'boomers' you see. We called them boomers. They didn't care whether they worked or they didn't care if the boss fired

them. They gloried you see, they had stamps in their book just like the
IWW had. They'd make donations into the IWW and they'd show us
[IWW and Machinists'] donations they had made in their book. They
worshipped that like the old soldier worshipped his medals or the CNR
fellows had the silver braid or the gold braid, and it was the same with
those boomers. They could show you that they'd been transferred from
[IAM] Lodge 122 in Winnipeg to 189 somewhere else and 484, and the
book would be full of stamps in different locals and they carried transfer
cards all the time. You know, the method they have in tracing them so
that they'd know that they were members in good standing. It was just
like medals to those guys and of course they'd see the world and they
were picking up experience because they were getting all kinds of experience. They'd leave Winnipeg, maybe work in the back [main machine]
shop for a little while and then they'd say, "Ah, I don't like this
regimentation. I'll get away, I'll move up to Calgary and get into a
roundhouse." They were more or less of a lone wolf. Every man for
himself. It's not a highly organized thing like what it is in the back shop.

And these people had a good influence, these 'boomers', and they were
useful you understand and any tough spot we ever found in the country
where we found a weakness in organization, like in Rivers after the
Grand Trunk strike, we used the boomers through there all the time. The
boomers were booming along. We kept them going in [to these jobs] and
we give them [transfer cards] to go in, and looked after them and they
were helped from Lodge to Lodge. They'd get a pick-up in Brandon, a
pick-up in Calgary or a pick-up in Edmonton or wherever, at Revelstoke
—all the big centres you understand. Quite a number of old country
fellows were boomers. They were the key to the organizing of the
unorganized.

HOMESTEADER AND HIRED MAN:
GETTING AHEAD IN THE WEST, 1911

*In the boom decades, 'nativists' often voiced their concern about the dilution
of 'British' Canada by 'alien' Europeans. A great campaign, of which A
Manitoba Chore Boy was a part, was mounted to attract the English
labourer to settle in the West. In this contrast between homesteader and
hired man; good boss and bad; between farmer's son, assisted immigrants
such as 'Barnardo boys', and 'remittance men' [black sheep of upper-class
families sent abroad], we see some of the hopes and difficulties of the
different types of workers.*

E. A. W. Gill, *A Manitoba Chore Boy* (London, 1912), pp. 38-43.

July 28, 1911.

MY DEAR MOTHER,

My letter is a little late this month, but I have been very busy between work and play. The work first. Big Ben says that is the secret of success here, and I guess he's right. This has been our haying time—not a bit like the old song, "Down in the Meadows amaking the Hay," nor like haymaking at the old Squire's, where we used to picnic in the Park, and wind up with a dance at the Hall. Little Ben and Regina are having their school holidays—and working from daylight to dark on the farm. The "wimmen folk," *i.e.*, Mrs. Gregory and Regina, are doing all the milking and dairy work, and most of my "chores," while "the menfolk," Big Ben, Little Ben, and myself, have been left free for the haymaking.... We have generally fed our horses and had breakfast before seven o'clock, when we start off in the waggon to the haying, taking our dinner and a big bottle of oatmeal water with us to drink; the slough water is impossible—too much animal life and embryo mosquitos. We each have our own work, Big Ben cuts the hay with a mower, Little Ben "coils" it into rows with the old black mare and a hay-rake, and I put the rows into "cocks" with a fork. The hay is quite dry in three or four days of fine weather here, and then we stack it out on the prairie, where it will be left till it is needed in winter, when it can be drawn home on the sleighs. We put a rough-and-ready fence of barbed wire round the stacks, to keep stray cattle from them, and plough a few furrows round, as a protection from prairie fires in the Fall. We have a kind of picnic dinner at eleven o'clock, and about four o'clock Regina generally drives over in the old backboard and brings us a "lunch," and some hot tea. We work again till it is nearly dusk, and take home a load of hay with us, all riding on top of the load. This load we leave at the hay-loft door for the night, and Little Ben and I put it in the loft before breakfast the next morning. As the "chores" are usually all done when we get home at night, it is supper and bed. The papers are very fond of talking about "the strenuous life"— Big Ben is a past master of the art of living it himself, and teaching it to the other fellows as well.

But we have had some variety and fun in this last month too; we have a football club in the settlement, and I am at my old place, "half back." ... We shall have a strong team when we have played more together, and get used to each other's game, and we represent all sorts and conditions of society. Four or five of our team are farmers' sons born in Manitoba of Scotch descent; one Welshman, a keen player, but with an immense idea of the superiority of Welshmen to all others, and a fine conceit in himself personally; two young fellows, working as "hired men" on farms near by, who came out as "Barnardo boys." I suspect they hail originally from the slums of London, but really they are very decent fellows, and have learned to play the game somewhere. They have been out three or four years, and must be good workers, for they are getting twenty-five dollars a month wages, and are saving up to go homesteading next year farther west. Then there are two old public-school men, fine football players and nice fellows, but somehow not suited to the life. One of them is a "farm pupil," which means that his father pays three or four hundred dollars a year, so that his son may do a little farm work when he feels like it, but I guess he does not feel like it very often. I should not care to pay for the privilege of doing the "chores." He may have an easy, pleasant time, but he'll never learn to farm or to make a living by farming in the West. The other public-school man is still more unfortunate—he does not like work, and his people will not send him any money. He tried for the army and failed, he tried office work in a country bank; it was too slow, they got him in a London office, and he got into debt; he hung around among his relations till they were tired of him, and finally gave him a few pounds and sent him to Manitoba. Some people "at home" seem to think that there is a keenness in the Colonial air which inspires the "home" failures with a keenness and a capacity for work which has never shown any evidence of itself "at home." Now he is "choring round" at a bachelor farmer's for his board and lodging, does the cooking, cleans the stables, cuts the firewood and probably does the limited amount of washing which is sufficient for a bachelor's shanty. He is six or seven-and-twenty now, and I do not suppose he will ever be anything better—a fine finish to an expensive education and good abilities!

It is not the fault of the West, and not half his own fault; he's been brought up to be above work, and now he is above it or beneath it. And yet he is an awfully nice fellow in lots of ways, and can play a great game of football when he gets roused up. Jack Dalton and myself complete the team. Jack is our goal-keeper, and a dandy one too. He has only been able to get out twice to practice, his "boss," different to most of the farmers round, has no use for football or anything but hard work for his "hired man." Jack likes the country well enough, but is not at all comfortable in his surroundings—a very rough "boss," who usually comes home "half seas over" and very profane and quarrelsome from his frequent visits to town, a houseful of noisy and unkempt children, coarse food, ill cooked, and work all day and every day. I can tell you I think I am pretty lucky by comparison. Jack says he will "tough it out" till the harvest, and then look out for another place, whether he can get his wages or not for the time he has been there. He was hired for the year, and will probably have trouble, as he had no written agreement about a month's notice. Regina has just called me to supper, so good-bye.

Your loving son,
TOM LESTER.

NAVVIES: ON THE RAILWAY WEST OF EDMONTON, 1911

The 'navvy' first appeared in the great canal diggings (thus the slang nickname, from 'navigator') and railway construction of nineteenth-century Britain. By the early 1910s some 50,000 Eastern Europeans a year were being brought in by Canadian railway contractors, ostensibly as farm labourers but in reality as 'muckers' and ditch diggers. Some were lucky enough to find a homestead, but most soon realized they must labour elsewhere for their 'cash stake'. For miners and manual labour generally, contract work was their introduction to free enterprise in the new country.

F. A. Talbot, *The New Garden of Canada* (London, 1911), pp. 26-9.

A railway contract is divided into stretches of 100 feet each. The basis of the contract is payment by the cubic yard, the survey plans and specifications showing how much earth it is necessary to remove from this point to be dumped at that. Instead of engaging a large staff of navvies working at so much an hour, the contractor encourages the labourer to become his own master. A man can take over a "station," as a length of 100 feet is called, and is paid so much a yard for excavation; this sum is, of course, less than that which the contractor receives, the latter's profit being represented by the difference between the two amounts. The scale of payment varies according to the nature of the earth worked: so much for ordinary earth, or "common" as it is called, a little more for loose rock, and higher rate for solid rock. The last, as it involves drilling and blasting, is generally taken over by the most expert hands, but anyone who can wield a pick and shovel is competent to tackle the other classifications.

Now, it is perfectly obvious that under this arrangement the more work a man does the more he earns; his prosperity is governed entirely by his industry. On this particular station it was mostly "common" and loose rock. The sole tools required were pick, shovel, crowbar, wheelbarrow, and one or two planks. The station men I saw here were three burly Galicians, raggedly clad—for any clothes suffice for this work—and they were toiling like slaves. They had co-operated on the job, and were wrestling with "muskeg"—in other words, swampy ground formed of water-logged, decaying vegetable matter. They were up to their knees in a viscous, black-looking slime, which had spattered them from head to foot. In appearance they were more disreputable than a mud-lark at home. But they were cheery.

As I swung down into the cut and plodded through the ooze with the resident they gave us a cheery hail, but did not stop a second in their task.

"Say, what do you get for shifting this?"

"Twenty-two cents a yard."

That was practically elevenpence. It seemed small enough pay, in all conscience, looking at it from the uninitiated point of view.

"And what can you make a day?"

"All d'pen's upon th' time o' year. Th' longer th' day th' more we can do."

"What are you making at the present moment?"

One of the trio paused and gave a sly look at the resident, as if he might be giving himself away. Then, as he resumed his labours, he blurted out:

"Well, the three o' us are cleaning up 35 dollars a day."

The resident nodded affirmatively; he knew by his returns of excavation accomplished. I figured it out. That meant excavating some 160 cubic yards, for which they received, roughly, £7 between them—practically 47s. a day each.

"And how long do you put in to make that?"

"From kin to k'int. An' we stop for nothin'."

It certainly looked like it, for they never slackened chopping out huge chunks of the sticky mass during conversation. The resident explained that the colloquialism meant from dawn to dusk. It was now past nine o'clock in the evening, and yet there were no signs of cessation. Those three Galicians certainly seemed bent on putting every minute of daylight to profitable account.

Working under these conditions is somewhat of a dog's life. The men are out on the job about four in the morning and slog incessantly until seven, when they make a short pause for breakfast. This is gulped down, and they are at it again until the mid-day hour compels another brief respite for a scanty meal. This is quickly digested, and then ensues a straight toil until six in the evening, when supper is disposed of, followed by a fourth spell of work till fading daylight compels abandonment until dawn.

Such is the round, day in and day out, with Sunday as the only break. The men live in little rude shacks, and the day of enforced idleness— from their point of view—is spent in washing what clothes they require and the performance of other domestic duties for the ensuing week. Their food, though wholesome, is reduced to the minimum, pork and beans being the staple diet, for these men have to board themselves, and consequently they reduce living expenses to the minimum. The work is hard, but it carries its own reward. They only ply their calling during the summer months, when the days are longest, and put in the other six months on a homestead.

This is one way in which Canada is becoming peopled with a solid backbone, for these men get their land practically free, perform the necessary improvements prescribed by the homestead law, and while the produce on their farms is maturing they are earning from £10 to £12 a week upwards. They carefully husband their wages, and by the time they have secured the patent for their farms are comfortably well off and have the capital in hand for the purchase of agricultural implements and so forth.

Galicians and a few Irishmen form the station men for the most part, especially where work is in "common." Scandinavians and Italians figure on the heavy rock work, for they are born "rock-hogs," as the drillers and blasters are called. The average navvy regards the station man and his work with disdain, preferring to toil for £6 a month all found, ignoring the fact that the station man is on the way to become his own master. Many railway sub-contractors of substance in Canada to-day numbered a 100-foot length as their first start, and had not a penny of capital to their name.

THE REVOLT OF THE BUNKHOUSE MEN, 1905-1913

The bilking of workers by railway contractors goes back at least to the 1880s; in the prewar railway boom, rising wages were more than matched by refinements of the 'truck system' (pay deductions for food and other items from a company store, at monopoly prices); and to this was added loan-sharking and graft by employment agents. Bunkhouse conditions had never been good, but by 1911-12 the wage-squeeze and demands for 'beds instead of straw' led to an unheard-of revolt in the mountains. All the ethnic groups united for the first time, in a massive IWW strike against the bosses. They seem to have won the promise of inspection of conditions by the government—the efficacy of which may be gauged from the final letters of 1913.

Letters to *The Voice*, Winnipeg, 26 May 1905 and 11 Sept. 1908; to the *Industrial Worker*, 6 Aug. 1910 and 22 June 1911; to *Solidarity*, 22 Mar. 1913 and *The Voice*, 8 July 1913. Courtesy of Professor Ross McCormack, University of Winnipeg.

The Voice, May 26, 1905.

To the Editor of The Voice.
Sir,—
Circulars have been issued by the superintendent of the C.P.R. at Winni-

peg to Extra Gang Foremen, not to give work to any man applying for it unless he boards on the company's cars at the rate of $4 per week. For myself, I consider it shameful that a working man is not allowed to spend his hard-earned wages in his own manner. What is the reason? Does not the C.P.R. make sufficient money without wanting a certain percentage off the wages of the men it employs? A man is employed at the rate of $1.50 per day, so that at the end of a week if he is at all lucky, he is $5 in pocket after paying board. Supposing there are two or three wet days in a week, where does the working man come in then, he is simply working for board and tobacco, and a man wants to save a bit of money if possible to tide him over winter. I have been boarding on the company's cars for one full week. During that time we have had nothing else but beef concocted up in several different messes. Possibly it may change shortly although I very much doubt it. The cook and cookees seem more like keepers than cooks, as if they pay you money to let them wait upon you, instead of it being the other way round. We are allowed one plate each on which to put meat, vegetables (potatoes in jackets) fruit or tart, whichever it may be. Asking for a clean plate is an unheard of sin, and of course, is not allowed. What are we, slaves or men? Have we got a will of our own? The sleeping accomodations is also something cruel. We are herded together in box cars like so many cattle—in fact, cattle are treated in a much better manner. There are 24 of us in one car lying upon straw in wooden bunks. We have no lamps for night time, neither have we brooms to sweep the cars out with (which are in a filthy state), neither soap nor towels nor pans in which to wash. When we want to wash we have to go to the nearest slough or ditch and wallow in it like pigs. For this we pay $4.00 per week. Shame. Work can be got in towns at the rate of $1.75 per day, and there you can be sure of a good bed to sleep in, soap, towels, water fit to drink and wash with, all for $4.00 per week. The C.P.R. must think that we consider it a great privilege to be allowed to work for the C.P.R. but they are greatly mistaken as they will find shortly. There has been already one extra gang quit work through this boarding business, others will follow, and small blame to them. I for one do not propose to live like a pig, and I hope others are to my way of thinking. I write this hoping you will find room to insert it in your columns, and so warn a man what to expect if he applies for work on a C.P.R. Extra Gang. Fight shy. Let every one kick against this boarding idea outrage. Papers please copy and insert.

Yours truly,
A KICKER.
Moosomin, Assa., May 18, 1905.

The Voice, Sept. 11, 1908.

Editor of The Voice.
Dear Sir,—
An article appeared in the Tribune of Saturday, 5th, re Difficulties of Charitable Work. I do not wish to argue on the subject as a whole, but would like to give a little more light on some of the statements made in the above mentioned article.

The writer seems to be surprised that English, Scotch and Irish will not work on the railroads in this country. Does he know the conditions that pertain in the different railroads in this country, especially as regards the C.P.R. Take the cars set apart for sleeping purposes for instance. Does he know that a good percentage of these cars are not fit for dogs to sleep in, let alone humans. These cars have been used for sleeping purposes for years, until they are infested with vermin, and it would be almost impossible to cleanse them, as a matter of fact the writer has never seen water used on the floor of these cars during his experience of over 8 years on construction, indeed water would make things worse, as you could not sweep it out of the cars on account of the bottom bunk being so close to the floor, it would mix with the filth and so cause disease.

Another trouble in connection with the cars is the over-crowding. Anywhere from 20 to 35 men are crowded in an ordinary 35-foot length box car, and I can assure you that the stench that protrudes from those cars about 11 o'clock at night and at 4 a.m. is enough to knock a man down. These are some of the reasons "white" men will not work on railways. There are of course other reasons. Such as the miserable wages paid viz., $1.50 per day with $4.25 to $4.50 per week for board, $1.00 per month for medical fees (sometimes you see the doctor, sometimes you do not), and when you do see him he doles out a few pills no matter what your complaint is. In regard to wages, a man considers himself lucky if at the end of the month there is $15.00 coming to him. What do you think of that ye financiers? Can you figure out how a married man can exist. Of course $15 or $20 is more to a Galician than a Canadian, but then a Canadian will not send his women on the streets to pick up or steal wood. He will not live in a room where eight or ten other people are also living and there are a good many other things he will not do to keep down expenses. There are still other reasons why Canadians will not work on railways, but I will quote them at a later date. Let us go back to the cars. The trouble with the cars is, that in the first place they were never intended for human habitation; they were built for carrying freight, for coal, lumber, cord wood, etc. Then when they have served their purpose, when they are old and shaken almost to pieces, when they are unsafe and dirty, in a word, when they are of no further use, they are turned over to the boarding contractor for working men to sleep in. They are good enough for that.

BRITISH CANADIAN.

Industrial Worker, Aug. 6, 1910.

Editor, Industrial Worker
On July 7th I went to the Logan employment office in Edmonton, Alberta and after giving them a hard luck story they booked me for a job gratis. A bunch of 100 slaves booked in that office the same day I did and each dug up $1 apiece. After several days we got a train. There were about 100 in the bunch and we were told that when we arrived in Wolf Creek the cook would be waiting for us with a good supper. We arrived in Wolf Creek about 3 a.m. and it was raining hard. We were all lined up after leaving the train and marched through the woods about three miles, wading through the mud and soaked by the rain. Before getting to camp we had to cross the McLeod river in a scow. When we arrived in camp we were wet to the skin and hungry as bears, but there was no sign of anything to eat. We were all so tired that we flopped down any place we could in our wet clothes and slept until breakfast time. The grub in this camp (Headquarters No. 1) was something fierce. It was so rotten and so poorly cooked that it made nearly everyone sick including myself. I hiked to Camp 38 (38 miles from Wolf Creek) and hit the boss for a job, getting a team of mules to drive on a dump wagon. I started to work about 9 a.m. and worked till quitting time. After supper I went to the boss and asked him where I was going to sleep. He told me that they didn't charge anything for flopping in the bunkhouse but that I would have to furnish my own blankets, and towels and soap. Upon enquiring I found that before going to work I was in debt to the extent of fare advanced from Edmonton to Wolf Creek, $1.25; meals eaten from Wolf Creek to camp, 50¢ each, $6.00; hospital fee $1; and mail 25¢ making a total of $8.50. If I had stayed on the job I would have bought a pair of blankets at a cost of $4.50 and soap and towels would have cost some more. I sat down and figured it out and I saw that if I held the job down the first twenty or thirty days I would have to work for nothing, so I told the boss I didn't think I needed the job. He tried to make me stay and work, as I had about $6.00 the best of it by quitting. The wages are $30 if you stay less than a month, $35 for over a month, and $40 if you stay the season. I worked just seven hours and started back to Wolf Creek. Going out on the job you can't eat unless you have an employment shark's ticket and go with a wagon to pay for it at 50¢ a meal. Coming back you have to pay 50¢ a meal as you are not supposed to quit unless

you have a stake made. The contractors have got it figured out so that it is impossible for anyone to make anything on the job because it will take you at least a couple of weeks to get square with the company and when you get ready to make a few dollars for yourself they fire you.

I went out on the job with Fellow Worker J. H. Coplin of I.U. No. 62. In going out to the job most of the slaves say they are going to make a stake and take up a homestead. As soon as they strike the job and see what they are up against they are satisfied to make enough to take them back to where they came from and after they have been on the job a few days they are satisfied if they can make enough to take them back to Edmonton again. I saw five men who worked at Shirley's Camp No. 23 who couldn't get a cent of wages when they quit. They had to hike to town without money to eat on, and wouldn't have eaten if the cook hadn't put them up a lunch. It is a rotten job all through and a man would be better off on the bum than working at it. The most of the slaves who work on the job get away with practically nothing to show for their work. There are several branch roads building out of Edmonton and they are all about the same.

ALBERT V. ROE

Industrial Worker, June 22, 1911.

Sir,—

Just a few facts relative to the conditions of the wage slave in this city of Tarpaper Mansions on the Grand Trunk Pacific railway, now under construction. There is no work in the city to amount to anything, with the exception of a little street grading. There is also a cold storage plant being erected. The wages are 50¢ per hour for carpenters and 30¢ for common labor. Board is $1 per day and $1 a month for hospital. The board is very "rocky" at that as it is let out on contract. It is a very bum job all around. There are two big slave drivers by the name of Lyons and Dillman. They go about here like roaring lions and if you work for them a month you will certainly need a hospital. The slaves don't work here more than five or six days. They cannot stand it any longer. It is a good place to be if you want to die soon. There is another cheap outfit here known as the Westholm Lumber Co. This hay wire company has cut the wages from 35¢ per hour to 30¢. Board is $1.00 per day and $1.00 hospital fee. The conditions up the Skeena on the G.T.P. are still worse.

The camps are of the usual railroad style—lousy and filthy, not properly ventilated, and so small that the slaves are tramping on each other's feet when they move about. They are packed like sardines in these filthy coops. The contractors have cut the wages from $3.00 to $2.75 per day and they anticipate cutting it more. The board is something horrible in those camps. It is not fit for savages. The meat is generally shipped from Vancouver, and you can guess what it is like when it reaches the camps 160 miles up the Skeena after it has been about four weeks on the way. Pork and beans is the general diet.

If you are travelling along the line in search of work you cannot have a meal for less than 50¢, and you would think they were giving it to you as charity. Hospital fee is $1.00 per month, but you never see a doctor and if you need medicine in camp you will have to do without as there is none there.

The checks that are issued by Foley, Walsh & Steward [Foley, Welch & Stewart] are not negotiable in any camp along the line. You cannot buy a meal with them and if you have no cash you can starve, no one will stop you. If you want to get your check cashed you must either go to Prince Rupert or Seelie, which places are 140 miles apart, or buy a ticket in one of the F.W. & S. Steamboat offices to some nearby point, whether you want it or not. They will not sell you a ticket unless a boat is in port. The free born British subject that thinks he is a free man finds out when he comes here that he is not free (unless to starve). The G.T.P. and Foley, Walsh & Steward can do just as they please with him and he is no more heard singing that old patriotic song "Britons never never shall be slaves" for he realizes that he is just as much a slave as any other nationality on this little planet. All the various necessities of life are twice and in many cases thrice the cost they can be purchased for in Vancouver or Prince Rupert.

Board is $1.00 per day in the camps up the line and it is dear if you got it for nothing. The slaves are practically working for overalls and tobacco. The banks charge 25¢ for cashing the time checks. The slaves are in a most deplorable condition up here. There are hundreds of them tramping up and down the line with their home on their backs in search of a master. Now if they would only unite in the One Big Industrial Union of their class they would soon make the big, fat parasite come to the union hall, instead of going to the "catch 'em and skin 'em" employment shark. Now, working men, don't be led into the wilderness by the shark. The slave market is overstocked here and is likely to be all summer. Fight the battle where you are. You will not better your conditions by coming up here in this miserable part of the globe. The real estate sharks are booming the muskeg and rock and that is more in demand than wage slaves.

Yours in revolt,
M. DOYLE,
I.U. 326, I.W.W.

Solidarity, March 22, 1913.

SIR:

Would you be kind enough to put the following few facts in your valuable paper, so that the public will be aware of the conditions men have to endure along the construction camps of the Grand Trunk Pacific. I shipped out to the G.T.P. through one of the employment offices of this city (Edmonton) about three months ago. After arriving at the end of the steel I had to "hike" with my bed on my back to Camp 148. When I got there I worked as a common laborer on the "dump". My wages were the munificent sum of thirty cents per hour, and I had to work ten hours per day, seven days per week. I was charged 25¢ per month for mail tax, although I never received any; $1 for hospital tax, and I may say that there are hospitals situated at the following points: Miles 52, 114 and 160. I pay $1 per day for board which was simply unfit for human beings to eat.

I would like to know why the B.C. police do not enforce the Lord's Day Act in regard to working on Sunday. Does their work only consist of hunting out "blind pigs" and looking after homes of assignation there? Have they locked up the laws in the safe or thrown them in the river? I have seen posters in the camp stating that if you did not work on Sunday one could "beat it" on Monday.

I know of a case of a workman who fell off a trestle bridge and was knocked unconscious. When he came to himself, he found he was relieved of $100, and after he was better he was turned out broke.

...Another case: A man at Mile 148 got his leg badly burned, and laid in the bunk house several days. When his funds were exhausted for board the foreman told him to get out. He started for the hospital at Mile 160, but was unable to continue beyond 150. He laid at 150 for five days. The men there fetched him a little to eat once in a while. After that time the superintendent was forced by the men to take the sick man to 160 in a sleigh. Another man was burned about the face by a carbon lamp and when he got to the hospital at 160 he was told that any man who could walk would not be allowed in there. The doctor (?) in charge gave him some talcum powder and told him to go back to the camp at which he worked. He had to lay around 13 days, and at the end of that time he was charged $13 for board for the time he did not work. A man got his fingers crushed at Mile 148 and laid off work several days. When his funds were exhausted he was told to get out by the foreman and had to go to Mile 114 to the hospital. The hospital would not take him in. Leaving 114 he walked to 152, during which time he had only one meal to eat, which he begged. At Mile 152 he laid his case before the officials of the company for whom he worked. They turned him down. He then went to Foley, Welch & Stewart's office and they gave him a line to take to his original camp so that he could get a soft job. The job was to take care of a sick mule. Oh, the irony of it.

The commissary is also a sore spot with the men. Shirts which cost $1.75 and $2.00 in Edmonton cost $5 from these contractors. Socks in Edmonton at 40¢; the company's price $1. Mitts at 40¢ in Edmonton; at company $1. Underclothes at $1.75 in Edmonton are $5 at company. Pants $3.50 and $5, respectively. Blankets $2 and $7 respectively, and so on. Will the government inspector, who is now making investigations, deny this?

We have had several government inspectors along this line during the last year which has not amounted to as much as the wind blowing from the south.

The first things done when arriving at the end of the steel was to made arrangements for a team to convey him over the road with F., W. & S. officials, which I followed to Mile 148. He did not enter one bunk house, but slept in the offices with fine accommodation. Eating with the foreman and timekeeper, not with the men; and all these so-called inspections are the same. What have they amounted to? Nothing. Conditions are worse than ever.

A WORKING MAN ON THE JOB

The Voice, July 8, 1913.

Sir:

The conditions under which the laborers and small sub-contractors are compelled to fulfill their contracts are worthy of more than a casual comment and should be placed before the Minister of Labor with a very distinct understanding that these conditions be investigated.

A little (but so very little) has already been published regarding the conditions which prevailed last winter, but which little caused the publication of an announcement to the effect that the Minister of Labor had ordered an investigation, but it was the old saw of "Shutting the stable door, etc.," for it was too late, the freight teams and freighters had gone, taking with them their tame vermin and "never again" impressions.

The men themselves were scarcely to be blamed for their personal uncleanliness for when one takes into consideration the fact that the "Camp 4" referred to was a log shack about 18 x 22 feet with sleeping accommodation for 16 men and a cook, the remaining space being occupied by a table stove, pots and pans and other cooking utensils (for cooking was done in the same place). Frequently both floor and bunks were covered with the sleeping forms of men, and I personally counted 43 men sleeping amidst pots and pans, filth and tobacco expectoration.

No provision was made for the washing of one's clothes or person, and that fact alone is chiefly responsible for the verminous condition of the men who, through lack of facilities were compelled to set down to meals unwashed, day after day, reeking with perspiration and the smell of stables.

This outrageous condition of affairs reigned supreme all the way from Camp 2 to 14, a distance of about 160 miles, until the freight teams were withdrawn, and no effort was made by McMillan Brothers to improve matters; on the contrary, it was treated as a huge joke, and to see the teamsters scratching themselves and picking vermin from their underclothing was regarded as a commonplace occurrence and was appreciated as a huge joke.

Inspectors for the prevention of cruelty to animals would have found enormous scope for their duties, for horses were worked until they died on the trail—girth or collar galled, calked or lame, all were treated with indifference; they were driven along with whip and curses until they were glad when merciful death intervened. One horse suffering from "greasy leg" was worked between town and camp 4 until it could not put its off hind leg to the ground. I put this horse out of misery with the merciful bullet.

True, provision was made for colic and other minor diseases, but it was not done for humanity sake, but purely as a means to an end, viz., working them to the last ounce of pull they were capable of.

One can well understand men resorting to such extreme cruelty when driven half insane by the "Gold lust," as in the Yukon, but a mere commercial enterprise does not usually tend to make one sufficiently callous and deficient to sit in one's office knowing full well that animals are being goaded along by almost inhuman cruelty and brutality.

I could write for hours on the above subject and only quote one of the many cases which came to my notice, as I propose to deal chiefly with the methods adopted by the contractors for the purpose of extorting the wages from their employees. I am in a position to verify any statement that I make in my effort to expose that which might be conscientiously termed "An Organized and Systematic Swindle."

System number one deals with the fact that it is compulsory for every man to pay $1 per month for medical attendance. This in itself would not be objectionable did we but derive any benefits.

During last winter several men were lying in what might have proved (and in one case actually did prove, the man dying suddenly on the trail) to be a dangerous condition—yet no medical attendance was to be obtained nearer than Le Pas, where the doctor calmly sat in his rocker in a comfortable house and drew his salary, disinclined to take a drive of 40 or 60 miles with the temperature at 30° below.

Few people would care to do so under such circumstances but probably there are a few whose conscience would prick them and whose hand would shake as they endorsed the check and drew the proceeds of a mutual graft.

I am not far out when I state that there are between 800 and 1000 men at the present time working under this firm and who are being subjected to this deduction.

Taking it for granted that there is but 800 employed – this means a total of $800 per month deducted for so-called medical fees and, presuming that the doctor's retaining fee is $100 per month, what becomes of the balance, viz., $700. Does it go to pay nursing expenses and patients' board? No! Most emphatically no!

For instance, a driller on the "rock gang" sustained a rather severe cut which necessitated his visiting the doctor, who was away; consequently he was detained at camp to await his return, which happened the following morning.

In spite of the fact that there should be an enormous amount of funds at the command of the hospital, this man's wound was bandaged, he was presented grudgingly with another two feet of bandage, and charged $1.50 for three meals.

This should leave a balance of $701.50 to the credit of the hospital for the month of May. I wonder if the hospital books credit the hospital with this amount? Perhaps the McMillan Bros. could produce a balance sheet.

It is since the appearance of a short paragraph in "The Voice" that a hospital tent has been erected and a doctor employed: the latter, young and inexperienced and just recently graduated.

I here give the estimated cost of these improvements:

Cost of Tent	$ 40.00
Doctor's retaining fee	75.00
Flooring tent	25.00
Total	$100.00
Presumed Capital	701.50
Disbursements	240.00
Balance Cr.	$461.50

In spite of the above total this man was charged for his meals.

System No. 2 deals with the practice of extorting 25 cents per month per man for delivery of mail.

During the winter there were approximately 75 teams freighting so that there was every facility for the delivery of mail to employees: books, magazines, papers or periodicals, etc., to which one may have been a subscriber.

I myself subscribed to two bimonthlies and have ample proof that these were delivered at the base office in Le Pas, yet in spite of the fact that I was only nine miles from town these were never delivered.

Taking the minimum number of employees paying this fee to be 800, this gives us a total of $200.

Since the teams ceased work three mail carriers were stationed at intervals of 40 miles. These men were paid $50 per month leaving a balance of $50. For what purpose is this utilized?

Last year about 700 men were employed and one mail carrier, who was paid $75 per month, leaving a balance of $100. But that is the dead past.

The disappearance of papers, magazines, periodicals, etc., should be inquired into by the postal authorities who, I think, are responsible for postal articles until they are delivered to the addressee. The erstwhile bookkeeper could give some account, were he so disposed.

System No. 3 deals with the employment of men from Winnipeg and distant employment agencies.

The men are engaged and their fare advanced. They go forth like lambs to the slaughter, for they are kept in ignorance of what they are up against, otherwise I very much doubt if they would go. Arriving at Le Pas they discover that they have a walk of from 64 to 200 miles, mainly over muskeg. No arrangements are made to feed these men on their way up until they cover the first 40 miles, where there is a boarding shack, indifferently presided over by a married couple. Here the extortion again commences, ad lit., 35 cents per meal is charged, and 25 cents per head is charged to be ferried across the Narrows.

One can actually obtain eight slices of bread and butter for $1.40 if one is not careful.

The next diningroom pasture is about 26 miles further on, viz., Camp 6. Here again 35 cents per meal is charged and by the time the men arrive at their destination they find themselves in debt to the firm to the tune of about $50.

To the best of my knowledge Camp 6 is the last eating place along the line.

These men are employed by the firm and though the firm is perfectly justified in demanding the repayment on the fares advanced, it is obviously their duty to provide stopping places for the men, at which they can at least obtain food, for it is impracticable to expect a man to walk 10 miles per day.

Each man packs from 50 to 80 pounds of clothing and blankets and the constant sinking in the muskeg up to one's knees wears out the toughest old railroader and should hardly be repaid by unfair treatment in the shape of poor food, if any, and unjust demands on the part of the contractors.

The price of provisions is so exorbitant that after a man has arrived at his destination he will probably have to work for at least two months before he can hope to get his time sheet in even a semblance to even, and thus the firm get two months work out of the man for next to nothing.

The sub-contractor, even provided he fulfills three-fourths of the requirements his contract calls for, is up against an extremely difficult proposition to board his men and clear anything like decent wages for himself, as his store bill will run away with whatever profit he may make on his contract.

I might write for days without exhausting the subjects but I think I have said sufficient for my purpose, pro tem.

Little, or no blame can be attached to the Government for this deplorable state of affairs but so long as the Minister of Labor continues to publish his resolutions in the daily papers with the obvious intent of pacifying and drawing a veil over the eyes of the general public and thereby warning the contractors, so long will this condition of "Systematic Graft" continue to flourish.

When an organized police raid is to take place on a doubtful house, do the police publish a paragraph in the leading daily to the effect that a raid is to take place on number 999 blank at 2:30 a.m. I presume not or they would invariably find that the birds had flown.

So it is with the Minister of Labor.

A paragraph appeared in a certain paper to the effect "That the Minister of Labor had ordered a board to assemble for the purpose of investigating the truth of said paragraph." This had the immediate effect of improving conditions a trifle, and when those dear, delightful, fireside, armchair investigators are landed in Le Pas so will they immediately be surrounded with doctors, mail carriers, etc., by the score who will have performed miracles of healing and walking fabulous distances to attend a sick man. The mail carriers will have all packed at least 150 pounds of mail per week, and have walked 40 miles per day.

George J. Rice

'EYE WOBBLE WOBBLE': THE IWW STRIKES FOR INDUSTRIAL UNION, 1912 AND 1917

Songs of the Workers (Chicago, Ill., Industrial Workers of the World, 1974), pp. 52, 58. Reprinted by permission.

Where The Fraser River Flows
(*Tune*: Where The River Shannon Flows)
(*written by Joe Hill, Fraser River Strike Camp) (1912 edition)*

(This is one of several songs Joe Hill wrote in strike picket camps along the line of the Canadian Northern in British Columbia in spring of 1912. The strike shut down 400 miles of railroad construction and made IWW stop shipments from Duluth and Los Angeles. Folklore has it that during this strike a Chinese restaurant keeper coined the term Wobbly trying to ask men if they were IWW members.)

Fellow Workers, pay attention to what I'm going to mention.
For it is the clear contention of the workers of the world
That we should all be ready, true-hearted, brave and steady,
To rally 'round the standard when the Red Flag is unfurled.

(Chorus)
Where the Fraser River flows, each fellow worker knows,
They have bullied and oppressed us, but still our Union grows.
And we're going to find a way, boys, for shorter hours and
        better pay, boys!
And we're going to win the day, boys; where the Fraser
        River flows.

For these gunny-sack contractors have all been dirty actors,
And they're not our benefactors, as each fellow worker knows.
So we've got to stick together in fine or dirty weather,
And we will show no white feather where the Fraser River
        flows.   *(chorus)*

Now the boss the law is stretching, bulls and pimps he's fetching,
And they are a fine collection, as Jesus only knows.
But why their mothers reared them, and why the devil spared
        them
Are questions we can't answer, where the Fraser River flows.   *(chorus)*

Fifty Thousand Lumberjacks
(Tune: Portland County Jail*)*
(13th edition, 1917)

(The 1917 lumber strike [in the West] changed the outcast, blanket-toting timberbeast into a highly respected lumber worker welcomed anywhere. No other strike in history has so transformed life styles.)

Fifty thousand lumberjacks, fifty thousand packs,
Fifty thousand dirty rolls of blankets on their backs.
Fifty thousand minds made up to strike and strike like men;
For fifty years they've packed a bed, but never will again.

(Chorus)
"Such a lot of devils,"—that's what the papers say—
"They've gone on strike for shorter hours and some in-
crease in pay.
They left the camps, the lazy tramps, they all walked out
as one;
They say they'll win the strike or put the bosses on the
bum."

Fifty thousand wooden bunks full of things that crawl;
Fifty thousand restless men have left them once for all.
One by one they dared not say, "Fat, the hours are long."
If they did they'd hike—but now they're fifty thousand
    strong   *(chorus)*

Take a tip and start right in; plan some cozy rooms,
Six or eight spring beds each, with towels, sheets, and brooms.
Shower baths for men who work keep them well and fit.
A laundry, too, and drying room would help a little bit.   *(ch.)*

100,000 JOBLESS: THE FORGOTTEN DEPRESSIONS OF 1908-1916

The panic of 1907-8 and the 'stagflation' of 1911-15 have been virtually ignored by Canadian historians, but they were as bad as the postwar slump of any period up to the mid-1930s. In fact, in 1914 thousands of 'enemy aliens' (mostly Slavs who had fled conscription into European armies) were herded into concentration camps in order to clear municipal relief rolls. On the West Coast there were protest parades of unemployed; and many 'British' enlisted in the army out of hunger. Unemployment did not ease until the middle of the war.

Canada, House of Commons, *Debates*, 1914. 19 Jan., pp. 18-19; 20 Jan., pp. 66-7; 22 May, pp. 41-56.

January 19
Sir Wilfrid Laurier, Leader of the Opposition:
"... For the first time since 1897, we hear of such a thing as non-employment in Canada. It is well known that at the present time prosperous establishments of long standing are reducing the number of their employees, that others are reducing the hours of work, that others are reducing the number of their employees and the hours of labour as well, and that others have closed down. And yet, in the face of that situation, when there are today, in Montreal, Toronto, Winnipeg, Regina, Calgary, Edmonton and Vancouver, not fewer than 100,000 men asking for work, the Minister of Finance says the crisis is over and that we can be as confident as we were before, and at this very moment when labour is scarce and when the purchasing power of the people has been reduced to its lowest point, the cost of all prime necessities of life has risen abnormally.... The Government [has] appointed a Commission to investigate the high cost of living and the cause of the depopulation of the farming districts...."

January 20
Honourable Thomas White, Minister of Finance:
"... My Right Honourable friend has certain delusions. One of his delusions, and I say it with all possible respect, is that the fifteen years of his administration were a sort of halcyon period in which prosperity was continuous.... There was a publication that I knew that my Right Honourable friend would not contradict, I have it here. It is the Labour Gazette for 1908 and bears the superscription of the Honourable Rodolphe Lemieux, Minister, and of W. L. Mackenzie King, Deputy Minister. I knew, Sir, that whatever I found in that publication would bear the hallmark of the living truth.... [From Toronto in] December 1907, Phillips Thompson reported,

'With the setting in of the winter season and the general cessation of most of the outdoor occupations, conditions are duller than those of last month, with large numbers of both skilled and unskilled workers out of employment. The continuance of the financial stringency has induced a slackening of activity in nearly all lines and the problem of providing for the unemployed has become serious.

'London, Ont.–A marked depression in the labour market this month especially in the building trades which were almost at a standstill. A large number of foreigners have left for their homes. As an indication of the number of unemployed, the military school here which for the past five years has only had 75 men, has now recruited up to 288 and more were coming in every day.

'Vancouver–There were more men out of work during the month than in the previous history of the city, there being fully 5,000 men idle. The building trade was practically at a standstill.'

In the issue of January 1909, I find the following:

'in British Columbia, the year opened with most of the mills, both coast and mountain, shut down and with heavy stocks on hand. These conditions continued throughout the season, production and sales falling far below those of 1907.... The world-wide commercial depression which set in during the latter half of 1907 and which continued during 1908, was reflected in the trade and revenue returns of Canada for the past year which showed a considerable falling off compared with those of 1907....'

'Niagara Falls–There are idle men in practically every class of labour.

'London–There are more employed men and women in this city at present than for years past and there is not a factory or a foundry that has a reduced staff.

'Brantford–The general opinion is that there is more unemployment at present than is usual at this season and also those that are unemployed are in a worse condition owing to a poorer season than last year.

'Montreal–Last year was a hard one for Montreal, poverty being more apparent than for a number of years back. This fall there have been a great many out of employment, as many factories and shops have been forced to reduce their staff owing to lack of orders, but in the past three months there has been a general industrial revival in the city and the number of workers who are walking the streets are now, but very little if any larger than is usual at this season.'

...I will refresh the memory of my Right Honourable friend by calling his attention to the fact that the Honourable Mr. Mackenzie King [then Minister of Labour] when introducing the Combines Investigation Bill in the year 1910, as reported in 'Hansard' [said]...

'We have during the past few years experienced a very serious and considerable rise in prices. This increase in the cost of living has not been confined to any one class. Rich and poor alike have had some experience of it but it has a very serious affect upon men of limited income, upon the wage-earning classes, upon those whose salaries are fixed and those who do not receive very much in the way of remuneration. It is this question of the cost of living which has helped to make the question of combines, monopolies, trusts and mergers, the possible effect they may have on prices so important. In the popular mind, there has come to be a gradual association between these two phenomena...'

May 22
Médéric Martin, [Mayor of Montreal]:
"I am not able to explain myself very well in the English language but I have never seen such a situation in Montreal since 1896. I heard this morning of a foreman employed in the Angus Shops [the locomotive shops of the CPR] who used to have 700 men working in his department but who has now only 25. Every day we meet on the Champ de Mars, about 4,000 people asking for work, and there are people sending me letters stating that, if I do not get them work, they will kill me. I am not afraid of such threats. Since I took office, the first week, I gave employment to 6,000 people, the second week to 8,000 and last week, I had 12,895 men working for the City. I think this week I shall have 15,000, but I am not able to do everything alone; I must have help from somewhere.... I have received a delegation, with Mr. St. Martin at its head, asking us to give the people vacant lots to cultivate. I think it is the duty of the Government to go down to Montreal and assist these people to go out West. The shoemakers have been out of work since last November. There is no construction going on, everything is stopped. I do not know what is the matter.... People are coming to Montreal because they think that Montreal is able to employ everybody in the whole country."

2
Poverty, Home Life, and Leisure

What was it like to be a worker? As well as the working man, should we
not look at the working woman or child? Should we not look beyond
'working conditions' to 'living conditions' in the home, the school, the
web of social customs? To raise these questions is to admit that much
basic research has yet to be done, and that the rich complexity of
Canadian workers' lives remains largely unexplored. What happened
outside the workplace, as much as in it, might be the major factor in
keeping the worker docile, or pushing him or her into radical action.
Working-class life must be viewed as a whole. Leisure activities, ranging
from organized sport to drinking, from religious festival to picnic, can be
surprisingly revealing of basic working-class attitudes. Unfortunately,
most eye-witness accounts were written by middle-class reformers. They
were outsiders who had not lived the life they described, missed much of
its hopes and fears, and some of its essential patterns.

Historians and sociologists have only recently begun to study family
life, real wages, and the anatomy of poverty. Sadly, the most representative source for these studies, census records over the last one hundred
years, are closed to the researcher. Almost all workers in this period lived
very near the edge of poverty. In most cases it was absolutely essential for
the survival of the family that all its members—parents and children—
work. And when the woman could not leave the house, or more likely if
she were widowed, the home was turned into a boarding-house. The
margin of security was thin: death, injury, debt, illness, unemployment or
conflict with the law could doom the entire family. Indeed it was not
unknown for a family to be pushed into actual destitution by such
common occurrences as the birth of a child, minor sickness, or a slight
accident. Occasionally workers reacted to crises with astonishing courage

and neighbourly solidarity. More often, they resigned themselves to religious fatalism or to drink.

The documents in this section were selected to illustrate some of the questions and problems that confront present-day scholars. What was it like to live in constant threat of destitution amid all the promises of industrial progress? What standards of life did ordinary workers have or expect for their children? Did these standards change as the century advanced? Beyond mere physical survival, what was working-class life about? What were the roles of religion, sports, fraternal societies, and the most important of working-class establishments, the public house? Was there much social mobility? If education was to be the solution to their problems, why did almost all working-class children never complete grade school? What was the impact on native-born workers of the annual tide of newcomers lured to the Golden Land by promises of high wages, free homesteads, a secure old age, and a better life for their children? And what about these disillusioned immigrants who found themselves trapped by unemployment in city slums, their wives and children condemned to a sweat-shop existence? Finally what underlay deviance from social standards-crime and prostitution? How did it change over time and how was it judged by the working class? Such questions—and the workers' responses wherever they can be gauged—may utterly overturn standard interpretations of Canadian social history.

Another major theme that emerges from these documents is the function of the state. Few of the workers whose lives are glimpsed here lived to see the welfare programs we take for granted: unemployment insurance, pensions, minimum wages, labour standards. Up to the 1940s the power of the state was most likely to appear in the form of the police, the poorhouse for the individual, strikebreaking and imprisonment for union members. It is not surprising that the older generation were rugged individualists or that most unions were self-help organizations providing insurance, sickness and death benefits, and highly suspicious of state intervention.

Finally these documents raise the question of the extent of class consciousness amongst Canadian workers. Were workers aware of themselves as a community in economic, cultural, or political terms, or were racial, regional, and religious loyalties too strong? How many really believed the myth of the 'classless society'? If they were conscious of being a class (and many were not, or rejected the label) did this necessarily lead them to form unions and radical parties? How much did the breakdown of paternalism and the bitter strikes against wage cuts help create a new awareness? There are no easy answers, but the questions are essential to an understanding of working-class history, and those who made it.

ON THE EDGE OF POVERTY: TORONTO 1900-1914

*There is a blurring of class lines in this story of a working-class neighbour-
hood. By the time the author was writing of his boyhood at the turn of the
century, he was a well-to-do Toronto newspaperman. Then as now, 'working
people' refused to think of themselves as 'lower-class'. They despised those
on welfare. Yet subsistence-level pay was accepted as natural: debt, drink,
death, illness, or unemployment could push a family over the edge into the
abyss of pauperism.*

J. V. McAree, *Cabbagetown Diary* (Toronto, Ryerson, 1948), pp. 1-12.

CABBAGETOWN is not to be found on maps nor is it described in surveys.
There may have been something slightly illegal about it, which would not
lessen the attachment to it of those who lived there some sixty, seventy or
eighty years ago. The word was applied to that part of Toronto lying
south of Gerrard Street, north of Queen and east from Parliament Street
to the Don. . . .

The people were mostly of English, Irish and Scottish descent. None of
them were rich in those far-off days. Most families were glad to add to
the yearly income the sale of fruits and vegetables that could be pres-
erved or stored for winter use. Cabbages we must assume were easily
grown, and when growing they had a lush and vigorous appearance
which appealed strongly to the residents. Or, it may be that one of the
early settlers began growing cabbages and thus set the fashion for those
who came later. . . .

. . . Northwest of Cabbagetown the greater density of population discouraged large gardens. North the city seemed to taper off and come to
what many must have thought would be its last resting place in St.
James' Cemetery. Going farther east and north, one soon came to market
gardens. There may have been districts on the borders of the city to the
west which had some of the outward characteristics of Cabbagetown. But
the west end at that time was held to be populated by upstarts or even
dudes. It did not have the old history of the east end, especially the
North of Ireland traditions which had developed there.

It is doubtful if I would be regarded by the pedants as having been
born in Cabbagetown, for I was born on the west side of the street. But I
spent most of my boyhood and early adult life within the strict canon,
and my home for most of these years was in the grocery store to which
my heart so often returns.

From this store, and members of the clan whose headquarters it was,
there came in later years a Minister of Finance of Canada, a mayor of
Toronto, a Speaker of the Ontario Legislature and a director of the T.
Eaton Company, besides others of lesser celebrity. So if it appears that

the store though small, and in a sense humble, was no ordinary store, and the family no ordinary family, it is my contention that appearances, in this instance at least, do not deceive.

My Uncle John, who owned the store, was a small, dark, wiry Irishman with a black beard and an unusually large and well-shaped head....

Uncle John's manners were courtly, and what success the grocery store had, owed much to the suavity with which he greeted his customers, literally bowing and scraping and rubbing his hands as he waited on them. There was nothing of the sycophant in him, for he was a fiery little particle, standing in no awe of size or authority. He blustered somewhat, but a kinder man never lived. At bottom he was weak and leaned much on the quiet, almost demure, strength of Aunt Polly who was the real backbone of the business.

It was she, not Uncle John, who took on the unpleasant task of lying in wait for a customer considerably in default, and telling him in low tones, and using words that took the flesh from his bones, that he was a drunken scoundrel, and had obviously planned to bring his family to disgrace and the store to bankruptcy. Oddly enough such outrageous charges never seemed to be resented and Aunt Polly could be depended upon to see that a growing debt was brought within bounds. I have turned white and shuddered when I have seen this little woman, in a voice not raised much beyond a whisper, talk to some hulking man in a way which to me seemed to place her life in jeopardy. But there was no temper behind what she said. It would be forgotten a moment later....

When dealing with customers who had fallen in arrears Uncle John would bluster and mumble, and wind up by extending more credit and parting on the friendliest terms. He and Aunt Polly used often to argue about the solvency of a customer. Uncle John always took the most optimistic view of it, and used sometimes to fly into a little rage when Aunt Polly insisted that the next order must be accompanied by cash. He never liked to offend anybody. Aunt Polly literally had no thought as to whom she offended. All she wanted was what was right. If people took offence at that, it was her opinion that there was something the matter with them....

...Uncle John and Aunt Polly were childless. With Uncle John's relatives, who were numerous and generally thriving, we in the store had little to do. Aunt Polly had two brothers and three sisters. The sisters died and two of their husbands remarried. The wives of the brothers died and the husbands remarried. There were also cousins and second cousins definitely accepted as members of the clan, and from time to time one of them or more would find it expedient to live with Aunt Polly and Uncle John.

When relatives lost jobs or went bankrupt there was the little store, like a stubby tug, ready and willing to give help to larger and more imposing vessels. My brother and I lived there off and on for twenty years. My sister, who cost my mother her life when she was born, lived there until she died. Cousins came and went. At one time three arrived from Western Canada after the death of their mother, the second wife of one of my uncles, and they remained there until they married. Another cousin became an adopted daughter of Aunt Polly and Uncle John.

Not having enough money to order and pay for a full-sized house, most people in Toronto sixty years ago built their homes by instalments. They would save enough to buy a lot. Then they would save enough to buy the material for three or four rooms; and then they would build what was intended to be the rear of the house. It was composed, generally, of lath and plaster, with gravel mixed in a sort of stucco effect, and this was called rough-cast. This part of the house would contain the kitchen, and perhaps two or three bedrooms. The more prosperous might run into a bathroom. Our store held its head up because we had a bathroom when the back of the house was built. The front was added later and it became the shop, with a hall and a couple of bedrooms above it.

I can recall seeing street after street of these unfinished houses, greyish white blocks, with an entrance on the side, many of which were never finished but stood like clumsy tombstones, as monuments to the unful-filled ambitions and broken desires of the owners. . . .

Our store was a small one but first class of its kind. It was small mainly because there was a grocery store in every block. We were considerably inferior in the matter of enterprise and business done to Radcliffe's at Queen Street and Parliament; but Radcliffe had the advantage of being on a corner and Queen Street was a considerable thoroughfare. We were in the middle of the block, and Uncle John was an older man than Radcliffe who had a staff of two or three clerks and kept his store extremely neat. Now and then when we would be putting price tickets on some article or other I would run down to see what Radcliffe was doing in this matter; and we were content to follow his lead. But we accepted no other leadership. I don't know whether our store was ever scouted in the same way. I never heard that it was. . . .

Our store, and the similar stores of the period and today, had one advantage over their big competitors. They had one thing to offer customers which was elsewhere denied them. They gave credit. I doubt if we averaged three dollars a day in cash sales. Somebody passing might see something in the window that attracted him. Or, he might have thought of something that he had forgotten, and would come in and buy it and walk away and we would never see him again.

Our regular customers were wage earners almost without exception. We had little or no professional or carriage trade. I have no idea, of course, what the average earnings of our customers would be, but I would not set it at more than $10 a week; but even sixty years ago there survived a popular slogan "A dollar a day is very good pay," and few of our customers were conscious of poverty. They lived plainly. They had all they wanted to eat. They had a roof to cover them; their children were going to school or were already at work, and on Saturday night they could relax with a can of beer. On Wednesday nights they could go to prayer meeting, and to church on Sunday. I doubt if half a dozen of them ever saw the inside of a theatre. On Saturday afternoon in summer they might go fishing in Ashbridge's Bay or see a ball game or a Lacrosse match in Rosedale. That would represent about the sum of their relaxations and cultural ambitions. They would work from ten to twelve hours a day.

They were paid on Saturday and on Saturday night the family would turn up at the store to pay last week's bill, or to present plausible reasons for not paying it, and order the supply of groceries for the coming week. They did not pay last week's bill nor for the goods they were ordering. They felt there ought to be moderation in all things. So they were nearly all at least a week in debt to the store. On Thursday, as likely as not, they would want some more groceries. Then on Wednesday the head of the family would drop in for a plug of smoking or chewing tobacco. We did not sell cigarettes, chiefly because Uncle John and Aunt Polly thought they caused consumption, and they would as soon have handled narcotics.

Nothing was commoner than for a customer to call about the middle of the week and borrow a quarter. I do not remember ever having advanced more than a half dollar, and I am sure none of them would have risked asking for a dollar. These loans were set down in our books as "Cash" and were added to the bill to be presented next Saturday. I have no idea what the cash was wanted for unless it might be for beer. Our customers lived and worked mostly in the neighbourhood and did not use the street cars much; but I suppose that even in the life of the humble working man, who lives from hand to mouth and who never had a bank account in his life, there might be circumstances in which he would feel happier with a quarter of a dollar in his pocket. Our store was ready to come to his aid, something Eaton's would not have thought of for a moment....

A man lost his job, and in two weeks was penniless. It was then that the small store did for him what no big store would do. It came to his rescue. It tided him over.

In our own store it would be unheard of to stop a man's credit just because he was out of work. That was the very time when he needed what help a little store could give him; and, if he could make arrangements for his milk and his meat, he could get everything else he required. So far as rent was concerned, it did not greatly distress him. He would not be evicted for falling a month or two behind. I never heard of anybody who had been evicted in those days. Some of our customers, of course, owned their own homes; but, if they did, as likely as not they had a little money put by and the temporary loss of employment did not spell disaster for them. A man might fall ill and be unable to work. Again our store would come to the rescue. It was not that illness was expensive at the moment. The sick man could get credit at the little drug store; the doctor did not expect to be paid for months, if indeed ever....

Then when he got on his feet again and was put back on a payroll he would come into the store some Saturday evening accompanied by his wife and, perhaps a small family, and mumble something about his bill. He would ask that it be made up. Then it would be presented to him, and he would say that he would pay perhaps $5 on account. He would then order groceries to the amount, say, of $3.75 and they would be put on a bill. So his account would be reduced by $1.25, and he would depart feeling virtuous. Now when a man earning $8 or $10 a week goes in debt to the extent of $50 or $100 how is he to pay it? The answer is that he is not to pay it, certainly not all of it, and morally does not feel under any obligation to do so.

The customers of our store were as honest as any similar group of poor people could afford to be. If one of them owing $100 had happened to pick up a hundred dollars in the streets, the chances are that he would have paid at least half of it to our Uncle. Lacking this windfall and still owing $50 how could he pay it? Probably the family would not have a dollar left at the end of each week after paying current expenses. If they paid 25¢ on the overdue account they might also reasonably be expected to pay something on other overdue accounts, which would be simply ridiculous. A man couldn't do it. Flesh and blood will stand only so much, and for the head of a family to reflect that he has less than a single dollar to keep him on the brink of solvency would be intolerable.

Of course there was the rare customer who had long ago been written off the books as a loss who would turn up and magnificently redeem himself thus restoring or strengthening our Aunt's faith in human nature. But, generally speaking, when a customer got credit to the extent of $50 the loss was the store's. When this happened, as it happened many times, Aunt Polly would have a long talk with the defaulter. She would satisfy herself that it was almost impossible that he would be able in any foreseeable time to wipe out the debt. So she would wipe it out. Simply to stop a man's credit would be not only to lose the amount owing but to lose the customer as well....

OVER THE BRINK: MONTREAL, 1903-1915

In contrast with the upward mobility of the family described in the previous selection, this document illustrates the cycle of poverty in which so many workers were trapped. The slums of great European industrial cities, and increasingly in North America as well, were a sort of killing ground. Thus Charpentier's book is doubly valuable. Not only was he one of the few to survive—for the sub-Arctic slums of Montreal had a death rate (including infant mortality) as high as Calcutta's—but his biography is the only first-person account written by a French-Canadian worker of his generation.

Alfred Charpentier, *Cinquante ans d'action ouvrière*, ed. Gérard Dion (Quebec, Les Presses de l'Université Laval, 1972), pp. 1-13. Translated by David Millar. Reprinted by permission of Les Presses de l'Université Laval.

I was the first of thirteen children born to God-fearing parents, who had all the human qualities and moral virtues to deserve the love of their numerous progeny. At the age of thirteen and a half I was called to share the family burden of my father; a bricklayer by trade, he could neither read nor write.

At the age of sixteen and a half, after having occupied a number of modest positions, I was apprenticed to my father. He instilled in me his love of the trade, and gave me my first education in unionism.

He took me to groups in which my labour education was greatly improved, sometimes to social gatherings of the Bricklayers' Union, sometimes to public meetings of the Labour Party of Montreal of which he was a member, sometimes to other labour demonstrations. On these occasions, I met the labour leaders of the period, both unionists and heads of the Labour Party in Montreal. Sometimes my father introduced me to them, amongst others Alphonse Verville, Joseph Ainey, Gustave Francq, Narcisse Arcand.* Their speeches greatly impressed me. I hoped one day to follow their example.

Therefore I resolved immediately at least to complete primary school. I

---

* Their lives are a short history of Quebec labour. All were AFL organizers. Verville (1864-1937) of the Plumbers led the breakaway Montreal *Conseil des Métiers fédérés* (1902) that doomed the labour party of 1900 and expelled the old *Conseil central* dominated by Knights of Labour; he became Dominion Trades and Labour Congress president and a Montreal MP. Ainey (1863-1940) of the Carpenters became a city controller and in 1918 headed the new Employment Service Bureau. Arcand (1871-1927), also a carpenter, became a federal conciliator for the Borden government; his son led the 1930s' Nazi Party with familiar oratorical thunder. Gus Francq (1871-1952), a Belgian-born typographer and militant socialist, became the grand old man of the Quebec AFL and president of the 1930-7 Minimum Wage Board. Paradoxically, their young admirer Alfred Charpentier would become a sworn rival; in 1934 he was elected President of the national Catholic unions.

attended the government night courses for three winters at Olier school [Ed. in the Saint Jacques district of Montreal]. I had not opened my textbooks for three years, but had never ceased to educate myself, and I read serious things. One book above all captivated me: it was an annual prize received at my first Communion, a sort of catechism entitled *The Arsenal of the Catholic*. I read it avidly. It awoke in me the sense of religious enquiry, strengthened my religious beliefs, and the piety I had learned at my mother's knee.

When I finished my apprenticeship in the fall of 1907, I was approaching 20 years of age. Now a full-fledged member of the Bricklayers, I was ambitious to perfect my knowledge of French and English, and especially of learning the art of writing in both languages. Besides my daily labour and the union activities to which I hoped soon to devote myself, it was the most I could hope.

In the spring of 1908 a heavy blow fell on my family. In 1904 my father had acquired a house which he sold two years later. He built one in 1906 and another the year following. He then became a bricklaying contractor, and took me as a partner. This enterprise was inspired by his fear of seeing us having to work below union scale during the economic depression of that period, a humiliation that many bricklayers were forced to accept, and that my father wanted to avoid. But we went bankrupt at the end of a year, as a result of errors on my part in calculating our tenders for the few contracts that we had undertaken. Thus we lost our properties. Forced to move to rented premises on Saint Denis Street north of Mont-Royal [Street], our family never recovered from its financial ruin. In the four years that followed, sickness was a permanent crisis in our home, striking my mother and several of the children. As the depression continued, both my father and I were frequently unemployed, quite apart from two strikes in the trade: the first lasting a week, in 1908 (when the union obtained a 10 cent increase in hourly wages and Saturday afternoon off); the second, six weeks in 1910 (this was a successful struggle against the open shop which the Montreal Builders' Exchange tried to impose). Thrust into poverty, our family was to remain in need for long years to come....

In 1915, having spent with my father seven long months without work (during which I spent several weeks on road construction in the north end of the city), I was forced to provide the necessaries of life for our family—unemployment insurance was unknown in those days—to take a position as a fireman for the City of Montreal. It was in the confines of the station that in the three following years I was gradually converted from the neutral trade-unionism of the Internationals to national and Catholic unionism....

At first, the principles of American trade-unionism were all I knew. I was then nineteen years old. They appeared useful, legitimate, fair and indispensable. Moreover, with the enthusiasm of youth I became its ardent defender. But understandably, I adopted its principles with naiveté. To trace them to their source, to analyze their truth or falsity, to see their consequences, were points I neither thought of nor studied. In short, I was taken in by these generous illusions, all the more easily since my father before me had taught and lived them.

But strangely, while this was my state of mind as a labour unionist, I had never accepted criticism of my faith and patriotism. In fact, in politics I was a Nationalist, and I could not see how this made nonsense of, or conflicted with, my Internationalism in labour. The day came, however, when I saw the flaw in my logic.

In fact, it appeared the more I studied the political Nationalism so ardently defended by Henri Bourassa, the more I weighed the need for all the forces of my people to collaborate in the selfsame common task: to revive our old political tradition, to allow our native land to develop naturally to its full independence. I began to realize that one of our several national forces was anti-national, and ever more menacing: it was American-dominated craft unionism. . . .

A MODEL WORKER AND HIS FAMILY: A QUEBEC TYPOGRAPHER, 1903

This is the first sociological study of Canadian workers. For many decades it was the only study of an urban family, and one of the few reports of their real earnings and expenses. The author was one of the young priests of the reformist Action Catholique movement whose writings helped spark Catholic unionism. Not unlike his Protestant counterparts, Lortie betrays clerical concern with drink, dances, and card-playing among the lower classes. This is a portrait of a model Christian worker. It is intended to show that despite near-poverty wages, the worker can work his way up to respectability by thrift and morality. But Lortie admits that business failures, the expenses of caring for children and aged parents, kept the family in poverty for thirty years.

Stanislas-A. Lortie, 'Compositeur-Typographe de Quebec en 1903'. Reprinted in Pierre Savard (ed.), *Paysans et ouvriers d'autrefois* (Quebec, Les Presses de l'Université Laval, 1968), pp. 83-9, 92, 95-8, 111-12. Translated by David Millar. Reprinted by permission of Les Presses de l'Université Laval.

Social Position of the Family
The family belongs to the working class, enjoying considerable respect owing to the moral virtues of its members. The perfect honesty of the patriarch, the distinction of his manners, his religious observance, give him practically gentleman status.

The prudence taken by the parents in giving their children a good education, and the unsullied conduct of their daughters, led to their contracting advantageous marriages....

How the Family Lives
The family was able to save little before the children came of age, and even then, in their first years of wage-earning the joint family income barely covered expenses.

But later, family savings were arranged in a rather special way. Once their income had risen sufficiently to cover household costs and other needs, the father had turned over control of their earnings, less contribution for room and board, to his children, who were thus able to lay up some savings [of their own].

Before their marriage, the girls had the benefit of their wages and bought their own clothes; they were thus enabled on the eve of marriage to buy, with their own money, a trousseau fit for a young woman of the town.

The boys now keep all their surplus earnings, paying any expenses, other than $2 weekly rent to their father, from their own pockets. Indeed, the family budget can thus be divided in three parts with some exactness...

YEARLY INCOME AND EXPENSES OF THE FATHER AND EACH SON

[NOTE: The amounts originally given by Lortie in francs have been converted to dollars, at 1900 exchange rates of 5f. per $1. Ed.]

1. The father's account:

Income		$
Interest on savings		7.50
Wages		468.00
Sons' rent		208.00
	Total	683.50

	Expenses	
	Food	305.41*
* Including $27.88	Shelter	171.70
beer and wine for	Clothes for husband	28.48
the family; all meals	Clothes for wife	33.50
eaten at home.	Laundry etc.	39.65
	Church, charity dues	24.95
	Tobacco	2.50
	Leisure, esp. Sunday	4.10

Taxes		2.00
Insurance		
($500 life, $80 union)		13.00
Savings for year		58.21
	Total	683.50

2. The elder son's account:

Income

Interest on savings		6.24
Wages		414.96
	Total	421.20

Expenses

Incl. death benefits:
*Union des prieres,
**Alliance Nationale

Rent		104.00
Clothing		43.08
Religious societies		1.00*
Tobacco		15.00
Leisure		30.00
Doctor		1.25
Fraternal dues		13.44**
Savings for year		213.43
	Total	421.20

3. The younger son's account:

Income

Interest on savings and use of tools		3.00
Wages		312.00
	Total	315.00

Expenses

Inc. death benefits:
*Union des prieres,
**Alliance Nationale

Rent		104.00
Clothing		35.90
Religious societies		1.00
Tobacco		15.00
Machinists' Journal		1.00*
Leisure		30.00
Capital amortization (tools)		3.00
Fraternal dues		13.44**
Insurance ($1000 endowment)		24.00
Savings for year		87.66
	Total	315.00

... Workers in each trade have their special societies which assure them of help in time of strikes, in return for monthly dues. These are called *Unions*, modelled on the British and American bodies of the same name, and have similar rules.

The head of the family belongs to Typographical Union No. 302; he pays 30¢ in monthly dues. There are 175 members of the local, whose goals are mutual protection and regulation of wages and hours. Voluntary contributions paid at the monthly meetings help to support members in need. At the death of any member, the society pays $80 to his heirs. It is affiliated with the International Typographers' Union whose headquarters is in the United States, and whose policy is followed by the local *Union* in setting hours and wage levels. To go on strike, the permission of the central office is required; it will do so only after conducting an enquiry into the facts, and only then will the International send strike aid, amounting to full wages for each man. Finally it offers a rest home in Colorado for members no longer capable of work. Since strikes are rare, these advantages are inconsiderable and of little profit to Quebec typographers.... In the last four or five years wages have risen from $7 to $8, then $9 weekly. Three years ago, the workday was reduced to nine hours. ...

Leisure

Leisure activities consist mainly in promenades and evening gatherings.

In addition, father and mother make three *promenades* yearly. These day-long outings are quite inexpensive. One is the annual pilgrimage to the shrine of *bonne sainte Anne* at Sainte-Anne de Beaupré; the remaining two are spent with friends at Saint-Augustin, a North Shore village twelve miles west of Quebec.

The young folks accompany them on pilgrimage, and promenade almost every Sunday to the outskirts of the city, by electric trolley, steamboat or buggy, for about 60¢ a day on the average. Such outings with chums offer certain dangers, not least to sobriety, but are averted by the fact that the friends of sons Loyola and Phileas are temperate and honest, belonging like them to the *Ligue du Sacré Coeur* and the *Congrégation de la Sainte Vierge*.

Once or twice a week, there is a concert on the Frontenac terrace or in a city park. The populace direct their promenade thence, and young men and women find chances to flirt.

A family evening is the most typical form of amusement. Neighbours, relatives and friends gather, providing their own entertainment. Card games are favoured—at home, however, they do not play for cash stakes as in certain clubs and restaurants, except among the better-off where the odious habit has intruded and even women take part (whose gambling can turn into a vice).

The old-fashioned soirees centred on stories and folk-tales. There were some renowned *conteurs* who used to come by special invitation. One was my great-grandmother who had a large repertoire of Norman fables and old French stories which delighted adults as much as children.... Today the fables have been replaced by quips and anecdotes, sometimes dubious, told for an easy laugh.

Music and song are also a traditional evening pastime. The *canadiens* adore music and many families, even workers, have pianos ... where the young gather while their elders sit at cards. The fashionable songs are like those of France, with patriotic ditties among the favourites.

In carnival time, cards may be replaced by dances, which may prolong the evening and even keep the company until dawn. However, the clergy see dances as a perilous amusement, above all among rural folk where they are often the occasion of licentiousness and intemperance. While the country priest thunders anathema, his counterpart in town merely demands abstention, from the dangerous excitement of the waltz or polka; his counsel is followed by most, who stick to traditional quadrilles, cotillions, lancers, etc.

At night's end, it is customary to offer guests a glass of beer or something stronger, some pastry and fruit. On gala evenings, the table is spread for a *reveillon*.

Besides these, family members may find enjoyment in religious ceremonies and fraternal meetings. The father, for instance, goes to monthly meetings of the Typographical Union, and weekly gatherings of the *Union musicale*, the parish choir of Saint-Jean-Baptiste to which he has belonged for years.

Last but not least, the Canadian is a smoker: of pipes mostly, but also cigars or cigarettes. His rest and recreation is to read the papers while puffing the ever-present pipe.

There is considerable difference between generations in the distractions and amusements they allow themselves ... young men spending on luxuries with an ease unknown by their father a quarter of a century before. ...

HOME LIFE AND LEISURE IN A QUEBEC COPPER TOWN, 1905

Some surprisingly vital social history is being written by geographers. Here Ross shows what can be done to reconstruct the patterns of behaviour and attitudes of workers, using not only the traditional 'documents' of the historian, but also maps, advertisements, photographs, and oral interviews.

W. Gillies Ross, *Three Eastern Townships Mining Villages Since 1863: Albert Mines, Capelton and Eustis, Quebec.* (Lennoxville, Quebec, Bishop's University, Department of Geography, 1975), pp. 56-62. Reprinted by permission of W. Gillies Ross.

Most of the miners live in company houses in the three villages. The houses are not fancy but are considered comfortable, look neat, and appear sound. Heating is by wood or coal stove. Lighting is by kerosene lamps, the wonders of electricity not yet having been applied here in the homes. Water is generally obtained from a well or spring. Garbage is usually burned. Toilets are conveniently placed within 100 feet of the houses. The rent is $3.00 a month. The three villages already have no fewer than nine telephones, located in the buildings of the mining and chemical companies, in the homes of their managers, in the rail stations and in the general stores.

The people do most of their shopping locally, paying by the month and benefiting from horse and wagon delivery, yet it is common for families to make a monthly trip to Sherbrooke to enjoy the larger selection of goods and bargain prices, at places like McKechnie's: (ladies' shoes and boots 98 cents, boys' sleds 10 to 75 cents, men's gum rubbers 50 cents) and to admire and envy the expensive furs at Cormier's (Bulgarian lamb coats $17, Astrakhan jackets $10). A butcher from North Hatley makes the rounds every week; a woolen goods salesman from Coaticook comes around regularly; a baker occasionally circulates (but if the housewife purchases baker's bread the returning husband inevitably declares "What! You call this bread?"). Itinerant pedlars, including Indians from Caughnawaga and clothing salesmen from Sherbrooke, arrive from time to time, as do the vendors of patent remedies such as Smith's Bucha Lithia Pills (for "sick kidneys, the bladder, rheumatism and the blood"), Bertrand's Creosoted Glycerine (for "congestion of the lungs and incipient consumption"), Dr. Mackay's Specific for Drunkenness, and Hurst's Pain Exterminator ("Dampen a cloth with Hurst's Pain Exterminator—bind it round the throat and gargle with a little of the liniment in water. My! How soon you get better").

Many families profit from the weekly visits of a music teacher at 25 cents a lesson, and painting lessons are available from Mr. Odell, the Eustis schoolteacher. Doctors visit frequently and although none of the villages can boast a resident dentist, Mr. Tamblyn, the blacksmith who makes the tools for mining, is said to be enterprising in utilizing these rather oversized implements for extractions. (That he may occasionally remove the wrong tooth should not be attributed necessarily to faulty technique but simply to errors in judgement.) Thus most of the basic needs of the villagers are satisfied either by local institutions or by itinerant services.

The villages have no banks, but cash transactions play a small part in daily life, with rent and purchases at the company store normally deducted from wages. The absence of taverns or other beer and liquor outlets is a more serious deficiency. Working in the dusty mine makes a man very thirsty and many yearn for something stronger than water or even tea. They generally find it too . . . in the iniquitous flesh pots of

Lennoxville and Sherbrooke. And in the process they usually make their presence known around the Albion Hotel and other spots, where their good spirits are not always appreciated. A newspaper account a few years ago reads as follows:

At about 10 o'clock last evening some five Swedes from Capelton, considerably the worst for liquor, proceeded to hold high carnival in front of Mr. A. F. Simpson's residence at Lennoxville.

Upon being ordered away, they showed their resentment of any interference by turning their attention to the house, which they attempted to enter.

Mr. Simpson, however, met them at the threshold, where he held them at bay with aid of his walking stick. This latter instrument, it appears, he wielded in telling style, keeping the intruders busy until Constable Dundin, accompanied by some of the no. 3 company men, arrived.

The foreigners were immediately hustled into custody, not, however, before one of their number realized the inelasticity of Mr. Simpson's walking stick.

Bootleggers operate in the villages, descending promptly on pay day to help their clients satisfy their baser wants. Blind pigs exist in some of the houses at Eustis, to which the company turns (most appropriately) a blind eye. Fighting frequently breaks out among the rougher elements at Albert Mines (chiefly the Irish and Scots) and it is rumoured that some of the lower classes even play at poker. A petition on behalf of the Capelton store seeking a license to sell spirituous liquor, which in the words of the submission, "would restrict the abuse which is now made of it", has been rejected by the Municipal Council of Ascot Township, so the bootlegging will certainly continue, to the great profit of Sherbrooke entrepreneurs.

What sort of social life is there in the villages? In reply to this question a miner tells us "Oh, about all you done was work, eat and sleep, I guess." A miner's daughter claims that visiting and socializing are limited because there is so much work to do on the job and in the home. The work week is six days long and Sunday is reserved for church-going or Sunday School in best clothes, for quiet walks or picnics, some visiting, and perhaps a few family pictures in the garden. Strict codes of behaviour exist, at least in some families. One girl, a miner's daughter, admits to having been chastised by her father for knitting on the Sabbath, that sort of thing being permitted only in time of war.

But in fact there is much more to the social and recreational life in the villages. There is certainly baseball! As one resident expresses it, "It's an awful place for baseball here. Gol, gee whiz, baseball; they trim every team everywheres." Capelton has emerged victorious once again in the Eastern Townships League, against teams from Sherbrooke, Asbestos, Windsor Mills and other towns. Frequently they are then matched against champions of other leagues "until late as hang in the fall... they'd wind up by playing with a bunch of niggers way down in the States somewhere."

The Capelton team is mainly composed of English and French Canadians, but people of other origins are invaluable as team supporters. Their enthusiastic support evidently commences well before game time:

They'd go there in the play offs. I remember they had a pitcher here, ...great big man, oh he was an awful pitcher, and as long as they'd leave him home on Saturday night, on Sunday they'd always beat.... And them Polaks, they'd come there you know on Sunday afternoon and they'd say, 'Joe, you beat them this afternoon and I'll buy you a bottle of whiskey'. Oh gee whiz, you'd see his lips start to curl.... He'd pitch something awful.

The success of the baseball team is out of all proportion to the size of the communities, as visiting players often have occasion to realize:

And late in the fall, you know, these teams from way outside would come here and they'd look around and they'd say, "Is this what they call Capelton?". Somebody'd say, 'yes'. They'd say, "Everybody must be baseball players here; they can't be much more than nine men living around here." They'd laugh, you know.... They wouldn't laugh after the game! They'd go home with their heads down.

In winter hockey is played but with far less success than baseball. According to a resident the team is composed mainly of Irishmen who join in order "to get somebody to fight with". Their skill in skating and shooting is said to be inferior to their pugilistic technique.

Aside from baseball and hockey games there are snow-shoe treks, band concerts, picnics, meetings of societies such as the Red Cross, Sons of England, the Orangemen, the Order of Foresters (formed only last year), and the Good Templars, and a variety of suppers, raffles and sales sponsored by church guilds. Recently a gramaphone has been demonstrated in a concert here; the phenomenon of a voice emanating from a machine frightened one child half out of her wits. Such contrivances happily have found no place in the home, and entertainment still depends largely on the resources of the individual. Amateur nights are frequently held and the performances on those occasions are said to be quite extraordinary. Adult education flourishes; in the evenings Mr. Odell teaches English to foreigners. The desirability of the divers nationalities communicating in some common tongue is borne out by the following experience.

> I got a job in the mines and near got killed the first day. I went down there. Some Russians were blasting and they hollered in Russian 'fire!' I didn't know what that was in Russian.... 'Boom! Boom!' They had about seven ... blasts went off and it hit the car—I was just coming round the bend—it saved my life. The stone hit the car and knocked me flat on my behind. My light went out.

Music plays a prominent role in the leisure activities of mine and mill personnel. Band concerts are held regularily at Albert Mines under the direction of William Tamblyn the blacksmith, with participants and spectators from Capelton and Eustis in attendance. Family social evenings and get-togethers almost invariably feature the music of a piano and perhaps an accordion, flute or mandolin. One family is said to comprise an entire orchestra! The richness of the musical offerings is in part attributable to the variety of nations represented here. One miner speaks of strolling up the hill behind Eustis on a Sunday and encountering a group of contract workers from North Carolina, well-known about the village for their minstrel music:

> And them niggers used to sit out there and sing. Oh they could sing good ... baritone, and oh but it was lovely.

SUPERSTITION OR SUBSISTENCE? TWO VIEWS OF THE ATLANTIC COAST

The contrast between these two accounts is deceptively simple: Millais attributes disease and starvation to the backwardness of the peasant; Dubé blames poverty and perpetual debt on the monopolies and the 'bosses'. Though clearly a middle-class snob on the question of the dirt and ignorance of pre-industrial populations, Millais rightly implies that backwoods habits could become lethal in a city slum, while Dubé, one of the very few French-Canadian Communist leaders, reminds us that religion is both consolation and social control.

J. G. Millais, *Newfoundland and Its Untrodden Ways* (London, Longmans, 1907), pp. 148-51.

The women work on the drying stages as well as the men, laying out the fish whenever the sun shines, and piling it into heaps under layers of bark whenever it threatens to rain. They all talk a good deal about their poverty, but personally I could hear of little genuine distress in this part of the island. One day two little boys, plump and well fed, but dressed in rags, stopped me and demanded cents. On asking them why they begged, and if it was for money to buy sweets, one of them said that they had had nothing to eat that day.

"What is your father?" I asked.

"We ain't got no father," the eldest replied, looking down. "He's got drowned."

"And your mother?"

"She can't do nothing; she's sick wi' the chills."

"Why don't you fish in the harbour?" I suggested; "It's full of flat fish."

This idea seemed new to them, and to present certain possibilities as yet undreamed of, and, after further conversation in which I found that their poverty was genuine, I was glad to give them some help.

It may seem extraordinary, but here was a bay simply crawling with beautiful flounders, but not a soul dreamt of catching and cooking them for their own use. Those who know best the outport Newfoundlander are aware of his conservatism and pig-headed objection to all innovations. Their fathers never ate flat fish, so why should they? They would rather starve than do such a thing. I asked a fisherman one day what his objection to them was, and he said, "People say they're poisonous."

I assured him to the contrary, and asked him if he had ever tried one, and he answered, "Yes, once, out of curiosity."

There are many other excellent fish, which they neither eat fresh nor cured, such as herring, wrasse (conors), skate, ling, hake, and halibut.

Like all seafaring people, the Newfoundlanders are exceedingly child-like and superstitious. Their fathers fished cod before them, and they do the same for four months in the year, often doing absolutely nothing for the other eight months, except to set a few traps for lobsters. If the Government offers them wages for making a road through the country they work splendidly—for one day—and then sit down contentedly and expect to declare a permanent dividend.

On the whole the men look strong, but the women are generally pinched and narrow-chested. Consumption is rife, and in no way lessened by the dirty practice of expectoration, so that if one member of a family acquires the dread disease it rapidly spreads, as the germs are fostered by hot rooms and damp weather. The purity of the air of Newfoundland is without doubt due to the fact that the people of the outports never open their windows.

Taking all things into consideration, the lot of the Newfoundlander who cares to work a little is an exceedingly happy one. He makes little or no money, but Nature offers him her gifts with no ungenerous hand. It is quite easy to go into the country in November and December and kill three deer. This can be done in a few days, the carcases being hauled out by dog or ox sledge. A supply of fresh meat is thus assured for the winter months.

When spring comes on and the ice breaks up, large numbers of the more able-bodied take to the woods for the purpose of cutting logs. In many cases they work on their own account in the virgin forest, cutting in such sections as have not already been claimed by lumber companies, and hauling or floating their logs to the saw-mills, where they sell them, wages averaging from one to two dollars a day. The majority, however, take employment with some of the larger or smaller timber owners, and they prefer this method, as they are housed and fed at the expense of the owners. A good "riverside" boss—that is, the man who keeps the others at work and superintends the movement of the logs on the rivers—will earn as much as three dollars a day. During the summer the men fish, mostly in "bankers," off the coast or away north along the Labrador, whilst the women attend to the home croft, and the planting and care of the land. In August most of the fishermen return and reap the hay or rough corn, which is only used as cattle food. On the east and west coast, in September, if the men are acquainted with the interior of the neigh-bourhood of their homes, they are often employed as "guides" for caribou hunting; at this they can earn from one to two dollars a day, sometimes even getting parties in October for the second season. No shooting parties—that is, sportsmen—enter Newfoundland from the south coast or northern peninsula, so this does not apply to them.

Thus we see that on the whole the Newfoundlanders, except the poor of St. John's and the islanders of the east coast, are exceedingly well off in the literal sense of the word, and would be in clover were it not for the over-powering taxes, for which they get absolutely nothing in return.

Evariste Dubé, in Stanley Ryerson, *French Canada* (Toronto, Progress Books, 1943), pp. 8-10. Reprinted by permission of Progress Books.

... In my childhood at Grande Rivière, on the south shore of the Gaspé Peninsula, I worked with my father and brothers who were fishermen, and grew up in the hard life of the Gaspé people. The struggle against the elements, to win a bare subsistence, was made harder still by the stranglehold exerted on our lives by the Robin & Jones fisheries monop-oly, which held many of our people in perpetual debt....

I remember how in the autumn my father, and my mother and three sisters as well, worked at repairing nets for the herring-fisheries of the coming spring, in order to earn a pittance that would tide us over until the Company paid its "advance"—payment in kind, made in the month of March, for the fishing-catch. I left school at the age of eleven, although I passionately wished to continue my studies; but the family's needs required that I go to work.

At fifteen I spent a year working in the lumber camps, then returned again to fishing. It was 1914; I remember that cod, which was rare and hard to catch, brought us no more than a quarter of a cent a pound. Once more I went back to the lumber-camps, alternating with work on the land, which brought us as scant a harvest as the sea. On the log-drives we worked thirty-six days at a stretch, with scarcely time to sleep, and up to the arm-pits in snow and water. Seeing how the companies grew rich at our expense, while we were paid so little for the work, I came to doubt and then to reject the precept I had been taught, that there must always be rich and poor, and that the duty of the poor was to remain obedient and submissive for all time.

After working in the paper mill at Chandler, ten hours a day for 32 cents an hour, I went to work in the lumber camps of Ontario. I found the workers there were better paid than those in our own province. But there also the great companies ruled the lives of the working people, and whether I worked for the Algoma Pulp or the Spanish Paper or other companies, the workers faced the same hard problems, and the same struggle. . . .

Later I worked in the building trades in Montreal. It was at that time that I began seriously to study the questions of economics and labor history. I went to meetings, took part in discussions, demonstrations of the unemployed, work of organization in the Left-Wing labor movement.

In 1935-36 I worked on the Montreal waterfront as a longshoreman. The shipping companies had introduced a system of speed-up, which was causing repeated accidents among the men. In May, as a result of a strike, we won an improvement of our working conditions and a wage-increase. The following year, a company union was set on foot by the Companies, and I and a number of my companions were black-listed and fired on account of the organizing work we had carried on in the men's behalf. In the years that followed I took an active part in the struggles of the unemployed. . . .

Evariste Dubé

Montreal,
July, 1943.

SELF-HELP AND NEIGHBOURLINESS: PATTERNS OF LIFE IN HAMILTON, 1900-1920

How representative are documents and anecdotes of working-class life? Historians are denied access to Canadian census records less than a century old, and no other records are as comprehensive, so it is difficult to analyse the working class. To overcome these problems, Professor Synge has pioneered an ingenious combination of anthropology and social history. She chose a statistical sample of working-class people who were at work in the first decades of this century and interviewed them at length. Some of her findings are corroborated in the Mathers commission testimony later in this chapter. These are excerpts from her study of working-class women in Hamilton, a typical industrial town.

Interviews by Jane Synge. Reprinted by permission of Jane Synge.

A native-born Canadian, Mrs F. was orphaned at the age of two, and she and her brothers were separated, and went to live with different relatives. Mrs F. went to her aunt, who had a boarding house. There would be eight or nine boarders, the 'mealers' who came only for their food, and a couple who helped out.

> Aunt had a couple, and for their board they worked in the house. And she had a baby, and aunt still kept her. And then she had a second. And aunt said, "I'm afraid not."

Mrs F. described the routine. Her aunt would be up at five. There would be three breakfast sittings, one at six, one at seven and one at eight, when the children also ate.

> Breakfast was cereal, toast and jam. Sunday—bacon and eggs. The ones that took their lunch were given their lunch—all packed up.
>   Dinner was according to the day. It was the same every week. Wednesday—always boiled beef and soup. Pork chops one day. There was fish. There was sausages. Sundays there was always a roast. Holidays there was a chicken. With boarders you were fed properly! There were potatoes, a vegetable, and a dessert—a pie, a pudding, or something—at noon.
>   At night we had fried potatoes, cold meat, relishes on the table, homemade, and fruit. And Sundays we had a homemade layer cake. My aunt, she had a way of dishing everything up by the spoonful, or the dab, that it went through everybody. She never run short. I never remember any leftover, but I never remember it short either.
>   My uncle sat with the men.... When the boarders were finished, all away from the table, then we sat down, my aunt, and my grandfather,

and us two children. . . . Until I was working, and then I sat at a little table in the corner.

There was money in boarders. . . . She (my aunt) had one interest, and that was to make a good living that she would never have to go to the old people's home. This was her great fear. It was just something that drove her to accumulate. She'd seen an old lady, when she was young, being practically dragged out of her house to be put in the home. The old lady was crying because she didn't want to go.

In the 1920s the aunt moved out to the country.

Times were getting bad. Some of the boarders were getting older, and they were living off her. And she just had to put a halt. So she traded the house on— —Avenue for a farm out at M— — —. . . . Even when she was seventy she had a boarder. She never had any help—I think she would have died rather than get help.

About her life in the boarding house, she said:

Others were a family. We were a business—it makes a difference. . . . That's why I couldn't make friends, I couldn't take friends home. . . . I always seemed to be so busy working that I never had time to really make friends. . . . Even when I was working, and had a day off, my uncle would holler at me to get up and help my aunt. On Saturday, when I got my work done, I would walk down and visit.

Mr U., born in 1900 in Scotland, arrived in Canada in 1909 with his parents and his four brothers and sisters. His father worked on a pile-driver, on the railway, and later in a factory when the boarding house business at home had grown to such an extent that he was needed at home more often. The family started in a six room house, but soon moved to a larger one so that they could accommodate more boarders.

A man from the old country came to visit mother, and said he wanted to board. So mother asked her neighbour. She said, "If you have him, have two, because your husband is away all week." Pretty soon she had four men in the big room upstairs. . . . The boarders paid $3.50 to $4.00 a week. Mother didn't wash for the boarders—they took it out to the Chinese laundry.

She was always making the odd dollar, which made her independent. Mother fed coloured men—horse attendants—at the racetrack. They slept in the barn with the horses.

When father complained about her 'extravagance' in children's clothes—

. . . She told him all he had to do was take his pay and put it in the bank, and she would run the house. Sure enough, his pay went in the bank every week, and she kept him in clothing as well.

At the age of 11 Mr U. was working school lunch breaks and evenings until 8 in a restaurant for $1.00 per week. Then he would go home and pack lunches for the boarders until 10. "I never got out to play."

... The way I worked and the way my mother worked, I could always afford to spend a bit more than the average boy.

He gave all he earned, even the tips, to his mother, and received pocket money from her. Once he forgot to hand over a tip.

Mother once found a twenty-cent tip in my pocket. She said, "I found something—twenty cents. Why wasn't I given that twenty cents? How long has it been there?"... Well, I began to think it wasn't right. At least I should have got ten cents.

When Mr U. was 11, his father died, and he left school to work full time in the restaurant set up for new immigrants.

These people had arranged with the immigration authorities. There was a lot of men immigrants coming from the British Isles—men like my father, coming out, and leaving their wives and their sweethearts, and so forth. And they had it so the immigration authorities recommended those men to come to this place to stay. Because they had two floors of bedrooms above this restaurant (in North End Hamilton). So there was always a turnover of strange men coming to stay.

Mr U. had been getting $1.00 a week, but when he left school, and was doing some bedmaking in the morning, he got $1.50 a week.

When I got that extra fifty cents school didn't mean a thing. I was kept in the kitchen as much as in the classroom—so much so that I quit going to school. Mother looked forward to that $1.50.

At the age of 13 he got a job as an assistant rivetmaker at a metalworking factory, working 55 hours a week, and being paid 20-23 dollars every two weeks. Pay was determined by the amount of work done by the group.

At this time (1913) if you go to any factory, and they needed you, they would take you in. If you could prove you were 14—that was all. Most of my chums were quitting school at 14.... You didn't keep your money. You took it home in the envelope. You didn't even open it.... And you got spending money. I was never short of spending money and I was always well clothed.

Mrs. D. was born in 1903 in Poland, and came to Canada as a small child with her parents and a younger sister.

They had relatives already in Guelph. They were going there but they had to change trains. They had to change, so the conductor said, "What are you going all the way to a small place for? Stay here in Hamilton. They need workers, like you." And they said, "But, they didn't know anybody." And he said that he knew of a German family. "I'll take you up to them so that you can get acquainted." Two days later he (father) went to work, up at the rolling mills.

After boarding briefly with the German family, they set up house and were soon taking in boarders themselves.

They (the boarders) bought their own lunch meats, and whatever they had for breakfast. In the beginning, I remember, they would bring home whatever they wanted to be cooked for that supper... If it was difficult financially he (a boarder) would just have his own meal. Most had one cooked. My mother made the potatoes, the vegetables, and the meat, but they all had their own bread.... I know they had bread-boxes, and everybody had a mark on his loaf of bread. They had two nicks, or three nicks, that was the way they went. That was the custom.

The girls brought in the wood, cleaned the lamps at noon in the school break, washed the supper dishes, and laid the tables.

My sister and I, we had to set the tables, and we had to set that loaf of bread in front of every person. And the first thing they did was check their bread.

Mrs. G. was born in 1901 in Poland, and came to Canada in 1904, with her parents and an elder brother. First they lived with an aunt who was already settled, then they moved to a three bedroom house, and began taking in boarders, generally about eight of them. Her father had built an extension to the house, "like a garage on the back, for sleeping." Her mother had five more children in the next years, while she was keeping boarders.

Father ate early with the boarders. Mother rose at five to cook for them.... The boarders ate before the family. In the evening it would always be soup. Mother would buy beef for the boarders, always beef, and have the butcher cut it in half pound pieces, [for each boarder] and we'd tie it up with string. [They] shared a drawer for bread and lunch foods.

Mrs. M. was born in Russia in 1902, and came to Canada with her parents when she was seven years old. Her father died when she was eleven years old, and her mother set up a luncheon business.

You could go into business and no one stopped you. We went to the city to see about the licence. But it was in a private home, just an open door, so we didn't have to have a licence.... Mother cooked meals, like a luncheon. We would get 30, 40, 50 people a day. And when they left I stood and washed the dishes. I had those dishes washed before I went back to school. I never got pay.

When she was 11, she started working in Woolworth's on Saturdays, from 8.30 am. to 11.00 pm. She got 75 cents a day, and after a few weeks there she was getting a dollar a day. As she says, "I was big for my age." She kept the Woolworth's money.

In the summer I got to work steady. That money I *had* to give her (mother).... If I wanted a pair of silk stockings I had to beg.

At the age of 13 she started work as a shop assistant at a wage of 7 dollars a week.

I went with a letter to City Hall to get leave to leave (School). Then I went to Eaton's factory as a cutter because you had Saturday afternoons off.

She was working 7.30 to 6pm. and till noon on Saturdays, making twelve to thirteen dollars a week on piecework.

It was very hard for a working-class widow to support her young children without help. One woman recalled her mother's plight in the early 1900s.

She did laundry work for wealthy people in town and we youngsters had to carry the baskets. Go and get it. And return it. She worked at home. That was the purpose, to be with us children. (Mrs. X)

Even with keeping a lady boarder this mother could not make ends meet, and the children were given to an aunt. The daughter was sent out by the aunt to work in a cotton mill at age eleven. Orphans were certainly more likely to earn their keep at very young ages than were children with both parents alive.

One man described how he took up his father's coal delivery round.

Mum managed after father's death by sewing. We had a truck. Dad was in the coal business. I knew the truck was sitting there. So after dad died the truck just sat there. And I knew that we weren't going to be able to carry on because things were getting pretty rough and I'd have to go out to work and help. So I took over the truck.... I wanted to keep them (the younger brothers and sisters) in school. (Mr. I)

Where there were no relatives who could offer the widow help or a home, there was sometimes no alternative to putting the children in the orphanage till they were old enough to work. One man remembered looking after his younger brother in the orphanage. His mother found she could not support them by doing domestic or factory work and reluctantly placed them in the orphanage. He remembered the strict routine, the grey uniforms, and most particularly, not being able to leave the orphanage when his mother came on the weekly visit to which she was restricted. By the time he was fourteen his mother had found him work with a family friend, and with two incomes, she and the two boys could again live together. (Mr. U)

Many of the respondents mention adoptions within their own families, and also instances of taking in the children of dead relatives. Many adoptions were quite spontaneous.

> I didn't even know him (the dead man). But I heard the story. That woman, she had three kids, two boys and a girl. So we went up to see the lady. And she was a beautiful girl. I said, how would you like to be my girl? And she liked me and she liked her (my wife). She had to go to orphanage. She bawled. What are we going to do about it? Well, we have no children ... How about if we take that girl, give her a home? O.K. I didn't oppose it. (Mr. X)

And in addition relatives and neighbours were quite aware of the consequences of not adopting a child who was left parentless, or not intervening to make sure that the child could remain with the single remaining parent. Orphaned children might well be working as early as eight or ten in the cotton mills should no one come forward to take care of them properly. ... With the high mortality rates that prevailed, many must have felt that there but for the grace of God went their own children.

Adopted children were often of direct use to their parents in family businesses. One woman described how a man attempted to adopt her son. The family were in poor circumstances at the time and he was selling newspapers on the streets.

> He said 'A man who has got a farm wants to adopt me.' He said, 'mum, I don't want to be adopted, I want to stay with you.' (Mrs. M.)

Boys and girls from orphanages were commonly sent out to work on farms once they reached the age of fourteen.

There were also less formal arrangements where relatives or friends took an interest in bereaved children. One upper middle class woman described how her mother had been asked to help with the upbringing of some girls who had lost their mother.

> Mother took a motherless family under the wing. Their father asked my father if she would take an interest in them. She said, send them up. We went to the same school. It was just a natural friendship. (Mrs. T.)

From the uniformity in the responses of respondents to questions about relationships with neighbours from working-class families it appears that there was an established code of neighbourly behaviour. There was little in the way of visiting in each other's homes, but considerable conversation over back fences, and from porch to porch. Clearly people saw most of their neighbours in the summer, and relatively little of them in the winter. Many respondents emphasized how their parents kept neighbours at a distance. However, neighbours could be relied on to help in an emergency.

> ...she (mother) never got too friendly with them. She'd pass the time of day, but not so much that they were in and out the house....
> In the neighbourhood...no one that would come in and visit. Talk to them outside, and if there was a death there, we all tried to go to the funeral. We were close in that way, but not to the extent of visiting. (Mrs. F)

There was, however, a great deal of help and social support given between neighbours in times of crisis. The kinds of help given to non-relatives was short-term non-financial help given by women, often at times of birth, death, or sickness. One woman described her mother's relations with the neighbours as follows:

> Just being neighbourly if anyone wanted her. If anyone died, she'd go and help lay them out. Anybody was sick, she'd go and help them. Jobs like that—if they wanted. Same with a child coming, and the doctor not available. She could help.

Another said:

> We were very close with our neighbours. If they were in trouble they'd come to mother. But not to visit.

Funerals were the most important neighbourhood affairs. The daughter of a commercial traveller, living in a lower middle class area commented,

> I seem to remember funerals as being an awful nuisance. Everyone in the neighbourhood would bake and take it in. And after the funeral everyone went back to the house. [Mrs. D.]

Not only were funerals important neighbourhood affairs, but mourning was expected to be observed. And adults, but generally not children, wore mourning clothes.

> Mother wore mourning (for grandmother)—black veil and all, just like the Italians today.... Of course, she'd be wearing what she had in the house.

> In those days you didn't go out after someone belonging to you died.

There was a lot of visiting—people knew you were confined, and they'd come in for a cup of tea in the afternoon or in the evening. It would be three months or so before you would be invited out. She (mother) might go to the sewing club, because that was for charity. But no card-playing—that was taboo! [Mrs. E.]

The introduction of funeral parlours, and the end to the practice of burying people from home caused strains in some families. Many people interpreted being buried from the funeral parlour as rejection by one's family and sought assurance that when they died they would be buried from home....

CHILD LIFE: SCHOOLDAYS IN HAMILTON, 1900-1920

Free schools brought about a revolution in working-class life. Yet despite a flood of middle-class reminiscences, there are almost no accounts of lower-class education. One of the few is this community history compiled by a local teacher, from memoirs by Hamilton North End oldtimers. It was, however, a limited revolution. The drop-out at Grade 8 seems to have been typical throughout urban English Canada; the children of French-Canadian workers seldom proceeded even that far.

Donald M. Oliphant, comp., *Hess Street School* (Hamilton, Aggus, 1974), pp. 36-9. Reprinted by permission of D. M. Oliphant.

...It was the custom in those days for a pupil to go to school till he was 14. If you passed your entrance at 13, you could quit and go to work. The boys were apprenticed to some trade except a bricklayer. Those days, an apprentice bricklayer had to be a bricklayer's son. All other trades were open. I think the rate was $4 a week, 10 hours a day, and 5 hours on Saturday. Night work hadn't been thought of at that time except for firemen, policemen, people to keep the fires going in factories, and night watchmen. The firemen slept at the fire stations....

Hess Street School had 4 rooms on the street floor. The Kindergarten was in the front on the south side.... The boys' washrooms were in the back of the school with a door on each side going into the yard. The yard had a big high board fence around it.... The yard was very small.

The second floor had a staircase near the back that went about halfway, then two staircases, one on each side, went to the third floor. There were 4 rooms on this floor with the principal's office in the front. A piano was located on this floor and when professor Johnson came, the teachers would get all the kids to sit on the stairs and then the sing-song would begin.

On the third floor there were 4 rooms. There was also a little room at the front which the kids called the punishment room. If on that floor it was decided that you needed the strap, into that room you went. On the second floor "Daddy" Cruikshank took over, and on the main floor they were too small to be punished.... Sometimes the teacher would raise up on her toes to get more leverage. "Daddy" would raise the strap over his head and wham! Some of the kids would go home and tell their father, and "Dad" would interview them. Sometimes he would win and sometimes father would, but it seemed to wind up in a yelling match most of the time....

If you went to school after you were 14, your old man was either a banker or a brewer or he owned a store or was quite wealthy.

School went from 9 to 12, and from 2 to 4. Recess for the young ones was at 10 in the morning and 3 in the afternoon. The older ones went at 10:15 in the morning and 3:15 in the afternoon. You just went into the yard. Some kids would play tag; others sat on the ground up against the fence; and others would yell their heads off. Boys were on the north side and girls on the south. We used to go to the Normal School between 9 and 10:30 once a week, the boys to learn woodworking, and girls to cook and sew. The teacher for the boys was Mr. Painter. We would arrive back at school at 10:50 or 10:55, depending on how fast you walked. Nobody hurried.

They had big bob-sleighs, and they used them on Hess, Caroline, and Barton. A big gang could get on one.... There were no cars in those days.... When a circus came to town, you got a note from your mother asking permission to go and see the parade. The teachers got so many notes that they sent all the kids out of Hess Street by 10 a.m.

"In the wintertime, once or twice the teacher would get the kids to bring a dime, and they would rent a sleigh off a man on Queen Street and ride to the top of Binkley Hollow and back. School fees those days were 10¢ a month, and I remember running the odd message to pay my dime.... The children used the carbon from the old carbon lamps to draw hopscotch on the sidewalks....

REPORT OF ATTENDANCE OFFICER

To the chairman and members of the Board of Education

Gentlemen:

I beg, herewith, to report for your information the duties performed as School Attendance Officer for the month of April, 1920.

Engaged each day from 9 to 12 noon at office work; afternoons, visiting schools and making inquiries respecting absentees, etc.

BREACH OF THE SCHOOL ACT

The cases against George Latham and John Nearn were dismissed and their boys were ordered to report to the Police Magistrate every Saturday morning to get their weekly reports signed.

Eli Gagnon was fined $20.00 for neglecting to send his children to school.

Number of children reported from the different schools as absent and irregular in their attendance, and investigated   133
    Number of notices served on parents   60
    Number of visits made to parents   67
    Number of boys who played truant   8
    Number of boys found selling papers during school hours   7
    Number exempted from attending school   1

Three boys and one girl were placed in the Children's Shelter. Their parents could not control them.

I remain, Gentlemen
Your obedient servant

Wm. G. Hunter
School attendance officer.

CHILD LIFE: THE PEASANT PATTERN, 1900-1930

The lifestyle of immigrants, and their struggle to survive, is seen here from two perspectives. One is that of the middle-class WASP teacher. The other, describing identical conditions but utterly different in its recognition of the courage and determination of the New Canadian family, is that of an immigrant girl.

Robert England, *The Central European Immigrant in Canada* (Toronto, Macmillan, 1929), pp. 81-5. Reprinted by permission of the Macmillan Company of Canada Ltd.

One teacher, who was sent to a school twenty-four miles from town in unorganized territory where the population was totally Ruthenian... in a letter dated October 6th, wrote of her experiences. It took her six hours to get to town by waggon and for that reason she seldom left the community. She reported that the last English-speaking person she had seen was on August 21st. She mentioned the insufficiency of clothing in the district and the coming of simultaneous epidemics of small-pox and diphtheria. Five homes had cases of small-pox.

"The doctor promised to come out on a certain afternoon to vaccinate and there were 76 children with a few parents at the school. The doctor did not appear and I have not heard anything of him since. I had diphtheria myself but luckily escaped the small-pox. Many of the children have never been to a town. They are shy and frightened of strangers. When the Inspector of Schools came the children were so frightened he could not have any classes.

I have found two classes of homes—the very clean and the very dirty. The houses are practically all two-roomed, log, or plaster with thatched roofs, and many with mud floors. Even in the houses which are kept clean, conditions are decidedly unhygienic, owing to lack of fresh air. They refuse to open their windows and owing to so many living in a room, the air is very bad. In one or two of the houses, conditions are unspeakable. One family of ten lives in a low one-room shack with one bed for the entire family. Numerous cats and several fowl also live in the same room. All the children of the family are badly infected with ringworm and eczema. I have obtained remedies for these which seem to be helping. However, the greater number of the people are very particular as regards personal cleanliness, with the exception of pediculosis, which is general. There are absolutely no nursing or medical facilities....

One of the things which has impressed me most is the amount of work done by the women and children. Not only have the women the care of the house and a large family, but they work side by side in the field with the men. All the children, even the very young, work in the fields, and look after the stock. They get up hours before school to get their work finished and are put to work again as soon as they get home. The only place they get any play or child-life is at the school. When they first come they have no idea of play. They are all bright, but as they get older one notices, especially among the girls, a stolid indifference. The women have no social life and have no time for anything but hard work. Once married they seldom leave their homes....

Their farms are small and most of them cultivated in the manner of the old country small farm. This spring many of the farmers seeded their grain by hand from a bag slung over their shoulders.

Another teacher, an acute observer, reports as follows:

Discounting the fact that 'rust' and 'hail', together with economic conditions, such as the price of grains of late, have come hard on the district, there is little evidence to show that in better times, they were much better off. True, where once they used oxen they now use horses, where once there were no telephones, they are now in 50 per cent. of the houses; where once all roofs were thatched, there are now a few shingle roofs to be seen:—there must have been a certain amount of improvement. But I do think the whole district would be better off if it had been better farmed. One cannot say that there is actual poverty, if one accepts the standards of the district. But certainly in comparison with an average Canadian standard, there is an appearance of poverty. I have been in several homes whose furnishings were of the barest. And in such homes, it is hard to say if thrift is practised deliberately. I should say not; it is more a 'hand-to-mouth' existence.

Hygiene and sanitation are very primitive in most houses of the district. There are no frame dwellings. (I leave the one English-speaking family out of consideration always in these remarks.) All houses are made of mud, usually white-washed outside and in, although there are several which are innocent of white-wash, either outside or in. Most houses have two rooms, and are one-story high. In a large number of cases, the floors are of mud in both rooms. Perhaps 50 per cent. of the houses have one room at least with a board floor. Windows are always small and few in number. They are usually nailed in permanently. Furniture is scanty, and in some houses is practically non-existent. There is a lack of cleanliness amounting to dirt in a few houses, but in most cases things are probably as clean as one might expect. Cleanliness in milking and dairying operations is in most cases doubtful. There are, however, one or two exceptions, where utensils are well scalded.

Food is in many cases primitively prepared. They do not appear to understand much of the art of butchering or of preparing meats. Meat is usually in "chunk" form. In one or two houses in which I have been there was no set table, nor adequate supply of utensils or dishes. There was no table that I could see—simply a pot of potatoes boiled in their jackets, some chunks of fat pork, and some chunks of dry bread. The sleeping arrangements in many of the homes are very wretched. In one house where there are ten children, from one month old to eighteen years, there are only two broad beds made out of boards and a sort of straw mattress in the garret. It is quite the usual custom for both sexes to sleep together in the same room as the father and mother. So far as I have been able to see, it is the usual custom in many homes simply to take off the shoes and sleep in their day clothes.

The doctor is rarely called in, and only in cases of extreme necessity. Then, as far as I have been able to find out, it is too late. In the one case of child-birth that has occurred since May 1st, there was no doctor. Complete ignorance seems to prevail with regard to contagious and infectious diseases.

I would say that the women and children of the district are distinctly under-privileged, and that this is a characteristic of Ruthenian homes. I would also say that if they were given a chance, in many cases, the home would improve. Certainly the women do more work than the men, and do it without complaint. The women and children do all the "chores" and in May when the roads were so bad, I have often seen the women-folk in bare feet trudging through the deep mud laden with full sacks.

There are exceptions, but this is the general rule. I have been shocked many times at what they expect in the way of work from growing young children. . . . Holidays are looked upon as good opportunities to get some manual labour out of the children. . . . Occasionally, there are dances but these are generally drunken brawls, and fights are not infrequent. "Moonshine" spirits of a bad order flow pretty freely, because it is easily obtainable in at least two places that I know of in the town. In this connection, it might be remarked in passing, that "justice" or the conviction and punishment of offenders is very lax. . . .

The only other forms of social entertainment that have come to my notice are the celebration of weddings and of saint's-days. A wedding is a great affair, at which there may be two to five hundred people from all around the country. Eating, drinking, and dancing occupy the time at these events. In passing, I might say that these celebrations are quite frequent, and that, lasting sometimes two days as they do, they cut a large and much-needed slice out of the already very short Canadian summer, when work should be the order. In general, I would say that this community has never held a social entertainment, which might be called morally or intellectually uplifting. . . .

All homes in the district have on the walls of the living rooms a collection of highly coloured pictures of saints, decorated often with coloured paper rosettes. . . . So far I have managed to get 90 per cent. of my children to school on "holy days", which is a small step in advance of other years. They come to school in their best clothes, and do all the usual work, with the exception strangely enough that though "plasticine" is permitted, "paper cutting" and gardening are "taboo". So far, I have not urged them to do these things. . . . "

Interview with an anonymous Ukrainian woman, in Russell Hann (ed.), *The Great War and Canadian Society* (Toronto, New Hogtown Press, 1977). Reprinted by permission of Russell Hann.

I was born in 1897. I remember the most when my father came to Canada in 1907. He was sick and tired of working for somebody else, so he thought he would make enough money in Canada and come back and start his own business. So that's how he landed in Canada. When he did come to Canada, I remember him saying that it was sort of the end of some depression they had just before 1907, so he couldn't get jobs. He walked from Kenora to Winnipeg, hungry most of the time. So then he landed in Winnipeg and signed up for British Columbia to build the railway, and I don't know how long he stayed there, but he didn't have a lot of money to send to us. Anyway, from British Columbia he came to the town of Saskatoon, Saskatchewan, and he got work in the city works department, digging ditches and so on. He thought he'd make enough money and come back home. Well, what happened then, he was illiterate, so somebody else had to write his letters. So one young smart aleck wrote a letter for him, and wrote what he said, then he added on his own: 'Sell everything and come to Canada.' Dad didn't mean it that way. He didn't want us to come. He still thought he'd make enough money to come back. Well, mother didn't think twice. She sold everything she had, and we landed in Canada in 1911. He was making twenty cents an hour then and worked ten, twelve hours: digging ditches. You know, they were putting in sewers and so on. Saskatoon was just building up then. That was 1911. See, this is the history of how we landed in Canada, and we did land here, and what can you do? He was working, so somebody else came and got us from the station. There was five of us. I was the oldest.

I was fourteen, and I didn't know what it was all about. I didn't go to school until I was nine years old in our country, when it became compulsory. You see, the peasants didn't give a darn, especially for the girl. What would she want with school for? Well, you know, I grew up. When I was fourteen, I was this size already. So how you going to go to school with kids? So I left after three years. So when I landed here, what can I do? I didn't have the language. It was terribly hard, and I had to go work right away, because my father couldn't keep the whole family. We had to have a place to live, so we bought an old shack and bought everything on time, and bought a lot, and moved the shack from somewhere else into a lot, so we had a home, but we couldn't live out of it. The first one we lived in, there was four families in the eight-room house, all immigrants, and we had to share one stove. That's the way we lived....

The first job I ever had was in a little Chinese restaurant in Saskatoon out of the way from the main streets, like. And what can I do? To his standard, I couldn't even peel the potatoes properly. I'd never done that sort of work before. I didn't fare very well. He let me go because I wasn't to his standard, I guess. I was a kid, you know, very thin. So then after that, I got a job in another restaurant. I think it was four dollars a week, and I worked twelve hours altogether. It was a split shift, we were off in the afternoon. I was washing dishes, scrubbing floors, and everything else that came along. I left there, and went to work in London Hotel. Gee, that was hard. It's a very, very busy hotel. That's where I began to learn all about what life is like. I worked with people that were grown up. I remember one day I was scrubbing a cement floor on my knees. I collapsed, and the girls carried me into a room, but I pulled through....

You had your room and board there. You get up at six o'clock in the morning, and you went right through, maybe you were off a half an hour or so before dinner, and then you come down to dinner, and then you go again, and you work until it's finished. Sometimes it would be nine, ten o'clock at night. I worked by the month, not by the week. That's the way they worked in the hotel. I was there for awhile. Then I was without work for awhile, and I remember some woman heard about me. She had a rooming house, so she came out to the house and she took me out to help her in the rooming house. That was in 1912, in the fall. I stayed there four years, and that's where I got my schooling. She helped me a lot....

I had three brothers at that time and one sister. There was five of us. My brother Steve went to work, but you know how boys are—they went for themselves. But my younger brothers had to stay home. That's the way they started. But with me, I don't know, all my life I've never had nothing for nothing. I worked very hard and I always have to get it the hard way....

At that time in Saskatoon there was no industry. The only jobs you can get was the private homes, restaurants, and hotels, maybe the odd sort of gardening that you could go and earn extra money. But there was no way of getting out. We had three rooms in our shack. The whole family slept in one room. And there was another room, quite narrow. There was three wooden beds, and six men boarders on top of it. That's how [my mother] supplemented some of the money we used for food and paid for the stuff they bought—the shack and the lot. So this is the way we lived when we first came. There was a small kitchen and a little cot in the kitchen—there was a man sleeping there. On top of it all, this lot that my father bought was a wrong lot. In about year's time he had to move the shack to another lot which was originally his, where he should have moved first. When we moved the shack there, there was a great big dilapidated shack at the back on this lot. So we got rid of the boarders from the house, and mamma put them all into this shack. There was about eight of them there. And she cooked and washed and everything else for them. I don't know what they paid her....

When I could spare a couple of dollars, I used to give them to my mother. She had to struggle. I remember a lot of times she used to get up very early in the morning and go and fish, try to get goldeye we had in Saskatchewan River. She used to fish so the kids would have something to eat. There was no welfare then. I don't know how she pulled through. She used to try everything she can, including selling booze—home brew—that's the fact! You know, I used to condemn her then, but when I analyze it now, I don't know if any body else could have done anything else....

She was illiterate, very backward, my mother was, but you know, she had a skill—she was a midwife, but not registered. I'll bet you that she delivered the babies of most of the Ukrainian women in Saskatoon, and you know, the doctors tried to prosecute her. There was one doctor. He says, 'Oh no, you leave her alone. There wasn't a child that she delivered that died or a mother that died. Just leave her alone.' She had her own way of doing things....

'SPARROWS AND BRONCHOS': BRITISH IMMIGRANTS IN THE BOOM

Even the WASP immigrant could meet with discrimination. Signs reading 'No English Need Apply' were a common sight before the Great War. (See John Bruce interview in Chapter 1.) Britons were often disparaged as 'sparrows'—that ubiquitous city pest imported from Europe—or as 'bronchos' liable to kick out at Canadian work-customs, blue Sundays... and anti-union employers. Despite this there was a persistent campaign, of which Copping's book was a part, to send more British slumdwellers to the 'Golden Land'.

A. E. Copping, *The Golden Land* (London, 1912), pp. 145-50.

... During the industrial depression that affected the American continent in 1907 and 1908, Canada suffered a check in its galloping development, and great workshops near Earl's Court, as elsewhere, were temporarily closed. Now, Earl's Court is a remarkable Toronto suburb that has sprung up during the past year or so, and is mainly populated by mechanics and labourers from London and other English cities. It happens that a majority of the Committee's emigrants came under the influence of that depression; and, as my inquiries at Earl's Court convinced me, there we have the chief cause of the disappointing 20 per cent. ratio of repayment.

When I was at Earl's Court, its 2,000 inhabitants had, almost to a man, outlived the consequences of that serious setback. The interesting process of transforming shacks into substantial brick or timber houses was proceeding apace. Nay, the "Shack Town" of a year before was already a town of villas, if of villas strangely mingled with nondescript wooden structures. And here and there the visitor is amazed to see part of one of those magnified fowl-houses projecting from an unfinished villa; for Canadian example encourages a skilful incorporation of the old home with the new.

A West Ham man made me acquainted with local usage as it affects land tenure, his testimony being confirmed by several neighbours...

"Ain't it all right bein' yer own landlord? My! that's a change from two rooms at Canning Town, and no nearer ownin' a brick of it after payin' seven bob a week for ten years and more. Only, mind yer, we was a long way from buying our own place at the start. Why, I hadn't been workin' more than a month, and jest beginnin' to think I was nicely fixed, when—bless me, if the foundry didn't close down, and all 'ands was thrown out. I tell yer, we 'ad it pretty rough for a time—but that's all past and forgotten now. Only when the shop opened agin, and I'd been took back, me and the missis figured it out that we'd be money in pocket if we bought our bit, same as everybody said we ought to. So I give the bloke five dollars for a start, and after that it was two dollars a month till the land was paid for.

"What's two dollars to a man when e's liftin' forty? That's what they pay me down at the foundry, and it works out two pound a week by our money. You've got to earn it, let me tell yer, but nobody wouldn't mind puttin' in a bit of graft for two pound a week. It's not gettin' the charnse of a job, more than might be an odd day a fortnight, and dog's wages at that—that's what takes the heart out of any one in the Old Country. A man can turn round, as you may say, on two pound a week—nice warm clothes for the nippers, a bit of finery once in a way for the missis, and a good bellyful all round.

"As soon as the land was paid off, 'Now it's time,' I says, 'to 'ave a nice 'ouse over our 'eads, same as others.' We'd made do up to then with jest a two-room shack—small, of course, but wonderful snug in the winter, and a lot more comfortable than you might think. By livin' quiet, and puttin' away a bit every pay-day, I'd saved pretty nigh half enough money to buy the stuff, and me and two others got to work on it, evening after evening, and very often an hour and a 'alf in the morning. But the lath and plaster and all the paintin' I didn't want nobody to 'elp me with. The rest of the money we're payin' off same as we did for the land, only five dollars a month instead of two; and be through with it, we shall, by next Christmas twelvemonth. Only me and the missis was puttin' our 'eads tergether to arrange if we couldn't pay 'em two months at a time, and so be through and done with it in jest over a year from now. Then it'll all be our own, and not rent to pay or nothin', and Sir Wilfrid Loreyer 'isself couldn't take it from us. I tell you, the missis don't half begin to fancy 'erself—goes to church of a Sunday, she does, with the best of 'em; and if I might 'appen to step into the parler, and forget to take off my boots, there's a pretty 'ow-d'yer-do over me spoilin' 'er nice noo carpet."

In the present trend of his life, that man represents hundreds of London labourers now settled in the eastern cities of Canada. The testimony of another West Ham enthusiast was typical of a new human interest that has been awakened.

"What d'you think of this?" he asked, with blushing pride, as he drew from under the table a clothes-basket full of small and rather muddy carrots. "Not bad for a beginner, eh? Before I come out here, it's a fact I'd never seen what vegetables look like whilst they're growing in the ground. I was jest a baby at it; but this year I've grown two sacks and a 'alf of pertaters—for we've got a nice bit of garden; and you ought to have seen all the cabbages and one thing and another we've been having. Then there's a nice lot of parsnips I've got to dig up before the frost gets hold of the ground. It's a hobby with me, more than work—I quite look forward to my couple of hours in the garden of an evening. Then, again, it's a big saving not having to buy vegetables, especially when you've got a lot of youngsters. And that's another thing about Canada—it suits the nippers. Our lot's got twice the go in 'em they used to have, and as for red cheeks and getting fat, why, you'd hardly know them for the same. I'll tell you, Canada's all right. For I've altered my opinion from the idea I had soon after we came out, when the big shops shut down, and there was a few months when jobs was as difficult to find, pretty near, as what they are in the Old Country. But we haven't had another spell like that for two years—and if we should cop it again at any time, well, I'll be better prepared, with house and land paid for, and a dollar or two put by."

GOOD-TIME GIRLS OR HARD TIMES?
PROSTITUTION IN TORONTO

Is it coincidence that many of the so-called 'prostitutes' were British immigrants on depression wages? For some, the promise of the Golden Land had failed. While much of what we know about the poor comes from church surveys, with their middle-class moral bias, there are cogent questions raised by these clergymen. Are poverty and class position the sole determinants of behaviour? Who 'falls', and why?

Report of the Social Survey Commission, Toronto (Toronto, 1915), pp. 34, 35-40, 43.

... [O]bviously the first step was to find what are the prevailing wages and living conditions of working girls. To this end the Commission had an experienced woman investigator spend some time in interviewing many girls, whose occupations included department and other stores, telephone exchanges, laundries and factories of various kinds. The investigation was made before the outbreak of the war and the consequent depression, and may, therefore, be taken as representing normal conditions. The results indicate that the wages most commonly paid run from six to nine dollars per week. It is difficult to estimate the average from the data obtained. A limited number earn ten, twelve or fifteen dollars, the last named sum being the maximum. Only two of the factories covered by the investigation and only one of the laundries pay more than five dollars per week to beginners. A very considerable proportion of factory workers seem to be earning less than six dollars. A low wage scale prevails in a number of shops, those in the large departmental stores being apparently better off in this respect than most others. The seasonal character of the work in the industries in which a great number of the woman workers are employed makes their living condition much more difficult.

A large number, probably the great majority of working girls, live at home. In some cases living at home may mean that the girl is only partly dependent for her living upon her own earnings. In other cases it means that she is one of several workers upon whom the maintenance of the home depends. In these latter cases, an advantage is that the girls are not homeless in times of unemployment or sickness. But at any rate it is the living conditions of the girl who lives with her own people which determine the wage scale, and that makes the problem of living so much the harder for the girl who is alone in the city and has to depend entirely on herself. Some of the investigator's visits among girls were made in the evening, in order to have opportunity for conversation. In some cases the girls were found in a class of boarding house that would not tend to raise their standard of living, but they said they could not get any better places, because they could not pay more out of their wages. And even those at home were often living under far from satisfactory conditions, being members of large families, in crowded quarters.

It is plain, therefore, that the pressure of poverty must be felt, often keenly, by very many working women and girls. How far is that pressure responsible for the downfall of those who become immoral? A very significant fact is that fallen women themselves do not often allege that they were driven to vice by the direct pressure of want. The director of one rescue mission in the City makes the following statement in this connection: "We have not had one case reported in seven years (in which time we have handled hundreds of cases) where it was stated that insufficient wages drove the offender to her misdeeds." The records for two years of another institution, where the history of cases is carefully recorded, were examined with a like result. Direct interviews with women gave somewhat different results. A group of volunteer investigators, whose results were placed at the disposal of the Commission, report interviews with twenty-five professional prostitutes. Twelve of these stated their reasons for entering upon their occupation, and two of the twelve declared the reason to be that they could not live on their wages. One of these had worked at making willow plumes at five dollars per week. The occupation and wages of the other were unstated.

In the direct investigations of the Commission there were thirty-seven prostitutes of the professional and semi-professional classes who made statements to our investigators of their reasons or motives for entering upon an immoral life. Of these fifteen were professionals and twenty-two were of the semi-professional or "occasional" class. Nineteen of the thirty-seven giving reasons for their immorality, stated that they could not live on their wages. Only four of these were professional prostitutes. The other fifteen were girls who worked in shops, factories or offices and supplemented their wages by prostitution. As to the wages received by these girls.

1 received $5.00 per week.
5 received $6.00 per week.
3 received $8.00 per week.
3 received $9.00 per week.
5 did not state the wages received.
2 received $20.00 per week.

These last were chorus girls who said they had to pay their hotel bills and expenses out of that sum.

As to the importance to be attached to economic pressure as a contributing cause of the social evil, the following considerations should be borne in mind:

1. It is obvious that insufficient wages is not the only nor indeed the chief cause, for if that were the case then wherever wages fall below a certain point, it would be found that practically all women whose wages are below that point would be immoral; and this is very far from being the case. In spite of the severity of the pressure of such economic conditions, most girls in such positions successfully resist the pressure and retain their virtue.

2. If insufficient wages and consequent inability to procure the necessaries of life were either the only or the principal cause of girls resorting to prostitution, we should expect to find domestic servants less frequently than any others among those who succumb, for the servant is less exposed then almost any other to periods of unemployment and when at work has always her board and lodging assured, and is not, therefore, driven to immorality as an alternative to starvation. As a matter of fact, however, domestic service contributes quite as large a quota to the ranks of the fallen as does any other occupation. The explanation of this must evidently be something else than the pressure of want.

3. While economic pressure is not the sole cause, it is one of the important contributory causes, as is evidenced by the fact that prostitution is recruited almost entirely from one social class, the class, namely, by whom the pressure of economic conditions is most severely felt. In Flexner's "Prostitution in Europe" a mass of facts and figures is given

which shows conclusively that European prostitutes come practically altogether from the lower working classes. The records of three hundred cases cared for during one year at Waverley House in New York shows that the previous occupation of the girls were as follows:

Housework	95	Cashiers	7
Factory work	72	Laundry girls	6
Waitresses	29	Trained nurses	3
Shop clerks	16	Telephone girls	2
Chorus girls	13	Milliners	2
Office workers	9	Manicures	2
Nurse maids	8	Miscellaneous	2
Dressmakers	8	No occupation	26

That the conditions in Toronto in this respect are not different from those found elsewhere, is indicated by the following statement of the occupations of seventy-five girls who were cared for in one of the institutions of the City:

    36 domestics.
    8 employed in hotels or restaurants.
    3 dressmakers, milliners or tailoresses.
    12 factory operatives.
    4 office employees.
    8 at home.
    2 sale girls.
    2 actresses.

It is noteworthy also that of the girls above referred to, who stated to investigators that they had been unable to live on their wages, none had received more than about the average wage and a number less than the average.

4. It is also to be noted that there were other cases than those who alleged the insufficiency of their wages as a cause of their downfall, in which poverty had plainly exercised an influence, such for instance as the cases of women who gave the death of their husbands as their reason for taking up this life, and others whose statements showed that the desire for good clothes, amusement, etc., which they had been unable to procure from their wages, have been inducements to immorality.

5. It is noteworthy that most of those who alleged that they had taken to prostitution because of the insufficiency of their wages were not of the professional, but of the semi-professional or occasional class. It is some evidence of the sincerity of their statement that though they had been initiated into an easier way of making money, they continued in the main to earn their living by honest work.

6. It is evident from the figures given above that some of those who claimed to be unable to live decently on their wages were getting as much as the vast majority of working girls in the City manage to live on respectably. On the other hand, a girl who does not get more than $6 per

week may very well find it insufficient, though many respectable girls are getting not more than that; but that some girls can maintain themselves and dress suitably to their position on a certain sum, does not prove that others can do so. A good deal depends upon the girl's ability and training. No sum can be specified which is just sufficient to avoid dangerous pressure. A specified wage may keep one person under such dangerous pressure, while the same sum would release another person from pressure.

7. Sufficiency or insufficiency of wages is not just a question of bare subsistence, but of a reasonably satisfactory life. The fact which has been everywhere found that the number of fallen girls and women who, though desirous, as all human beings are, of excusing their mis-steps, claim to have been driven to immorality as an alternative to starvation, is comparatively small, may indicate not so much that the cause was something else than poverty, as that this cause operated in ways of which the objects of it were not directly conscious. In other words, the case in which a woman deliberately determines to sell herself in order to procure things which all normal human beings crave and which her earnings are not sufficient to procure, is probably a comparatively rare case. The commoner case is probably the one in which a girl debarred by poverty from reasonable and wholesome pleasures and indulgences, makes up for them by "good times" of a questionable character, thus lowering her moral tone and incidentally placing herself under obligation to her male associates, and thus comes gradually and by a process, the significance of which she may not herself clearly apprehend, closer and closer to the danger line. Following such courses for a certain length of time a single fairly easily made step takes her across the line—and the remainder of the downward course is easy and rapid. Cases of this kind in which poverty has certainly been an important contributory cause, are undoubtedly very much commoner than the cases in which the downward step has been taken all at once, because the girl realized that she either had to do that or to starve. . . .

Housing and Sanitation.

Undoubtedly overcrowding exists to a great extent in Toronto. Those mentioned below are but a few of the many cases that might be furnished, but they will suffice as examples to show the role played by improper housing in the problem of prostitution in Toronto.

Dr. Hastings, the Medical Officer of Health, reports as follows:

"In regard to the influence of overcrowding on the moral conditions of our City, I might say that many cases have come under the observation of our Inspectors from time to time in which grown-up sons and daughters occupy the same sleeping apartments, and in some cases grown-up daughters occupy the same rooms with their father and mother, or with the father alone.

"In every case they have been notified to secure separate sleeping accommodation for the male and female adults in the home.

"In a recent investigation made by my female inspectors there were some fourteen places found in which conditions of this kind existed. One small room was found to be occupied as a dwelling and workshop by a man and two daughters, both grown-up; in another instance one small room was used as sleeping apartments by a man and wife and two boarders; also, one room used as a dwelling by a man and daughter, age 18 years; one small room used as a dwelling by a man, son aged 14 years, and a daughter aged 18; one room used as a dwelling by a girl about 20 and a brother about 15. In another instance there was found a room used as bedroom only, by a man, wife and baby, and a woman, baby and man, whom it was found was not her husband. . . .

. . . The large proportion of British immigrants indicates that a grave danger exists in relation to the British immigrant girl. Of course, in comparison with Canadians it may not prove that there are not more Canadian girls erring than the others. It may only mean that the Canadian girl, when in trouble, has other resources than the rescue home. As compared with other nationalities, the explanation no doubt is that girls of foreign birth do not so often immigrate alone, but come, for the most part, with their families. Still, the fact remains a serious one that so large a proportion of this social wreckage should consist of young women who have recently come to this country from the motherland. It shows conclusively either that the conditions surrounding these young women in their adopted country are not what they should be, or else that sufficient care is not being exercised in the selection of emigrants, so that this country is getting too many girls from Britain who are not of the best class. It seems probable that both these conditions contribute to the result.

Closely connected, probably, with the problem of immigration, is the fact, noted already, in another connection, that the commonest occupation of girls who go wrong is that of domestic service. The common notion that the domestic leads a very sheltered life, secure from the temptations by which girls who have to earn their living at other callings are beset, does not seem to be borne out by the facts. As a general condition, this may not be easy to explain. It has a bearing, as has been noted, upon the question of economic pressure; for so far as girls are driven to immorality by poverty, we should scarcely expect the domestic to be the most numerous class to succumb. On the other hand, it may indicate that other conditions, such as confinement, isolation and loneliness, drive servant girls into dangerous associations.

THREE DAYS FROM STARVATION: THE URBAN POOR IN 1919

The stenographer's transcript of the Mathers Commission hearings across Canada is one of the fullest and finest sources we have for the whole period between the 1880s and the 1930s. In the hearings the actual voices of workers are heard. No one should suppose, however, that they constitute a statistical sample of public opinion. Rather, excerpts have been chosen to show conditions and causes of unrest in each major region. In the West, the unrest was to climax in the Winnipeg Strike.

Transcript of Testimony to (Mathers) Royal Commission on Industrial Unrest, 1919 (PAC), pp. 82-3, 1211-22, 1189-92, 1059-65, 1690-1, 2368-72, 3148-63, 3536-8.

Reverend William Ivens, at Winnipeg, May 10th [later imprisoned as a strike leader]
What they [the Canadian Manufacturers' Association (and government) Reconstruction Committee] mean by 'thrift' is that the workers shall wear their overalls just a little bit longer, that they shall carry just a little bit less in their dinner pails, and that their homes, which to-day are not kept warm enough, shall be kept one or two degrees colder.... I have stood by the graveside and buried little tots, and have said over them these significant words, "Forasmuch as it has pleased Almighty God in His great mercy to take unto Himself the soul of our dear one here departed," when I knew that they were being buried because their parents did not have the sustenance to nourish the bodies of these little tots. Furthermore, I have buried women in this city, mothers of tots, wives of husbands, where I have known these women were working when they ought to have been resting.... More 'thrift' means less medical attention....

Reverend Hugh Dobson, Field Secretary of the Methodist Church in the four Western Provinces, at Regina, May 8th
My work takes me steadily through the four Western provinces, I have just come back from two months in British Columbia and of course the extent of unrest is very great.... In this Province the types or the groups in which there is the greatest unrest is somewhat different from the group in British Columbia. This is an agricultural province. British Columbia is more what we would call an industrial province. There is [a] difference between urban unrest and rural unrest. [I]n both cases it is quite large. ...The causes of the unrest seem to me to fall in these forms: 1. the unjust distribution of wealth and income, 2. the unemployment and denial of an opportunity to earn a living 3. the denial of the right of opportunity to form [e]ffective organization, 4. insecurity, the insecurity

of life ... and the really bigger aspiration for a higher standard of living. On the other hand, there is the resentment of the obstacles that are back of getting that freer life, and the two greatest obstacles that I find in the country and have found in the last 8 or 10 years on this point are indifference and stand-pattism and a few irresponsible extremists. The last would not be a factor were it not for the former two. . . .

What machinery has been prepared for dealing with the high cost of living appears to be a farce. . . . With regard to housing and speculation, we have a very serious housing condition. I would ... call attention between a man who works on a wage, and the other. This is just one map of one city. Every black spot represents a dead child there in the city of Toronto in 1912, there is part of the city where there is a very abnormal death rate, that part of the city is where the greater part of the wage earners live. A man earning wages in Vancouver does not live on Shaughnessy Heights, the wage man does not determine the part of the city where he lives. There is a map of the City of Halifax, there is one part of the City where they have six or seven times as many living as in the other part of the City. . . . This is another map of the same city showing the infant mortality and this is the area where the greater proportion of the wage earners live, . . . where there is an abnormal amount of deaths and disease and delinquency. . . .

In Ottawa, one ward in the City of Ottawa—while London, England has a death rate of only 87—Ottawa, our capital city has a death rate of 88. . . . While in Ottawa, I went over this later with the mayor and other officials of Ottawa, in the Victoria Ward of Ottawa out of every 10,000 children born 220 died before they were a year old; in another ward 226; in Ottawa Ward out of every thousand children 300 died before they were a year old, and that is part of the city where the wage earners live. We will then come to the Rideau Ward, where they take care of folks, where they do not get industrial unrest, the death rate there is only 46 per thousand while in Ottawa Ward it is 300. Men receiving wages are acquainted with these facts and their lives and families are limited owing to the conditions that exist of having the ordinary expenses of mankind. They have the expenses of sickness and funeral expenses, and the high cost of living is only exceeded by the high cost of dying. . . . Ill health and accident and non-employment are the three great evils. Ill health is really the thing that causes the most discontent and that is due to the indifference of people to the slum conditions of their own City. That is due to the fact that the comfortable people do not take the time to take an interest in those things. . . .

It has been proved by study here and abroad that there is a direct relation between poverty and the death rate of babies. The rate at which poverty kills was not known, at least in this country until very recently, when it was shown that the babies whose father earned less than $10 a week died during the first year at the appalling rate of 256 per 1,000, on the other hand those whose fathers earned $25 a week or more died at the rate of only 84 per 1,000. That is, the babies of the poor died at three times the rate of those who were in fairly well-to-do families. The last of the family to go hungry are the children, yet statistics show that in six of our largest cities, that 12% to 20% of the children are noticeably underfed and ill-nourished.

In each of four industrial towns studied by the Bureau of Labour Statistics, more than 75% of the children quit school before reaching the 7th grade. The great seriousness of this condition is even more acutely realized when it is known that in the families of the workers, 37% of the mothers are at work and consequently unable to give the children more than scant attention. Of these mothers, 30% keep boarders and lodgers, and 7% work outside the home.

I have here an illustration of... the benefits accruing to the workman in Great Britain. In Great Britain they have old age pensions, invalidity insurance, health insurance, industrial accident insurance and unemployment insurance... and [in Canada] the people are quite aware of it.... Our most fundamental institution in Canada is our fireside and... the family. [T]hat is why men fear; the man who employs men under our present system employs them feeling he has a right to dismiss them any moment.

Mrs Regina Asals, representing the Women's Labor League of the Trades and Labor Council, at Regina, May 8th
Take a girl to-day who is not experienced, she starts work at $7.00 or $8.00 per week, and in some cases less, can you tell me how that girl lives? The cost of living and of clothing have gone up in price to such an extent that if she is not living at home, she must turn elsewhere, who can you blame for that?... In some cases, when a girl or woman commands a fairly good wage she keeps that position by being immoral.

Now take a working man's wife, she toils from morning to night trying to make ends meet, what is her life, what enjoyment does she get? Very little, with the result that she becomes irritable and cross, thereby making herself and everybody else that she comes in contact with, miserable; in some cases she has to go to work and leave her family to get on best they can. I ask why? I think I can answer that, being a working man's wife, also the mother of four children: in the first place we have to have a home to live in, which to-day means approximately one-third of a working man's wages is confiscated for rent, the majority not owning their homes.

Then the big item, food; really when one comes to think of this great problem we can hardly say how we eat; while the war was on, it was because of the war, now we have to pay even more than in times of war because of the large demands; there must be something radically wrong, this not only applies to food but includes clothes, [the] prices of which are still advancing, not only advancing but very inferior in quality; can anyone answer the question why all this bleeding and crushing of the working people?

Can you wonder why a woman would rather die than bring children into a world like this? The present struggle for an existence is one of the reasons the birth rate is declining. There is only one thing that the workers have to thank the capitalists for, and that is that they have tightened the screw up so much that they are awakening the worker up to the fact that he is the most important factor, and that until we produce for use instead of profit this unrest will still prevail. Let the working man, the one who produces, have control, and then we shall see the light of a new dawn . . . .

John J. McGrath, President of the local Plumbers' Union, at Saskatoon, May 7th [Ed. note: a conservative craft unionist]
The cause of unrest among the workers, in my idea, is due entirely to education. There have been a few people for the last forty years who have been studying economic conditions and who are known as Socialists. These men have been telling us things that the majority of trade unions have regarded to a certain extent as bunk, but since this war has started and conscription was brought in this country and the United States and workers were conscripted into the Army at $1.10 a day and certain privileged individuals were allowed to conduct business for production for the needs of the country and were making abnormal profits and at the same time these fellows were on top of the house, crying out, "Go on, we will see that you are well fed and see you get all the meat you want," and so forth, and the workers were beginning to think that some of this bunk that the so-called Socialists were driving at them was not all bunk, . . . the worker was only getting 16% . . . [to] 20% of the wealth [he] produced and that someone else was getting the balance of it. Now that was a cause of unrest . . . .

There is no man who kicks because he is unemployed occasionally, that is if he had proficiently laid by [to] . . . tide himself over, but the trouble is that the worker is getting so little of what he produces and is not enabled owing to the high cost of living to have anything saved up, and when old age strikes him he has nothing but absolute poverty to face. Secondly, when he is laid off and obtains work again, the first thing he has to do is to pay up a bunch of back debts, and by the time he has the bunch of debts paid up and is trying to save up a little more, he is laid off again. . . . As far as a remedy is concerned, I feel of [sic] suggesting of profit sharing plans of some kind. . . . There are men in the employ of Ford to-day that own their own houses . . . [more] that own their own house than . . . in most of large industries. There is one thing against the Ford system and that is that a man has to lose great deal of his individuality . . . but at the same time I think that if a man is working under conditions where he is a great deal better off than what he ordinarily would be [then] he must lose some of his individuality and I think myself that it is a good thing for him. I believe it is a good thing for a man that he is placed in such a position that he doesn't squander his money . . . .

A great many men earn good wages, but a great many of them when the pinch comes haven't got a cent, that is one of the great troubles we have in Union matters. When it comes to a strike . . . they have not got enough to rely on and that's the reason they cannot last. While I hesitate at saying it, I believe that some of us have too much individuality at times. As to a remedy, I believe that possibly means could be worked out, a kind of co-operative, a co-partnership system of some kind . . . that at the end of the year the profit of the industry be divided amongst the employers and among the employees on an equal basis. . . .

J. Grant, Chairman of the Executive Council of Boilermakers, Shipbuilders and Helpers of America, at Fort William, May 13th
On this last conference [with Eastern Canada shipyards] we are now to meet the employers in our different localities, separately. That, I take it as Chairman of the Executive Council, is a direct slap at us to divide our organization. If that is the kind of co-operation the employers are going to give to bring about better conditions for the working man, I want to inform you that that is the way to start trouble. We are determined that the living conditions of the working man must be improved. At the present time, the workers through the shipyard at Port Arthur are getting 42½ cents, with an increase according to the prices in the Labor Gazette. That was granted, a 5% increase on April 1st. . . . Even the Government does not print the truth in its own Gazette . . . butter is given at 50¢. That is ridiculous. I travelled throughout the city, and in no case have I been able to purchase . . . butter at less than 60¢ or 65¢, or margarine any less than 35¢ or 40¢. . . . The working man gets 42½¢ for nine hours' work, and an increase at about 2½¢ on his wages. The ordinary worker in the shipyard on that salary is the unskilled man, but the hardship of that is that the unskilled workman is the man with the largest family. I went through the yard and got the statistics of married men with children. Out of 431 in this organization, no one has less than 2, and they go as high as 6. I myself have 6 children. The rents in this district, contrary to what one of the speakers told you, a fully modern house in this city cannot be got for less than $35 or $40. That would be six or seven rooms. Therefore, when the worker realizes he has to go to work and when he brings home his cheque at the end of the week, if he works every day and has no

sickness or drawbacks, he has a cheque for approximately $22. I tried very carefully and tried myself to keep myself, and at the end of the week I found I would be from $6 to $8 in debt; nothing for sickness or life insurance, nothing for the day when the crash comes, which every employee knows is surely coming. . . .

The worker coming home sees his children under-clothed. He dresses them up the best he can, and across the road he sees the people in the heights of luxury, driving around in limousines. I had this remark passed about my children; . . . their children came across the road to play with mine, and a woman came to the door and called them back, "Come away from those children, they are liable to be diseased." That remark was made to my children.

For the best part of my life I have been fighting for my country. I am drawing a life pension now. During the War I fought against labour organizations. There were placards: "Fight this War, and then come back and fight your own war." We are here to-day to fight our own war. . . .

Allan Snape, individual testimony, at Hamilton, May 21st
Q. Are you a mechanic? A. I am working as a boiler fireman now, labouring.

Q. Let us have your views. A. Well, I came to represent the lower grade, the grade that I will be in if I have the misfortune to lose the job I am at. As long as I work 77 hours a week and 365 days a year, I can keep myself from getting into it.

Q. What wages do you get? A. 33½, 2½ [cost of living] bonus; I am privileged.

Q. That is 36¢ an hour? A. Yes. . . .

Q. When did you get your last increase? A. I could not remember; it was just before the conclusion of the war.

Q. Is there any unemployment in this city? A. Oh, it is full of it. . . .

Q. How many would you say are unemployed? A. Over a thousand of my class.

Q. That is of unskilled labourers? A. Yes . . . .

Q. To what do you attribute that [unrest among the unemployed]?
A. Man's work has depreciated. I could work a couple of hours in 1914 and earn a screen door. Now I have to work 7 hours to earn a screen door. In 1914 I could earn a suit of clothes in a week. Now I have to work two weeks to earn it. . . . if I would go to work 5 days a week or 5½, I am ruined, but I tell you I am favoured; I am amongst the better class of labourers; the others get 30 and 32½ cents with the 2½¢ bonus. All over the city there is special firms that has a lot of money at their back, and they employ a lot, but it is not natural that a man would hire our labour at 36 if he can get them for 30; well, he can get them for 30; he can get them for anything . . . .

Q. Do you rent? A. No, I am trying to buy a house. I have tried to build it. I have borrowed money and built what I could myself; it is on the outskirts, but it is in the city, we have to live away back where land is cheap.

Q. Do you have sewer and water? A. Yes.

Q. What did the land cost you there? A. $300 for 25 feet, but that was in 1914. You have to pay $18 a foot for it now; it has gone up from $12 to $18.

Q. In the majority of cases that kind of land has gone down since 1914? A. But this has gone up. My house cost me about $850 to build . . . to build the same house now, I would have to pay $2000.

Q. But that is giving your own labour in building? A. Yes, I never counted my own labour in.

Q. And you think nobody else does? A. The plumber does; the lawyer and the doctor. My wife took sick . . . and of course after about six hours running about persuading the doctor to come, I got one, and I have got to save up now for six years to pay him for his half hour's work . . . .we have got to employ the skilled men and we have got to pay. We have no organization and have no representatives . . . .

Q. Then you think the lower class of worker is in a despairing condition? A. Yes, absolutely despairing. I just took one man and reckoned him up. He drew an average of $15 a week, if he was not sick . . . and before I allowed him any food, he had to spend $13 out of that $15, which left him $2 to dissipate on, but he had to buy food with that for himself and three children.

Q. Are you a married man? A. Yes.

Q. Wife and children? A. Yes; wife and one child now; I have had two; I have had sickness and lost one. . . .

Mrs Rose Henderson, non-Catholic Probation Officer of the Juvenile Court, at Montreal, May 29th

In the majority of these homes which I have investigated the father is earning only from $12 to $15 a week. Now, if we spread that $15 per week—if he works all the year, which in the majority of cases he does not on account of slackness of employment, one or two weeks out for sickness—and if we deduct from $60 a month, $12 for a three-roomed house, we leave an amount which approximately amounts to 8¢ a meal for feeding himself and his five children (average number) and for fuel, clothing, education, doctors' bills, transportation, amusements, etc.

We have just had a Baby Welfare Exhibition and during it mother after mother has come to me and said: " . . . what I want you ladies to tell me is, not what we are to do, but show us how we are to get the means to do it . . . " The wife of an organized machinist came with a baby of three months old. She said, "Where are we going? What is going to happen? How can I support my family? Before my baby was born my husband was earning $16, now he is earning $18, but before this baby was born we had to sit up nights to figure out how to meet doctor's bills; I had to keep my oldest girl at home from school—a very bright girl—she is behind in her studies and my husband is furious to think that we cannot send her back to school so she might get an education that would put her above the domestic servant class or perhaps allow her to be a school-teacher"...

...[T]he mothers are going out every day to help supplement the father's wage; the oldest child must stay at home to look after the family; the younger sons run the streets with no education or training, and so they come into the Court....

...[T]he dollar of 1917 [is worth] to-day between 38 and 48 cents... from 1912 to 1917 you could get 18½ lb. of bread for a dollar, to-day you can only get 11 pounds. Sago, tapioca, beans, sugar, rolled oats, herrings, halibut, potatoes, and all these things; cabbage in 1917, 20 heads for a dollar in 1912 and 17 in 1917, in 1918 only 8 heads. Potatoes, 4-5 pecks; now 2¼. The price of clothes is even higher.

All this, to my mind, is one of the most important and far-reaching of the causes of the present industrial unrest.

We might say that this unrest comes from two classes in particular: one is what I will call the "underdog", living on the verge of starvation—not removed three days from starvation; the other, the organized mass of labour who have had ideals of democracy dinned into their heads for the past four or five years and now realize that their sons fought for this democracy while they themselves remained at home and worked in munitions factories.... They are determined to have a greater measure of what they produce and greater advantages for themselves and their children....

The first law of life is self-preservation, we all must live, and we know from the statistics that the largest number of women who take to the streets are recruited from the domestic servant class. I think the domestic servant problem is the work that the woman is expected to do, the wages and the stigma attaching to it.... We have practically no labour laws. There are certain industries that have inspection but in a large number of industries children can work at almost any age, and often until eleven and twelve o'clock at night; take for instance messenger boys.

Q. What is the average wage of the woman worker in this town? A. I have never made an investigation that would be a good criterion; I investigated certain individuals in stores. Not long ago I found in the Montreal Light, Heat and Power Company they were paying as low as $6 a week.

Q. Adults? A. Yes.

Q. What were they doing? A. Various things; they have to live.

Q. Then you favour a minimum wage? A. Absolutely.

Q. You have not got one? A. Not yet....

The children we see in the Juvenile Court would generally be the children of men like elevator runners, men doing labour work, men in warehouses or driving trucks; men who are doing all sorts of unskilled labour.

Q. You said there were considerable numbers of boys and girls working for $3.50 a week; what age would they be? A. From 10 to 15 years.

Q. They are allowed to work at that age? A. Yes.

Q. There are no restrictions as to age? A. I believe that we have passed a law—I don't know if it is passed or will be passed next year—where they were raising the age to 16.

Q. You spoke of a 45% increase in the Juvenile Court cases this year. What number of homes would your investigation cover in 1918; what number earning $15 a week? A. At least 3500 homes.

Q. With an average family of? A. Five would be a moderate average, some eight and ten....

Q. Would it be fair to double the number of homes you have given us? A. Yes, absolutely.

Q. That is the class you say are but three days removed from starvation?

A. Yes.

Q. What would you say would be a typical house of that class? A. In what way?

Q. In the way of rooms. A. The average home has three rooms, some four.

Q. What sort, any water laid? A. Yes, but the sanitary conditions are very poor—no baths. Eighty percent, at the very least, have no hot water in their houses.

Q. What rent do they pay? A. The cheapest shack of three rooms is $12 at least; if in the centre of the city, $15 and $16, and in the latter case there is a roomer or two taken in....

Q. Have you made any survey as to the mortality of the children? A. ... The wards producing the greatest number of cases for the Juvenile Court also produce the greatest number of deaths—the two go together. Infant mortality continues in spite of the Child Welfare Societies and the Pure Milk Stations.

Q. You have the highest mortality in Canada here? A. Yes... I might also say that in a great many houses that I visit it is not the father who expresses himself; I find the real revolutionist is the mother—not the man. She says openly that there is nothing but Revolution. I was in a store the other day and heard two women talking. One of them said: "It is come, it is here." The other said, "What is here?" She said: "The revolution—look at the discontent—how can we feed our children? We never have enough money for three days!"...

Alex MacKay, representing steelworkers of Eastern Car Co., at New Glasgow, Nova Scotia, June 5th

...Although our plants in some respects are in good sanitary condition, in other respects conditions exist that imperil the health of the men. At the [railway car] Car Plant for instance, and the Car Plant is immeasurably better than the Steel Plant, numerous furnaces used for heating rivets and all sorts of iron, pour their smoke through the plant in a wigwam fashion. There are no chimneys or smokestacks to carry the smoke out of the Plant. It finds its way out or into the lungs of the men at its own sweet will. The smoke sometimes becomes so thick that it is difficult to see more than thirty feet, the windows become coated and sunshine cannot enter. The ground floors, tramped to dust, are never oiled, and when a compressed air line bursts, and it is a common occurrence, this dust is blown into clouds and is breathed in by the men....

[T]he press reports of the Winnipeg trouble are so incomplete that we are unable to decide just what is meant by "collective bargaining," but if it means that employers shall be compelled to do business with their employees, through the medium of a committee of representatives from the Union in which the men are organized, then that meets our needs and we give it our support. In the Steel and Car Plants the Companies meet our regular men's committee and many troublesome questions have been successfully negotiated. In spite of the fact that these committees are entirely Union men the Company refuse to recognize them as union committees.

The 8-hour day has been recognized by the Peace Conference as a justifiable work day throughout the world...[but] men are working here from 10 to 12 and 12¼ hours per day. Much of this work is near furnaces, rolling mills, and machines where the men work very hard in hot and poorly ventilated positions. At the end of the day these men leave their work tired and exhausted and needing 10 hours' sleep as a preparation for the next day's work.

What is left for the worthwhile things of life? Three hours! No wonder the workingman's yard is not turned into a garden, no wonder his children hardly know their own father, no wonder the merchants and idlers run the towns, no wonder the churches are empty of men.

This is an existence, but not a life. It is the heartless grinds of thousands of men who begin to work when they should be in school and keep it up until they are broken-down old men. No wonder men strike under such conditions....If we had the 8-hour day and Saturday afternoon off there would be none of this. Strikes would then be worked only as a last resort and not in any spirit of having a holiday.

POVERTY IN THE MIDST OF PLENTY

The 1920s brought prosperity to a few, but there was still disparity among the regions and massive poverty among the unskilled. Who was to blame? What was the minimum level for a 'living wage'? These were some of the questions investigated by this committee. It had been formed in response to the International Labour Organization conventions of 1919-20, and was spurred on by a tiny group of labour spokesmen, M.P.s J. S. Woodsworth, Rev. William Irvine, and A.A. Heaps. They found it almost impossible to shake the complacency of the middle class and the rural-born, whose solution to poverty was harder work and longer hours. What the committee did achieve was to educate some of the public on the absence of government welfare policies, the cycle of illness and poverty, and the need for minimum wages. Its positions were gradually accepted over the next two decades.

Canada, House of Commons, Committee on Industrial and International Relations, *Minutes of Proceedings and Evidence,* 1926. *Sessional Papers,* pp. 43-5, 83-9, 20-1, 102-12.

Testimony of Miss Margaret Gould, Research Director, Canadian Brotherhood of Railway Employees
...For some time before I went into research and cost-of-living work, I was a social worker in the city of Toronto, and had charge of a Family Welfare department which took care of all parts of the city. Toronto is a typical industrial city in Canada, perhaps the most typical together with Montreal. It is an industrial city, and workers live there to a great extent. There are typical working-class sections and typical poverty sections. The social worker sees the poverty sections because she is in a position where she has to deal with those who are down and out, who somehow have lost or missed their step in the race for decent living.

I found in hundreds of cases which came under my care, and that of my assistants, that there was a tremendous connection, a most vital connnection, between the amount of wages received in the family, and the effect on that family if wages are not enough to buy the things they need. I found that 50% of the cases which came for charity were those who were ill, and when I took the trouble to make a digest, in most of my families I found the cause of that illness was not enough food, and bad housing. Most of my cases were tubercular, and were undernourished, and we all know that many ills come from undernourishment....

In my own experience, which is only one of many in the country, I found that most of my families were in ill health or poverty because they never had enough to live on, throughout the time they were working or living. A lot of ill health was due to occupational diseases. I had one carpenter, for instance, who had blood poisoning, who was compelled to work at every available opportunity, and was not in a position where he could take a rest. If he had had enough leisure and sufficient air, with a decent house to live in—he lived in a hovel because he had eight children and earned $16.00 a week—if he had been able to go away annually for a few weeks, he might have headed off the disease which finally resulted in his death, the widowhood of his wife, and the orphaning of his children. . . .

There are two most important points with regard to poverty: insufficiency of food, and improper housing. Of course, improper clothing comes in too, because if you are not sufficiently warmly clad in the wintertime, you are susceptible to pneumonia, bronchitis, and you have neglected colds which result in tuberculosis. . . .

Another type of family which fell into poverty are those which are unemployed a good deal of the time, so that you might say that three-fourths of the poor families are suffering the ill effects of poverty simply because they never earn enough to make a sufficient living and keep themselves in health. . . .

Testimony of Mr C. W. Bolton, Department of Labour
Q. I want to interject something which is perhaps my own idea but based on my knowledge of social work, and I would like to know whether you can confirm this, that a very large number of lower-paid workers must certainly buy their clothing second-hand, some of it not very fit for wear? A. That is perhaps the third chief source of economy. I have mentioned economies in their food and housing. Then they will economize in their clothing in two ways: by going without what they can, and getting what they must have as cheap as possible, even if it is second-hand. There is another thing I was going to mention about the lack of food. It is well known, and I do not need to give it as my own opinion, and it is constantly referred to in this investigation, that children who are not properly fed do not get along at school, but leave school before they ought to, for instance when they are 14 they are only in Third book instead of being through. They never dream of going to high school, and they do not learn trades because they have not got the stamina and ambition to learn a trade. They drift into blind-alley occupations in order to supplement the family's income, and in many cases they come to a bad end, even getting into crime. . . .

Testimony of Mr Albert Hewitson, departmental superintendent, Canadian Colored Cottons Limited, Cornwall, Ont.
Q. How long have you been working in Cornwall? A. Twenty years next spring.
Q. And previous to that, were you employed at Hamilton and Dundas? A. Yes, Hamilton, Dundas, and Meritton. . . .
Q. How many women and girls would you say you have in your

department? A. Between ninety and a hundred in all. . . .

Q. What is the lowest wage you pay to any girl? A. In my department, $10 a week, that is, for an inexperienced girl about 13 years of age, that is the minimum. The law is that we cannot start them at less than $10 a week, that is $9 a week for the first six months and $10 a week for the next six months.

Q. And they can work up to what maximum? A. The maximum is $11 for an experienced adult female. . . .

Q. With regard to the minimum wage for girls, your opinion is that it is a reasonable amount to keep a girl in decency? Has it worked out apparently as a reasonable proposition? A. I have not tried to form any opinion on that. I cannot say right offhand, but I have never had any complaints of dissatisfaction. In fact, I have absolutely no trouble in getting girls. They prefer to work in my department for $10 a week, rather than some other department for $11 or $12. . . .

Q. The reference in our Resolution before this Committee is to the effect that the principle of the Minimum Wage as it applied to female labour should be extended to male labour. You have male labour in connection with your factory too? A. Yes.

Q. Do you think it would be a reasonable thing to set a minimum for the male as well as for the female? That is what we are getting at in this Committee. A. Well, I hardly agree with that, because as I say being head of a department, and having no trouble at all, I see no necessity for it. It appears to me personally that it is not giving the good man a chance. . . .

Q. What do you think a man ought to receive in your town in order to keep a family in decency? Have you any idea of the wages [for a family of five including three young children not old enough to become self-supporting]? A. I have young married men of that description working for me, and I have no trouble with them at all. They seem to be living. Some of them own motor boats, and they go down the river fishing on weekends and holidays, and all I have to pay them is $15 a week.

Q. Sixty dollars a month? A. Yes.

Q. You pay them $15 a week, and you pay all unmarried girls $10? A. Yes.

Q. Would you say that the expenses of a man and his wife and three children would not be greater than one-half as much as a girl's? A. Of course, but I am speaking about dissatisfaction. . . . I don't suppose they have any luxuries, but they seem to be quite happy and contented. . . .

Q. How many young unmarried men in the town that you live in, that you know, are running motor boats worth anywhere from $300 to $600, but also running automobiles, men working in your mill? A. I cannot say how many; I know there are two in my department.

Q. Do you mean to say that a motor boat has been purchased out of the earnings of a man who is getting only $15 a week? . . . How can a man and his wife and three children live and run a motor boat on $15 a week? A. I cannot see how they can, really. I am often amazed at what they do and just how they do it. I know they do it, but just how they do it, I cannot understand.

Q. Have you any idea of the monthly rental for the houses these families live in? A. There was a man working for me, with whom I was talking, who said he was paying $15, and they raised his rent to $17, and he said it was pretty hard, earning $15 a week and paying $17 a month rent. . . .

Q. What do the young unmarried men have to pay for room and board? A. $8 a week. . . .

Q. I know of a case at home [in Halifax] of a prominent firm who had two employees getting $17.50 a week, and who had motor cars. The firm feared pilfering and stealing, and they investigated. They found there was no opportunity for stealing, so the manager sent for these men and questioned them. Their explanation was this: they managed to buy the car, and the gas they used did not require as large an expenditure as going to the movies, and floating around the city. On holidays, and Sundays and evenings, they went out into the country and probably took their kettle with them, and some bread and jam, and it kept them from going to the movies, and they spent their extra money on the car rather than on the town sights. . . . They saved a little to buy it. They could buy a second-hand car for $500 or $600, or perhaps a new Ford. . . .

(Witness) The same condition exists right in Cornwall. You can go uptown and see the same faces from the industries. They cannot miss that moving picture, just as this gentleman says. Those who don't go to the movies spend their money for gasoline, for running down to the river to fish, and they would probably catch enough fish to feed them for half a week.

Q. Do any of them cultivate their own gardens? A. Yes, a great many of them. . . .

Q. Would these men who start at $15 a week gradually work up to $50? A. I am one of them. I started weaving in Dundas. My sister taught me to weave. From weaving I got to the loom-fixing, and from loom-fixing I got to second hand, and from second hand I got to be foreman, overseer of the loom. They took me from the weaving and put me in the finishing department. That is how I progressed in business. . . .

Q. How many of these men with lower salaries own their own homes? A. There are more at low salaries that own their own homes than there are with big salaries. . . . They do a lot of work themselves at night. They put them up much cheaper than I could put up a house myself. They would get together and have a "bee" and say, "We will put up another storey," or "we will put on the clapboards," and finally, they have mighty nice living quarters. . . .

Q. Have you had much of a migration from Cornwall to the States on account of the higher wages? A. There has been a lot go to Detroit, particularly the young men, but I would say 90% of those who went have landed right back home. That is not this year, but in the last two years. There have been a lot of young men that went to Detroit when the boom was on, but I think I am safe in saying that yes, 99% of them have come back home.

Q. What would you say about the appearance of the young women on the streets—the young women who work in your mill—as regards dress and comforts, compared with the best people in town, the very best citizens in the town? A. There is no question about it, if any of these gentlemen happened to take a walk through the town, they would say, "There is some dress here, some money here somewhere." They are getting their dresses from somewhere, and they are certainly dressed as good as my children. My children are not dressed as good as some of the others....

Q. Does not one of your sons work in the paper mill, or did for a while? A. Yes.

Q. In the machine shop? A. Yes. I think he gets 45 or 48 cents an hour or some thing like that. Of course, in the paper mill their wages are about the same as ours. We have to keep the standard of wages pretty close to one another, because if we did not there would be too much changing.... There are higher-paid men in the paper industry than in the cotton industry because there is heavier work.

Q. And steady employment? A. Yes.

Q. Twelve months a year? A. Twelve months a year. There is absolutely no appearance of poverty in Cornwall....

Q. You work 50 hours a week? A. Nine hours for 5 days, and five hours on Saturday....

Q. Would the average family connected with the industrial establishment about which you are giving evidence have sufficient money to see to the education of members of the family, if any of the members wish to go forward in school? I think that is an important thing, that there be something in that family with which to equip the children of that family, if they wish to go into another channel of life, and not be tied up forever and a day to a particular industrial establishment. A. There are a great many of which I know in the east end of town who are sending their children to high school or to business college at the present time.... There have been a good many, but my idea is different from some others. Take my own two boys, for instance: there is no man who would have done more than I would for them. I would have gone without shoes to help them get an education, but they would not have it. You find in most families in Cornwall, there are some who will not have an education. They see other young fellows who are working out with their motor boats and having money to spend, and they want to get to working themselves. A working man cannot send his boy to college and give him a college education and hand him out money to spend, and there are many boys who will not sacrifice that little pleasure for an education. My own two boys would not have it. . . .

'STANDING THE GAFF': CAPE BRETON STRIKERS' FAMILIES, 1924-1925

For Cape Breton miners and their families, the mid-1920s were not a time of prosperity but a continuation of the crisis of 1919 (referred to in Mathers commission testimony). The Maritimes had never been really prosperous since the 1850s; and there were no alternatives but subsistence farming and fishing, or exodus. This article reminds us of the terrible suffering that prolonged unemployment or strikes could bring to workers' wives and children.

K. Crone, 'Twelve Thousand on Rations', *Canadian Congress Journal,* vol. IV (April 1925), 13-14.

Twelve thousand men, women and children in the mining districts of Nova Scotia, most of them within a radius of twenty miles, are dependent for their existence on the rations issued by the relief committees.

At that, the rations, in the words of Rev. Dr. McAvoy, Chairman of the Central Relief Committee at Glace Bay, are "just enough to hold body and soul together."

If the relief in money and kind that is being contributed from many parts of Canada were to slow up or stop, under present conditions, there would be wholesale starvation and God knows what else in the way of tragedy.

SITUATION BECOMING WORSE

The Glace Bay Committee was two thousand dollars in the hole last Saturday; that is, the members of the Committee had felt obliged by the urgencies of the case to buy food costing that much, although they had no means to pay for it.

The situation is becoming worse every day, as more and more families reach the limit of their scanty resources. Heroic struggles to keep off "the relief" from a sense of pride and independence are numerous.

While I was with a relief worker yesterday a man came up to us, hesitatingly, and with evident dislike of his mission. "I have stood the gaff for five weeks," he said, "but I'm beaten at last. You know we said we'd be damned if we'd take anybody's charity. The Lord only knows what the missis and the four kids and myself have stood. The children are wondering why other children can get food through the relief stations and they get nothing to eat. The missus and myself can suffer, but it's hell to see the youngsters suffering. So I want you to put my family on the relief. Some day, maybe, we'll pay it back. We'll try, anyway."

NO FOOD FOR SPARROWS

Even the sparrows have a hard time to live in the Sydney Mines and Glace Bay districts. Every accumulation of garbage has been picked over by human beings who needed food. Women and children have been on the railway tracks gathering the seeds of grain that have fallen from the cars en route to the stables of the pit ponies. Roots of all sorts have been dug out of the ground and cooked into messes that had a resemblance to food.

Fortunately coal can be got by digging the outcrops on the hillsides. Groups of miners get together and make small shafts of their own, while women and children carry the coal away in bags or boxes. Much fuel is needed, one reason being that many of the houses are so damp that fires must be kept constantly going, and another is that the soft coal of the districts burns away quickly.

CLOTHING AND BEDDING

Clothing and bedding—mostly second hand, of course—are beginning to arrive at the relief stations in fairly large quantities from different parts of the Dominion. Local resources in that line have long since been exhausted, and it will be some time before the outside relief begins to meet the local necessities.

It has to be remembered that the destitution is a matter of growth across three years of short-time work, that in the last four months thousands of the miners have been able to get only one to three shifts a week, and that the complete stoppage of the mines in the beginning of March was merely a culmination of a long siege. Practically no bedding or clothing has been bought for three years,—the people have been lucky if they had food and fuel alone—and the result is that a large proportion of the population is in dire straits for bed and personal covering. Many children have been all winter without shoes and stockings, many without even a stitch of underclothing. Bedding, where it exists—often it is non-existent—is frequently a mixtures of rags. Some of the most unusual costumes, improvised out of any fabric handy, are worn by miners and their families. A rather extraordinary feature of this situation is that practically every house has clean white curtains, even if they are only of cheesecloth or have more patches than original material. It is not until one gets inside the houses that one has any adequate idea of the misery behind the clean white curtains. It is a tribute to the natural decency of the people that most of them try to conceal their difficulties from the outside world.

BAD HOUSING CONDITIONS

Housing conditions as a rule are third-rate. It is not expected that mining towns and villages will resemble the prosperous, or at least nice and comfortable, suburbs of large cities. One might expect them to be some-what crude and frowsy. But one hardly expects the meanness, the bleak-ness, the wreckage and the insanitary conditions that are to be found in rather large and oppressive measure.

There is comparatively little sickness in the mining districts, much less than might be anticipated to go with the other conditions of life there. This is partly explained by the fact that the homes are on the edge of the Atlantic Ocean, that the people are obviously a hardy lot hereditarily, most of them descendants of Highland Scottish crofters who were immigrants a century and more ago, while the process, too, of the survival of the fittest has doubtless played its part in moulding the present genera-tion.

A DECEPTIVE QUIETNESS

As in matters of physical hurt, where the noisiest are usually the least injured and the most dangerous cases are the silent ones, so is it with these mining localities. The streets are quiet, there is no excitement in the spoken word. It might almost seem, in a casual look around, as if the clear fresh winds of the sea were aiding in the telling of the tale that all is peace and tranquility. But the close examiner knows how utterly false and misleading are outward appearances, and how grave a disorder lies behind apparent patience and contentment.

General business, and the ordinary activities of social and municipal life, are almost at a standstill, for nearly everyone and everything depends more or less directly on the mines, which, with the steel indus-try, are the basic industries of Cape Breton. Merchants have failed; others merely grub along. Most of the municipal taxes are unpaid and uncollectible. School teachers, and policemen and firemen, are a month behind in their wages, and thank their stars things are as good as that. The churches no longer take up collections for purely church purposes; practically every sort of collection is for the immediate meeting of human necessity. At the close of a Salvation Army meeting on the main street of Glace Bay, after the band had played and the "testimonies" had been given, the officer in charge said to the crowd around: "There will be no collection, friends. We know you've got no money."

DAILY PAPER A LUXURY

A daily paper is a luxury. A pipeful of tobacco or a cigarette is a gift of the gods. No one drinks strong drink because there is no money to pay for drink.

Nearly every soul in the communities is either "on relief" or voluntarily "working in relief"; many miners are both "on relief" and "in relief".

Clerics of all denominations, Y.M.C.A. workers, Salvation Army workers, bankers, miners, editors, aldermen, postmen, lawyers, shop-keepers— all sorts and conditions of men and their wives and grown-up children— are working together in the relief stations. Misfortune has developed a fine community spirit and very efficient organization of relief forces and methods.

The merits of the strike or lock-out itself do not matter. Human beings are in great need and all kinds of hearts have opened to think of human service.

WHO IS TO BLAME? CHARITY IMMIGRATION UNDER ATTACK

The abuses of contract labour were not only inflicted upon adults. This speech by Woodsworth as leader of the Ginger Group in the House of Commons makes clear that immigration schemes for pauper children by charitable organizations were often a thinly disguised form of slavery.

J. S. Woodsworth, 'Child Labour', *Canadian Congress Journal*, vol. III (May 1924), 9-12.

The Department of Immigration attempts to give the impression that in encouraging child immigrants we are actuated by high and disinterested motives; it appeals to our patriotic and humanitarian sentiments....

But is the welfare of these children the real object of the Department?

As we read on in the report there grows upon one the suspicion that the real reason for developing our juvenile immigration is that we may be provided here with cheap child labor. Expressions are used with regard to the distribution of young workers, with regard to their services. It also says:

"The importation of thousands of boys and girls of ages varying from fourteen to eighteen years, will in a large measure meet the needs of Canada in respect to farm and domestic labor."

The report further points out that of these children who come 1,426 are wage-earning. The total wages paid to the above children amount to

$173,190; that is, they are employed at an average of a little over $100 each per year. It is a serious situation; as I have said, we import these children under the guise of philanthropy and turn them into cheap child laborers.

As regards these children who come from respectable homes of the workers of Great Britain, I may say that at the present time in England there is a very strong protest being made against allowing their migration. It is being felt over in the Old Land that children should not be forced to leave respectable homes there and be sent to this country.

Again quoting from report:

"There are openings throughout the Dominion for British children of all ages but of course these openings are affected by the positions the children are expected to fill on arrival here, viz.; helpers from ten to thirteen years of age placed under principle of adoption or boarded out— various ages up to fourteen—workers fourteen to seventeen and over."

And again:

"The most suitable ages to send a child to Canada for service are from five to fourteen years for boys, and from thirteen to sixteen for girls."

Do we propose in Canada to import children for service from the tender age of five years up to the age of fourteen for boys, and of the age from thirteen to sixteen for girls?

We have had within the last twelve months, both in western Canada and in the province of Ontario, a very considerable number of cases in which children who have been brought to this country have suffered very greatly at the hands of some of the foster parents and of their employers, a few of the children having been driven to commit suicide. The problem was discussed at great length last autumn at a Child Welfare Conference held at the city of Winnipeg at which reports were presented from the various child caring agencies in all parts of Canada. From the statistics there presented, and the investigations which were subsequently made, I should like to quote a few statements. The question was asked very clearly at this conference: "Does Canadian public opinion countenance importation of child laborers into this country?" And then the report from which I quote goes on to say:

"The social workers of this Dominion are more than half convinced that, under the guise of child immigration, child exploitation is not only tolerated, but actually assisted by Canada's present juvenile immigration policy which has been followed for the past twenty years."

If the idea is to settle children in farm homes across the country, the question that the child welfare workers asked in this conference was "Why not so settle the children that are already in our own homes in Canada." . . .

This brings us to our second problem. What affect has the coming of these immigrant children on the welfare of Canada?

We have from time to time had a good deal of discussion as to the character of the live stock we admit into this country. We have had a good deal of discussion with regard to the maintenance of a high standard of seed grain and that kind of thing, but apparently we have not yet taken it into consideration that it is tremendously important that we should have as high a class as possible of human beings if we are to develop in this country a high grade of Canadian citizenship. For some years I had considerable to do with the immigrant people of western Canada, perhaps particularly with the younger people among the immigrants, for some time having to make investigations with regard to the character of these immigrants. No one can come into close contact with the peoples coming to this country without recognizing that we have been altogether too slack in regard to the character of our immigrants. I do not wish to impress my own personal views upon the House, but propose rather to quote a few passages from the second interim report of the Public Welfare Commission of Manitoba, as printed by the order of the legislative assembly of Manitoba, in February, 1919:

"A careful study of the figures regarding the nationality of the various persons examined makes it more than evident that Canada has received an undue share of immigrants who, under a proper system of inspection, would not have been allowed to enter this country. Those familiar with social conditions among the defective classes realized that the welfare of the nation is seriously threatened by the influx of undesirables, and a brief survey of the facts obtained in Manitoba are of interest. Let us consider those in regard to illegitimacy, defectives and delinquents, as under these three headings we shall find grouped the worst of the imported classes. In considering these facts it must always be remembered that the Canadian population of Manitoba is 46 per cent of the whole. In other words, the foreign born outnumber the native born by almost three per cent. . . . To deal with the jail population of the province, taking 400 consecutive admissions to the jails, what do we find? Twenty-three per cent are of Canadian birth, while the Austrians, who should, under normal conditions, only number eight per cent, rise to thirty-three per cent of the total; and the Russians, who should number 1 per cent, contribute 11 per cent."

It is not clear from these figures as to what is the underlying reason that these foreigners should contribute a larger per cent to the jail population. It may be, and in my own judgment, it is, very largely owing to the fact that we have rather bad social conditions to which these people come, and we have not yet provided the machinery for welding them into our Canadian citizenship; but it may also be, and to a certain extent I think it is, true, that some of them come of a stock that is not altogether desirable, or that their children when first introduced into this country are not able to fit into our life here.

Taking another table—there are a number given here, and I shall quote from only a few:

"Nationality of 269 unmarried mothers in Grace Hospital and Misericordia Hospital during the past year: British, 44.23 per cent; Canada, 25.76 per cent; United States, 9.23 per cent."

And so on. I will not give the smaller percentages. The comment is:

"It is somewhat surprising to find such a proportion of British born among these mothers of illegitimate children, but comparing the figures with those of a study of 266 cases in the last two years in one Ontario hospital, we find the most striking similarity; in Manitoba, 44 per cent; in Ontario, 40 per cent. When we study the character of much of the immigration we are in a position to make clear some reasons why such burdens have been imposed upon a long-suffering public. In the craze for numbers we have allowed quantity rather than quality to be the slogan, and no better illustration can be brought forward than that furnished by a brief survey of the 266 Ontario cases. Eighteen (22.75 per cent) of the British born mothers were brought to Canada by one well-known home which has already foisted an immense number of defectives on the Canadian public, as the records of criminality and deficiency will show...."

Quoting from the report of the Supervisor of Juvenile Immigration:

"The children come largely from overcrowded centres of population, London and the surrounding towns supplying the greater proportion of the children in the homes."

Some of us who have lived in the slums of East London and have visited some of the institutions there, who have lived among the people in their homes, while having every sympathy with the poor there cannot view with any great equanimity the bringing over of that class into Canada with the idea of building up a strong Canadian public.

On the question of mental deficiency let me bring to your attention data collected by Canadian social workers.

"We submit the evidence of a few of the clinics maintained in Canada, in support of our contention that adequate precaution is not being observed in this field of immigration.

"In one general health clinic in Toronto alone, 128 cases of juvenile immigration brought out in recent years by the same agency have required attention. Of these 23 were boys and 105 girls. Their story of social disaster is briefly summarized,—

"Of the girls, 105—40 per cent confirmed prostitutes, 25 per cent venereally diseased, 70 have had 94 illegitimate children, 95 per cent examined mentally abnormal.

"Of the boys, 23—2 known to have had venereal disease, 95 per cent examined mentally abnormal."

'FREE LAND DETERMINES THE MINIMUM WAGE':
A POLISH HOMESTEADER, 1926-1933

In the 1915 Report on the Cost of Living, government officials argued that free land made minimum-wage laws unnecessary—there was always employment on the agricultural frontier; most native Canadians had been brought up on hard farm work. In the 1920s Canada was still a paradise for those from middle Europe, and for many peasants, emigration was an escape from feudalism to the exalted status of landowner. Yet with the best land taken, mortgages at almost three times normal interest rates, and the great drought at the end of the decade, the dream was fading. The writer is typical of the post-1919 immigrant in his Catholic conservatism, ethnic pride, and aspirations for his children as 'new Canadians'.

Pamietniki Emigrantow Canada (Institute of Source Economy, Warsaw, 1971). Memoir 9, dated 18 Nov. 1936. Courtesy of Professor A. L. Balawyder, Saint Francis Xavier University.

Wonderful was the morning of August 4, 1926. . . . when I left my parental home. My parents, brothers and sisters cried and lamented on my departure. And when I sat on a wagon which took me to the train almost everybody from the village for about one kilometer cried as if it were a funeral. My parents felt that we would never see one another again.

I arrived at Lvov and immediately went to the Immigration Bureau. It was extremely crowded here. Despite the chaos our documents were processed and we were on our way to Warsaw from whence we travelled to Danzig, where we took a boat. After twenty days of journey I saw the shores of Canada. When I arrived at the port of Quebec I felt that at last I was on "firm footing." Leaving the ship I entered a reception building where my documents were again examined. And from here a day later I left for Edmonton to which destination my ticket was paid. Here the Bureau of Immigration was to provide me with gainful employment. The times were good and work was plentiful. As the saying goes: "the worker did not have to search for work, work searched the worker." Everywhere salaries were favourable, factories were in full operation making Canada a paradise. On the second day after my arrival I was despatched to a Czech farmer. . .

After finishing my work at this Czech's place I travelled to another town where a distant relative lived. Unfortunately the harvest seemed to be over as snow began to fall. I worked for a German farmer who spoke Polish. During the winter months I received ten dollars a month and from spring to October I was paid fifty dollars. I worked here for two years and earned eight hundred dollars. Indeed I had enough money to pay a deposit on a farm which I purchased [about 1929] near Landis

Saskatchewan and to bring my family to Canada.

When we operated our farm we did not have much. We bought immediately a bed, two chairs, a cast-iron stove ... All of this cost us one hundred dollars; the stove itself cost us fifty dollars. For a long time we used a trunk for a table until I made one. I also made a cupboard, a clothes closet and a washing cupboard. The lumber, paint and the nails cost me ten dollars whereas new ones would have cost me sixty dollars.

When I arrived on the farm I did not have horses, or machinery. Since I did not have enough money to pay cash I bought on credit four horses at three hundred dollars, harnesses for forty dollars, a wagon for sixty dollars, plough for thirty dollars and harrows for sixteen dollars. For all of this I paid a deposit of one hundred and eighty dollars and the rest I agreed to pay in due time with eight percent interest ... In spring I bought another horse because I needed five horses for ploughing.

I cultivated one hundred acres ... Because of the short growing season grain stocks were frequently left on the field over winter. In spring farmers had extra work. In April I would begin to cultivate my land; it took me twenty days to plough one hundred acres. Once ploughed I borrowed a seed-drill because by hand it would have taken too much time. By the seed-drill I was able to seed twenty acres daily ... Once sown I begged God for good crop for it was with such a good crop that I could pay my debts. I paid one dollar and twenty cents a bushel for seed grain.

Generally speaking the land yielded about twenty bushels an acre ... some 2,000 bushels in all. Half of the money I received (a bushel sold at fifty two cents) was paid for threshing; machine and other expenses; some for defraying the loan on the farm. I paid the thresher ten cents a bushel for wheat and seven cents per bushel for oats.

The year which is deeply engraved in my mind is 1933. The winter was cold with little snow. Already we felt that things would not turn out right. The spring was early as people began to work on land in April. When I was seeding rain interfered with the operation making it difficult to complete my work. I managed to sow one hundred and fifty acres of wheat and forty acres of oats. The people rejoiced at the appearance of the crop. At the beginning the people rejoiced at the sight of the new growing crop; but this joy was turned to sadness as time went on and no rain came. On several occasions we thought that the black clouds would bring us rain. Instead they were but clouds of dust. During the entire summer the sun poured down scorching every semblance of vegetation. From one hundred and fifty acres I was able to thresh but one hundred and eight bushels. There were no potatoes, no cabbages. I was unable to pay my taxes; I had no money for clothing. Finally I did accept government "relief" ... We received one hundred and twenty bushels of oats for the horses and some thirty bushels for seeding. We also received two tons of coal and warm clothing for the winter... There were four of us, for we had two children now. We received from "relief" two dollars a month. Thanks to the fact that we had two cows and about one hundred chickens... therefore we were able to get eggs and butter. What type of relief was it when one had to repay it at eight per cent interest... To make it worse my wife got sick and was laid up for three weeks. I brought a doctor from a small town. I was unable to pay for the medicine. The doctor who knew me arranged for the municipality to pay for his service and for the medicine.

And although I lived among strangers I was well served by them. They willingly lent me things and brought me the mail from the post office. The neighbourhood consisted of Poles, Russians and Doukhobors. The children were taught in English but after school hours they received Polish or Russian tutoring. Religion was taught by the priest in the parish church. And I am extremely satisfied to know that my children will be brought up as Catholics as I am... I think it is much better here than in Poland for there is opportunity for poor men as well. There will always be bread, potatoes and meat. A number of our friends did go to Poland only to return to Canada.

I am glad that [my children] will be able to speak and write in Polish. Our children speak both English and Polish. Although we subscribe to English newspapers, we do read Polish ones as well even though they are rather expensive. When the children grow up they will be able to read Polish books which I brought with me to Canada.

WHY DO WORKERS REJECT RADICALISM?

Despite the sufferings of the Dirty Thirties, why did so few join the Co-operative Commonwealth Federation, the Workers' Unity League, or later the CIO unions? Immigrants might hesitate to for fear of deportation, but what about the native-born? Ingrained conservatism was a traditional work-ing-class attitude, as this study of farm boys and small-town workers in Canada's industrial heartland makes clear.

L. A. MacKay, 'The Ontario Small-Town Labourer and Farm-Hand', *The Canadian Forum*, vol. XII, no. 37 (Feb. 1932), 174. Reprinted by permission of The Canadian Forum.

I have no qualifications for a formal or statistical survey of the condi-tion of these people, but the fact that I was one of them for the greater part of my life, and that I have still many friends and relatives among them, gives me, I believe, some right to speak as one of them, of their mental attitude towards some social and economic problems.

I believe that our fundamental approach to this problem is often quite misunderstood both by our critics and by our would-be defenders. Neither, it seems, realizes sufficiently how small a part avarice and ambition play in our outlook. Our strongest impelling motive is simply fear, a haunted quest for security. When that shadow falls for a moment into the background, we think of little but the immediate enjoyment of life. We have, in the mass, comparatively little rancour, and not much interest in general ideas, political or other.

We do not feel that it is degrading to work for a boss; our self-respect is too robust a plant to be affected by such an irrelevant consideration. Rather we enjoy being free of his responsibility. We are not envious or resentful of greater wealth, except in a very superficial way. We admire and envy the skill of the man that can amass riches, as we admire and envy the skill of the musician or the artist; but we do not resent it, unless we feel ourselves to have been outrageously victimized in its acquisition— which we seldom do.

We have an extremely realistic, moderate, and philosophic attitude towards wealth and leisure. All we want is to be reasonably sure of comparatively simple food and housing, with a decent amount of leisure for our rather inexpensive amusements, and we can look on with an amused tolerance at the struggles of our betters for wealth and power. If it amuses them, very well. To us, the reward doesn't seem worth all that effort. We can attain with much less trouble than that, the forms of happiness which we value most; and the formal living conditions that financial success seems to bring with it, would be frankly distasteful to us.

We are vaguely suspicious of Socialism, as involving too much regimentation and too much responsibility. If our masters would only get together and add to the existing system, by whatever means they chose, some provision that would exorcise the fear of destitution, and loss of our simple pleasures, whether in old age or in the prime of life, we should go on doing a reasonable day's work for them, quite readily, with a reasonable amount of holidays, not caring in the slightest how much money they made for themselves in the meantime.

If they are worried about our numbers, let them give us the necessary information, and we will soon limit our own increase to the most advantageous proportion. In the matter of procreation, we, like them, are far more interested in the process than in the product. It is not we that would raise the religious objection. Whether we belong nominally to the Protestant, the Anglican, or the Roman communions, we are far more free from the domination of our spiritual guides, outside the field that we vaguely but firmly mark out for ourselves as properly spiritual, than even our own fellows of other communions ever realize—a fact that any priest or minister will regretfully corroborate. Our practical ethic is a far older, more selfish, more easy-going ideal than that of Christianity.

Let our masters only free us from the driving obsession of destitution, assuring us of a reasonable amount of wages, freedom, and leisure—and our idea of what is reasonable is quite amazingly moderate—and they would find us quite docile, though not at all servile, and much more simply and sustainedly happy than themselves. We have no idea how it is to be done. It is their job to figure that out; they have that kind of brain, and we haven't. We can't speak for the city-workers either, whom we feel to be somehow different, though we suspect them to be fundamentally very like ourselves. We know that we throw up occasional biological sports who belong by temperament to the ambitious class. These we feel should have every opportunity of exercising their talent; these too we admire tolerantly, somewhat condescendingly, but do not really envy.

If our masters will only secure us, as we feel they could if they put their minds to it, some system that would give us the maximum of security, with the minimum of responsibility and the minimum of inter-ference, Private Capitalism may go on to the Day of Doom and after, for all we care.

THE MAKING OF A RADICAL: WINNIPEG IN THE 1930s

The class consciousness of North-End Winnipeg stands in sharp contrast to that of the WASP small town. Left-wing politics was often a family tradition. Radicalized like many immigrants of his generation by the Russian revolts and pogroms of 1905, Jake Penner was thrust into prominence during the 1919 Winnipeg Strike, and became a 'red' alderman in 1932. His son Norman followed him into the Party, and was one of its inner circle until his break with the Communists in 1956.

Norman Penner Interview, by Steven Penner, at Toronto, 1972.

—We lived in [West Kildonan] a suburb of Winnipeg, a little north of Winnipeg. It was very sparsely populated. Most of the people who lived in this suburb were war veterans from Britain who had emigrated to Canada after the First World War with their families. Although my mother and my father had come over to Canada—my father in 1903 and my mother in 1905—these people considered us as foreigners. One of my earliest recollections is of them very often throwing stones at our house and calling us foreigners and telling us to go back where we came from. Another recollection I have is of these same people deciding that they were going to rescue myself and my brother from atheistic parents. They were going to get us into church and they got us into church. They got us into Sunday School and they got us into revival meetings in the church, which was not too far from where we lived. My father knew nothing of this.

—How did they get you to go?

—Well they just persuaded us, they'd come over and talk to us and made it sound very attractive. They mentioned the fact that I shouldn't tell my father about it, and they showed us lantern slides about the life of Jesus and all that. I might say that it didn't make too much of an impression on me except the solicitude of these people, and the fact that we had to get all dressed up, and the fact that there was an element of conspiracy about it. One Sunday my father was passing the church and saw my brother and myself coming out, and when we got home he sat us down and said, all right, I don't want you to go to church any more. If you're going anywhere, go to the Young Pioneers. The Young Pioneers was a communist children's organization that had been set up after a pattern that they had used in Russia. It was the Russian version of the Boy Scouts with uniforms and red kerchiefs and so on, that type of activity plus communist indoctrination. So the next Sunday, instead of going to church, we went to the Pioneers. We found it quite attractive. We learned songs, revolutionary songs. We learned all about the life of Lenin and, after being in the Young Pioneers for about a year, I was asked to make a speech at the Lenin Memorial Meeting. . . . I was eight. I was about a month away from my ninth birthday. My father wrote out my speech, I memorized it, delivered it with great enthusiasm to an audience of about 500 people, and after that I became in demand as a child speaker, a silver-tongued child orator. At the age of 12 I addressed a meeting of about 10,000 unemployed workers in front of the Manitoba Legislature just before a delegation had gone in to see the premier, Bracken. I did quite a bit of speaking in those years, from the age of nine when I started, to about the age of fourteen when I was featured on the program when Tim Buck got out of Kingston Penitentiary and came to Winnipeg. He was given a tremendous reception, about 6,000 people at the C.P.R. railway station. When he spoke that night in the Winnipeg Auditorium, I greeted him "on behalf of all the people of Winnipeg". I was 14 at the time. . . .

—How did you feel about being treated as a foreigner by the people there, being ostracized by the people in the community?

—I was quite mad and I used to fight back because I had just as much right, if not more so, to be in the country. I considered myself a

Canadian. I considered my father a Canadian and my mother a Canadian.... We lived in a small house. It was one of several dozen houses
that were owned by the Reeve of West Kildonan. He used to come
around once a month to collect the rent. We paid $25.00 a month. By
present standards it certainly was a poorly equipped house, no hot water,
no basement, a Quebec heater, but as compared to some of the houses
that were in the slum areas of Winnipeg, it was not too bad. My father
never earned very much money. He was always rather on the poor side.
But we never did live in the slums. He always managed to get us a
modest place, but clean and, well, maybe I wouldn't use the word
comfortable, but at least half-decent. What I do remember is that when I
was a child, for some reason or other, I got one sickness after another,
diphtheria, scarlet fever, and a number of other things that required
hospitalization. And because we lived in the suburbs, we had to go to the
hospitals in Winnipeg and pay. Of course my mother and father didn't
have the money to pay and they were saddled with a great debt as the
result of the excessive hospitalization of mine, which they never did pay
off until after the Second World War.

—How was your father making a living at that time?

—When we lived in West Kildonan he was a salesman for a wholesale
hardware, although my mother used to tell us that every time he earned
commission, half of it went to the Party and half of it went to the family,
and that he spent more time propagandizing his customers than actually
selling to them. When we moved into the city, Winnipeg itself, in 1930,
the Communist Party opened up a creamery in Winnipeg and my father
became the accountant in the company. That was the first good job he
had had up to that time that I know about.... He was working as the
book-keeper or accountant at this Creamery and making a fairly good
wage by depression standards, and then he got elected to the Winnipeg
City Council in 1932, took his seat January 1933, and lived off the
alderman's wages, which were not terribly high but at least better than a
lot of people who were on relief or working in a factory were getting....

North Winnipeg was actually a sociologist's dream. I mean, you had
every type of person there. It had a unique flavour of militant radicalism.
There were an awful lot of Jewish people living there and Ukrainians
and Germans, and then there was a sprinkling of Anglo-Saxons. The
place was dotted with immigrants' halls both of the left element and of
the right element. People took their politics very seriously there right
from high school up, and that area produced a lot of labour leaders,
members of parliament, members of the legislature. In fact, at times
during the depression, there were six elected from each ward to the City
Council, three each for a 2-year term. My father was elected for 2 years
and then at the next election, next year, there would be three running
and they would be elected for two years, so out of the six, probably, at

one point, I think, all of the six were Labour and Communist, but at any rate the majority always were....

One thing happened the year that we moved that only coincidentally was connected with the fact that we moved. I was in Grade 4 at that time and in the school to which I was transferred, they had manual training which they never had in the West Kildonan schools. [North Winnipeg] had a very well equipped wood-working shop and I went there once a week with the rest of the class. We made scissor-holders, window props, little end tables. The wood-working instructor was a fascist. He was actually a member of an organization that had sprung up called the Canadian Union of Fascists led by a man named Whittaker, and wearing brown shirts and swastikas, and this man was one of them. He was a tall, strapping-looking fellow. He looked something like Horst Wessel, and used to beat me up regularly in the wood-working class. He would call me up to the front and before the whole class would say, "Well, Penner, I hear that they shot poor people in Russia for stealing some jam." As soon as I opened my mouth to answer him, he whacked me over the shoulder with a stick. He was a sadist. So finally I couldn't stand it any longer. I went to see the principal. I told the principal that not only was the man persecuting me, but hitting me, inflicting terrible corporal punishment on me, and everything I used to make he'd break, so the principal said "Why is he doing that?' I said "Because I'm a communist." He said "You're a what?" "I'm a communist." He closed the door and he said "So am I." He wasn't a member of the Communist Party because I asked my father, but he was caught up in the radical politics of North Winnipeg and especially at that time in the midst of the depression, there was a very big upsurge in radical politics in North Winnipeg. The beating stopped although this fascist teacher remained as a teacher, so that was my first introduction to the city of Winnipeg....

But I wasn't really involved in politics in the schools until I got into high school, and the high school that I went to, St. John's Technical High School, was a radical's paradise. A lot of the teachers were radicals, a tremendous number of the students were. One of the teachers was the very famous radical R. J. Johns, who was leader of the 1919 general strike and had been fired from his job as a machinist, but got a job later as a vocational instructor and became a pioneer of vocational training in Winnipeg. At that time he was a teacher of industrial arts in the shops, the wood-working and metal shops in the St. John's Tech., and he was looked upon as quite a hero by a lot of the students.... I was President of the Debating Society and the debates had become a very popular activity. As president of the Debating Society, I always used to arrange the topics and decide in such a manner to give my side the advantage. I remember one debate "Resolved that Communism is a Menace to Society," where we had the very best debaters in the school take the negative and the worst debaters take the affirmative. We would have 400 or 500 kids out for the debate and this became a weekly feature. We had some tremendous debates. Then we used to run for school council under political slogans. I was elected vice-president of the school, running against the principal's son, although the principal was not a bad fellow at all. He was a CCFer and later on became a member of the board of education as a CCFer. A lot of us, communist and non-communist radicals, used to consider it was necessary for us to point out to the students where the teachers were going wrong in history or literature and to put forward a radical point of view in contradiction to what the teacher was trying to put across. I remember once the history teacher said we were going to have a lecture on Irish history. None of us knew anything about Irish history but six of us got together the night before and went over all the communist publications we could get our hands on about Ireland, and we kept peppering this guy with questions that he had never heard before, and we used to consider that this was part of our duty to do that. . . .

I had joined the Young Communist League when I got into high school, and became very quickly the Y.C.L. High School Student Organizer, responsible for developing the Y.C.L. "cells" in all the high schools in Winnipeg. And then I also got involved, as part of this, in the work around the Spanish Civil War, which started in 1936, and we had quite a wide variety of activities in high schools in aid of Spain and then later on in aid of the Mackenzie-Papineau Battalion. I developed there, as a leader of the Y.C.L., what we called the High School Parliaments where we simulated the actual operation of the House of Commons. . . .

3
Women's Work

Though women were an essential part of the Canadian working class, their status both at home and at work was that of a group separate and unequal. In the first sixty years of this century only a handful of women wage-earners were organized, and still fewer held union office. Indeed the woman worker was widely regarded as marginal, temporary, and lacking in militancy. That this could be a misleading assumption is shown not only by the occasional strike early in the 1900s—textile workers, garment workers, and telephone operators participated in hard and partly successful battles—but by the choices that thousands of women over several generations made by moving from one occupation to another. In this respect they, like the vast majority of unorganized males, were 'voting with their feet'. It was virtually the only choice they had. At home and at work women faced incredibly long hours, sweated and often dirty conditions, and starvation wages; above all, they had virtually no control over their own lives.

In 1900 the largest number of women workers were domestics. Since a cot and food were supplied, their wages were pitifully scant—pennies a day. And because most household service had a very low status, entry into a factory was a kind of liberation.

Industry, however, was characterized by the sweatshop and the smoke-blackened textile mill. In earlier days, and on the fringes of the still-expanding factory system, it was possible for women in small towns to combine factory work with their traditional roles in family and community. Hours were flexible, and home close by. But by the early decades of this century the scale of industry was often becoming too large, its pace and discipline too intense.

The wage-earning girl and the working mother were nineteenth-century traditions. For the poor, female wages had become essential to survival, even while the entry of more women into the industrial work force depressed the levels of pay.

The major changes of the twentieth century in the employment of women were in the types of industry in which they worked, and in the widening of the labour market. Since the 1880s, lower-class city girls in their teens had been expected to earn a wage. Now women in rural and coastal areas were drawn into the textile plants and canneries. With the coming of the Great War, married women joined the work force *en masse* for the first time, and a revolution occurred in middle-class life as many girls entered the greatly expanded occupational ranks of secretaries, clerks, nurses, and other service work; all were sectors unorganized by the unions, despite some movements among shopclerks, housekeepers, teachers, and others towards the end of the war.

What held women workers back? Because of the all-pervading tradition of their domestic role, women were treated as future mothers and eternal servants. They were seen by employers, fellow workers, and even by themselves as temporary wage-earners holding down jobs because of permanent poverty, or until marriage and motherhood took them out of the labour market. Yet despite the celebrated theory that the 'two-stage' working life (before and after marriage) was an invention of the 1960s, and despite contemporary assurances that working mothers were only in industry 'because of the depression', or 'because of the winter unemployment', they seemed always to be there in the factories and shops. The 'two-stage' working life was a permanent feature of the battle against starvation. Only in the 1930s, with its massive dislocations, were many women let go—in order to keep male breadwinners at work.

In the twentieth century there may have been some shift of working-class girls into genteel white-collar work. There may well have been improvements in the general level of education. Women seem to have almost completely rejected the domestic occupations by 1914, except in dire poverty and need. Such a change implies a dramatic assertion of their equality by sections of the female working class. It may be the working girl's equivalent of the middle-class battle for the suffrage. And the beginnings of union militancy during the First World War, and again in the late 1930s, marked another major change in attitudes.

Women workers had little chance to express their militancy through AFL unions. Those organizations were at their most unstable in industries characterized by 'women's work'. Radical industrial unions before the CIO were largely the creation of single men who had less to lose, and therefore included relatively few women. There is however a great deal of evidence of picket-line militancy by women *as part of the family unit*, going back into the nineteenth century. Women were not only long-suffering helpmeets and mothers; they could be the 'real revolutionaries', as Rose Henderson observed in her testimony to the Royal Commission of 1919, provided they saw some chance of genuine change. Out of the ferment of 1919 came the Women's Labor Leagues, which attempted to organize where the AFL had so signally failed, but on a sex rather than a craft or industrial basis. They were eventually absorbed into unions or destroyed in the depressions of the 1920s and 1930s.

The women of the Labor Leagues, at once typical and outstanding, fought the battles of the 1920s for decent working conditions and a living wage. Their courage and humour deserve better than being relegated to the category of lost causes—or worse still, of association with the half-hearted palliatives acceptable to middle-class clubwomen.

Not until the 1930s did most female and ethnic workers find an organizational form to express their revolt against a century-old pattern of exploitation, which had at this period returned to its worst 'sweating' practices. Revolutionary as they were for many women, the strikes and industrial unions of the 1930s, however, were not the end of the story. As the final selection in this chapter shows, at the present time the battle is still far from over.

HOW THE SWEATSHOP SYSTEM BEGAN:
'HOMEWORK' IN TORONTO

One of the reasons why women in the garment industry—and even skilled male cutters and tailors—fought a losing battle against low wages and miserable conditions was competition from a reserve army of semi-employed, paid 'by the piece' and fired at will. Factory laws did not cover the sweatshop—a few workers under a sub-contractor, in a slum room. The sweatshop in turn faced competition from workingmen's wives and daughters doing 'homework' at even lower piece rates. For single girls and widows it was a desperate battle with starvation. The vicious cycle was not broken until the drives to form unions in the needle trades in the late 1930s; even today it continues in some small shops, as shown in the Arnopoulos articles that close this chapter.

K[night]. of L[abour]., 'Where Labor is Not Prayer', *Walsh's Magazine* (Toronto, 1895-6), p. 111-16.

The political economists who base their calculations upon the living wage, that is to say, the smallest sum upon which human life can be sustained, would be surprised to find how small this sum may be. Theory and fact do not harmonize because any theory that supposes the possibility of living, supposes also a moderate amount of comfort. It has fallen to my portion to find in this city, conditions of work, such that the living for which the work is done is only questionably desirable.

Where a dozen men and as many women are crowded together into a room not too large for two persons, ill-lighted, unheated, unventilated; where women work night and day making trousers at sixty cents a dozen pairs; where young girls work long hours for no pay, that they may learn the business; where girls are not even respected, but are sworn at and driven by brutal task-masters, the conditions are not the most desirable. The deplorable results are manifest to those whose charity, or whose duty brings them to the aid of the fallen.

Some account may here be given of a recent investigation of the system which makes these conditions possible. Generous minded people will be interested in the story.

Anyone whose business regularly brings him down town, knows that there are large wholesale clothing warehouses situated on Bay, Front and Wellington streets.

From these warehouses are continually plying a number of wagons, which are seen to contain bundles of clothing, made and unmade, which are being collected and delivered in all parts of the city, either at the regular workshops or at some private house. Recently a visit was paid to one of these workshops, considered to be one of the best of the kind in Toronto. A poster containing rules and regulations is posted on the wall, showing that the factory inspector has been there, and that, so far as sanitary arrangements and working hours are concerned, things are about what they should be. About a dozen girls and women are working at sewing machines, and expecting that it is not difficult to detect the effects of constant and unremitting hard work, where it is all hurry, with not a moment to lose, the young ladies appear to be happy enough. The overseer is a pleasant self-satisfied sort of person, who willingly furnished the information asked for.

He said that his work was of the finer grade of the wholesale work.

"Though," he said, "even for this class of work, the prices are so terribly cut down, that it is hard to make it pay at all. When asked what wages he paid, he said: "of course that depends on the ability of the girl to turn out the work. Some of the best hands, get as high as five or six dollars a week: the others less, ranging from two dollars and up, according to the length of time they have been at the business, and their own expertness." They work by the week, the hours being ten per day, and five hours on Saturday. Continuing he said, "of course the work is hard, and they have to keep on the hustle."

He wished he could pay better wages, but it was not possible with the low prices paid by the wholesalers. It was all the fault of the sweaters, said this "contractor," as they are constantly undercutting the prices in order to get the work, and the wholesalers are continually playing one lot against the other.

From this cause prices are lower now in some lines by fifty per cent than they were five or six years ago.

Four or five shops of this kind were visited where the conditions are very much the same as in the first one. All alike complained that prices were getting lower and lower, and that excepting the two or three very good hands they could not afford to pay higher wages than from two to four dollars per week.

The next place visited was a shop where things were evidently being run at a higher rate of speed. The girls are paid by the piecework system; and how they worked! The machines could scarce move fast enough, as with stooped shoulders, heads bent forward, the rapid movement of hands and feet, with furtive and momentary glances in the direction where employer and stranger stood talking, the work was rushed along, as though life depended on every stitch made by the whirring machines.

It was the same story, prices were so low now compared with what they used to be. His work was principally boys and youth's clothing. He got thirty-five dollars per 100 coats. Out of this he paid eighteen dollars for labour. The rest was for express hire, rent, fire, light, and so on.

The wages ranged, he said, from three to five dollars per week, though the beginners, of course, did not earn so much. The visitor subsequently learned more about the "learners," with whose case I will deal later.

The blame for the bad condition of affairs was again all laid on the shoulders of the "other fellows," and those women who persistently take out the work for less than the regular contractors' prices, and ultimately force the general rates down.

"For these same coats for which I am getting thirty-five cents," said the contractor, "a woman whose husband works at another trade, has this week taken some out to do in her own home for thirty-two and a-half cents. The next thing I shall be told is that I must make them for the same price, or somebody else will." . . .

I then went further west, and after some difficulty discovered a place of which I was in search, and what a place it was! The ceiling was very low and black with age, the light was poor, and the ventilation miserable. . . . There were seven men and seven women in the room. Their appearance was certainly in keeping with the place, looking as they did, more sad and dejected than any I had yet seen. The employer claimed to be a victim of circumstance and deplored the low wages of his employees, which he said were from one-fifty to three dollars per week.

"How can they possibly live on such wages?" was asked.

"Well I'll tell you how it is," he replied, "their brothers or fathers, I suppose, have to help to keep them."

All these women were of adult age.

He showed me coats and ulsters the prices for which were thirty-five cents and eighty cents respectively.

Coming back east, I visited two more places, in one of which was a young girl under age, who had no business to be there. She was pulling out bastings, and doing other light work. When spoken to about it, the employer made very light of the matter, and said she was not regularly employed, but that she came in occasionally for her own amusement.

There were ten other girls employed in the same place, but they were all so busy and intent on their work that they evidently had no time to even think of or notice anything else.

In the other place, about the same number of hands were employed. The employer in this case, a very intelligent man, most willingly furnished me with all the information in his power. The wages, he admitted, were very low and the work very hard. But that could not be avoided so long as the trade was conducted as it is under the present system.

The indiscriminate giving out of work from the wholesale places, and the eager readiness to take advantage of every one's necessities in order to force the price down still another notch, was the prime cause of the whole trouble. He showed me several of the tickets given out along with the work, which describe the work and give the price. For the benefit of those familiar with the technical terms of the trade, I will give a couple of samples:

1. Double Breast Overcoats, edges swelled, one-quarter, seams raised, three-eights, five pockets, cloth, quilting, silk stitching—price $1.45.

2. Fly Front Overcoats, edges narrow bound, five pockets, velvet collars, quilting—price $1.45.

"When I began seven years ago," said the contractor, "the prices for the same class of goods were about double what they are now, and the work must be done even better now than it was then. I have to buy my own thread and silk, and I expect we will soon have to furnish cloth as well."

Another bill of particulars differing slightly from the two given showed the price to be $1.35.

"All these goods are of the very best class and the work must be perfect or it will not be taken.

"You see this ulster here," showing a fine garment, a full size Irish frieze. "Now, everything in that has to be first-class and it is a single order. It is for Mr.—," mentioning a well-known clothier, "and all he will give me for the making of it is $1.75. How he thinks we are to live I cannot tell."

In my tour of the sweating shops I visited a great many places, but to relate my experience in these would be simply a repitition of what I have already said, the prices varying slightly in some instances.

In one place, the basement of a house, though it is tolerably well supplied with light and ventilation, thanks to a former visit of the factory inspector, there were eleven girls and two men besides the contractor. The work was principally on boy's or youth's coats and overcoats, the prices ranging from thirty cents to one dollar, and some men's coats for forty-five cents.

"It's the workingmen's wives who get the work at cheap rates," said the [contractor], though he evidently appreciated the services of the workingmen's daughters whose wages he admitted were very low.

Every one has seen the large number of women and children wending their way up or down Bay street, carrying bundles in their arms or on perambulators. Several of these women were called on at their homes. In some cases the work is a matter of absolute necessity with them, as they have themselves to support and others dependent upon them. In other cases it happened that though they had husbands working at their trades, yet from one cause or another they were sometimes glad of an opportunity to help meet the financial requirements of the house by earning an extra dollar or two.

I also called on several of the young girls who work in the shops. I will relate my experience among them as I was particularly anxious to get their views of the case. It is difficult in most instances to get them to state what they know, from fear of losing their places. One girl said: "Yes, indeed, it is very hard work, and very poorly paid for. I think I get the highest pay where I work and I get four dollars per week, the others get from two dollars per week to three or three-and-a-half. We make sack coats. They are what are called double-breast, double-stitch, with five pockets and flaps. There are three buttons on each sleeve, and two rows of buttons down the front. So you will see that there are numerous buttons to be sewed on, say, forty coats. The price for these coats is forty-five cents each, and, of course, out of that our boss has to pay express hire. They call these coats, boy's coats, but I think that is only done to keep the price down. I know one place on King street that is a very hard shop to work in. The boss will go up and down the shop swearing at the girls. I have seen some of the coats with very little less work in them than the forty-five cent ones—in fact, you can scarcely tell the difference—made for thirty-five cents each. We often lose a lot of time through having to wait for work. We often work Saturday afternoons when there is the work to do. Some parts of the year we can get no work at all."

Another girl said she was one of the highest paid girls. "I get four dollars per week. I like the work, though some times my head gets so dizzy I can scarcely see what I am doing. I know many of the girls come as learners, getting very little wages indeed, then they leave and their places are taken by other learners."

This simple account of a round of visitation, will give some faint impression of the conditions, almost unbearable, under which great numbers of our population, here in Toronto exist, for it is existence and nothing more. To work, cook, eat and sleep in the one room is not uncommon. The song of the shirt has not been sung for the last time. It would astonish the knowing ones to learn the number of those who work out a bare subsistence in "poverty, hunger, and dirt."

A TRADITIONAL ROLE

Born in 1922 in Chipman, New Brunswick, Elizabeth Brewster commemorates, in realistic and sympathetic glimpses, older patterns of Maritime life.

Elizabeth Brewster, *East Coast* (Toronto, Ryerson, 1951), p. 3. Reprinted by permission of Elizabeth Brewster.

ANNA

ANNA, being the eldest of nine children,
Had always much to do about the house,
But, being stronger than most girls, was ready
To help her father plough or cut the firewood.
Her body was clumsy, but her bony hands
Were light and kind with babies or with horses.
She married, when she was no longer young,
A widower with five sons. She thought him kind,
Though sometimes wishing, when he snored beside her
For the swaggering lumberjack whose dancing eyes
Had awed her tonguetied girlhood. When she woke
And lit the lamp for breakfast, all her mind
Turned to her day's work, to the milking and baking,
Washing and ironing. She had little time
For rest, except nights when she mended
And thought with half her mind; or cool June evenings
When walking through the hayfields in the dusk
She smelled the summer round her; or the Sundays
She went to meeting in her one good dress
And, kneeling with the parson's voice above her
Like a fly buzzing somewhere in a corner,
Thanked God she had been luckier than most.

A PLEA FOR STATE INTERVENTION: QUEBEC TEXTILE WORKERS, 1908-1910

This is one of many such petitions to provincial governments protesting nineteenth-century conditions of work for women and children. The child workers of 1900 could legally be as young as 12 (boys) and 14 (girls); but many poor parents falsified ages for the Factory Inspectors. Indeed, entire families joined this early Catholic union, which in 1910, after many a bitter strike, finally won shorter legal hours for women and children.

Quebec, *Sessional Papers* (1910), No. 87, pp. 8-9. Excerpt.

FEDERATION OF TEXTILE WORKERS OF CANADA

Montreal 18th February, 1908.

Hon. L. A. Taschereau,
    Minister of Labour,
        Quebec.

Sir,

I am directed by my executive council to call your kind attention to the following points:

1, Women and children who are obliged to earn their livelihood in factories are subjected to labours whose weight and duration are beyond their strength.

2. In a great many factories, the working day for women and children begins at 6.10 A.M.; half an hour or three quarters of an hour are allowed them for the mid-day rest and the working day ends at 6 or 6.10 P.M.

Such a working day is too long and too hard for women's physical strength and for children at the growing age.

For many years, the inspectors of the Province of Quebec have, with a persistency deserving all praise, pointed out the existence of the evil in their reports and have represented it as a danger to the future of our nation.

To arrest or remedy the evil they have several times requested the necessary intervention of the law.

Basing itself on this authority and upon uncontested experience, the executive council of the Federation of Textile Workers of Canada, on behalf of the local unions affiliated with this council and of a great many other labour unions or associations;

Respectfully ask you.

To give your kind and sympathetic attention to the question which affects to the highest degree the safety and future of workmen's families in our Province;

It expresses the hope that new provisions regulating the hours of labour for women and children will be asked for at the next session of the Legislature.

It suggests that the Industrial Establishments Act of the Province of Quebec, now in force, be amended in the following sense:

The working hours for women and children in factories shall not exceed 55 per week and shall be distributed as follows:

1. The working days for women and children in factories shall never begin before 7 a.m.

2. At noon, they shall have one hour for their meals with liberty to go outside the factory.

3. The working day shall never extend beyond 6 p.m.

4. Saturday afternoon shall be declared a legal holiday and all work shall cease at noon for women and children.

I have the honour to be,

Sir,

Your obedient servant,

(Signed) L. A. GIRARD,

General Secretary.

A QUESTION OF STATUS: MAID OR HOUSEKEEPER?

Most books aimed at prospective immigrants were outright propaganda. Ella Sykes' is a refreshingly sharp portrait of Canadian and English snobberies in a supposedly classless society. The federal government made various attempts to import British domestics. At best these women treated the scheme as if it were a marriage bureau. At worst they fell prey to the white-slave trade (see Chapter 2 for items on prostitution and child labour). Here we have an eyewitness view of the brighter side. In 1916 there was even to be a Housekeepers' Union in Alberta!

E. C. Sykes, *A Home-help in Canada* (London, 1912), pp. 174-7.

The time of my arrival coincided with the departure of the last "girl," and the leave-taking between mistress and maid was anything but cordial. Mrs. Downton then led me into the kitchen, and, pointing to a paper fastened to the door, said, "Here are my rules for the work of each day," and showed me my room, comfortable save for the lack of a chair or any place to put my things, except a few nails on the door, and told me to prepare supper as soon as I had taken off my hat and jacket.

This was eaten at seven o'clock in the dining-room, and, in my capacity as lady-help, I sat at table with the husband and wife and the "man," a depressed youth, who never opened his lips. As Mr. Downton, kind and pleasant from first to last, was conversationally inclined, I quite forgot my inferior position, and chatted away during the meal, though I had had rather a blow as I entered the room. "Does *she* eat with us?" had been the remark of Master Tom, the elder hope of the family, and he stared at me, greatly surprised, as I took my place!

I cleared away after supper, and during the washing-up Mrs. Downton looked into the kitchen and asked very stiffly whether I would care to sit with them in the drawing-room. I politely declined this honour, and immediately my employer's manner became less glacial, so great was her relief, poor woman, and indeed I could sympathize with her. This was the first and last occasion that I was invited to enter the family circle, save at meal-time.

Next morning I was in the kitchen by half-past five to start preparing the breakfast. To my relief the stove behaved well, and I lit it with no trouble (here, as in many parts of Canada, only wood was used), and set about cooking porridge and bacon, making toast and laying the table. All was ready by half-past six, and the family assembled.

When I got into the dining-room (I was always a little late, as I had to wash my hands and remove my apron after dishing-up) everyone was eating busily and there was no chair for me. I straightway forgot that I was a home-help, and was greatly annoyed at the discourtesy of the men. "May I have a seat please?" I asked in a tone that brought them to their feet in a second, and Mr. Downton rushed into another room to supply my need!

When breakfast was cleared away, I started on my daily round of sweeping. Carpets had to be cleaned with one implement, the linoleum and matting had a special broom, and the rooms with only bare boards another. Then all the skirting had to be wiped around with a dry cloth, and it was in vain that I begged leave to use a damp one, as the dust merely flitted from one place to settle in another. After this operation I was told to do the bedrooms, and when they were finished it was time to peel potatoes for dinner and supper, and to begin preparing the substantial midday meal.

That over, and the washing-up accomplished, I made a cake and blancmange for supper, and, as it was now four o'clock, I was allowed my freedom for an hour and a half. A good part of this precious time was occupied with my toilet (it was very cursory in the mornings), and then I rested as I had a "crick" in my back. A friend was expected for supper that evening, so we had soup, fish, meat, and sweets, and I had to change the plates, bring in the dishes, and wash up the fish plates to do duty for the pudding course as the crockery ran short.

My fellow-hireling and I were left entirely out of the conversation—not that my employers were in the least unkind, it was merely that we were dependents and therefore did not count.

During my stay I met a home-help who spoke enthusiastically of the way in which her employer treated her, but on inquiry I found that the lady was a Canadian, and therefore had not the British "caste" ideas. My acquaintance assured me that she would not have been treated as well as she was in any other household in that district, and said that she would dissuade all girls from coming to this particular neighbourhood as lady-helps, and I quite agreed with her.

Certainly the English do not always appear to understand the home-help in the way that the Canadians do, the reason being that she is not a British institution.

A girl I met, who was acting in that capacity to an English family in another part of the Dominion, told me that not only was she cook, parlour-made, and housemaid combined, but that she had actually to wait upon the children's nurse, a woman socially much her inferior.

The master of the house came home for week-ends, and during his spare time used to chop a quantity of wood which he imagined would last until his return. As it only held out for three or four days, my poor friend was reduced to "grovelling about" for fuel, as she expressed it, before preparing any meal, and not only had she to cook and serve the usual three meals a day, but this family insisted on having a substantial afternoon tea with cakes and scones.

'AS MUCH A LADY AS YOU ARE': A CALGARY CHARWOMAN, 1909-1914

These memoirs are a rare document indeed, and extraordinarily frank. Jean McDonald was no middle-class journalist, but the orphan of an Irish steelworker. Hers was a childhood of brief rural idylls—gathering rushes by the river, her father's songs, her mother's piety—and brutal poverty. She helped bring up her orphaned brothers, married at last a man with whom she dreamed of running a small dairy farm, and while following her husband and the dream to Canada in 1907, was raped on the immigrant train. As the tale starts here, their dream was fading as the difficulties of getting a cash 'stake' increased. Mrs McWilliam (as she was then) saw her homesteader husband forced to enlist by the depression of 1914. Later she organized soldiers' wives, raised a family, cared for her shell-shocked mate, and eventually remarried. Meanwhile, she had become a founder of the Women's Labor League in Alberta, which criticized middle-class club-women reformers.

Jean McDonald, *Memoirs, 1877-1969* (Unpublished MS., Glenbow-Alberta Institute), pp. 30-9. Courtesy of Veronica Strong-Boag.

The next house I rented was a little red brick cottage across the street from the Paget Hall and Pro-Cathedral of the Redeemer. The Carlyle Dairy was a little cottage on 5th Avenue and 1st Street East and Weldon and Tom Carlyle were beginning their adventurous task of a big concern, which now bears the name of The Union Milk Company. Unfortunately the homestead my husband had picked was not a success. Of course he never had been a land farmer always in Scotland it was dairying and he did not know the value of good land, so try as he would he could not make a go of it. So he came to town to discuss the situation with me. He said he had the chance of work with a farmer in the district if I could help him get some shoes, etc. as his money was finished. He had used what he had for a grub-stake during the winter months, so he had to have shoes. However, I gave him ten dollars—it was just about all I had, and I too had been having a struggle to pay the rent of the house and buy coal and light. So next day he went back to Munson. Of course in those days every homesteader was practically in the same plight.

Well I went to see Mr. Weldon Carlyle and asked him if he could give me some work to do. He kindly gave me the office to clean. I had to get it cleaned before seven-thirty in the morning before the staff came in, so I slipped out of the house about six in the morning while the children were asleep (my little girl was with me again by this time), but I would be home in time to give them their breakfast and dress them. One morning Mr. Carlyle asked me if I would care to go to his home and help his wife one day a week from nine in the morning until five. I took the work—sometimes I took the children with me. I really appreciated the chance and as Mr. and Mrs. Carlyle never treated me like a common charwoman. I felt much at home there. I can always remember a neighbor they had. Her husband was an army captain—very English. They kept a Chinaman to do their charring but he had taken sick and Mr. and Mrs. S – – – had rented their home as they were leaving for Miami. She asked Mrs. Carlyle if she would do her a favor and ask me if I would give her a hand to clean her house. I said yes. So I made arrangements for a neighbor to care for the children, I would pay her. She consented and I went to Mrs. S – – – about nine in the morning. I was a little late as I had cleaned the dairy offices earlier then had to care for the children. She met me at the door. She said "You are late—it is near nine-thirty". I said "Yes, but I had to wash and dress my children and give them their breakfast, but I did not wait to eat anything—I'm sorry, but I'll make up the time." She never said "Make yourself a cup of tea", so I started upstairs and had to clean the three bedrooms and bathroom and a large hall. After a chinaman I found places he had never cleaned so I made a thorough job. I was just finishing upstairs and going down the stairs when the lady called to me she had put on a piece of meat for my lunch. It was near one o'clock by then. However, I thought I would finish the stairs. I had just reached the bottom when she came and said to me "Why did you not come and cook your lunch? The meat is burned." I picked up the pail, went upstairs and emptied it in the bathroom and came down and said "Mrs. S – – –, any lady I have been cleaning for always made my lunch and set it in a clean place. I am neither a pig nor a Chinaman. I am just as much a lady as you are. I only came here to oblige you as I made a practice not to work on Saturday as I work every other day for ladies in Calgary. They all treat me like a human being, so here is your pail, you go get me my money and clean your dirty house yourself." She ran to the phone and phoned her husband who by the way was at the Ranchman's Club. She said "Oh, captain, captain, do send me a Chinee boy. Mrs. McWilliam is leaving because I would not cook her dinner. You know, dear, I never cooked for a charwoman in my life". When I heard her call me a charwoman my Irish blood boiled, I said "Now I'm not a charwoman, so you get my money". I put on my coat and collected my one dollar and a quarter for nearly five hours' hard work.

I decided then just what I would have to face working for such ignorant upstarts. I had believed there was no class distinction in Canada, but here it was in full. I decided to be on the look-out for that type and found them aplenty. The exploitation I had left as I thought in Britain was right here, with all the traits of snobbishness. But that dollar and a quarter was all I had to feed my children for the week-end. However, I was determined to starve rather than let them get me down.

I kept on working each day until I gathered a few beds and dishes then I started to keep boarders. As there was a building boom on in Calgary it was easy to get boys. Board and room for six dollars per week. I soon got my house filled. Most of the boys were Scotch and I could cook good healthy meals. I took the house next door and finished up having from eighteen to twenty boys. I hired a girl to help me. She was an Icelander and she was a good girl, just another immigrant, but we were very happy.

The Chief of Police was Chief Mackie, and as I lived so handy to the city hall he asked me if I would act as matron for the police when they arrested girls. The city hall was under construction and the police headquarters were in the basement of the city hall, and I lived about a half-block away from there so it was handy and I consented. It brought me in a few dollars per month and it was mostly two or three in the morning when these girls were brought in so I was always home in time to get the boys their breakfast. Gradually things got better for me until one day the landlord came and said he had rented one of the houses to a Chinaman for double the rent I was paying, so that meant I must leave. Well houses were hard to get to rent and I had no money to buy.

I told half of the boys they would have to move as I would have to move myself. I tried to locate somewhere and finally a real estate dealer said he had a house to sell. He asked me how much money I had and I told him I had about two hundred dollars. "Well", he said "That will pay the year's taxes and my commission". I then asked what price was the house and he said fifty-five hundred dollars. I told him I would take it so I gave him my two hundred dollars and signed the contract to pay one hundred per month.

When I went home a man was standing there, very well dressed with a little black bag like a doctor's bag. He said "I am glad to see you" and I asked him what he wanted. It was about three in the afternoon. I knew the hired girl was in the other house setting the table for supper and would not be expecting me home just then, and my little girl was playing in the back yard. He asked to come in and I kept asking him what he wanted, but as soon as he got inside the house he said "Oh don't be afraid of me, I really did not intend to kill the man, but I did it in self-defence. You look like my mother so I won't kill you, but will you show me where I might lie down to rest?" I was really afraid I'll admit, but I knew I had better humor him. I did not expect any of the roomers home till five o'clock and there was a room close to the door so I told him he could rest there. He said "If I lie down there will you hold my hand and I'll tell you my story". However, I sat down beside him and he said the man he killed was an engineer. He was on the train coming from Maryland and this man went to look out the door and he pushed him out. They stopped the train and he slipped out the other side. "Promise me you will not tell the police I am here". I promised and he dozed off to sleep. I tried to slip my hand out of his but as I did so he woke up and said, "You just try and get away and I shall kill you." There I sat and in a short time my little girl came skipping into the house. I shushed her, but motioned her to me and very quietly whispered I needed help and to run to the police station. The children and the police were very friendly and the little ones visited the station all the time so it was not unusual for her to run there and in a very few minutes two policemen arrived and took him into custody. He looked at me in the maddest sort of way and said "I'll get you for this". However, the police found him to be a dangerous lunatic who made his escape from Ponoka and they felt I had had a very narrow escape. So much for that—I was sure relieved.

When the men came in for their supper I told them of my wild experience and then broke the news that I had just bought a house for fifty-five hundred dollars. They told me then that I was also crazy and should have gone to Ponoka with the lunatic as I would never be able to pay for the house. But I then remembered an old song my father used to sing—it ran: "O proud and undaunted stood bold Brennan on the moor". So I just laughed them off and said "It may take me one hundred years to pay for it, but I have bought it. Now I'll be a real taxpayer and a real Canadian" and we moved up to our new home, which by the way when I bought it was occupied by a Baptist minister, and it was in a nice district close to Victoria Park. It was in a better section than the first house I went to when I came in from the farm, which I mentioned earlier and which I thought was in the red light district.

So I got settled at last and I had a nice new house.

It was 1912. The Stampede was beginning—the men had sports, pole jumping, tug-of-war games, for which prizes were given by the merchants in town.

When I finally got established I had some notable characters amongst my boarders. Two brothers named McPherson, Dan and Alec. Both working on the Palliser Hotel—one a stone-mason the other a carpenter. They quarrelled one evening upstairs. I heard Dan say "Alec, I am going to shoot myself!" So I went upstairs. Dan was crying because Alec had left him uptown and he had to come home alone. Another funny episode. It was around Christmas time and the boys were holidaying and being Scotchmen they had been imbibing a bit. After supper one evening the hired girl and I had already gone to bed as we thought every one was either in bed upstairs or had gone out, when I heard the most awful commotion upstairs. I said to Nora "I'd better go up and see what's going wrong. The bathroom and toilet in the house are separate, so as I got to the head of the stairs I saw one of the men, a Scotchman named Archie, a blacksmith, on his knees at the toilet door. I asked him what he thought he was doing and he said "Hughie is in there and he can't get out". I said "Why" when from behind the door the voice of Hughie said "Mrs. Mac, let me oot o' here". I said "Where is the key?" and he answered "I locked the door and put the key outside". I stooped down and picked up the key and unlocked the door. In his hurry to get out he fell over Archie. He said "Och ye fool, what were you kneeling there for?" Archie replied "O Hughie, I was praying to God Almichty ye widna dee in there." I came downstairs and my hired girl, Nora and I had a good laugh over the incident. However, my nature was to laugh. There were eight boarders upstairs. The next morning I found out one of the men had a birthday and they were celebrating. I maybe should have been cross as I did not touch liquor myself, but in the years that followed I was often glad I did not get angry at the boys. We were all a very happy family, but of course this was not to last. They were sure a jolly bunch and we had many good times together. We kept up old country ideas and as the district had few houses we could dance every night from Christmas to the New Year in my new home. There were lots of Scotch lassies in town and Scotch laddies on the police force. The police on the beat used to join the crowd and they too can remember even now the good times. The boys brought their Scotch lassies in and we had the bagpipes skirling at two o'clock in the morning. Square dances and all our old country reels and strathspeys and Highland fling.

That was the year the first "black Maria" was brought to Calgary. Often during the night the "black Maria" would come for me to go and act as matron. My few neighbors then thought I was a pretty bad character getting arrested so often. However, I got acquainted with them as time went on and we used to laugh over their worries when I explained my position, and they used to join in our dances. Maybe we were a noisy crowd but we were a harmless bunch. As I never could be coaxed to imbibe I kept order.

However, a couple of years were not long slipping by and one by one the tool kits were brought home. Some of the boys were socialist-minded and they knew what was in the offing, and I heard all the arguments pro and con until I too learned what was ahead. Unemployment was rampant. Soon the battle drums were playing. Soon the pipers were playing like the pied-piper of Hamelin to get the armies marching and the black shadow of 1914 took the once happy boys into the ranks.

A LITTLE INDEPENDENCE: FACTORY GIRLS, 1912

Despite a few middle-class sentimentalisms, the 'Videre' articles are amongst the best accounts we have of the life of factory girls. To understand the lure of the factory not only for young women from the farm but for city girls too, we should bear in mind that wages meant not only a relative independence from the tyranny of father or husband, but adult status, as well as liberation from the chores of home, farm, or boarding-house. For the very poor, it was not a question of independence: children's earnings were simply part of family income. And there must have been many poor families: as late as 1921, some 7 per cent of the industrial work force were children under 15 years old.

'Videre' articles in the *Toronto Star*, June-July 1912. Courtesy of Wayne Roberts, McMaster University.

June 1: How I got my first job in a Toronto biscuit factory
"If only one of us would go and work as a factory girl, we should understand better the real conditions..."All winter, the committee of

our University Women's Club delegated to study industrial conditions had been at work. We had gathered statistics, read books, held meetings, ... been addressed by speakers, ... gone through factories by the kindly permission of their owners.... But we still felt there were some things in the life of a factory girl that we had not yet gripped....

I have called myself 'Videre' because I went "to see" the land. I have been practically a wage-earning woman as much as I have been a journalist drawing a regular salary, and have also been to some extent an employer of others' labour, in that I have had from time to time stenographers doing special work for me.... In fact, I feel that I could no longer afford the cheaper line of labour. I have also been connected for some years with the work of a downtown church, and have in that way become acquainted with many whom I am glad to call personal friends, in all ranks of labour. I have, too, had something to do with the investing of money, and realize that a man has a right to expect a certain income from the wealth he has amassed ... If I may put my creed in such form, I believe in the right of the individual to acquire an honest fortune if he has the skill. I believe also in the brotherhood of man, though I do not interpret it to mean that God made all men free and equal, as has been stated on the American dollar. If He made men free, He never could make them equal....

I arrayed myself in a $1.25 shirtwaist, a ten-cent collar, a hat once good but a little tawdry from the dew and dust of last summer, and confronted the foreman of one of our biscuit factories.

I had to wait standing for half an hour at a desk in the hallway for him, when I stated my object, but I remembered that of course a working woman's time did not count for very much, and that I would probably have to stand all day when I succeeded in getting a job.

"What have you worked at before?" the foreman asked.... "Worked on papers," I answered meekly.... "Well, you'll find the work here very different from that you've been used to...." "Yes," I replied, "they say it's healthier to work on biscuits than on paper." "Yes, that's right." I think I finished plaintively, "If you gave me a chance I think I could soon get onto the trade."

"Well, all right. Be here at 7.30 Monday morning," he said, and abruptly left....

It was scarcely 5 o'clock when I awakened that Monday morning, but I dared not go to sleep again for fear of losing my job.... I tied up my necessities for the week in a brown manila wrapping paper and with my bundle under my arm and $5.00 in my pocket I stole away from my little world.

A mite of a girl was standing at the foreman's office where I waited myself that morning for directions. "Are you waiting for a job?" I asked. ... "I was told to come," said the mite. "So was I," I replied confidently.

"How old are you?" "Fourteen." That was an irrelevant question, I have since learned. All children applying for work at factories know enough to be fourteen.

"You go over to the dressing-room," said the foreman, approaching me. I went meekly. Ten minutes later I was installed in a big cotton apron at the table where the jelly wafers are made. . . .

The forman passed a few minutes afterwards, and I dropped my little jelly-scraper and seized an opportunity. "You didn't tell me," I said, "whether I was to be on time work or piece work." "Oh, I'll put you on time work," he said in a kindly voice. . . . I was too unsophisticated yet to comprehend the advantage he was affording me. "How much will I get?" I asked. "Oh, I'll give you $5.00 a week. . . . "I went back attentively to my jelly-box and scraper. My thoughts, if fully concentrated on my work, would read something like this: "Dab-a-jelly, turn-a-biscuit, dab-a-jelly, turn-a-biscuit, dab-a-jelly, turn-a-biscuit."

But you soon begin to work mechanically. Most of the workers seem inclined to sing while working, though singing is against the rules. I found myself contracting a habit of ceaseless humming. Fortunately my weird melodies were drowned by the whir of the machinery.

. . . These are selections I heard sung on my first day as a factory hand: "I love to tell the story." "Count your many blessings." "Blest be the tie that binds." And a snatch of a love song that I did not recognize. I have listened to the singing of many hymns, but I seldom had them go to my heart more deeply than did these under the circumstances. To offset this, I was given to understand that several little misses of 15 and 16 could tell quite shady stories.

Being an inexperienced worker . . . before an hour I had my hands and the handle of my scraper all daubed with jelly. . . . I was directed to a sink at the other end of the room. A woman joined me there, with a marshmallow pail to wash. "Been here long?" I asked. "Over a year," she answered. She was a patient, earnest-looking woman of about 30. "How much do you get?" I asked. She turned her eyes full upon my face. "Five dollars a week." I shall never forget, I think, the look in those eyes. It could not have been a look of appeal, for I was but a fellow-worker. It was just a long, long look.

June 4

I joined a group for lunch at noon. There was a moment of silence as they waited for the forelady to ask the blessing. We don't have blessings in boarding houses, so naturally I felt it was not a bad crowd I had fallen among. . . . There seems to be a continued shifting in these occupations. The workers grow tired of the monotony of their labour, and change from chocolates to lace, and from lace to gum, and from gum to feathers, and so on. . . . Quite a percentage of my fellow workers in this factory were new employés of a month or so. One would think it would be to an employer's advantage to pay higher prices to those already trained in his service, and prevent thus this system of eternal change. . . .

It was decided finally that a girl I shall call Alma had better take me in hand in a search for a room that night. Alma was one of the most relied-upon employés, had been six years with the firm. She drew a salary of $6.00 per week. She paid $1.25 rent for a nice, but tiny box of a room at the end of a hall. Her meals cost $2.25 per week. She had thus $2.50 per week for clothing, laundry, and other expenses. She was one of the best provided-for of the employés. . . . The average wage paid these women was from $4.60 to $5.25 per week. . . . I found a number of girls who had left other factories because they were paid lower wages than they were paid here, for instance $3.50 in the chocolate industry, $4.00 in the cigar trade. The few getting $6.00 per week were mostly boarders. Among the most interesting of my new friends was one I shall call blue-eyed Alice, a girl of 14, getting a wage of $4.50 per week. I met her also at the sink at the close of the day. She was elated and sparkling. "I got a hustle on to-day," she said. "I packed seven trays. They are 15¢ a tray piece work. Perhaps they will make it up to me on pay day. But the others tell me I mustn't go so fast, or they will cut the price on the trays when they find out how many we can do." And next day, acting on the hint, she did but five.

I found this sentiment very common among the workers, that an unusually quick worker was likely to cut the price of piece work. . . . Next day I learned from Alice that though she was only 14 last November, she had left school two years ago, and has been employed in four different industries: chocolates, gum, feather, and biscuits. . . . I noticed that she could not read the typewritten directions hanging about three feet above her head in the dressing room. Her face was pale and anaemic. Is it possible that the grim red walls of our factories are red sometimes with the life-blood from the cheeks of our children, as well as with bricks from the Don Valley?

"How would Alice manage to get away from school at 12 without the teacher noticing her disappearance?" I asked of a couple of other little girls.

"Oh, it would be like this. She would move and be transferred to another school and then never turn up after transferring."

There was a slightly festive air about the factory on pay day. "I never care for pay day," said Alice, "I give all my money to my mother. She lets me have a quarter, generally."

Her father was living. There were but three children in the family. The eldest was employed in paper-box making. The night of that same pay day, I took Alma to a five-cent show. At 9.20 my Alice came marching in with a younger child. . . .

I cannot leave my companions in the factory without speaking of the many little kindnesses they showed me as a stranger, the sacrifices even, that they were willing to make. I was late, for example, the second morning. Alma waited for me rather than let me go in alone. I noted the flush on her face when the foreman asked her what was the matter. This being late means docking 10¢. During my last afternoon I had a misfortune. I upset from the top of the pile a wooden box containing about twenty pounds of biscuits. . . . My Alice left her work and scraped up biscuits with all the strength of which she was capable, that I might not get into trouble with the foreman when he came upstairs.

June 6

I went at the close of my first factory day with Alma to the house where I could get my meals for $2.25 per week. The meals were really better than I had expected at this rate. We had spare ribs, potatoes, tapioca pudding, and tea. This was, I later learned, a meal a little below par. The next night we had fish, potatoes, and raw tomatoes (the second week in May). Breakfast consisted of porridge, steak or bacon, and fruit (sliced oranges, jelly, etc.) . . . The linen was coarse but clean. As descriptive of the social surroundings, I will give just a sentence I heard the other day from the lips of a stenographer. "In those cheap boarding places the girls are usually a great deal nicer than the men, for you find so many real nice girls in the city on very poor pay." [Many cannot afford these meals and just "take something."]

We went out on our search for a room. . . . I could not, at the outside price, pay more than $1.50 a week. We found a very nice clean little room a few doors from my boarding place at this very rate. It was over the kitchen and heated by a stove-pipe, but a fair size and with a good closet. The landlady impressed upon me that I must buy my own soap and matches. . . . My landlady told me in a very kindly way that she could not afford to let the girls have hot water for washing and gas for ironing in the summer. She did not mind at all in the winter time, when the fire was on. She even gave them the privilege of cooking some things then.

I believe she told the truth. She could not afford it. She was paying $35.00 a month for a nine-roomed house. . . . It had taken often two tons of coal a month to heat the house during the past winter. . . . Her rooms would sometimes be vacant. You can readily see . . . the difficulty she would have been in had she not herself had children at work. Her daughter was a book binder, getting $7.00 a week. She paid $4.00 a week at home for her board, she told me. She aroused my envy with her pretty velvet waist and lace collar. That "paper business" I had left was not so bad.

I should consider myself as well and safely lodged in this house as in most houses. We did not have the use of the parlour at all, and took our gentleman friends to our rooms. But that is so in almost all rooming houses.

"Do you shut your door when you have a gentleman in?" I asked of the girl in the next room. "Oooh, yes," she said expressively. "Shut it and lock it."

My oft-reiterated complaint in this house was that the bathroom was in such a dangerously unsanitary condition. I presume it was the landlady's fault....

I sat down at my window that evening and went over the things I had to be thankful for as a factory girl. There was a glorious view of the sunset between the chimneys.... I was thankful for a nice clean room in a nice house and on a rather nice street.

But I began to see myself confronting certain financial difficulties. I had just $1.25 weekly left for clothing and other expenses.... I must have soap, coarse soap.... So many of my companions lived at home, helped the family by contributing $2.50 or $3.00 of their earnings, but they had their laundry done, and had all the rest for clothes and pin money.... At night they changed their working skirts and put on nice quiet suits and hats to go out into the streets. I would not have recognized them as the same girls passing in a crowd. I like new clothes as well as any girl, and I wished very much I could afford things like theirs. I wanted also to take Alma to the five-cent show....

I used to think that any girl who worked all the time should have something laid up in case of sickness, and not be dependent upon charity, if she were ill a few weeks. It looked to me as if she were not very provident... but it is hard to save when the necessities of life are demanding every cent. Then too,... I wanted church collection. I had paid at least 25¢ too much for my room to begin with. I could not afford $2.25 for my meals. I find I can't afford three meals every day.... By going without breakfast one morning a week, I could afford Sunday dinner.... I had begun to know what it was to be "just a little hungry." ... Nibbling at occasional biscuits while at work no doubt allayed my appetite too.... I discovered that eggs, even at two for five, were rather expensive. It would be cheaper to get three bananas for 5¢ and make them last three days for lunches, and thus save difficulties about cooking. I remembered then the words of a barrister in the flat across the hall from my old room. I had told them I was cooking an egg for lunch that night before I left for my job. "Eggs!" called the barrister, "you can't afford eggs! Eggs are dear. It's bread and tea you want."

June 11

I applied to a forelady this time. The only question she asked was, "Have you ever run a power machine?" I answered in the negative, but said I thought I could learn. That was the only question asked me. I began work next day amid the buzz and whir of the long vista of the whitewear trade [lines of sewing machines]. . . .

I made a bad mistake that first morning I began as a whitewear operator. I took off every bit of jewelry I had. I was somewhat cha-grined when I saw two seats from me a girl with nearly five inches of brilliants in her hair, a wristwatch, a locket and chain, a gold belt buckle, long pearl ear-rings, a few other like accessories, and a chew of gum. Out of nine girls sitting near me, five wore gold lockets. The girls kept a little aloof from me that first day. . . .

Next day I put on all the rings I had, and several other additions of a like kind. I meant them to see there was "some class" to me. It worked like magic. I was much more at ease, and found the girls a great deal more friendly.

We must not imagine . . . that my bejeweled little neighbour is typical of the average whitewear girl. I discovered, on looking around later on in the day, that there were scarcely any lockets except those in the immedi-ate neighbourhood. I forthwith dubbed ours "the jewelry section."

I was greatly hampered in my investigations in this factory . . . [there was no sink at which the girls could meet and chat]. There had lately been made a new regulation, that girls were not to walk about to the others' machines during working hours. I should think this a wise regula-tion on the part of the firm, though as one . . . girl said, "It rests you a lot if you can get up sometimes for just five minutes and go around." We talked, of course, to those on the machines near us, though you have to speak loudly, for the factory is very noisy.

I greatly appreciated in this factory the lunch room. Dishes and spoons were supplied free of charge, cups of tea at one cent. . . . There were tables supplied with the best of our current magazines. . . . Our work-rooms seemed perfectly ventilated, light, and sunny. The hours were better here too, from 7.45 to 5.30.

I have heard that there are "class distinctions" in the whitewear trade. The girls who do the more skilled work do not associate very much with the girls who do the cheaper work . . . It recalled a statement I once heard from a girl who sold ladies' suits . . . "The suit girls don't have anything to do with the shirtwaist girls," she said.

June 13

There were any number of girls making less than $6.00. Skilled girls were some of them making as high as $15 to $18 a week . . . There are of course slack seasons when the piece worker has to take holidays at her own expense . . . One needs a little capital to start in the whitewear trade at piecework, as you cannot possibly make a living wage the first few weeks . . . I had here an opportunity of noting especially the difference between the time worker and the piece worker. In the other factory, where they had been nearly all time workers, I had often heard a girl washing her hands opposite the clock call down to the others, "Five minutes to twelve, Annie," or "A quarter to six, Lizzie." Here all was piece work. The gong seemed a sort of custom of the past, like the curfew bell. When it sounded, everybody was at work on their machine ... On the other hand, some of these girls who are better paid feel they can afford a half-day off when they like ... I am afraid that the presence in the factories of married women who have husbands to support them has a tendency, by over-filling the market with labourers, to cut down the wages, more even than the girl living at home. They are unconcerned about what they get.

[One employer said] "If we pay the workers more we have to charge a higher price for the goods, and these other firms, who are paying the lowest possible figure to employés, will undersell us every time and get the trade." One can easily see here the wall the employer is up against, without some kind of governmental or municipal supervision of the prices paid the workers in the different industries.

I have submitted this article before publication to a girl who has been a number of years in another whitewear factory ... She had her doubts about the average wage being as high as $6.00 to $9.00 a week. She believes that is overstated....

When a girl is working from 7.45 a.m. to 5.30 or 6 p.m. at, say, a power machine, there is not much danger of any question of "morals" obtruding itself. Of alleged conditions as portrayed by melodrama, where the villain is a wicked foreman or employé, I found absolutely no hint....

"Here," says one girl, "is how I spend my evenings." Monday night, an "occasional." That means a man who just calls upon one sometimes. Tuesday, my "steady". Wednesday, another "occasional." Thursday, "steady." Friday, another "occasional." Saturday and Sunday, "steady." The "steady" worked three nights a week, so she filled up her programme as above, according to her own words. She was a very attractive girl, around whom the attention of our boarding house seemed to gravitate. And again, if I may put myself in another girl's place, "Monday night Will comes; Tuesday I sew; Wednesday night Will comes again; Thursday night I sew; in short, I sew every other night, for Will and I are engaged." You see, there is the light of love and romance in the life of the girl worker just as in the mansions of Rosedale....

Do not think, though, that we can spend our evenings all at church. We have clothes to launder and mend, letters to write, and other things to do. Do not think, either, that when you have opened up the church evenings for us, you have done all there is to do. What you need is not so much a place to go into as a place to go out to. We need open-air skating at a lower rate. Regular rink charges are so high that we can't go unless John or Jimmy takes us . . . Outdoor ball games are good for us, if they do not necessitate too much expense, as tennis often does. We like gymnastic apparatus, and after a hard day's work you'll pardon us for saying that we like something more exciting than a sermon or some lectures. We are fond of music, and often wish that there was a popular music hall in Toronto, like we hear of in Germany.

But do not think that we want to take all these things and give nothing back. In a certain young people's society of a certain downtown church in this city, . . . [$760] was given by less than a hundred of Toronto's young workers, mostly girls (it is safe to say, generally, on small salaries). They were contributing also to the pastor's salary and other funds . . .

June 20

I had worked in the average and the almost-ideal factory. I decided for my third experience I would look up a place, well, say not too near the celestial regions. I applied for a job in a little office on one of the upper floors . . . It is no exaggeration whatever to say that one needed a shovel as well as a broom to get the dirt and dust off these stairs . . . There was a manager and a forewoman in the office, though I learned later that the forewoman was usually in the work room. "Had I any experience in edging or lining boxes?" she asked. "No, but I think I could learn," I said.

Again no references were required. "Come on to-morrow at eight o'clock," I was told. This sounded quite luxurious. The hours were 8 to 6. I was to get $4.00 a week, time work . . . Beginners were taken on, it is true, at $4.00 a week, but as soon as they could earn over $4.00 a week they were put on piece work. . . .

It was by no means a light or pleasant room, however, and the lowness of the ceilings, and the machinery whirring overhead, added to its depressing effect . . . There was a good deal here of the same spirit of kindness among the employés that I had found in the other factories. They seemed anxious, all of them, to see me pick up the work quickly and do well at it, ready to tell me how slow they had been at first and how discouraged. The work room was divided into four sections of four workers each. It is in these factories where people work in little sections in handwork, that you get a chance to know the mental and moral fibre of your work-fellows. Where they work on busy, whirring power machines, there is not much opportunity for morals to get in. But a small section of handworkers can have its own little chats and exchange of ideas. . . .

They seemed to me to be in need of more workers. I found out later that they had to work evenings sometimes. I shuddered at the thought of these little kiddies of 14, 15 and 16 coming back to work at night at nine or after in a section [of the city] like this. . . .

There was no lunch room. I did not expect it after the stairs. I ate my lunch on a window sill looking down into the back yards across the lane. ... old barrels, and boxes, and rusty scraps of tin, and old hat-brims, and worn-out shoes ... Wouldn't the air be cleaner, I wonder, for us all to breathe, if the back yards of the city were looked after once in a while? ... I turned my back directly towards the window in order to gulp down and keep down the rest of the lunch.

I walked over after eating it to an end of the factory where a few girls were grouped about another window. A group of men were reposing during the noon hour on the other side of the street below. I perceived there was a code of signals of some kind passing. I also perceived that I had put somewhat of a damper on things, and was not wanted in this select circle, though the girls said nothing rude or unkind ... I fled to the only remaining side where there were windows. This time I was more fortunate. Down in the side street below, a group of kiddies of our factory were playing ball with two or three of the boys from adjoining industries. The ball game looked clean and health-giving. I drank in the sunny air of the south window [and] found there the little golden-haired girlie of the table behind me, eating her lunch alone. She smiled in a friendly way, and I began to chat with her. She had been there less than a year, and was not making very much, somewhere between $4.00 and $5.00 a week.

"I used to work upstairs," she said, "but there was only three girls up there and two of them left, and I didn't want to be the only girl up there working among the men, so I asked the foreman to put me downstairs."

"Do you find the work hard?" I asked. "Oh no, it's easy work," she said. "That's nice," I answered. "If you're not too tired at night, you feel more like going to night school or something like that." "I used to go to night school," she said, "but father said that if I worked all day that was enough for me. I shouldn't go to school at night."

June 25
Bert, I will call her, isn't a bad sort of kiddie if she were headed in the right direction. She is certainly unusually quick and clever, one of the best workers in the factory. Her pay card brought her $8.70 that week. She looks about 16. Her eyes are big and brown and beautiful, but I am afraid they have seen "ower much".

"I just hated it the first morning I was here," Bert told me, "I went home and I just wouldn't go back, but Mother said I might just as well finish my day out, and I did, and then I stuck out the week and now I like it."

"I can make meanings with my eyes," she said in the course of the afternoon's conversation ... She jumped off her stool and faced me and went through a series of flashes with those big brown orbs ... The display of fireworks ended with an alluring lift of the eyes and brows. I could not interpret the look, and she refused to do it for me. . . .

Sadie, the girl who works at the other half of my table, is older, much more mature looking, has "puffs" all over her head, and wears a soiled net-waist. I discovered I can learn a good deal of life from Sadie. Her knowledge of life is much greater than mine, that is if as some people think, knowing life is knowing the seamy side. Sadie is one of the girls who has a home in the city but does not live in it, prefers to board. She boards just now with a sister, but the home is too far away, so she is coming downtown to live with friends. Her pay card this week amounted to about $6.00 Last week she stayed off most of the time, and her pay amounted to $1.20 . . . I got quite a few pages of romance from Sadie, too. She told us all about Georgie, who used to work upstairs in that same factory.

. . . "[Mother] thought an awful lot of him. Now that I'm not livin' at home she doesn't know that we're not goin' together yet. She says to me sometimes when I go home, 'When are you and Georgie goin' to get married? You've been going together three years now. It's a long time.' and I just say, 'Oh yes, it is rather long.'"

"How does she like Jimmie?" Bert enquired. "Oh, she doesn't like him at all, she hasn't seen him but once, but I daren't let her know I'm goin' with him."

The announcement of a fortune having fallen to two working girls filled up a good deal of an afternoon's conversation. Each girl spent it in her own individual way. They all seemed to agree about a nice house, and furniture, and an automobile. . . .

Looking back on my memories of this factory, one thing stands out pre-eminently in my mind. The working girl needs more than a living wage. She needs often to learn how to live on the wage . . . Sadie, for example, needs to learn not to buy expensive cuff-links on the instalment plan, needs to learn that she does not need a $9.00 hat . . . Kiddies such as these around me should not be coming back to work in the evening in the district below Queen. No employer should be allowed to require that.

The 14-year-old stage is really the most important educative period of a girl's life, and just at that stage she is liberated entirely from the schoolroom and sent into the industrial world . . . Would we not do well to look at the educational system of Germany, under which the employer of labour is compelled to have given a certain amount of daily instruction to his employés? We believe there are great potentialities in our Technical school along this very line. We are beginning to believe that we need more than technical schools.

July 2
I was sitting in a group of my 14-year-old factory friends at noon hour

when I propounded the question rather tentatively, "Wouldn't you rather do housework for somebody, girls, than to work in a factory? You get bigger pay."

The young faces around me drooped a little. Instantly I perceived that I had offended. I had made what is called "a break."

"Mother says," said one, "that I cannot do housework unless I do it in my own house." This "mother says no" reason is a very common one for girls not going into housework. Mother does not like the social standing for her daughter. Besides, the little girlie helps by bringing a part of her money home when she works in a factory, and the family are kept together.

"You are not thought as much of," says another. "You have to work harder at it," says a third... "It is every night in the week but one, and Sundays too."

I put the same question to Alma, the more mature girl, in her little $1.25 room. "I don't like being bossed so much," she answered. "At the factory, when your work's done, your time's your own. You can go where you like."

Aside from the reasons given, there is a lure about the factory... The girls like to be where there is "something doing," where things happen, where the joke is being bandied and the bit of gossip, good-or ill-natured, whichever it may be, passed along. The kitchen looks a lonely place down behind the board fences and between the brick walls....

Our pretty sentiment about the servant girl's good home is more or less flimsy farce. The home where she is employed is not in any sense her home... Home is where love is, where they have a community of interests. The servant girl occupies no such place in your dwelling. Which one of your home circle would feel he "belonged," if he or she had to eat alone in the kitchen and live apart from the rest?...

One must allow too for the mating instinct... The girl in the factory has "bows" in her hair and "beaux" in her train. The girl in the kitchen is shut away from these lords of creation... She is only out one night a week and altogether she feels that the back gate is a sort of limit to her prospects... Besides, when John calls on your servant girl, he has to go in by the back gate. If he is a somewhat proud young man, he does not like it. A month later, when she has taken a place at the factory, he can call at the front door of the boarding house and ask for "Miss Samson Johnson," or whatever it is. They both feel that she now has a different standing in the world.

Above all, it is this loss of caste, this social slur that women themselves have put upon housework, that accounts for the unwillingness of our girls to do it....

MUNITIONS PLANT: WOMEN WAR WORKERS, 1917

Until the middle of World War I, only lower-class females took factory work. Many working-class women had been drawn into the war plants established by the Imperial Munitions Board. Then, according to these memoirs, 'all of a sudden' middle-class women moved from 'pretty work' for the Red Cross or YWCA to the new shell factories. The change was caused by the crisis of the Western Front. Similar shifts, on an even more massive scale, would take place in World War II; in both cases there is some evidence that women who learned that wage-earning meant a new independence tried to stay in the work force. More questionable is Mrs Nelson's middle-class assumption that extravagance and luxury were the main motives for their behaviour.

Interview with Mrs Elaine Nelson [pseud.] in Russell Hann (ed.), *The Great War and Canadian Society* (Toronto, New Hogtown Press, 1977). Reprinted by permission of Russell Hann.

Someone asked me one time—it was either the YMCA or YWCA—if I would join a team that was going to serve in the canteen in the big munitions factory, which was the Fairbanks-Morse, which was on the corner of King and Lansdowne. Well, it was about two hours' journey for me by streetcar, and we were on an all-night shift, but I went, and found it very, very difficult to stay awake. There were certain hours of the night that were very, very hard to stay awake.

The people would come in perhaps off and on all week. There was always a rush before and after the time when they were going to work. For instance, in our case, we were working the night shift from eleven to seven. If they came in at eleven, they were cold, they'd been on the streetcar, they wanted a bowl of soup. Then when the machine broke down, they'd come in again, and then when they were through, before they'd go home, they'd want to have a bowl of soup because it was still slightly dark and miserable, and they could have that and go home and go right to sleep and have a bit of rest, before they woke up for something to eat.

Was that common for that service to be offered in munitions?

No, I don't think so. I think probably Fairbanks-Morse decided they were going to have as many conveniences for their workers as possible, and probably offered it to the 'Y' and said, "We'll give you this room and equip it for you.' It was just a huge, long factory room. It could have been forty feet long. There were tables and chairs and the big counter and coffee urn and that kind of thing, and ways of heating the soup up.

It was all Campbell's soup—can't *bear* the smell of it to this day. (I wasn't used to canned soup at any time anyway. Ugh! Terrible stuff.)

We were all very annoyed because the supervisor—I imagine she was the only paid person—was determined that we were going to give very skimpy ladles of soup to the workers who came in. We felt it was *not* fair. They had to go from their factory building across a long area in the cold or the heat or the rain or storm to get to the building where this canteen was. And they were cold, and they were tired, or they were hot and tired and hungry. And I felt that they needed that good generous bowl of soup, and I ladled it out regardless, until finally we really came to a thorough understanding. I told her that I thought that they were getting that soup either for nothing—it was canned soup—or at cost certainly; that the factory supplied the great big room completely equipped for them to work; that all their workers were volunteers, and that it behooved them to be very generous to these people who were making the shells with which we were going to help win the war. And I resigned promptly.

What was your reaction to seeing big industry for the first time?

I didn't see it until I started to work. I just arrived at the canteen and never got anywhere else. Then, when I asked if I could get a job there, then my first experience was when they said, 'We'll allot you the first set of the howitzer shells.' The foreman met me at the door, and he just beckoned to me. The reason why he couldn't say anything was because you couldn't have heard him! And I just had to follow him. I went through all these avenues and avenues of clanking, grinding, crashing machines. Some of them were so close together that in order to get to their machines they'd built a kind of a stile—several steps up, and then you walked across, and then you went down again. On the line that I was on, some of the people had to get to their work that way.

Well, the foreman just led me in behind this machine, and I stood by the wall and watched. He demonstrated how to do *one* shell, and then he stood aside and pointed to me. And so I very gingerly walked up to the machine and did what he had done. Then he stood there and said, 'Again!' and I did another one. Then he just waved me goodbye and off he went. I was *panic-stricken*. But I got used to it, so used to it that pretty soon I was looking around me seeing what my fellow workers were like.

You couldn't talk to anybody—that was another thing! When you got up to the rest rooms and the cafeteria it was bedlam there, because no one had been able to talk all day or for the eight hours. So you were just jabbering for all you were worth, jabbering and eating because you were hungry, you were cold, or you were hot, one or the other. The canteen was a godsend for those people, that and that restroom. We had to punch a clock when we went in, in the morning. The offices and that, and the little cupboards that we kept our clothes in—I always forget their name—but those were all in one building. Then when we got dressed, we had to go across this big yard to the other—oh, it was literally a hellhole! It was terrible.

What was the process like?

I imagine the shells came out of the blasting furnaces first, and then they would have to be put out into the yards to cool. And then gradually they were brought in and they were put on this conveyor belt. I was near the end with my back to the wall. Those things came along there, and there was a woman in front of me and on the side opposite to me, she did the first cut and I did the first cut. We pushed a lever and that lifted the shells up onto this conveyor belt and then a man—I don't know how he got there, I don't know what he did—but I just remember that he did something that lowered it onto our machines. When the shell came, I pushed this lever and the belt caused a knife to go just against the shell, and then it would start to peel. The shell was turning all the time. I pushed that lever against it. It would turn, and you had to *quickly* knock off these jagged long pieces before they got as far as your face, because they would just wing around, back and forth. You just knocked them off, and they fell behind the machinery. I imagine that every once and awhile they had to go and clear all this jagged stuff out. Then the next machine to me did the next cut and so on until it got to the end of the row. Then it was just like a beautiful piece of polished steel. Then it had to go some other place for other things. Oh yes, and right over there where this thing was—it looked like a great big chisel—was this little tap. Just before you put your machine on, you turned that little tap so it was pouring chemicals over that thing. And then you started. It poured all the time, and as these jagged pieces came out, it splashed this stuff. And that's what got all over us. It was really a miserable thing. There was a duckboard around our feet. It was right across this pan. I guess they were made of iron or something, because they would be about, oh, five, six inches deep, and it was full of that stuff. Now there must have been something that caused the suction for that to come up through the little tap when we turned it on. But we were standing over this wet, and our feet were wet, and the duckboards were slimy. There were little spaces in between so that all this stuff could go back in there. It was quite an endurance test, let me tell you.

I worked there almost a year and then I worked three months, perhaps four months, as a government inspector of these caps for the shrapnel shells. It was still a long journey for me and it was worrying me too much. I just had nightmares that I passed a shell or somebody else with me had passed a shell that had been imperfect and might kill our own boys. There were terrible accidents from the American shells in the First World War and in the Second too. But that was just a game. People were kibitzing, talking and laughing. That's why I couldn't stand that inspector's job. I couldn't stand it because some of the girls in that group—and some were my friends—were laughing and talking too much and not watching exactly what they were doing, and that worried me. I wanted to get out of it.

Were there many injuries?

The machinery was all open. The one thing they were terrified of was the belts and our hair, so we had to cover our hair. I used to wear a red bandana because the caps that they had—yellow caps with a frill on them —were ghastly things. We used to call them 'mob caps,' and they were made out of the same thing as our uniform. You looked so terrible. I wore a bandana, and I was called 'Gypsy.'

I don't remember any great tragedy but there could have been, your clothes getting caught or something getting caught. Certainly these jagged little things—I used to get a little panicky sometimes if I didn't break it. After it got a certain length it could just slash you. If it wouldn't break off you were literally fighting for your life almost. But gradually you became expert at doing that. Also you learned right from the very beginning that there was no fooling, there weren't any second chances with machinery like that. Oh, and on the other side of the wall where my back was, there were great big blasting furnaces that these shells came out of, so if ever there'd been a fire, there was absolutely *nothing* would have saved us. *Nothing* could have saved us. . . .

If I hadn't been as healthy as I was, I'm sure I would have had pneumonia for sure. Because you had to go wringing wet like that across this long courtyard before you got to the place where you could change all your clothes. It was bitterly cold. Your feet were frozen and the rest of you was just roasting because all the machinery was hot. You could smell this heat coming from behind you but you couldn't feel it. You could smell the hot molten metal and when we were on the way out there was one great big doorway where you could look and see. They'd open the furnace and it would just look like hell.

Why did you decide to go into munitions instead of working with the Red Cross?

Because anybody can do those other things—the older people could do that. It took young vigorous people of a good will to do that kind of work, you know. Things were bad for the war, for us, and we just felt we had to get our shoulder to the wheel and get down to business. When you're young, you do what everybody's doing. As soon as a few girls go in, then they all want to go in. It was the thing to do. But then when you got in you were interested, just as I happened to be. I think a lot of the girls—there's always some that are miserable and stupid and badly behaved—but on the whole they were a wonderful bunch, and I see so many of them to this day. It enriched my life really.

There was everybody, every single class, from the squire's lady to Judy O'Grady and some a few shades lower than Judy. I thought it was fascinating. You get in the canteen or up in that big restroom there and hear them talking. It was very, very interesting. And there's every kind: wonderful, brave women who were saving every nickel they could so they'd have enough money to buy a home when their husband came back; and some flighty, silly little fools that were running around with other men. You'd just see every kind.

I used to get a little cynical because I used to kind of feel that some of the good men had rotten wives and vice versa. I can just think of some of the experiences. One girl, pretty, little, empty-headed thing, ran around with some fellow. I couldn't see any reason at all why he wasn't in the war. She apparently had a very devoted husband, and he eventually was killed. She put on the fanciest widow weeds you could imagine and continued to go around with this fellow, but he didn't marry her. And I just thought it served the darn girl right. He just thought, 'Well, if you can try that on your husband you can just try that on me too, girlie.' I was very glad.

In meeting these people that we had never had any opportunity to meet before, and finding they were just the same as we were, but they just hadn't had the chances that we'd had for education and that kind of thing, we began to realize that we were all sisters under the skins. Wars do bring every class together and I think we need to do a little bit more of that without war if we can.

Another thing too: there's nothing that draws people together more than mutual trouble. When you read the newspapers and you see columns of deaths, of boys being killed, you read those names and you say, 'Oh, So-and-So's gone,' and then somebody's husband's gone, and somebody's fiancé's gone. And things went so much against us so often, so long that we just felt we *had* to. The boys are doing that for us, what are we doing for them? You just rolled up your sleeves and you didn't care how tired you were or anything else. It's a terrible thing that it takes a war and a national tragedy to pull things together....

When I first started I just wore the underclothes that I would wear ordinarily. In those days girls who had money wore what you call [crepe de Chine]. They were real silk underwear. Of course they just rotted in a week. When they got wet with the chemicals they just rotted. Of course they were stained hopelessly, so that I smartened up pretty quickly about that. And incidentally anyway, they weren't warm enough. So I had my brother's longjohns—he was six feet tall—and I had to roll them up to here and turn them back on the sleeves, and I was darn glad to have all that extra warmth.

I was amazed because the people who had never had anything much were the ones who were most careless with their clothes. I was simply astounded to see this one woman who had been our cleaning woman. Every week she would come and she'd perhaps pay $25.00 for a blouse. Well, that was an outrageous price to pay in those days. And she'd put that on, a beautiful blouse all beaded and everything. And the style was pearl grey or beige or white kid boots, and she would buy those and she'd wear them right into the machinery because she wanted everybody to see them. She'd leave the smock open a little bit so you could see this beautiful blouse. Of course the shoes were ruined the first day she was there and so was the blouse. But then the people who were used to good clothes looked after them, and the ones who weren't used to it just spent money like water.

Was that because they were making more money?

They'd never had much money before and they would probably have had to pay a neighbour or someone to look after their children. But they wanted to get this extra money so they'd have a lot when their husband came back. And then, incidentally, they had never had much so they did treat themselves to some things, and they deserved it—but not the extravagances. The cleaning woman wanted to wear the kind of clothes that I would have worn. You could hardly blame her, she had never had them in her life. But she didn't have sense enough to look after them. Well, I would have been tickled to death if she had had all those things—she deserved them because she was a hard-working woman. But she thought that if you were rich, you waste, and rich people don't waste. The reason they're rich is because they have never wasted.

GARMENT INDUSTRY: THE SPEED-UP AT EATON'S, 1929-1934

Speed-ups, wage cuts, and starvation pay in the needle trades were typical of an industry long subject to depression. Competing small shops and subcontractors could be played off against each other by big business. Unrest had been endemic since at least 1912, when men and girls staged a losing strike against Eaton's. For some years Eaton's had run its own garment shop with 'model' working conditions, but in the depression of the 1930s it began to revert to sweatshop practices. To placate business lobbies,

the 1920 Female Minimum Wage law had allowed certain industries to pay
a fifth of their workers less *than the weekly minumum: the '20 per cent*
class' who were supposedly learners or part-time girls. Such exceptions
made a mockery of protective laws when they were most needed. The
collapse in the garment industry at large began in 1926.

Royal Commission on Price Spreads (H. H. Stevens, Chairman), *Report*
(Ottawa, 1935), pp. 4410, 4417, 4426, 4442, 4448, 4518, 4520-2.

MRS. ANNIE S. WELLS, called and sworn.
   By Mr. Bullen:
   Q. Mrs. Wells, you reside where?—A. In Toronto.
   Q. And were you ever employed by the T. Eaton Co. Limited of that
city? A. Yes.
   Q. When did you first go there?—A. In the spring of 1916.
   Q. And you were employed until what date?—A. The 11th of July,
1934.
   Q. In what capacity?—A. I began as an operator.
   Q. By an operator you mean what?—A. I mean that I sewed up skirts or
blouses, or dresses, whatever were given to me.
   Q. And did you continue in that capacity throughout?—A. No. I oper-
ated on skirts, and then on dresses for three years, and then I was made
a teacher.
   Q. And then you were made a teacher?—A. Yes, to show the other girls.
   Q. And how long did you work in the capacity of teacher there to the
other girls?—A. Around twelve years.
   By Hon. Mr. Stevens:
   Q. How many years, I didn't quite catch that?—A. Twelve.
   By Mr. Bullen:
   Q. For twelve years you were a teacher there, and then when did your
vocation as teaching the other girls cease?—A. Well, that must have been
in 1931, so far as I can remember.
   Q. In or about 1931?—A. Yes, sir.
   Q. Then, in 1931 what did you do?—A. I went back on the machines
and made dresses.
   Q. Back as an operator again?—A. Yes.
   Q. Now, when you first went there, Mrs. Wells, how were you paid?—
A. I was paid $8 a week.
   Q. Yes?—A. I was paid $8 a week straight, you see. If I made $8 I got
$8 and if I didn't make $8 I still got $8.
   Q. That is to say, irrespective of what you made you got $8 a week?—
A. Eight dollars a week, and I was told that if at the end of three weeks
or four weeks I couldn't make the $8 I might lose my job.
   Q. Well, were you able to make the $8 a week?—A. I sure was.

Q. Well, without any undue modesty on your part, you say you were able to make $8 a week?—A. Yes. I made $10, $12, $14 and $16.

Q. In other words, you became fairly proficient on the machine?—A. Yes, sir.

Q. And were able to make good?—A. Yes.

The CHAIRMAN: She was paid those amounts over and above the $8, was she?

By Mr. Bullen:

Q. You were paid those amounts over $8?—A. Yes, sir.

By Mr. Young:

Q. If you made $16 you got it?—A. Yes, sir.

By Mr. Bullen:

Q. Yes, so that you were able to make your minimum right up to the time they put you on as instructress?—A. Yes.

Q. Teaching the other girls?—A. Yes.

Q. Well, we will come back to that later on. Now how were working conditions when you went there in 1916 and say on through 1920, 1924, 1925?—A. They were exceedingly good.

Q. Working conditions were good?—A. Yes.

Q. And did they continue in that shape throughout to the end?—A. Well, no. They were very good indeed until Sir John passed away.

Q. That is Sir John Eaton?—A. Yes, Sir John Eaton.

Q. What difference did you notice when he died?—A. Well, things were not so easy for us. We could not make our dresses and things quite so comfortably. We were not looked after quite so well; we didn't have the same help, and around 1929, 1930 and 1931 the prices were cut and cut and cut.

Q. What do you mean by prices cut and cut and cut?—A. The prices on each unit. You see, they made out a bundle, say at $5 or whatever the price might be, and they gradually worked it down until it was a great deal less than that, $3 or $3.80 a dozen.

Q. That is $5 per dozen?—A. Yes, and then, of course, they began to use the speeding up system.

Q. Well, do you want to describe to the Commission what the speeding up system consisted of?—A. Well now, I cannot say when the stop watch began exactly; I think that began in 1933. But in 1932 and 1933, and the short time I was there in 1934, we were badgered and harassed and worried.

Q. In what way, Mrs. Wells?—A. Well, you were told to work and work so hard at these cheaper rates to make the $12.50, and you were threatened if you did not make $12.50 you would be fired. You felt insecure with your job....

Q. What difficulty had you then?—A. Well, for one thing dresses were very much more elaborate, there was a great deal more to make on them; the styles were far more elaborate and, well, as I say, we were unable to make so many for the same price to make $12.50.

Q. Well, you say the styles were getting more elaborate. What about the price?—A. Well, so far as I could see the prices were extremely poor.

Q. Well, did they go up or down?—A. No, they went down, steadily down.

Q. The prices went steadily down?—A. Yes.

Q. And how was the price per unit on which your wage was based fixed?—A. I don't quite understand you.

Q. Well, who set the time and who set the price per dozen dresses that you had to make?—A. Well, we have an estimator, a lady called an estimator, Miss Lewis, and she sets the price.

Q. Yes. Did she make any test or anything of that sort?—A. No.

Q. She just set the price?—A. Yes.

By Mr. Young:

Q. For each operation?—A. There is an estimator, you see.

Q. And she sets the price for each operation?—A. Yes, for everybody, yes. She set the price and we did our best to make money on that, naturally.

By Mr. Bullen:

Q. After 1931 were you able to make the minimum?—A. No.

Q. You as instructress were not able to make it?—A. No, I never made it.

Q. Why?—A. Well, I was not able to make it because, I suppose—I am being as fair as I can be, Mr. Bullen,—I was slow at first because I had not been on piece-work for so long.

Q. Yes.—A. Well, I soon picked up speed and I could make around $11, $11.75, $12, $12.25, $12.35 and $12.40 but I never somehow made $12.50.

Q. Up until the 11th of July, 1934, did you ever in any week make the minimum?—A. No.

Q. You have never made the minimum?—A. No.

By Hon. Mr. Stevens:

Q. In 1916, when you were making the minimum you would recall the tension at which you worked?—A. Yes.

Q. The speed?—A. Yes.

Q. And the effort it took?—A. Yes.

Q. Would you consider that in 1931, when you went back on the machines as an operator that you worked as hard as you did in 1916 to get eight or nine dollars?—A. A good deal harder.

Q. Would you say from your experience in all those years as a teacher that you were giving more physical work and effort in 1931 when you went back than you were before?—A. Yes, I did.

Q. And for less pay?—A. For less pay.

By Mr. Bullen:

Q. Did you find, Mrs. Wells, any other girls in the same position of not being able to make the minimum who had easily made it before?—A. It appeared to be the common complaint that they could not make their minimum.

Q. Yes? Do you know why?—A. For some reasons. The prices on each bundle were too low and we were harassed. I suppose girls are foolish in that way, but they soon get nervous and upset, and we were harassed too much, badly harassed. . . .

By Mr. Edwards:

Q. You spoke about a stop-watch?—A. Yes.

Q. Was it an efficiency expert who stood behind you with a stop-watch?—A. Yes. Miss Lewis stood behind you or she had a seat nearby, and while she never did it to me, thank goodness—

By Mr. Bullen:

Q. Did you see it?—A. Yes.

Q. What was the effect on the operator?—A. Well, she was no good for the rest of the day.

Q. Did she do it under the same conditions you had to do your work?—A. No, because the bundle would be brought to her with the thread, and it would be opened for her. It would have everything all ready, and there would be no flaws, and she could do it as fast as she could, without any trouble, whereas we would have to hunt around for thread and maybe wait a quarter of an hour or twenty minutes to get a bundle. . . .

Q. Was it complained of, Mrs. Wells?—A. Yes, it was complained of constantly.

Q. Well now, what other steps were taken to make you speed up? You have told us about the stop-watch. What about the lists?—A. Well, we came out in July, and I should imagine that for about seven or eight months, the whole of 1934, and I should say part of 1933, lists were hung up at the back of the forelady's table with the numbers of the girls. Each girl had a number.

Q. You did not go by name but had a number?—A. No. I was No. 151.

By Hon. Mr. Stevens:

Q. Miss 151?—A. I was 151. The list was hung up there and a note against it showed the amount you had done the week before.

By Mr. Bullen:

Q. What do you mean by that?—A. Well, that you had not made your $12.50, that you had made $11.75 perhaps, that you were short. That was up against you. That was a bad mark.

Q. And what happened the next week? Did they make that 25 cents or 75 cents up to you?—A. No, they never made it up to me. I have never had that money made up to me.

Q. Did you not receive it any time you were there?—A. Never.

Q. You were only paid—A. What I made.

Q. All the time you were there?—A. Yes.

Q. And from 1931 until July, 1934, you never made the minimum?—A. No.

Q. So you were always practically in the 20 per cent?—A. No, not always, Mr. Bullen. I daresay quite frequently I was in the 20 per cent class because I was out. I would be sent home for a day or a day and a half when we were slack. Then you could not expect $12.50. You only got what you made. Other weeks I would make $12 or $12.25 or $12.35. That is not the 20 per cent class, is it?

Q. You did not work all week?—A. Yes.

Q. You worked all week?—A. Yes.

Q. And you only made $12.25?—A. Yes.

Q. And they paid you $12.25?—A. Yes.

Q. Did you make an hourly rate of 28 cents?—A. I never calculated it that way. It was beyond me. I leave that to the office.

By Hon. Mr. Stevens:

Q. But you would work 44 hours for that $12.25?—A. Yes.

By Mr. Bullen: [referring to lunch-time]

Q. Did you always get the hour?—A. From 20 to 12 to 20 to 1. The bell would ring for lunch and the bell would ring to go in again but you had such a terrible time getting up and down stairs in the elevators that you would lose a quarter of that hour. The time office was moved from the main floor to the ninth floor.

Q. Where did you work?—A. On the 6th floor.

Q. What did you have to do when you went in, in the morning?—A. We went up to the ninth floor, took off your hat and coat, and clocked in. Then you would go down in the elevator or walk down to the sixth floor. At noon you had to take the elevator up to the ninth floor and clock out and then come down again to the main floor, and then when you came back from lunch you had to do the same thing in reverse.

By Mr. Edwards:

Q. Four times a day?—A. Four times a day.

By Mr. Bullen:

Q. How many people used that elevator?—A. Everybody in the factory.

Q. How many is everybody?—A. I would not like to say everybody, but four or five thousand.

Q. And how many elevators?—A. There were four freight and two passenger, and they would use the freight in the morning and the two passenger elevators, we used them, too, going up in the morning, but at noon, somehow or other, there was always a fight among the elevator men as to who would take us up and down and you had to run around with the others to find an elevator. Perhaps there were only two running. It was a muddle.

By Mr. Young:

Q. Some of the elevator men would refuse to take you up?—A. It was in their noon hour. You could not blame them.

Q. But did they refuse you?—A. I would not say they actually refused us, but they fought amongst themselves, and then you lost out....

Q. When did it start? When did this speeding up process start?—A. You mean the stop-watch?

Q. Yes, all of it?—A. You see, it gradually—you cannot say it began in any one particular week or day. It gradually accumulated from the depression, from 1929. It accumulated, got worse and worse and worse as time went on, until it was unbearable.

Q. Then the depression——A. Started it.

By Mr. Bullen:

Q. Now I see in Mr. Gordon's report that conditions seemed to be a little better as far as the girls were concerned, particularly the girls who were involved in what is called the lock-out——A. Yes.

Q. It has been referred to as a strike?—A. No, it is a lock-out.

Q. We will develop that later on. Conditions improved from the 2nd of March to the 2nd of July, 1934, over a period of the 29th September to the 1st of March, 1934?—A. Yes.

Q. Do you know from what cause?—A. We joined the union.

Q. You joined the union? When did you join the union?—A. We started going to the union and listening to the lectures in February.

Q. Then would you tell the Commission just what you say is included in this speeding up, just give us the items?—A. Of the speeding up?

Q. Yes.—A. Well, you have to work extra hard. You had to sit at your machine from a quarter to eight until twenty minutes to one and go as hard as you could. You had no time to get up and have a drink of water or powder your nose or look at anybody, you just went on working. And, of course, they expected you to make and make more than you really could....

Miss JEAN CHAMBERS, called and sworn.

By Mr. Bullen:

Q. Miss Chambers, were you ever employed by the T. Eaton Company Limited?—A. I was.

Q. For what period?—A. Probably ten years....

Q. Did you notice conditions improve at all at any time from 1929 and 1930 on?—A. In about the first of 1934, at the time this Stevens investigation was going on and Mr. Cameron broadcasting over the radio—

Q. What about?—A. About conditions in this particular place where I worked, although the name was never given.

Q. And who was Mr. Cameron?—A. Who is Mr. Cameron?

Q. Yes—A. Ross M. Cameron, of the Presbyterian Church.

Q. He was the minister of the church and he was speaking over the radio on what?—A. On conditions.

Q. And you say as a result of that something happened?—A. We noticed that we were not told to work so fast to make up the $12.50, we were not told that we were going to be fired, it seemed much easier.

Q. I see, you were not told about having to make up your $12.50 and were not told that you were going to be fired?—A. It was a little easier on the nerves.

Q. Was there a decided improvement along that line that you really noticed?—A. There was in conditions of driving.

Q. Yes?—A. And we joined the union, of course. We had asked for $15, for our prices to be raised so that we could make $15 a week but our prices were not raised so that we could make that, but we received $14.20 whether I made it or not.

Q. That is after you joined the union you got a better salary?—A. After we joined the union.

By Mr. Sommerville:

Q. You received it on that basis for the hours worked?—A. Yes.

By Mr. Factor:

Q. Why did you leave Eatons? Did you leave them of your own accord?—A. Yes.

Q. Why?—A. Well, my mother was in the hospital sick and she passed away and I never went back.

Mr. BULLEN: That is all, thank you.

The WITNESS: I would like to mention to you, in that nerve-racking I found the elevators very nerve-racking, and we had to wait so long after our time clocks were changed up to the ninth floor to the time office from the main floor; we had to waste so much time in the mornings when one went in there, waiting around for elevators, and at the noon hour when we came out and at the noon hour when we came in.

By Mr. Bullen:

Q. What happened then? You walked up to the time floor on the ninth floor at a quarter to eight?—A. If you were half a minute late in the morning, well then your number was taken.

Q. And what did that mean?—A. It was sent to head office....

Miss WINNIFRED WELLS, called and sworn.

Examined by Mr. Bullen.

Q. I believe you were employed by the T. Eaton Company?—A. Yes.

Q. What year did you go there?—A. In September, 1916.

Q. As what?—A. As an operator.

Q. How long did you remain?—A. Until 11th July, 1934.

Q. Now, did you find conditions any different during, we will say, 1916 on for a period, than you did in the last three years, 1932, 1933, 1934, when you were there?—A. I found conditions better, very greatly better, in fact very good.

Q. Conditions were good up until what time?—A. Up until 1929 and 1930.

Q. Then what happened?—A. Well then prices began to be cut. . . .

Q. Did you always make your minimum wage, the $12.50?—A. Yes—the odd once and awhile that I fell down on it. One time when I fell down was the beginning of January, 1934, on one day.

Q. Did you find it any more difficult to make it in 1933 and 1934 than you had prior to 1929 and 1930?—A. Yes, I did.

Q. Why?—A. Well because prices being low, you had to do a great deal more work. You had to do more garments to make your $12.50, naturally and then of course, at that time we had no lady to give out the work. We had to go and take our own work, and it was a matter of who could get the most work. You would have to go and take your own work, keep on going and getting it.

Q. What effect physically had it on you, if any?—A. Well, I was tired right out. I would go home at nights and I would be so tired I could not eat my supper. I could not sleep at night; and another thing, examiners had to stand all day. You are not allowed to sit. And I would be so tired and stiff going home on the street car, I would just dread getting a seat, because if I sat down, I could not get up again, my knees and my legs would be so stiff. . . .

By Mr. Bullen:

Q. Well then, are you able to speak from your own knowledge as to the effect of this lowering of prices on the other girls in your own factory?—A. Yes I can.

Q. Can you instance to the Commission any instance of the effect of it? —A. Well, the girl that worked beside me was away for two months with nervous exhaustion, and I would go around—

Q. What was her name?—A. Carrie Cuthbert.

Q. Miss Cuthbert?—A. Yes.

Q. Yes?—A. I would go around to the operators, you know, if I had to take work back to them or anything many times, I would go back to them and find them crying, and I would say, "What is the matter; what is wrong to-day"?

Q. Probably my friend will object to what was said. You found the girls crying?—A. Crying, yes.

Q. Any thing else?—A. Well, they were generally in a very high strung condition.

Q. Besides the cutting of prices, was there any other evidence of speeding up of the work that you know of?—A. Well of course that is—the work came in at the last minute. We were the last people to handle it, you see, and we had to speed up to get it out in the time.

Q. Did you see any lists?—A. Yes.

Q. What were on the lists?—A. Long foolscap paper.

Q. What did they have on them?—A. All the girls' numbers and the amount of special money.

Q. What do you mean by "special money?"—A. Money that they had not made, was supposed to have been given to them.

Q. When?—A. For a period of six months.

Q. Do you mean money which was given the week before?—A. Yes.

Q. Do you know for what purpose?—A. To bring them up to the $12.50.

Q. The difference between what they earned and the $12.50?—A. Yes.

Q. Where was this list posted?—A. On the forelady's table. . . .

Q. Was there any comment made to you about the times you had fallen down?—A. Yes, I was sent home.

Q. What? How long had you been there? When did you go there?—A. 1916.

Q. In 1916?—A. Yes.

Q. You were sent home when?—A. On January 2, 1934.

Q. 1934? You had been there 18 years?—A. Yes.

Q. You had fallen down how often?—A. Very seldom.

Q. Did you fall down on this occasion when they sent you home?—A. Yes, for one day.

Q. Will you tell the Commission about that?—A. Well, it was the 2nd of January, 1934, and so far, nothing had been said to the examiners about having to earn $12.50, like they did to the operators, you see. Well, on this day—New Year's day was Monday, and this happened on Tuesday, and Mr. Jeffries came to us right after lunch, and he asked each one of us in turn had we made our money for the Friday, the previous Friday, and I said, "No, I have not." I think I was about 30 or 75 cents short.

Q. On the Friday?—A. On the Friday; and we had not any too much work that week, you see. Well, he went away and he came back again in about half an hour's time, and he said: "You go home; go home and don't come back until I send for you; take a week anyway, and we will send for you when we are ready." Well, he did not say why I was going home.

By the Chairman:

Q. Was that with pay or without pay?—A. Without pay. So I went to him and I asked why I was being sent home, and he said he did not have to tell me. I went to him again and I asked him. I said, "I refuse to go home unless you give me a good reason why I was going home for a week." And he said if I wanted to know I would have to go to Mr. Conroy. Mr. Conroy was second man in the department. . . .

Q. Who was the head? He was ahead of Mr. Jeffries?—A. Yes. So I had to hunt around a long time. I found Mr. Conroy: I asked him. And he said that was a new system that we are bringing in, every time a girl fell down on her work she would get a week's holiday, go home for a week. And I asked him if he thought that was quite fair; that that was the first day in the week; I had the rest of the week to make up to the $12.50. And he did not seem to consider that was anything at all. And I asked him how he thought I was going to live. I said to him, "If I come back at the end of the week and I fall down again on my money, what is going to happen then. He said, "You will go home again the second week."

COMPETING STANDARDS: HOMEWORK AND SWEATSHOPS IN QUEBEC

Scott and Cassidy were closely linked to CCF social reformers and to the industrial unions in the garment trade. Their carefully researched report fleshed out the Price Spreads inquiry and had an explosive effect on middle-class opinion. In bitter strikes two years later, these unions were victorious in Toronto and Montreal factories. However the competition from rural and small-town workers continued into the 1950s; the flouting of minimum wage laws and the exploitation of immigrants by unscrupulous employers still exist.

F. R. Scott and H. M. Cassidy, *Labour Conditions in the Men's Clothing Industry* (Toronto, Nelson, 1935), pp. 5, 23-5, 27-8, 29, 30, 32-3. Reprinted by permission of F. R. Scott.

Prior to the depression, from 1926 to 1929, the number of employees deriving their support from the men's clothing industry was somewhat over 11,000 and of these about 10,000 were wage-earners. The number of women in the industry was slightly larger than the number of men. About 4,000 of the employees were in Ontario, and more than 6,000 were in Quebec. The largest single group of the clothing workers in Toronto and Hamilton is Jewish, while there is also a certain number of Italians, Ukrainians, Poles and other immigrants among them. In Montreal, the Jewish group is also by far the most numerous, while there are various Eastern European immigrants and some French Canadians as well. In Quebec country districts, there is a considerable number of French Canadian workers employed. It will be noted that the working force has been recruited largely from immigrant sources.

The major problem with which the wage-earners in the industry had to contend before the depression was unemployment, on account of the irregular seasonal operations of the clothing factories. Naturally, the climatic factor makes for seasonal variation in the manufacture and sale of men's clothing—heavy clothing being made in the late summer and early fall for the winter months, and lighter clothing in the spring for the summer. The fact that the industry was made up very largely of small establishments competing furiously with one another made it practically inevitable that each enterprise should guide its production policies by immediate considerations of marketing, with little or no attempt to overcome seasonal fluctuations by careful forward planning of output. . . .

While the industry, as has been shown, is concentrated largely in the City of Montreal, the competition of the shops in other towns and villages in Quebec is a very important factor in determining working conditions generally. The country shops have lower rents to pay, operate under lower minimum wage schedules, are undoubtedly less supervised by government inspectors charged with the enforcement of hours and wages regulations, and can obtain an abundant supply of cheap labour amongst the French Canadian population. They compete in the Montreal market, and the Montreal employer, particularly the better type employer, is continually under pressure to meet their competition by reducing his labour costs.

Two other factors have tended to lower the standards of the workers in the Province of Quebec. One is the great importance of the contract shop. We have seen that most of the work in Ontario is done in "inside" shops, that is, by workers employed by the manufacturer on his own premises. A great proportion of the work in Quebec, both in Montreal and elsewhere, is done in contract shops. From information supplied by the Montreal Clothing Contractors' Association and the union we estimate that at least 2,000 workers in the province were thus employed in the autumn of 1933. By its nature the contract shop lends itself to the worst evils of competition. It is small (the average number of employees for 95 contractors we found to be 20) is housed cheaply, can easily be set up, moved or closed down, and requires very little in the way of overhead. The contractor's principal concern is the cost of his labour, since he neither buys materials nor sells completed garments. Consequently competition between contractors becomes almost entirely a question of competition in forcing down labour standards, and this process has proceeded unchecked during the depression. This means that a shift from town to country is a comparatively simple matter for the contractor. Cheap labour is the magnet that attracts him.

The other factor which helps to explain the poor conditions in Quebec is the union situation which prevailed until September, 1933. From 1929 the Amalgamated had grown progressively weaker in Montreal, until finally in 1932, it was practically displaced by a rival union, the United

Clothing Workers. Employers could, and did, play one union off against the other, and the competition between the two made any systematic enforcement of wage agreements impossible. This condition was overcome by the strike called by the Amalgamated on September 5, 1933, to which 4,000 workers responded. At the end of four days a new agreement was reached with the employers calling for a 44 hour week in Montreal and a 20 per cent increase on existing wage rates, with further concessions from employers to take effect from December 1, 1933. The Amalgamated now has control of about 80 per cent of the industry in Montreal. The country districts, outside of Joliette and a few isolated shops elsewhere, are still non-union. . . .

Our interviews with some of the individual workers in these shops only help to fill in details. In one Joliette shop we found a family of six (two female and four male) employed on various operations. They stayed every night till closing time, and put in hours running as high as 72 in a week. Their wages were listed in the books as four at $2.00, one at $5.00 and one at $7.00 regardless of hours worked. One young girl of 19, in Ste. Rose, had been receiving $2.00 for 55 hours' work before the strike, or less than four cents per hour. She was an orphan, with two young brothers in a local French Canadian academy and one sister working. At that rate she could not even pay the $4.50 per week which her room and board cost her, and had to be helped by the sister. After the strike her wages rose to $6.00. In the same shop a widow of 39, sole support of four children, was earning $9.00 to $10.00 for about 60 hours' work. As she lived in Montreal she had to take another hour or hour and a half each day, and pay the cost of transportation to and from her work. We have 31 envelopes from four women workers here; they range in amount from $1.72 to $5.54. The latter amount was for 68 hours' work and the hourly rates of the four ran from eight to ten cents. One of them was the daughter of a farmer with six children; her efforts added about $3.00 per week to the family budget. There seems little doubt that in the country districts of Quebec girls from farms are obtainable at very low rates owing to their ability to live at home. Every additional dollar is to them so much money found. The farm itself is thus in effect subsidizing the employer and assisting him to drive down living standards in the industry as a whole. . . .

In concluding our account of wages and earnings in Quebec we may say that we had no opportunity to determine to what degree the manufacture of garments is being carried on in private homes. Mr. W. L. Mackenzie King found this practice to exist in 1898. We have some evidence that it has not died out. One worker we found who had been, until 1932, working at home with her mother for the previous ten years, making boys' pants for a contractor. A social service official in Montreal informed us that a woman who had applied for relief this year was discovered to be working on boys' garments in her home, performing an operation for which she received 25 cents a dozen. Mr. Francq of the Minimum Wage Board stated that he had heard of garments being delivered in vans from door to door, like milk or bread, and collected later by the contractor. One of the writers was taken to a house in Montreal, where in a basement room lit only by a glaring electric light, a man, his wife, and a girl were working beside a pile of garments. To trace this kind of work would be extremely difficult. We refer to it simply as being the sort of competition which is always possible in the present uncontrolled state of the industry. It may safely be assumed that, to the extent the practice exists, it is being carried on at wage rates below those obtaining in the ordinary shops. Neither the Minimum Wage Laws nor the Factory Acts extend to private homes where no strangers are employed. . . .

In the matter of shop conditions, as in wages and hours, the difference between the better and the worse shops is very great. We visited two well-run establishments in Montreal, where the layout of the machines was carefully planned, the lighting and heating arrangements were fully satisfactory, the toilets modern and clean, and the comfort of the workers was clearly an important consideration of the employer. One of these shops had a lunch and rest room, but this had been abandoned under pressure of competition during the depression, with the result that we saw a number of employees during the lunch interval sitting beside their machines to eat their scanty meal. Even in these good shops it must be remembered that piece-work is general, so that the pressure of work upon the employees is severe. The writer was struck by the appearance of haste, strain and anxiety on the faces of many of the workers working under what are called good conditions.

The ordinary small contracting shops in Montreal also varied considerably in their facilities and conveniences. A number of them are located in some of the large buildings—such as the Caron Building on Bleury Street, and here the conditions are relatively good. Overcrowding was usually the main difficulty. Besides these better located shops we saw several in poorer parts of the town, where the conditions were definitely bad. One shop on St. Lawrence Street was reached by two steep and dirty staircases, leading into a room lighted only by windows in the rear. The toilets here were filthy, and entirely boxed off from daylight and ventilation. One sink provided drinking facilities. The whole surroundings of the workers were drab and sordid.

Another shop, definitely in the sweat-shop class, was carefully inspected by two of our assistants. It belonged to a small coat contractor, who worked there with his wife and eleven employees, eight male and three female. It was situated in the basement of a house, the only sources of ventilation being two doors, which were normally closed, a front window and a back window, the latter being partly boarded up by two toilets built around it. There was no plan to the lay-out of the machines, each worker being given just enough room for his or her operation. Piles of garments and scraps littered the floor, making it difficult to pick one's way across the room. The only heat came from a small stove in the centre and artificial light had to be used at all hours. A single sink served for washing and drinking purposes. The general impression left by the disorganized overcrowding, foul air, absence of sunlight and piles of cloth was one of complete and utter disregard for the welfare and comfort of the workers. Driven by the iron law of competition, the employer could think of nothing but keeping down his costs.

The fact that struck us most about this shop was that the workers, when questioned, had no complaints to make about their conditions of labour. They were all Poles, most of whom had never worked under any better conditions, and who, going home in the evening to rooms for which they were paying from $4.00 to $7.60 per month, must have found little contrast between their day and night quarters. By such shops the pace is set in the relentless process of driving down living standards.

ORGANIZING THE COCKROACH SHOPS: MONTREAL, 1937

Leah Roback, Educational Director of the International Ladies' Garment Workers' Union (1937-9) recalls the crisis in middle-class reform in the 1930s. Working-class militancy was a grass-roots phenomenon, not merely the work of Communists of the Workers' Unity League, the 'new unionism' of the CIO, or Catholic nationalists. As the well-educated daughter of Jewish immigrants—traditionally a central group in the needle trades—Leah Roback was in a unique position to understand conditions and the need for labour education.

Interview by B. Ferneyhough with Leah Roback.

I had done a stint from '32 to '34 as an Educational Director at the YWHA, and there I used to find it so difficult because we were right in the slum area where kids had nowhere to go, and some of the board members, felt that we shouldn't do too much. There were problems of adolescence, and so on. . . .

Well, the dressmakers were going on an organizational campaign, and I had been asked if I would want to come in and take on the educational director work. I thought that would be fine. I would be in my milieu, and I felt very good then. They had a very fine person, a woman, Rosa Pessotta who was a hard-working organizer, who had organized the length and breadth of the United States, and she was very co-operative and gave us carte-blanche. And I also want to say that there was a young secretary we had there, Yvette Cadieux, a young French Canadian, who did a lot of work in the French field, a girl who came from a middle-class background, brought up by the nuns, but who did a magnificent job. As Educational Director we had the programming to do, but it was not only programming, there was organizing. You had to meet with the workers, go to the factory, help them to understand that it was the Union which would bring them better conditions, because the conditions were vile. Well, first of all, the conditions in the factory—I remember there in '37 when we started organizing in January, the girls (I was especially working with the girls), because they had no defence, and at that time most of them were French-speaking, who were the operators, and the Jewish girls, some of them were operators but most of them were finishers, drapers and examiners. And naturally, it was a dog-eat-dog industry. Now, I don't know why it was, but it seemed anyone, if he had a couple of hundred dollars or knew somebody who would write a note for him, he could open up one of these sweat-shops in the Jacobs Building, or in the Wilder Building. The French girls used to call them *les cocrons* and a *cocron* is a French-Canadian slang expression. What is a *cocron* in English? It's slang, it's a slang for "a hole in the wall", you know, but *cocron* is much more descriptive, than a "hole in the wall", and most of these places were infested with cockroaches. The girls sat and worked one near the other very closely. There was no such thing as rest period, of course. Your lunch you ate at your work and you worked as you ate. The boss—there was this favouritism—and it's a very sad thing to say it, because as a woman I always felt so lousy about it—it was the fact that if you were "dans la manche" as the French girls say it, if you were on the right side of the boss and the foreman, you had the bundles. You see they'd get bundles, and most of them they'd take them and work them together, but the girl who was willing to give the very fine intimate favours to the boss, she got the big bundles. There was no such thing as division of work, and remember, it was during the days of the depression, and if you worked 2 days, 3 days, a week, you were lucky, for $9.00 a week, or $7.00 a week. There were two girls who would be working, and the rest of them, if there were ten girls for a bundle, the favourite, she got it, and she felt so fortunate, and the workers were so envious. You know the favour that the boss did for her? She took that bundle home with her. Mama and grandmama and the little sisters and everybody worked on that because they had to turn the belt. She ran them up on the machine in the factory, but they had to turn them to get them back there. The belt, the buckles had to be sewn on, the buttons to be sewn on—all that was done at home. And they weren't paid for this homework; this was all counted in the bundle. This was what happened, and it shows you—no pay at all, not for work at home. You were supposed to have done it at the factory. If it wasn't done in the factory, take it home and get the family to work at it; and this is what went on. It was a miserable industry, and the workers didn't know any better, I mean, let us put ourselves in their places. They had no money, it was that or starve, and so, if you had to give favours to the boss, well, you gave them. What else could you do, eh? So you did, and you ate in this horrible place. There was no such thing as a cloakroom. Your clothes, you had to shake them out so that those cockroaches weren't on your coat or you wrapped them up in a box right near your work, and your sandwiches you ate them right there, and you had to do this, shove off the cockroaches, because that's the way it was in that Jacobs Building; and the Wilder Building the same thing, and the Bleury Building the same thing, and those other little bedroom—so small we used to call them "bedroom" factories.... So that when we taught organization, we mustn't forget that there had been the WUL Union before this time who had done a terrific job, but naturally they had not won. You know, many of the people thought that the French-Canadian workers with their Church and with the priest, and so on, that they wouldn't listen to the Unions. They'd be afraid, because let us not forget at that time you had the Catholic Syndicate who were also trying to organize the dressmakers. They were in this industry, the Catholic Syndicate led by Father Bertrand who was chaplain. They were working with the priests who on Sunday would preach in the north end where most of the dressmakers lived; "Don't join the Union, it is perfidious, you will not be able to live as Christians, as Catholics", and so on. But as some of the women said to us when they joined the Union: they said—"Look, that's all very well for him to talk from his pulpit on Sunday, but we have to feed ourselves, we have to pay rent, we have to dress, we have responsibilities to our children. My husband isn't working, so"—And they said. "It's all very well to talk, but if we can get a better way of living, all right, we'll join the Union." And they did, 4000 of them joined. The 1937 strike was a fine demonstration, and it was at the height of the season, when the spring orders had to get out. And it was very interesting to note the militancy that was developed in some of them. Naturally, they were afraid of their jobs, and some of them we had to sort of help them to understand; and so they did, they stayed away. It was at the time of Duplessis, and that was a very difficult time. I used to laugh because Duplessis, who was in cahoots with—I think his name was Stein, who was the representative of the bosses at that time—and they were known to see to it that their status was maintained. And Duplessis, I think for certain money for *la caisse électorale*, adhered to their request, and came out and said, "We're not going to have any of this kind of anarchy and this business of Communists, these organizers." And I used to laugh because Raoul Trépanier who was the leader of the Union at that time helping us to organize, *cher monsieur* Raoul Trépanier was anything but a Communist, believe me. [The leader of the Union] Bernard Shane, . . . saw Reds under the bed all the time, and to call him a Communist was a laugh, you know. But that was the emblem of the politics of Duplessis. And it was not easy to organize because it got around. You'd go to the people's homes and you'd talk with them. Naturally there was the problem of—"Yes, but what is going to happen? My daughter has to work," and so-and-so, and so it meant a lot of talking, a lot of talking.

This was a policy of the ILGWU, you always established an educational department, which was a good thing because it made them feel that they were getting something, and our Educational Department of the ILGWU had headquarters in New York. Naturally, you could not use the method of New York—most of them Jews, Italians, who had long been in the industry, who knew about Unions—you could not use that for the French-Canadian mentality, which is an entirely different mentality, to what they were doing in New York, and so, of course, there were times when it was rather difficult. For instance, we set up a Sunday morning class for the Jewish cutters, the Jewish pressers, I should say, some of the cutters who came, and we had a very dear man. He was a writer for the *Jewish Daily Eagle*, and he was the labour reporter. He went from Union to Union. This man was an honest man and a man who understood the political situation in the Province as well as the Trade Union Movement—he understood it very well. Now, he taught Sunday morning classes to the Jewish pressers and some cutters, as I'm saying, the men, and gave them labour history, which was what I wanted to do with the French girls, because you cannot just learn that you fight for five cents an hour increase if you don't know the economics and if you don't know the labour value and the price and the profit and everything, and that can be taught in a very simple manner, and so this was one of the things that I felt we needed. Unfortunately, this was not possible, and I could have stood on my head, I could not make the officials of the ILGWU, at that time, understand that that was important, because once we were able to teach them what their rights were, and how come these things are happening to them, and what they had to do, well, it was a sort of a superficial education. However, we started out with a library, something that had never been before was a library on the Trade Union Movement, and I was greatly helped to get the books, English books, through McGill University, and I loved the French books. This was the problem, so I went to the Ecole des Hautes Etudes. At that time they were where the Dawson College is now in Old Montreal, and there was a librarian, a Mr. Houde. He was a very lovely man, very fine person. He let me go through the stacks, and here—I laughed on the other side of my mouth, because so many people were being visited by Duplessis' police, where all the Marxist books were being taken out of their homes, Marxist, not Marxist, anything that did not agree with Duplessis, they were being hounded, and here was this beautiful library stacked with books on Marx, Engels, Lenin, all what you wanted, and I said to Monsieur Houde, I said, "Oo la la, you've got a gold mine here. Does Duplessis know?" He said, "Ssh! We don't want him to know." But there were the books, and I was able to take one or two books out, on labour and on price. And also they had a very fine collection of good literature in French which we were able to have. We didn't have many readers, because nobody read in those days. Who read? Who bought books? By the time you bought bread and so on, well, you just didn't have money for books, and so we had the library and we also had some courses. I taught English, because you see at that time there were many of the Jewish people coming out of the eastern European countries, and they were coming to Montreal and they were in the industry, and some of them were highly cultured people from Europe, and here they couldn't earn their living because they couldn't get into their fields where they had been trained, so they went into, as we call it, the "schmata" trade, you know, and the French call it "industrie de la guénille". And so, they wanted to learn English. So I ran an English class, and I ran a French class for the English-speaking workers who wanted to learn French. And that was very interesting, but we were able to get to know one another so well. And then we had classes in dancing because it used to be so sad. We'd run a dance, and the men would line up on one side and the women on the other side, and they'd sit down and they'd stare at one another. They didn't know how to dance, unless they danced their own type of dancing. And so we had dancing classes, and we also had some speakers come out. And then we inaugurated the first "Bal des Midinettes". This takes place every November, as it does in Paris. And I was the one that started that with the workers and with our officials, and I had my experience at describing dresses, but there we were. We asked a favour of the bosses, and I'm not that kind of a Trade Union organizer. I don't like favours from the boss; if I have to go on a grievance to discuss with him, I don't want him to throw at me—"Look at all the favours we gave you, the dresses for your ball." I don't like that kind of thing. However, this was the one ball that I had been responsible for. They lent us the dresses, and we elected the woman who was the best one, La Reine, the Queen. Anyway it was a very lovely affair, and it was highly enjoyed. Then of course, as I said before, there wasn't a need for educational department work a full day, so we would look after grievances. Workers would come up from a shop, a shop steward—You see, this was where we needed lessons for them in the field of Trade Unionism, because if they had been able to read these things, you know, they could have really developed, they could have had definite classes....

And we go on now to 1939 when things were not so good and there was talk of war, and I felt that I had done as much as I could do in that Union, and I felt that the opening up of heavy industry and other industry that perhaps one could go and help to organize there. And so I left and went to organize in another industry....

IMMIGRANTS AND WOMEN: SWEATSHOPS OF THE 1970s

These articles raised a storm in Montreal, but the conditions described are by no means restricted to Quebec; and as we have seen, they go back to the 1890s and perhaps generations before. Forty years after the pioneering victories of the 1930s, the exploitation of women and immigrants by sweatshop operators continues, only slightly mitigated by poorly enforced minimum-wage laws, and by unions that seem reluctant to put huge sums into organizing drives. The problem is due in part to the weakness of Canadian industry in general and small firms in particular, to international competition from cheap labour, and to the presence of large numbers of 'illegal' immigrants who dare not complain for fear of deportation. Here are the old problems of the early 1900s in a new guise.

Sheila Arnopoulos articles in the *Montreal Star*, 27 March—6 April 1974. Reprinted by permission of Canada Wide Feature Service Ltd.

$1.85 an hour; $74.00 a week; $296.00 a month; $3,848.00 a year. Way below the poverty line for a family of four. That's what a quarter of a million people in Montreal make for a forty hour week if they're lucky and know about the minimum wage. Thousands however, aren't aware of the legal minimum and these people can spend fifty or sixty hours a week toiling in a hot restaurant kitchen or a factory at sixty cents an hour.

Who are these workers making the minimum wage or less?

Mainly they are immigrants from the Caribbean, Latin America, India, Pakistan, Greece, Portugal and Italy. Most come from villages and have no skills or basic education. Some cannot read, write or do simple arithmetic.

A large number speak neither English nor French even after a number of years in Canada because they are not exposed to either language on the job or at home.

Fast urban living and the alien ways of North America is a frightening experience for them.

They may never escape. Low wages, long weary hours and poor housing but they hope for a richer more rewarding life for their children.

While they dream of "tomorrow", they man the clanging textile and clothing factories which line St. Lawrence and Park. They clean toilets in glittering highrises, wash dishes in grimy restaurant kitchens, pull switches and operate machinery in fuming plastics and chemical factories, abattoirs, machine shops.

An unskilled labour force toiling at low paying, dirty jobs, unwanted by native Canadians, goes back to the early days of Canada's history.

In the 1830s for example, the exploited group were the Irish... who reportedly worked like horses and died like flies.

Today, it is the newly arrived unskilled West Indian, Latin Americans, Asians and Southern Europeans who stand on the bottom rung of the social and economic ladder.

To find out how these people fare on the job, I decided to work where they worked at their hours, and at their pay.

To job hunt, I put on some baggy corduroys and an old duffle coat, carried a plastic purse and creased grocery bag containing my running shoes and lunch. [As an English Canadian] to avoid suspicion, I had to appear uneducated, unkempt and weary. My journey into the world of exploited immigrant labour began at the South end of St. Lawrence Boulevard at the 55 bus stop. The St. Lawrence 55, starts at graceful Place D'Armes which separates the financial district from chic old Montreal. It ends miles and miles later, way past the Metropolitan near Louvain, a long street of squat, spreading factories with tall smoke stacks, belching steam and smoke... For middle class gourmets the "Main" is Saturday morning at Waldman's Fish Market or Louis Tucker's Live and Dead Poultry. It is an amble through Portuguese pastry shops and Greek grocery stores, followed by a smoked meat at Kravitz's or a steak at Moishe's.

But for the Portuguese, Haitian or Italian immigrant who starts work at 7:00 a.m., and sometimes finishes as late as 8:00 p.m. on forced overtime, St. Lawrence is not exotic at all.

It is where the factories are—it is where you get $74.00 a week, working 8 to 5 on the minimum wage—or even less if you don't know the law... St. Lawrence's crooked buildings, with warped doors, narrow wood staircases and grimy sectioned windows, revealing clattering machines, steam pressers, greasy cardboard boxes and harsh fluorescent lights.

It is the monotony of the assembly line, the exhaustion of pumping

away at one mechanical task a thousand times an hour—ten hours a day
—five, sometimes six days a week—with only 15 minutes for a bite of
lunch over a machine.... It is hardly the Canadian dream but it is where
one must begin in a new country....

In my pocket was an ad from the Montreal Star which read,
"Pantyhose packers and general work. Good salary."...

"You have jobs?" I asked. A short man wearing a peaked cap padded
out from behind the door at the back. "Have any experience?" he
demanded in a thick unrecognizable accent.

"No." I said.

"Where do you come from?"

"Out west." I replied.

"Vancouver?"

"No, Alberta."

"What kind of work you did before?"

"I worked in a store."

"You married?"

"No."

"You live with your parents?"

"No, with friends."

"You staying here long?"

"Six months," I said, "maybe longer."

"Okay," he said, looking me over, "piecework—follow me."

That was it. He didn't ask for my name or social security number. No
forms were filled out. The good salary was not mentioned.

He took me down some rickety wood stairs to a black windowless
basement smelling of oil and dust where about sixty noisy machines were
making snow-white stockings. Piercing lights shone on the machines but
the rest of the place was in semidarkness illuminated here and there by a
swinging light bulb. There didn't seem to be many workers around, just
three men keeping an eye on the machines and two women at one end
counting and bundling the stockings.

Across one wall behind the machines, there were piles to the ceiling of
bulging plastic bags containing white stockings. At one end stood rows of
greasy cardboard boxes. Weaving in and around bags, boxes, machines
and stray tools, the man led me to a dingy corner where a Greek woman
in a housedress and open shoes was frantically counting stockings.
"Watch her." he said and disappeared. Next to her was a young black
woman also counting hose.... Surrounding the women counting the
number of stockings were old steel oil drums. On top of the drums there
were discarded tools, dirty rags drenched in grease and puddles of
scummy oil, half filled oil tins, broken jars, plastic tubing, crunched
metal waste baskets, cigarette butts, wads of gum, cast-off stockings and
hunks of cardboard littered the black cement floor... There was a No

Smoking sign. However, while I was standing there, one of the men walked in among the oil tins with a cigarette.... My job was to put the stockings open at both ends, in bundles of twelve pair with the plastic ends up. After each bag full, I was to mark the dozens I had counted on a special sheet. I tried to strike up a conversation with my two co-workers but it was impossible since we had to keep counting all the time.

It was by now 10 a.m. By now, I had done about twenty dozen. At noon I went over to the foreman, "How much do we get an hour?"

"It's by the piece—three cents a dozen—but I wash my hands of it." He smiled apologetically. "You have to check with the boss—after you learn to go fast—you can make some money." He shrugged his shoulders. "It's hard to make money these days."

I estimated that I was making sixty cents an hour. My back was killing me and my feet were sore. There was no chair to sit on, it smelled musty. I was afraid that someone would drop a cigarette, the whole place would go up.

At 12:30, the Greek woman left her counting "table", picked up her small paper bag and went to a stool near the furnace room to eat lunch. Ten minutes later, she was back furiously dumping her plastic bag—counting, bundling, stuffing the stockings back in the bag, marking her sheet—another plastic bag—count—bundle—stuff—mark—another plastic bag—count—bundle—stuff—mark.

One o'clock. "Are you going to lunch?" I asked Joan the black woman from Guyana. It turned out it was her first day too ...

"I'd better stay here and keep working." said Joan—"only bring me back an order of toast on your way back" ... Joan had worked in a box factory on Jean Talon where they paid minimum wage ($1.85 an hour) and "conditions" were nice. "But I kept cutting my hands on the boxes and I just couldn't take it any longer." she explained. "I saw this ad so I decided I would try it here."

We trekked upstairs. "What are we going to get paid here?" I asked the secretary.

"Well—you know—it's by production—piece work." she said carefully. "Don't expect to make much the first month." She put on her fur coat hurriedly adding, "the Greek lady down there—you know—you made very little at the beginning—but now she makes—well about $98.50 a week."

"What are the hours here, Joan", I enquired.

"Well the Greek lady starts at seven in the morning and finishes at five in the afternoon."

We walked out. "You know," Joan said on the way back to the 55 bus, "I think I'll have to bring some Ajax to clean that bathroom." I can't eat anything after I've been in there. What do they think that we are, horses or something—no breaks, no chairs—and it's filthy—if we start at seven," she went on, "I'll have to get up at five. It takes me an hour and a half to get here"....

I went over to the Greek woman who kept picking away—never looking up—count—bundle—stuff—mark another plastic bag—"how much are you making here? I asked her. She was about three times as fast as Joan or I.

"I do 500 dozen a day, three cents a dozen, $15.00 a day," she said in halting English.

"From seven in the morning until five at night?—every day"? I asked.

"Yes," she nodded picking and bundling without stop.

Up at 5:30—at work at seven—ten minutes off for lunch—finish work at five—home at 6:30 at night totally exhausted—50 hours a week—for $75 bucks—over $22.00 a week under the mandatory minimum wage....

"I can't make enough money here." I told the secretary. "I'm leaving. Could I have my pay?" She totalled up the dozens of stockings I counted over my nine-hour stint at Atlantic Hosery. A little less than 200 dozen—$5.80.

A tall man with long thin fingers plunked $5.80 on a chair. "Sign here".

"Goodbye," I said but no one responded.

MINIMUM WAGE LACKS TEETH

Luigi M. is a dish washer in an Italian restaurant working a 60 hour week for $50.00

Maria V. is a sewing machine operator who used to work for a Greek sportswear contractor on piece work rates. After her first three weeks and 135 hours, she had cleared $37.00.

Francine M. is a young Latin American working at a knit mill on a working permit. Every day her boss picks up her and other employees at 7 a.m. and returns them at 9 p.m.—after 12 hours work and no overtime pay.

These people are immigrants prepared to do almost anything to earn their living, unable to speak English or French, unaware of their rights.

Their employers are flagrantly violating the provincial minimum wage act and are sure that they are going to get away with it.

Why? Because the minimum wage commission does not have a time enforcement system.

It will go after employers when complaints are registered but a minority of underpaid workers complain.

Most employees will not file a claim against an employer while they are working for him.

"Anyone who files a complaint with the commission always does it after they've left the job." said Dennis Adamou who works with the Greek Labour Association to help immigrants. "If they complain on the job, they're usually fired or conditions are made so intolerable for them, they have to leave. Employees hesitate to complain unless they're prepared to look for a job elsewhere."

Moreover, many immigrants don't know the minimum wage act, or a government commission where they can seek redress, exist.

There are 400,000 workers in Quebec supposedly getting the hourly minimum wage at $1.85 for the first 45 hours a week and $2.78 for overtime.

Roughly 250,000 of these workers are in Montreal, employed by non-union clothing and textile factories, machine shops, plastics and chemical works, furniture and electrical appliance firms, restaurants, abbatoirs, and office buildings as cleaners.

Thousands of these people do not earn the minimum.

Last year, as a result of complaints registered by workers, the Minimum Wage Commission collected 1.5 million in unpaid back wages from employers who had cheated 40,000 workers. This sum was just the tip of the iceberg.... Welching on the legal wage takes many forms. One of the worst is the imposition of the piecework rate, whether the workers are capable of reaching the basic $1.85 an hour with it or not. The employer may keep no record of hours worked.

"Piece work of course, is allowed," said Paul E. Germain, Chief of the Minimum Wage Commission Office in Montreal. "But records must be kept of the employee's hours and he must receive at least $1.85 an hour."

Some piece work employers make sure the employee never makes more than the minimum. As soon as the workers produce faster to make more money, the employer lowers the piecework rate.

Another common trick is to ask fast workers to hold back some of their "tickets" representing pieces completed and be paid for them at "some other time." Often the employer never intends to pay.

One woman working for a clothing contractor who had a reputation for going in and out of business, accumulated $700.00 worth of tickets. When she decided to leave and demanded cash for them, the employer refused to pay...

The Minimum Wage Commission apparently has no real teeth. It relies on employee complaints because it doesn't have enough inspectors to hunt out abuses... Non-union workers in certain industries do not seek redress for underpayment through the Minimum Wage Commission. They go to special "Joint Commissions" run by Union and employer representatives of the industry concerned. Each joint commission has a mandate to oversee a particular industry such as the dress industry which is largely but not completely unionized.

After collective agreements have been signed in a particular industry, unions and employers ask the government to issue a decree setting some minimum conditions and wages for the non-union sector. These are

always less than the union rates but better than the legal minimum wage
... Often an arbitrary wage is decided by the employer for work weeks
that may reach 80 hours when it can be hidden from the authorities.
Many workers are paid in cash, with no taxes deducted...

Before job hunting, I dropped in for lunch at a clean cheerful restaurant called Rio De la Plata on Saint Viateur, run by two sisters from
Uruguay who came here four years ago with their husbands. "We're a
month in our restaurant—just new," one of them said slowly. Their husbands work at a Montreal North factory where their shifts end at 6 p.m.
Then they work here until midnight. "When they come—we go home,"
one of the women said. "No speak good English—but learning," the other
commented with a smile. "We open at 8 in the morning and close at
midnight." These two Latin American families weren't going to slave in
factories all their lives. Getting up at six in the morning and going to bed
after midnight is a gruelling life but the long hours, they hoped, would
be worth it. Rio De la Plata would be theirs and they could forget the
factory.

POOR GOVERNMENT INSPECTIONS ARE PART OF THE PROBLEM

Recently I got together with about twenty Italian immigrants, all of
whom told stories about working conditions either in their present jobs or
in those they held when they first came to Canada. Perhaps the most
bizarre tale came from a young man I will call Mario who works in an
abattoir owned by a fellow Italian.

"Well to start with, the place is full of flies," said Mario, one of the
few present who spoke English. "We eat in a room where a lot of flies
keep falling dead on the table."

He went on to describe this abattoir's night guard. "You see, the boss
didn't want to spend money to hire a night watchman and he felt he
needed one so he's got this wolf in there guarding the place. Well it looks
like a wolf," he said, "—and supposed to know everybody, otherwise it
attacks and bites. Some workers have been bitten. You know Pasquale?"
He looked around the room and everybody nodded. "Well, he was bitten
quite badly and had to go home."

"Lots of strange things go on in this abattoir. During the day any meat
declared rotten by the Food Inspector has to be thrown in the garbage
but at night when we come in, we're told to dig it out and prepare it for
a sausage factory."

A common complaint is unhealthy working conditions. Victoria Caparelli works as a lathe operator in a Montreal East machine stop. "The
pay is okay," he said, "$4.00 an hour, but there is no ventilation in the
place. We use these special solvents to clean machines, which are very
dangerous if you inhale them. I have been intoxicated, light-headed,
three times already from these solvents."

Some Greeks who work at a vinyl factory also complained about air contamination. "There's a lot of smoke from the polyurethane and vinyl machines," said one man. "Last year some people had to go to the hospital because of it. It's a lot better this year because the factory has expanded so the pollution has spread out. We have a union and it's in our contract that vents and fans are supposed to be installed, but nothing has been done about it."

Gruelling dust in a hosiery factory made another Greek worker Costas Brakas now with the Greek Labour Association "feel sick all the time" and he eventually left.

Filthy toilets and general lack of cleanliness was mentioned by many factory workers interviewed for this series. No toilet paper, soap or towels, and stopped sinks, broken cubicle locks and dirty floors are common.

Insufficient safety measures is another complaint. Many immigrants, it appears, are not adequately instructed by employers in the operation of dangerous machinery. A Centre for the Haitian Christian Community spokesman said, "there are far too many accidents concerning immigrants." Since the Centre's inception 16 months ago," he says, "there has been one on-the-job death and 12 accidents involving Haitians." "Most of the accidents take place in plastics, metals and the textile industry," he said, "where there's no union, no protection. Workmen's Compensation always seems to take a long time to come through. . . . "

Montreal has only 40 Fire Inspectors to police the city's 88,000 commercial establishments. Routine visits are few and far between and inspections are often made only after a complaint. . . .

While doing this series, I also heard of two women being assaulted by their bosses. One case involved a Haitian woman at a clothing factory. When she began work, she asked what her hourly wage would be and was not told. At the end of the week when she asked for her money, she was accused of stealing a dress. She protested and the boss struck her. With the help of the Haitian Centre, she is going to court.

The other case involved a Latin American woman who wanted to leave her knit factory for a few hours to visit her son who had been in an accident. The boss protested and said that she was unreliable. An argument ensued and the man punched her. The woman was so shocked, she fainted, couldn't be revived and had to be taken to hospital in an ambulance. She too is suing with the help of an immigrant aid organization. Factory work can also involve crushing boredom and fatigue which even adequate pay does not ease. . . . There is a constant turnover because "workers can't stand the jobs.". . . . Psychiatrists and social workers who treat immigrant factory workers report that many take pills to keep going. Some women quit for two or three months to "recuperate," said one social worker. "They're exhausted all the time." The Greek Labour

Workers Association says that many immigrant workers quit for health reasons. They want to keep going but they just can't. On their medical certificates which must be submitted in order to get Unemployment Insurance, anxiety neurosis is often marked. "These factory jobs make mental and physical wrecks out of people."

GRUELLING WORK POVERTY CAN'T KILL CAMERADERIE

After only a week on assignment for this series, I was a wreck. The long hours, tedium and fatigue of low paying factory work had gotten to me. At night I lay in the bath and drank hot rum toddies to wind down and prepare for the next day. It was impossible to imagine a month—a year— ten years, of factory work at poverty wages—it was far too much of a nightmare.

There was only one consolation. In the areas dominated by factories and slums, public baths and tiny lunch counters, there was a warm feeling of community among the army of factory "hands," the truckers, and delivery men, short order cooks and grocery men. Even the bus drivers seemed different.

Fellow workers said hello and goodbye and tried to be helpful. At lunch counters, you could strike up a conversation with the man who made the french fries. When you paid for your coffee, the cashier said, "au revoir," and meant it.

It was like a small town where everyone felt linked in some way, to everyone else. Call it "working class solidarity," if you like.

FACTORIES FIGHT TOOTH AND NAIL TO KEEP UNIONS OUT

The unions face a difficult task. To start with, immigrants are often confused about what a union is. Some, for example, are convinced that unions are illegal or "communist." Many come from dictatorial regimes and the idea that they have the right to challenge the boss is unheard of.... To rebel in any way, they believe might jeopardize their position in Canada.

Some immigrants of course have tried to form unions. However, many who have had a taste of it are thoroughly discouraged, if not a little frightened by the outcome. Attempting to organize is often a long tortuous process with the employer using intimidation, firings and Labour Board proceedings in his attempt to block union certification.

Once the union is in, negotiations are often long and frustrating. Frequently, the boss decides simply to close down and the workers go to similar jobs in other non-union places. Later, often in a month or two, the boss reopens under a new name and a new place with new employees and—no union.

The story of Crystal Hosiery Factory which closed in February is a good example of what happens regularly. According to Angela Pitzakas and Dionysia Mouralatos, who worked at Crystal and were union executives, workers wanted to make the management up the piecework rates, improve the physical conditions and pay them on traditional holidays.

"Between 1969 and 1971," said Mrs. Pitzakas, "Crystal cut piecework rates two or three times so that workers had to work harder and harder for less and less pay."

According to Mrs. Pitzakas the following took place:

In March, 1972, the Crystal workers organized and quickly got a majority for a union under the C.N.T.U. Trouble started mid-April when 36 workers were suddenly fired. However, a complaint was quickly filed with the Labour Board which resulted in the rehiring of the workers two months later and in order to pay the back wages. "We have yet to receive this back pay," said Mrs. Pitzakas. The employer stalled certification until March 1973 and negotiations did not get under way until June.... In November, the company suddenly notified the government it would close in February...

"Crystal workers who had not joined the union had jobs in other hosiery factories on the recommendation of the Crystal management" said Mrs. Pitzakas. "The ones in the unions have been refused in all the hosiery factories and are on unemployment insurance or working in other types of factories." "The unionized are on a backball list being circulated around to all the hosiery owners", said Mrs. Mourelatos, who is President of the union.

At a few other hosiery factories where workers are trying to unionize, intimidation and firing is allegedly continuing... "Most people don't contest these firings," said Jean-Guy Frenette, Research Director of the Quebec Federation of Labour," because even if they are reinstated, the company makes life miserable for them, especially if no union has yet been formed."

To ward off the union, some employers quickly set up "company unions" or "employee associations" with "Yellow" contracts. Such associations have little muscle because they do not have the backing of the big union organizations that can provide strike funds. Although the big unions are in principle, sympathetic to non-union shops, there doesn't seem to be much effort to organize them. I have yet to hear of union organizers taking jobs in some of these shops and trying to set up a union from within. The tactics seem to be to distribute union pamphlets outside the factory door.

Prohibitive costs are often cited by the big unions as the reason for failing to dig in and do something for these exploited workers. "It costs a lot to organize the small shops," said Mr. Frenette of the QFL. "One is constantly in court—everything takes a long time."

In many cases, say the unions, an employer will close down and all the organizing work goes down the drain.

Only 35% of the Quebec labour force is unionized and in some industries where the unions are active, workers often complain they are not doing a good job. Two of the big unions in the Quebec Garment Industry are International Ladies Garment Workers of America with 20,000 members, and Amalgamated Clothing Workers of America with 6,000 members. Complaints about both unions are rampant. Until recently, Amalgamated Clothing hadn't had a general membership meeting for years. It took a wildcat strike to get one called. Immigrant aid groups claim that some immigrant members of both the ILGWU and ACWA aren't even aware that they are union members. "Some of them have never seen their contracts," said Costas Brakas of the Greek Labour Association which does translations of labour contracts for Greeks. "They are also totally unaware of procedures for grievances."

GRIEVANCES

Maria D., 50, is a Portuguese sewing machine operator who works in a new building in a unionized dress factory which is known for its good wages. However, Mrs. D. who was terrified of having her name used when she called me, felt that there was a lot wrong with working conditions in the needle trade, even where there are unions. "I came to Canada 25 years ago and I've always worked in the dress industry," she said. I don't work in a so-called sweat shop. It's a new building but it's badly constructed and always cold and extremely noisy because of all the factory machines. I make about $3.00 an hour which is considered very good pay but I've paid for it in terms of health." Mrs. D. explained that she has always done piece work. "To make money, one must go very fast. There is always tremendous tension to produce . . . produce." As a result, she has suffered a number of nervous breakdowns. "I'm not the only one who has become sick because of the factory conditions," she pointed out. "The International Ladies Garment Workers Union which I belong to has a medical clinic for workers. If you look at their files, you'll see a very high percentage of workers suffering from respiratory diseases from synthetic fibre dust and nervous breakdowns. Many people are on pills to help them get through the day in the factories. A number of the older ones have become alcoholics."

Maria D. also complained of total inadequacies of the International Ladies Garment Workers Union which she claims "ignores grievances from employees." "The union even makes deals with employers not to pay the minimum wage to some workers." This happened she claimed in the case of workers 50 and up who are "burned out and can't go fast any more on piece work." "These women are scared that they won't be hired anywhere else so they agree to sign cards [renouncing] their right to the minimum wage at the request of the employer and union." This of course, is totally illegal. . . . Many of these women should be able to retire at 55 because they are "too tired" to keep up the "tense pace of the factory". However, pensions are "not geared" for early retirement, she said.

The piecework, she added, makes for bad atmosphere in the factory. Some piecework jobs pay better than others and there is a "constant battle" between workers for "favours" from the boss to secure the better paying piece work position.... "The union," she claimed, "keeps the immigrant workers in the worst paying places. I was very lucky to battle my way in."

Another caller was a French Canadian bookkeeper making $170.00 a week in the St. Lawrence Boulevard Men's Factory. She said that she adored her job and claimed the factory conditions where she worked were "excellent".

However, she said that in the same building, the Knit Mills were paying immigrants who don't know any better, $40.00 a week. "They won't hire Canadians because they know their rights. Everything is cash under the table with no records and no taxes paid. The government is losing a lot of revenue. Physical conditions are horrendous. Mills will wait until the water pipes burst in the faces of their workers before they fix them"....

PRISONS

I decided to work one more day, but at a pen factory which had advertised for help in the Star.

9 a.m.—Meilleur Street. Another row of buildings which looked like prisons, about five streets north of St. Lawrence north of Cremazie.

Lined up outside the buildings were a handful of long shiny expensive cars, sandwiched between honking delivery trucks. I went further down and into 9292 Meilleur. There was a sign in the lobby in English, French and Italian saying, "No loitering or eating." Up to the fifth floor. There was no sign for International Pen, just a door with "Office" on it.

"You have jobs?" I asked.

"Okay," said a woman in a white sweater, "put your coat here." She pointed to a crooked locker... "You leave your purse in the locker—bring only your wallet." She didn't ask my name or Social Security Number.

The factory itself was on the other side of the tall wire fence. We walked through and two minutes later I was at a table putting red pens in tiny plastic bags—premiums for All soap boxes.

"What's the wage here?" I asked a girl during the ten o'clock break.

"You married?"

"No," I lied.

"You got any kids?"

"No." That was the truth.

"Well in that case I guess you'll get the minimum—$1.85. I get more because I've got a kid."

"You gonna stay?" she continued. "Yesterday a black girl and a Filipino came in but they didn't come back. Some people say it's too boring." The door opened a well-turned-out girl with a plaid mini-coat, blue A-line skirt, nail polish and eye make-up walked in. "Gee, wonder what she's doing here," said a girl with chalky face and straw-like hair. "She looks like an office type."

10:30-11:30—there were five people at my table but no one was talking and the time was going slowly. I was doing 1,000 pens an hour. Noon—I had decided not to stay for the afternoon, I just couldn't take it any longer.

I picked up my wallet and put it in my purse in the locker. A quick trip to the rest room where the sink was plugged and the water was flowing on to the floor.

I threw my duffle on, my boots, put my running shoes in a shopping bag. I could hardly get out fast enough.

Down the elevater, into the sunshine—and out. This time, for good.

4
Working Conditions and
the Rise of the CIO
1919 – 1940

This chapter takes the story of the development of trade unions from the collapse of the One Big Union to the founding of the Canadian Congress of Labour in 1940 (the Canadian central allied to the CIO). With the CIO —the Congress of Industrial Organizations—international unionism once again dominated Canadian labour, as it had during the expansion of the AFL in the early 1900s.

The 1920s, however, were lean years for the Canadian worker. Organization was at a standstill. Union membership fell before the onslaught of business-sponsored 'open shop' drives. The crushing defeat of the Winnipeg Strike had set the pattern for unholy alliances against industrial unionism all across the West, and labour was demoralized, its leadership divided, its idealism and vitality sapped; the only chance of improvement seemed to lie in co-operation with the boss.

There were some fresh initiatives from nationalists in the 1920s. In Quebec new Catholic unions formed the Canadian and Catholic Federation of Labour (CCCL) in 1921. English-Canadian workers also broke with the international unions, founding the All-Canadian Congress of Labour (ACCL) in 1927. And there was a rebirth of left wing militancy in the Workers' Unity League of 1930. Though it was dominated by Communist leaders, the WUL reflected genuine rank-and-file demands for a Canadian industrial union movement to meet increasingly desperate needs.

Ethnic labourers were in a particularly bad position after 1919: excluded from the AFL, harassed by self-styled 'white' workers, penned up in company towns and slums, and threatened with blacklisting for union activity or deportation for participating in radical political parties. It is not surprising that some "Bohunks' (as racists called them) joined the underground Communist party. Others, though non-Communist, were powerfully influenced by the new ethnic pride of an Eastern Europe freed from Czar and Hapsburg; they found it natural to join cultural front organizations set up by the Communists, and eventually more activist groups like the Farmers' Unity League or the WUL.

After the explosive unrest of 1919, the company town was re-establishing its hegemony. In the coal districts of the West and of Nova Scotia; in the fish and fruit canneries along both coasts; in pulp and paper towns; and in logging areas, the old patterns re-emerged. It was as if the gains of the early twentieth century had been erased and the clock had been turned back to the nineteenth century.

Even the skilled workers of the AFL and (for a while) highly paid assembly-line workers in the new mass-production industries, though temporarily better off with the promise of profit-sharing, incentive, or spread-the-work plans of business and company unionism, were soon cowed by the speed-up for the good worker, the blacklist for the rebel, and favouritism for spies and toadies. But even these were preferable to the conditions wrought by the Depression.

With the great crash thousands of Canadian men, women, and children were thrown onto the streets, without jobs, without income, their meagre savings exhausted, and most of all, without hope. More than a third of the work force had lost their jobs, and even those lucky enough to hold onto theirs suffered as pay dropped below starvation levels. Many of the more scrupulous employers had gone bankrupt. The remainder were able—and most were quite willing—to cut wages and increase hours without fear of strikes. For the hungry unemployed there was no social welfare or unemployment insurance. To qualify for relief they had to go into bankruptcy (or sign over what they owned) and submit to humiliation by petty bureaucrats and jealous neighbours. Most family men faced the soup-kitchen and the wood-yard; the single were sent to remote work camps under army rule.

It was in conditions such as these that the radicalism of the WUL, and later of the CCF and the CIO, took root. Nor was it necessary for the worker to be a radical to understand his need for union protection against the power of the employer. It was not until the swelling of war and lend-lease orders in 1940 that the life of the Canadian worker improved.

The war was to change organized labour permanently. In 1937 the CIO had been labelled a foreign intruder. By the mid-1940s tens of thousands of Canadian war workers had signed union cards. Their fight for legal recognition gave new impetus to radical parties, though many of these workers were anything but radical. Catholics, evangelical Protestants, stubborn individualists, farm boys, and old-party supporters found themselves demanding new rights under the banner of the CIO. In the process the CCF and Communist parties gained new sympathy for their proposals of immediate reform. The Communists had been almost crushed by deportations and arrests in the early 1930s, but had nonetheless led many of the first demonstrations for social justice and union rights. But the CCF, with a strong core of Christian socialists, British Labour party supporters, and allies in the farm movement, was more acceptable to the average worker. After 1937 it contributed an increasing number of organizers to the CIO.

The CCF became the political midwife of the labour reform movement. Together with the CIO, it raised a storm of hope—and of protest—that forced the hands of the old parties. By 1943 British Columbia and Ontario had legislated collective bargaining, and in February 1944 the federal cabinet decree (P.C. 1003) established a charter of legal rights for most industries. This was labour's Magna Carta.

The reform was not without a certain cynicism, however. Only those groups of workers strong enough to threaten political upset were granted union rights. For the unskilled, the immigrant, and the female worker in major urban industries it was a revolution. For workers in agriculture and in the service and public sectors it was not. For some of the latter groups, excluded by law from union certification, the Depression has never really lifted, as the last document in this chapter makes clear.

THE 'UNHOLY ALLIANCE' AGAINST THE OBU

A major obstacle in the way of labour unity was the conflict between ethnic workers and their brothers of British stock. In this strike vigilante squads of returned British veterans (financed by the bosses) battled East European immigrants supporting the One Big Union. These were the same 'foreigners' who had been interned at the outset of the war, were released to work for the big companies in 1917, and then saw their union meetings, newspapers, and socialist parties barred by the government. The OBU was one of several attempts in this period to organize skilled and unskilled, WASP and ethnic. It was doomed not so much by its own contradictions and weaknesses as by an 'unholy alliance' of government, business, and the AFL unions.

A. B. Woywitka, 'The Drumheller Strike of 1919', *Alberta Historical Review* (Winter 1973), pp. 1-7. Reprinted by permission of Anne B. Woywitka.

The year 1919 was a period of industrial unrest in many parts of the world. The war had ended but not the tension nor the anxiety for a better post-war deal. No sooner had World War I ended when the labour war began, accompanied by strikes and violence. In March of 1919, at a Western Labour Conference in Calgary, a new union was organized for Canadian workers. Though the idea for the union originated with the trade unions of Great Britain, the new union itself was to be all-Canadian and for Canadian workers only. The aim of this "One Big Union" was to unite all workers, both white collar and manual, under one leadership. It was to work in the interests of labour and was to be totally disaffiliated from International Unions.

At first, the One Big Union's success was striking. It appealed to the majority of workers. Strong union detachments broke away from parental bodies to join the O.B.U. Among them were the miners of Drumheller Valley who had been members of the United Mine Workers of America, District 18. One of the sore points was the collection of miners' dues which were sent regularly to the head office in the United States leaving a shortage of funds for local union work.

The organizer and secretary of the Drumheller branch of O.B.U. was Jack Sullivan. He was a dynamic man who was liked and respected by the majority of miners. On the other hand the mine operators regarded Sullivan with suspicion and labelled him as a dangerous revolutionary. They refused to have anything to do with the new union that he represented. In their stand against the O.B.U., they had the full support of W. H. Armstrong, Coal Commissioner for Alberta.

Production of coal was interrupted when the Drumheller miners went on strike on May 24, 1919. They requested the mine operators formally recognize the O.B.U. as their legal bargaining agent.

In reply, Coal Commissioner Armstrong said: "I decline to conduct negotiations or enter into negotiations with O.B.U. The present contract is with U.M.W.A. and with them we will conduct business with regard to resumption of work and negotiations of a new agreement." (*Calgary Herald, March 24, 1919*).

The Coal Commissioner's reply became the signal for the start of the war between the unions and was to last through the summer of 1919. When the miners walked out in support of O.B.U. the companies retaliated by closing down the mines. Being in the middle of the slack season, the closing of the mines caused no hardship for the mine operators. But for the miners it was a crucial period; many of them were forced to disperse in search of other work.

At the same time, the great General Strike of the O.B.U. was underway in Winnipeg, culminating in the so-called Bloody Saturday of June 21st that ended in death for two people and various injuries to thirty others. The strike that paralyzed Winnipeg for more than five weeks ended officially on July 3rd, 1919.

However, by late July the Drumheller lockout was still on when winter orders for coal began to arrive. The mine operators were anxious to resume operations and word went out that the mines were being opened for work again. The miners then called a meeting and the majority voted in favour of continuing the strike for O.B.U. recognition.

The thirteen mine companies, including Drumheller, Newcastle, Western Gem, Manitoba, Atlas, A.B.C., North American, Scranton, Sterling and Midland, joined forces and flatly refused to recognize the O.B.U. They also began to lay plans to break the strike. They asked for and were given official government permission to hire special constables to "protect" their property.

At this time general post-war employment was at a low ebb. The labour market was flooded with returning veterans in search of jobs. Lacking mining experience, the veterans had been by-passed by the mining companies in favour of experienced "foreign" miners—Belgians, Italians, Swedes, Romanians, Ukrainians, Hungarians and Poles—who had kept the mines operating throughout the war.

Playing on the veterans' resentment against aliens, the companies set out to hire a sufficient number of unemployed service men as "protectors of mining property" knowing it would be an important factor in the veterans' dealings with the strikers. The companies paid them $10 a day and let many of them become plied with liquor. Then they gave them pick handles, crowbars and brass knuckles before they sent them out in company cars to round up the strikers for work.

Several old miners who took part in the Drumheller strike of 1919 recall the events that led to the terror that stalked through the Drumheller Valley that summer. One of these men, Nick Gill, had left Drumheller to work on the railroad after the mines closed down in late May. When word reached him that mines were to open again, he returned the first week of August to find the strike still in progress.

Daily, fresh news came of individual miners being picked up for work by force. If they offered no resistance, all was well. They were sent into the mine to work and nothing more was said. But if a striker showed resistance, he was driven out into the country 30 or 40 miles away, beaten and left on the prairies as an example to others.

With each passing day, the atmosphere in the Drumheller Valley grew more tense. The striking miners had to be on the alert at all times. During the day they roamed in packs as there was safety in numbers. At night they slept with one eye open. Living in their small shiplap and tarpaper shacks staggered along the river banks, they soon learned by the grapevine of any happening and in turn, passed it along.

As the struggle progressed, the U.M.W.A. and the mine operators brought in outside agitators able to speak several languages. These silver-tongued orators left no stone unturned in District 18 in favour of the U.M.W.A. Their aim was to turn the "foreign element" against the One

Big Union. But the hard-core strikers included not only the foreigners but many English-speaking people, too. These stood fast with the leaders of the O.B.U.

On Saturday, August 9th, Jack Sullivan, who lived in the vicinity of Newcastle mine, was awakened by thunderous knocks on his door. As he dressed hurriedly, five men forced his door open and surrounded him. One of the men grabbed his arm roughly, growled: "You're coming with us, Sullivan!"

Sullivan had no choice but to nod. By his gesture he admitted that he knew he was outnumbered. "Let me wash myself and I'll be with you in a minute," he said quietly.

The men watched him closely as he went to the washstand. Sullivan, scraping the bottom of the pail deliberately with the dipper, filled the basin with cold water. He splashed loudly as he washed. He then wiped himself. Picking up the basin to throw the water out, he took a couple of steps out of the door before he flung the basin away from him. A split second later he was sprinting across the yard to his neighbour's shanty, the ex-soldiers at his heels in pursuit.

"Rogers! Help me!" Sullivan yelled.

Rogers was a Negro fireman in the steam boiler at the Newcastle mine. He had been standing in his doorway wondering what would happen to Sullivan when he saw him come running toward him. As Sullivan rushed past him into the shack, Rogers reacted instantly. He grabbed the gun standing inside his doorway and pointing it at Sullivan's pursuers, he warned them: "Stop! If you come one step closer, I'll shoot! You have no business coming on my property!"

Leaving them no choice, the "special constables" backed away, swearing angrily. Thanks to Rogers, Sullivan was spared that day.

That same morning, word got out that a number of strikers were gathered at Rosedale mine to prevent workers from entering the mine. Two hundred veterans were rushed in touring cars to break up the picketers who were then forced to scatter in all directions.

All day Saturday, August 9th, hundreds of striking miners milled restlessly through the streets of Drumheller. There were frequent exchanges of obscenities and name calling as veterans and strikers stalked around. Tempers flared as the hired strike-breakers taunted the strikers, yelling, "Bohunks, go home! We don't need you here!" The strikers yelled back in return: "You dirty scabs!"

The cauldron bubbled and boiled, fed by hatred and distrust of the opposing factions. On one hand was the veteran glowing with patriotism, returning home after years at the front, expecting a hero's welcome and reward. Instead he found himself facing frustration, unemployment and labour unrest. It angered him to find men of foreign extraction holding jobs while he remained unemployed.

On the other hand, the immigrant who had left the poverty of his homeland and the tyranny of the Austro-Hungarian Empire, arrived in Canada in time to help in developing a raw, new land. He, too, was faced with frustrations and disappointments and the heavy work of opening land, building railroads through the mountains, digging sewers in the cities, mining, etc. When the war began in 1914, he was immediately dubbed an "enemy alien" and required to register with the police and was kept under surveillance. He was sent to fill essential jobs or faced deportation if he refused. Thus each party felt justified in its stand.

The Drumheller police under Sergeant Skelton patrolled the streets and issued repeated warnings to both sides: "Be careful! We will not be responsible if anyone gets hurt or killed!"

The unrest lasted late into the night, when the strikers and the veterans finally dispersed. Early Sunday, August 10th, 500 striking miners gathered in the vicinity of the Newcastle watertank where Sullivan had gone into hiding. To prevent any surprise abduction of Sullivan by the veterans, the strikers took him into their midst and marched with him down the tracks to the Miners Hall.

They found the door padlocked. Refusing to be halted, they lifted one of the men to their shoulders to open a window. After crawling inside, he opened a side door to permit entry of the remaining strikers.

That day, Sullivan, Kent, Browne, Christopher and other O.B.U. leaders addressed the meeting. Discussions followed, touching on many of their problems. In closing the meeting, they passed a resolution to send a telegram to the O.B.U. head office in Calgary for further instructions.

Leaving the hall, the mass of strikers proceeded to the station house where they ordered the stationmaster to send a telegram. He refused, saying it was Sunday and he was not working. But mob pressure changed his mind. The message was sent and instructions were received to hold a special meeting with an O.B.U. representative from Calgary on Monday morning. Once again, the men dispersed for the night.

The miners' shacks were strung along the valley, separated by brush, sometimes a bit of a garden, maybe a fence here and there. In each of them lived at least two or three people, and sometimes as many as could put their bed rolls on the floor.

With Mr. and Mrs. Gill lived an elderly uncle and the old man, being a poor sleeper, was up early Monday morning. He dressed himself and went out into the milky whitenes of early dawn. Except for the singing of the birds, the valley was sleeping peacefully. The old man sighed. At this hour it was hard to believe the harshness of preceding days. As he stood contemplating the austere beauty of hill and valley, his ears caught the laboured chugging of approaching vehicles.

He peered into the valley, waiting. Within minutes, the cars stopped and he heard a commotion as of people thrashing through the brush accompanied by loud whoops and cries of outrage. He did not need to be told what was happening but hurried back to the shack to warn his nephew.

"Wake up, wake up!" he called from the doorway, his voice rising with the sense of approaching danger. "They're coming our way! Hurry!"

Gill was up and dressed in no time. Stepping outside, he heard heavy thrashing through the thick growth of chokecherries and saskatoons that grew along the valley. Presently, he saw men running and recognized his neighbours. Close behind them were their pursuers, rending the morning air with their cries. They were heading in the general direction of Gill's shack.

Halfway between Gill's shack and the bush was Mike Babyn's shanty. Back of it, firewood was stacked neatly making a fence several feet long and four feet high. The fleeing miners headed for this shelter. They were joined by Mr. Gill, his uncle and several other men who'd been drawn there by the early morning disturbance. Each grabbed firewood, rocks or whatever was handy and when the pursuers came into view, they were met by a furious barrage of flying missiles.

The unexpected counterattack was enough to stop the startled pursuers. No doubt the cries of pain accompanied by loud swearing meant that many of the missiles found their targets. Unable to cope with the attack, the ex-servicemen turned about and started running back to their cars. Immediately, the strikers taking advantage of the retreat, started after them in hot pursuit. They headed them off, forcing the veterans to run for the hills.

The chase was finally abandoned when the ex-servicemen scattered in all directions on top of the hills. As the strikers began to make their way back to the valley, they heard rifle shots reverberating through the valley. Realizing that all was not well, they paused on the edge of the hills overlooking the town of Drumheller. It was then they saw that reinforcements had arrived for the ex-servicemen. More cars and men had come and the valley rang with their shouting. They recognized numbers of their own men running for the safety of the hills. Turning on their heels, they headed the exodus.

A number of strikers were captured that morning, but the majority gained the hills. Here they sought vantage points for observation, and hiding places in the deep gullies and crevices scattered over a large territory. It was apparent that the special meeting scheduled in the hall for that day would not take place. However, many of them hoped that a meeting could be organized in the hills. Then, as several hours went by it was apparent that there would be no assembly in the hills after all. Sullivan was nowhere to be seen; sometime during the melee, he had disappeared.

As day drew to a close and night began to fall, men began to emerge warily from gully to hilltop, seeking contact with fellow strikers. With the coming of darkness, several men offered to make their way down for further news of what happened and for food and water.

Eventually, when they came back, they brought with them news that the hired strike breakers had returned to Babyn's shack, hoping perhaps to capture Babyn in retaliation for the attack suffered at his place. Mr. Babyn was not home but his wife fearing an attack on herself, met the intruders with a .22 rifle. She fired two shots which went astray and hurt no one. (Later Mr. Babyn was convicted of illegal possession of arms by an alien and was sentenced to three months in Lethbridge jail.)

Among those captured that day was a man named Thompson. He was taken to a barn at Midland mine, strung up by his feet and offered horse urine to drink. A report in *Calgary Daily Herald* denied mistreatment of captured men but there is a cryptic item in the paper saying: "He (Thompson) was given a drink of water and was told not to spit in it."

In another instance two other men, Gulka and Malowany were assaulted and strung, feet up, in the same barn. Gulka, who was almost totally deaf, was presumed to be stubborn and un-cooperative and was treated accordingly.

The *Calgary Herald*, August 12 observed: "Legally, the course adopted on Saturday, Sunday and Monday last, may be gravely questioned but the valley people are not splitting hairs in connection with this matter."

Those who had gone down into the valley secretly Monday night brought back the news that the mine operators were threatening to run the strikers out of town if they did not return to work by Tuesday morning.

It was a sleepless night for the strikers on the hills. They were cold and tired. By daybreak, the groups began to congregate again. Their spirits were flagging. Left without a leader, they were at loose ends as to their next step. Tuesday morning arrived and from their vantage points, men watched the valley for further developments, half expecting reprisals. The sun rose higher. Thirst and hunger increased as it grew hotter. Disillusionment grew with every passing minute.

Presently, they noticed what appeared to be a party of police officers making their way towards the hills. Word was passed along and soon the men were ready to disperse should it become necessary. They watched warily as the party of ten provincial police officers and a Drumheller constable approached. The striking miners figured that the mine operators knew the strikers did not trust the local police and deemed it advisable to bring in outside help.

The party of policemen spread over a wide area so as to contact as many strikers as possible. Using megaphones, they assured the men there would be no reprisals if they returned to work. "We are here to help you! It is safe for you to return to your homes. There is work for you at the mines. Do not be afraid!"

The message was repeated. Strikers exchanged looks and some nodded. They could not hope to stay there indefinitely. Others withdrew to regroup, preferring to wait for further developments. They did not trust the mine operators' promises nor their "hired constables" who were only too eager to carry out their instructions.

It was noted in *Calgary Daily Herald* that on August 12th, the Drumheller mines were operating at only quarter capacity. This was a long way from full operation which the companies needed in order to fill their winter orders. "So far none of the alien element has returned to work," the newspaper observed. "Those who have returned are the better class miners who up to yesterday have been guided blindly by O.B.U. agitators."

The strikers who returned were soon approached by the companies' "special constables" and were made to sign papers accepting U.M.W.A. as their bargaining agents with the mine operators.

As for the remaining strikers who stayed behind in the hills, it was suggested that they all be run out of the valley. The veterans went to their homes with the message that O.B.U. men had the alternative of signing up with U.M.W.A. or clearing out. On Wednesday, the companies decreed that "preference will be given first, to returned soldiers, next, white men who had mining experience and last, the alien element."

Within a few days, the remainder of striking miners had returned to their homes. The companies had resumed operations with the help of ex-servicemen, their sympathizers and those miners who had given up hope of winning the strike. There was every indication that the strike was broken. However, the "special constables" continued their search for O.B.U. leaders, including Sullivan whom they could not locate. Christopher, Kent and a third unidentified man were captured by five carloads of veterans raiding a secret meeting at Wayne. They brought their prisoners back to Drumheller, held a "court-martial", roughed them up thoroughly and ordered them to clear out of Drumheller.

On August 21st a Drumheller correspondent to the *Calgary Daily Herald* reported, "Considerable excitement prevailed here last Monday when the returned veterans went to the Miners Hall where a meeting was in progress and took Sullivan and Roberts for another ride. Sullivan returned to town on the morning train from Calgary and the vets decided to get rid of him again. Roberts who had also returned, was taken along, too. The two men were taken to Rosedale where the vets at the Moody mine joined forces with the Drumheller boys and set the two men on foot heading towards Calgary."

What the report failed to mention was that Sullivan and Roberts were beaten, tied to telephone poles and then tarred and feathered. They were later released and ordered to make themselves scarce. As the men took off, the mob of veterans howled after them, promising more of the same should they return.

This latest incident sounded the final death knell to the O.B.U. in Drumheller. The strike was over. The triple alliance of government, mine companies and U.M.W.A. had triumphed over the wish of the miners for One Big Union. The United Mine Workers of America was again the legal bargaining agent for all the mine workers of District 18.

The veterans who had played the major role of strike breakers were hired by the companies as promised. But in a short time, the majority of them proved to be indifferent miners. The companies, interested only in production and amount of turn-over of coal, soon released many of them from work. The so-called "alien element", being experienced miners, were eventually re-hired under contract with U.M.W.A. and peace returned to the valley.

CHEAP LABOUR: ETHNIC EXPLOITATION IN WESTERN CANADA

Nowhere was the ethnic worker more exploited than in the company towns of Western Canada. Phil Christophers was an OBU organizer in the Alberta coal fields. The ad reprinted in the Canadian Unionist, *the journal of the All-Canadian Congress of Labour, is an example of the exploitation of contract labour by ethnic bosses and employment agents. Many of these down-trodden ethnic workers were soon swept up by the Communist-dominated Workers' Unity League in a last stand for industrial unionism and improved conditions. Some of these men were shot down in cold blood by RCMP troops during a WUL strike in the lignite fields around Estevan, Saskatchewan.*

Phil Christophers' letters to *The Searchlight*, 9 July 1920, and the OBU *Bulletin*, 17 July 1920.
'Hard Work and No Questions Asked! . . . The Hungarian-Slovak Colonization Board', *The Canadian Unionist*, March 1929. Reprinted by permission of the Canadian Labour Congress, Ottawa.
Cecil Boone, 'Estevan', *The Canadian Miner*, 30 Jan. 1932. Reprinted by permission.

The men are in some cases paid as low as forty cents an hour and work ten, twelve and in some cases as much as 14 hours per day. The mine boarding houses and stores are all run by the companies and all houses in which the married couples live are company houses. The rents and board, as well as the prices in the stores, are the highest in the district. The miners claim that they have no recourse except to deal with the store of the company by which they are employed, as they are told that these stores are kept open for the benefit of the workers and the cost will be borne by them whether they patronise the stores or not.

The houses in which the families live are mere huts and absolutely no provision is made for sanitation, this being left altogether in the hands of the tenants. As far as living conditions are concerned Drumheller valley in its worst days was a paradise compared to these camps [Taylorton, Estevan, and Bienfait].

The majority of the miners are Galicians who are still kept ignorant of the fact that internment camps are a thing of the past and are generally given to understand that war conditions still prevail, and the few English-speaking men employed are there because they find it impossible to get the means together to get out. . . .

One of the mines belongs to the Hon. Senator Watson. The mine tipple was burnt down some time ago and has not yet been repaired and in consequence the mine is at present not producing coal. Notwithstanding the fact, the new briquette plant being built by the Dominion is being erected close to the Senator's mine. . . .

P. M. Christophers

Hard Work and No Questions Asked!

HOW CANADA IS BEING COLONIZED

Hungarian-Slovak Colonization Board
10200-97th St.,
Edmonton, Alta.

Gentlemen:

Can you use some husky Slovaks in your mill or camp? Young men not afraid of work, hard, efficient workers, eager to get jobs and are satisfied with fair wages and grub.

The Slovaks are from the Carpathian mountains and feel at home in the woods. They are good swamp and axe men, handy with the chain and know how to handle logs on the river or in the woods.

The Penticton Saw Mills, Ltd., and several other firms who tried them are well satisfied and putting our men to work as they need them.

Right now jobs are scarce in the Alberta camps on account of lack of snow, and we could supply you good, steady men, willing and eager to put in a good day's work. They don't belong to the I.W.W. fraternity.

We have two blacksmiths who understand steam engines and want jobs in camps, and two cabinet makers who would be useful to sash and door makers but who will accept any kind of a job anywhere in a saw mill or box factory.

Let us know how many men you need and for what kind of work, the wages you pay and how to reach your camp or mill. Your orders will be appreciated and promptly filled.

Hoping to be at your service soon, we remain,

Yours very truly,
JOHN FRITZ,
Secretary-Manager.

Phone 6404

ESTEVAN

In a little mining village
Scarcely noticed on the map,
Bourgeois guns were turned on workers
And their life blood there did sap.

No one dreamed of such a slaughter
In that town of Estevan,
That armed thugs with guns and bullets
Would shoot men with empty hands.

Just a protest from the miners,
And boss bullets then did fly,
Caring not who was the target
Or the number that would die.

Blazing forth, nine hundred bullets
Bodies full of lead did fill,
Murdered three, and wounded twenty—
But the Cause they could not kill.

Three more martyrs for the miners
Three more murders for the boss
Brutal laws, to crush the workers
Who dare fight in Freedom's cause.

As those workers lay a-dying
In their agony and pain,
Whispering, "Though we die for freedom
That we do not die in vain."

"For we knew our class will triumph
When they shall united stand;
They will take the world for labor.
And the workers rule the land."

"Then the workers' day of vengeance
Will be proclaimed with each breath;
Labor's cause is right and mighty
And beyond the reach of death."

—Cecil Boone

THE POSTWAR DEPRESSION IN THE WEST

In this article Woodsworth, one of the leaders of the Winnipeg General Strike, and soon to be elected to Parliament, warns of the onset of the long-feared postwar depression. Woodsworth was one of the few middle-class reformers to understand the point of view, and speak the language of the ordinary worker.

J. S. Woodsworth, 'The Coming Winter', *The Canadian Forum*, vol. II (Sept. 1921), pp. 362-4. Reprinted by permission of The Canadian Forum.

"What"? I asked a Labour Man, "is the subject of greatest interest to Labour Men to-day?" Without hesitation, there came back the reply—"The coming winter".

Labour, in the West, is still deeply interested—and divided—on the question of industrial organisation. Labour was never more concerned over the political situation. But the immediate pressing problem is that of holding or securing a "job".

The demand for harvest hands has somewhat relieved the situation. A large number of mechanics and other workmen, who have been more or less unemployed since last autumn, have gone out to the farms. About eight hundred are to come from Vancouver, out of some four thousand who applied for the special transportation rates. In the neighbourhood of twenty-five thousand have been brought from Eastern Canada. But in the majority of cases the farmers will not require these men after the "freeze-up". What then?

In any case with wages varying from three dollars to four dollars a day, with deductions for wet weather and transportation, the amount that harvest hands can earn during the next few weeks will not go far towards supporting their families during the coming winter.

Under normal conditions, there is a considerable influx from the prairies to the cities during the winter months. This year, it will undoubtedly be swollen by numbers of English immigrants who came out this summer to go on farms, but whose services will not be needed after threshing.

Again, what then?

According to press reports at the conference now being held in Vancouver, the authorities admit that there are in British Columbia between eleven thousand and twelve thousand unemployed men, and that this figure will soon be increased to twenty thousand. Many of these men have been idle, except when engaged on relief works, for almost a year. Aside from the demoralising effects of such long-continued absence of steady work, any little resources in the form of money reserves, stocks of clothing, household effects, etc., are sadly depleted.

From Alberta has come a protest against any more people being brought into the province under existing conditions. Some Alberta farmers have come East to Saskatchewan and Manitoba to find work during the harvest.

In Winnipeg, the railway shops, which are the largest employers of labour, have during the summer been running part time. Here again the men have been drawing on reserves. As yet there has been little actual suffering.

Many men in the building trades have been idle for a considerable part of the season. It has been asserted by business men that had wages been reduced in the spring, there would have been extensive building operations this summer. Whether or not this is so—and the standing of business houses hardly warrants the assertion—and, whether or not the labour men were warranted in not accepting greater wage-cuts, the fact is that many will face the winter without the customary summer earnings. Absence of buying power will still further depress local business.

As the mental attitude of the workers is an important factor in the problem, perhaps I cannot do better than to relate a little incident that occurred a few days ago. This illustrated the position in which many a mechanic finds himself to-day, and also his view of his own problem.

A working man, shabbily dressed, gaunt and apparently ill, accosted me on the street.

"You are a *Canadian*, did I not once hear you say?" so he began. "Well, so am I", he continued, bitterly. "But a stranger in my own country. Nearly all the men I meet with in the shops are "old-country". It's only now and again you come across a real Canadian these days. This country was spoiled when they brought in those foreign Galicians".

"I haven't had a steady job for months. I always could find a job up till a few years ago. But since we were laid off, I haven't been able to get more than a few days. I guess the fellows that get the odd jobs must be members of some Order or fix it up with the boss."

"It's not only that the shops are running part time, but the staff was cut right down and lots of the men are out altogether. It isn't as if there wasn't plenty of repair work to be done. The Roads will not be able to handle the crop. But that will play into the hands of the Banks, and the farmer will get soaked as usual. No railroad should have the power to turn men off that way. That has been my job for years."

"The employment office? It's only a bosses' institution. It's convenient for them to call up for a man, but the office does nothing to provide work. My name has been on the list since May. Lots more like me. And still they bring in hundreds of thousands of immigrants. Yes, I suppose I shall have to go to work on a farm, for a few weeks during harvest. But what good is sixty dollars a month to a man with a family? The Loan Company will get after me the harder, too, if they know I'm working."

"I have a cottage half-paid for. I can't keep up the payments. They will take that from me. Then what can I do? I'm too old at forty-seven to save up enough to get a start on another. Down East, in the old days, a man could at least have a little house of his own. They said it would be all right after the war, but it's worse than ever!"

"You can't get any credit either. I've been buying from the Creamery Company for years and now they will not leave me a single bottle of milk without the cash. Fine, pious, respectable citizens, aren't they?"

"Look at that stream of automobiles! A prosperous country for some folk. Why the gasoline it takes to run one of these cars would almost keep my family going."

"Then there's the wife and kids! I've been worrying about them and the house till I'm hardly fit for a job. What am I to do?"

"Come", I ventured, "and have lunch with me, and we'll talk things over". His voice hardened, as he replied shortly, "I had dinner before I left home." I had not misjudged my man!

That face and figure has haunted me. I have not "investigated the case". What is the use? There are hundreds similar. I lived in the midst of it, all last winter. I dread the hardships and demoralisation of the coming months. Is this the price of the deflation of labour? Theories aside, what can I do for that hungry worried man, vainly wandering the streets in search of a job?

He may, possibly, on occasion, have been intemperate. He may not be 100% efficient. He may have been a little more "independent" than some, and refused to curry favour with "the boss". I do not know. It does not materially affect the situation. The outstanding fact is that here is a

Canadian workman of Scottish ancestry, anxious to maintain his family and keep his little home together, and in the length and breadth of Canada he can find no work.

What can be done? Apparently nothing will be done till the crisis is upon us. Then, in spite of good intentions, we shall be forced to give doles on an unprecedented scale. Although taxes are already high, this may be the cheapest safety-insurance scheme that can be adopted. But such a policy only staves off the evil day; makes the solution of our problem, in fact, the more difficult.

THE DIRTY TWENTIES IN QUEBEC: CATHOLIC UNIONS AND THE SOCIAL QUESTION

This is the story of the lockout (contre-grève) of its employees by the E.B. Eddy Company of Hull, Quebec, aimed at a Catholic union belonging to the Canadian and Catholic Confederation of Labour, founded in 1921.

In one sense it is typical that the Eddy dispute was not a strike. Catholic union leaders opposed strike action and favoured collaboration with the employer. But here, as in other disputes of the 1920s, they were forced to take militant action; and significantly, the story begins with a common tactic of union-busting companies, the 'yellow dog' contract (a document in which workers agreed as a condition of employment not to take part in union activity).

'La Contre-gréve chez Eddy', *Le Droit,* 30 Oct. 1924 and *L'Action Catholique,* 3 Dec. 1924. Translated by David Millar.

The city of Hull has just been the theatre of a labour struggle which will go down in history. For nearly 3 months several hundred members of the National Catholic union have been struggling fiercely to claim their legitimate rights against their powerful employer, the E. B. Eddy Company.

This dignified and energetic resistance by a group of workers, the majority of whom are girls, has provoked a strong movement of sympathy in all parts of the province. Several papers have spoken most favourably of the attitude of these workers and the justice of their claims. From various quarters and the most diverse groups have come encouragement, support and precious resources which the locked-out workers were far from expecting at the beginning of their difficulties. All this proves the obvious justice of their cause and its common interest to all workers.

Conscious of the justice of their claims and stimulated by such powerful auxiliaries the Catholic unions' members have remained "firm to the end," according to the watchword of their leaders, at price of what sacrifice only they know. The struggle was long, exhausting and nerve-wracking. They have persevered in the face of power and pettifoggery combined. Honour to the brave, thanks to their benefactors and friends...

Nature of the Conflict: Mistakes

On the 2nd of September last, posters signed by the match department manager of the Eddy Company, Mr. Arthur Wood, warned of a coming cut in employees' wages. This wage cut was exorbitant, and the procedure used unjustifiable, since it constituted a grave violation of the agreement concluded between the company and the union back in 1919.

Having already seen, on more than one occasion, important clauses of this contract undercut by Superintendent Wood, the workers on their own accord and without prior consultation with the officers of the union, quit work forthwith until such time as the offending matter be removed, and the author promised that he would launch no such further ultimatum without agreement with the Catholic union as stated in the contract, still in force and signed by him in the name of the company in 1919. It was the first defeat for Mr. Wood. But he would bring yet another on himself by his unjust actions.

Jobless

Four days after this incident, new posters announced this time the closing of the match department for an undetermined period. In order to justify this unusual proceeding, the company claimed urgent repairs were needed to machinery, overstocking of matches in its depot, and a slackening market.... What credence to attach to these reasons for unemployment we cannot say. But the lockout has proved that the match stockpile was exhausted in a few weeks although the Deseronto branch plant was working at full capacity all during the time of the difficulties.... Too soon the rumour spread that this layoff period was only the beginning of a lockout campaign by the company, in other words an attempt to impose new working conditions on its employees when the company recommenced operation. Having learned to be wary, the unemployed did not break ranks. Two and even three times a week, all those concerned met at the labour exchange. The union directed all its members, "Don't accept new working conditions without checking at the union office." A prudent counsel, as events were to prove.

The "Yellow Dog" Contracts

The 23rd of September the company, ignoring its foreladies, sent people to find the girls for the opening of the match operation. All union members were at once informed of these strange proceedings by the bosses. A strong group of unionists accompanied the girls and requested to go to the factory. To the astonishment of the employees, once in the company's offices they were presented, although already duly engaged as employees, with the following formula to sign.

Application for Employment with the E. B. Eddy Company Limited

I _____ name in full herewith seek employment as _____

I agree that in accepting the position requested I will not discuss the organization of a labour association during the hours of work nor urge others to become or not to become members of such union or association.

I further agree that if I am not satisfied with salary, working conditions or hours I will not leave my work without prior notice of one full day to the company.

Department _____ Signed _____ Date _____

How can this be only a request for information, "an employment record form," as the company claims? The text does not permit this interpretation. An impartial study by any just reader must lead him to support the employees, who have seen in this formula an individual contract pure and simple.

This unfortunate formula is the immediate cause of the difficulties. If the union members had signed it, what would have been the force of the collective agreement signed with the company by the union in 1919? Would that contract, still in force, not have become according to the Prussian formula a "vile scrap of paper"? The workers so claim. Let us examine the facts.

Lockout

In its declarations to the papers, as in its correspondence with the union, the company has always denied that the difficulties in the match department were a lockout. In the *Citizen* of October 27, President Millen said, "There is no strike of the employees of our match company.... There is no *lockout* for the company has always been ready and willing since the end of September to operate its match factory to a limited extent." Understandably, the company wished to reopen its operation, since its match stockpile was almost, if not totally exhausted at that date. Which does not prove, however, that it is not responsible for the lockout.

What is a lockout or "contre-grève?"? It is the action of an employer closing his own factory gates and imposing on his employees new working conditions before he re-engages them. Is this not the case at the Eddy Company?... Furthermore, the employers admit themselves that the contre-grévistes were duly engaged under the contact of 1919. The president has written, "I hastened to assure Father Bonhomme that the company had no intention of terminating its agreement with the union."

Then why the new contracts?...The company insists on radical changes in the conditions of work and further, closes its doors to its employees. That is a 'lockout'. Whether it will or no, the company must bear its responsibility before public opinion.

War on the Union

...as we have said, there is abundant evidence that Superintendent Wood has always led an undeclared war against the union since its foundation. It was with his back to the wall that he signed an agreement with this legally constituted body in 1919. But as for respecting his signature, that was something else again. Sometime before the closing of the plant, had he not the audacity to offer a raise in pay and a holiday to one of the foreladies if she agreed to renounce her union? She was one of the same ladies that he obstinately refused to re-employ at the company until the 20th of November.

What is the 'individual contract' quoted above? An underhanded attack on the union. How can we explain the energetic refusal, the stubbornness of M. Caesar and others to re-employ the foreladies and union officers during negotiations? Would these negotiations not have succeeded the 4th of November had it not been for their thirst to make victims in sacrificing the leading figures of the union?

Finally what should we make of these two statements of M. Caesar, the dictator during the proceedings, "The union has thwarted my plans of re-organization," and this laconic phrase excusing his rejections, "We want to be at home"? For those who have eyes to see, it becomes extremely clear that a fight to the death against the unions has inspired this whole frameup.

Some have seen in this attack a blow against Catholic unionism, anti-Catholicism. We would not go that far. Moreover, it must be said that Mr. Millen [the former chairman] has always prized the friendship of the Catholic clergy with which he has had long acquaintance....As Omer Héroux says in *Le Devoir*, "It is in the general and highest interest of the company to promote by all means possible the Catholic union of match workers. The Catholic unions tend to social peace and to the raising of professional standards...."

A Moral Problem

In their despairing fight against the exercise of union rights by their employees, the bosses have ventured on a most dangerous territory, that of morality. Their error has singularly favoured the struggle against the lockout. A serious moral question has been raised concerning the first case of nearly 300 young girls, and thus has been created a strong resistance not only on the part of Catholic parents but on that of their priests. Here is the moral side of the Eddy lockout.

For years the immediate supervision of female employees in matchmaking was confided to foreladies. This policy seemed quite normal. No clause was inserted on this point in the 1919 contract. Bosses and unionists alike shared this view on the necessity of foreladies for young girls.

But as we will see, as negotiations began the union representatives found the company obstinately decided to replace foreladies by a matron and several foremen. Why this innovation dangerous to the security of young girls? "The industrial revolution of our plant demands this change," replies the company. But it is a grave danger for morals.

Position of the Curé

Father Philémon Bourassa: ... "It is not my habit to speak from the pulpit of conflicts from which our city suffers from time to time. But at the present hour the moral question is the basis of the difficulties, and since morality is our domain as well in the factory as at the school or on the street, it is my duty to speak. As you know, last winter when to save some dollars on the production of each ton of pulp the company closed a plant and put 250 employees on the sidewalk, of whom many had grown old in the service of the company, I did not raise my voice. Morality was not directly in question. And I contented myself with aiding the most needy families. Again this spring, when by proceedings which I leave you to judge, the powers that be placed on your shoulders both increased municipal expenses and a ten-year tax-exemption, I did not breathe a word. Morality was not directly in question. Today it is another matter.

[Looking at the Eddy company's new contract], twist this unfortunate document as you will two conclusions are inevitable. 1. The company is systematically ignoring the existence of a professional union duly constituted, and with which it has dealt in the past and to which it is still bound. 2. The attempt to murder this legitimate union by inviting its members to sign, individually, the contract and its conditions which by rights belong to the union, and forbidding them to talk union at the factory as if it were an anarchist conspiracy—that is called respecting Catholic unionism. The boss may be master of his plants, his machinery, his capital, but he is not the master of the health, the virtue and the family of his employees. We are no longer in the time of slavery. To endanger workers' lives beyond their capacity to avoid, is a crime for which the boss may be punished by our civil law. Is then the soul of the worker worth less than his body? Shall the virtue of a young girl not be protected as well as her lungs? The demands of health, its security and protection are ensured by civil law and by divine law; this security and protection must be given to virtue. The promiscuity of the sexes in the factory is already a grave moral danger. But still more intense is the danger of the subjection of girls to some foreman. What can a weak girl do to defend herself against an influential and cunning foreman? She has no choice. It is dishonour or the door. Once you know a man who can say, "If a young girl takes her chances that's all right, as long as she works well I'm satisfied," you can imagine the rest.... I shall not recount here the history of some shops, rather on this question as priests we know what we are talking about. And our experience will not be denied by those fathers who know certain places of work.

For the rest, when it is a question of the honour of our children, of their future, there is no risk to be taken ... "

The Second Negotiation

The 22nd October Messrs. Marois and Guyon arrived at Hull in the name of the Quebec Labour Minister. After having investigated the claims of the strikers, the government representatives came to the company to hear its grievances and propositions for peace. Two days were given to this delicate work.

Instead of holding out its hand to this intermediary, and putting an end to a conflict as disastrous for employers as for employees, the company broke off relations. But let us read its war-like declaration.

Monsieur Marois

Dear Sir: This will advise you that at its meeting yesterday, the 22nd of October, the board of directors of the company unanimously adopted the following resolution:

"Given the violation of the criminal code of the country by a certain number of members of the national union of matchmakers and their assault on the person of the superintendent of the match factory ... the company refuses to undertake any negotiation with the union or any other body of law breakers.

Yours truly, the E.B. Eddy Limited ...

Monday November 20th. Mr. Wood was driven to work in his automobile, supercilious as ever. Several of the young girls on the picket line jumped in front of the superintendent's car. The driver stopped, then backed up in order to get his machine up to speed and break through the ranks of the girls at the risk of crushing them to death. "Run through the bunch," Wood ordered. A labourer not a member of the union, going to work at J. R. Booth's ... jumped on the running board of the vehicle, threw on the brakes and tried to strike the imprudent driver. Monsieur Gauthier, a member of the match union, fortunately averted the blow. The auto was pushed with its two occupants toward the Eddy Company stable, the police intervened and took Wood under protection and urged him to return to Ottawa for his own good, since the employees of J. R. Booth who saw the whole thing were about to settle accounts with that unpopular gentleman. The author of the match conflict, A. Wood, the official 'victim' of this terrible assault ... escaped with a good fright.

The Picket Line

... In good weather, in bad weather, under the cold rain, in the wet snow or under a soft sun, groups of 50 and sometimes 200 girls regularly picketed from 6:30 in the morning until 5:30 at night. Those who were on guard left the labour exchange to go picketing and came back to the same building, their chore accomplished ... The men had one regret only, that they could never use their fists. "They let the girls stop in front of the factory but they make the men walk on. The girls say that they are afraid and if we stand up for them the police threaten us. That is really shocking." But these, under firm orders from the union, mastered their feelings and remained calm. For two long months of picketing only a couple of small incidents ... How many strikes of the "international" could show an attitude as calm and blameless? The bosses, supposedly scandalized by the girls' picketing, would do well to contemplate the truth ...

All Hull Supports the Unionists

The resistance of a solidly structured union, the disastrous immobilization of a factory by the refusal of its employees to return to work under unacceptable conditions, these certainly are indispensable elements of victory. But they are however not enough to assure the triumph of a legitimate cause. The bosses are rich and capable of bearing heavy losses. The workers live from day to day and in times of crisis must count on the aid of their neighbours. Let us add that all the local commerce suffered from the prolonged unemployment.... But it is rare that labour difficulties have received such proof of support from every class of society....

Unquestionably the population of Hull in its entirety stood with the contre-grèvistes. Public bodies such as City Council and the Chamber of Commerce supported them by word and deed. The Saint-Jean-Baptiste Society, the Commercial Travellers' Society, laymen's associations and other groups protested to the Company and generously subscribed to the strike fund. Individuals also did their part. A tag day organized by the "Godmothers" of the women's "syndicat" brought in almost $1,000. A voluntary campaign subscribed several hundred dollars. Merchants sent the needy stocks of food. Finally, several organizations in favour of the unions had unexpected success ... Assuredly, the moral side of the conflict played a preponderant role in this shoulder-to-shoulder stand against the company, but to be exact, it must be said that Hull profited from the occasion of the lock-out to give large course to its sentiment of discontent toward the Eddy company. This popular unrest depends on several fairly recent developments: the fact that French Canadians are no longer represented in the ranks of management, that the late Madame Eddy's bequest and company subscriptions to local charities were considerably less than those of the Booth company, and the dismissal of some 300 pulp workers during the winter to take advantage of lower prices elsewhere, the municipal tax exemption which depended on Eddy construction work going to Hull workers which was observed more in the breach than in the observance (The company paid only 30 cents to labourers and 50 cents to carpenters).

The workers speak of the time of Eddy and McMillan as of the golden age, a paradise lost. Those self-made men understood their fellow workers and knew how to make themselves loved by their men. Today the men and the methods have changed. The relations with the managers are no longer stamped with confidence and respect.

Even the press is passing rather severe judgement on the conduct of the managers of the company. It has ramifications in the political world, for one of the directors of the factory is Mr. R. B. Bennett of Calgary, Minister of Justice in the last Meighen cabinet and celebrated for his attack against Meighen himself in 1914. At that time, he accused the man who later became his leader of being the mouthpiece of MacKenzie and Mann and the two old parties, of receiving secret funds from railway companies to which they truckled in giving public subsidies. Mr. Bennett has been at Ottawa, it goes without saying, since the beginning of the strike.

THE WHOLE STORY

Wednesday, 3rd December, 1924. Our paper has once again spoken in its Labour Chronicle of the dispute between the E.B. Eddy Company of Hull and its Matchgirls' Union. Apparently, at least, this difficulty was settled some days ago to the satisfaction of the factory girls and the entire population of Hull who sympathized fully with them.

The impact of this contract, even rather less than more respected by the company, was considerable. The factory girls' Union having received life from this establishment, was now able to supply services. What is more, it was soon installed in a large fully-furnished hall where its members could go to pass some of their free time, to learn sewing, housekeeping, English, French and arithmetic and to this union was attached a Credit Union in which the working girl could amass a small dowry. While in the syndicate, the members could prepare their future role as good working-class mothers, in the factory the presence of fore-ladies protected them against the dangers that some experienced eyes had foreseen... The work accomplished by this union was so obvious, not only to the eyes of the girls' parents but to the entire population of the town, particularly the pastors who rejoiced in possessing a model union, that the community as a whole raised its zeal to encourage and defend the factory girl. All the associations, the public bodies, took their side. Expressions of sympathy were so numerous that they included other localities and even Protestant groups. Thanks to the action of these associations and public bodies, thanks to the zeal of the Reverend Father, Chaplain of the Syndicate of the Fathers of Notre Dame and the other curés of the city parishes, thanks to the repeated efforts of the City Fathers who finally succeeded in playing the role of intermediary, a solution was found to put an end to the unemployment and that, to the satisfaction of the working girls who fought for nothing else than their moral protection . . . Thus, it is not from an eyewitness that our colleague at the *Telegraph* got his information of Monday, 1st December: "The young girls employed at the E. B. Eddy Factory at Hull who had been on strike for some time, returned to work having entirely lost several weeks of work. Although sadder than the day when they quit work, they had become considerably wiser." The *Telegraph* shares the opinion of a French newspaperman who says, "We do not see why this strike was declared, nor why it lasted so many weeks. We would have thought that the conditions obtained by the girls for their return to work could have been more easily won by peaceful and friendly negotiations than by striking. Thus, poverty would have been avoided in many families and losses both to the company and to the city. The strike instead of being the first means employed by the working girls should have been the last but somehow there always seem to be some hotheads in the population."

If the *Telegraph* had taken the pains to inform itself properly, it would have learned the full story, . . . especially, it would have learned who were the alleged hotheads. With the dust out of its eyes, it would have easily described the cause of the dispute, the urgent need to safeguard the moral health of the young girls who will be mothers of tomorrow.

A JEWISH RAGPICKERS' UNION, TORONTO

Exploitation of immigrant workers was not confined to the west. The role of the ethnic workers in Canada in the 1920s and 1930s was a miserable one, and for none was it worse than the orthodox Jews. Here we see one of their few successful attempts to organize.

M. Biderman, 'Father and Friends Organize a Union', *Fraternally Yours*, Nov.-Dec. 1970. Reprinted by permission of M. Biderman and *Fraternally Yours*.

One of my father's favourite stories, and also one of mine, was the way in which he and his fellow workers organized and formed a union. My father was a rag picker or a sorter, if one wants to use a more elegant term. He worked for M. Granatstein and Sons on Wellington Street. His boss was Mendel Granatstein, the founder of the firm—and referred to by the men who worked for him as Reb Mendel. Reb Mendel himself started as a rag peddler with a push cart. When we arrived in Canada in 1920, and for many years after that it was common to see Jews with long beards pushing their carts and buying old clothes and rags. If one of them had a horse and buggy, he was considered the aristocrat of the peddlers.

The old clothes and rags from all over the city were brought to Granatstein, dumped on long tables where they would be sorted, baled and taken to the mills for reprocessing into cloth.

The sorters worked in dirt and filth all day long. I visited my father at work one day. It happened that he forgot his sandwiches and my mother asked me to take them to him. Reb Mendel himself met me at the gate and escorted me to my father. At first I couldn't see any people at all. The haze created by the dirt rising from the rags and clothes on the long tables, could be compared to a haze in a steam room.

The working week was long, 60 hours—12 hours longer than the prevailing average working week of 48 hours. The wages were lower, too, in comparison with the prevailing standards and conditions of that time. All of the workers being religious Jews, they would leave work early on Friday to prepare for the Sabbath. But to make up for this, they would have to come in and work after sundown on Saturday night. Having to work "Shabeistzunacht" (Saturday night) was particularly aggravating to the men and in the synagogue on the Sabbath they would discuss this. Little by little the idea took hold of doing something about it.

The first meeting took place in the home of one of the workers. Only a very few of the close friends and the most trusted were called. My father was among them. Two points of view were put forward at the meeting. One was that they should leave things well enough alone. Where, some argued, are religious men of their age going to get other jobs if they should happen to lose the one they have? On the other hand—others argued—where will the boss get such slaves to work such long hours at such miserable low wages? Among the latter was my father.

At the end of the meeting it was finally agreed that every man present should talk to one at work who was not present, acquaint him with the discussion and bring him to another meeting to be called. They all swore each other to the strictest secrecy by giving each other "Tkias Kaf"—a very sacred religious vow not to betray one another.

This was the beginning of union organization. What followed is another story.

After the initial meeting which was limited to a very few intimate friends, many more get-togethers took place. These served a very useful social purpose. The men at Granatstein's, you must remember, were all "single"—they were here in Canada alone, separated from their families and unable to bring them here because of the war.

Little by little all the men at Granatstein's began to attend the social meetings and discussions, in the course which they gave voice to their bitter lot. Slowly the idea took hold to unite and organize. But forming a union was no simple matter in those days, especially for newly arrived immigrants from Poland, with their religious, social and economic background. Working for a living was in itself an entirely new experience, entailing great hardship and suffering for them.

Much discussion on how and where to look for help in their efforts to organize took place. Perhaps we should go to the Rabbi, was the opinion of some men. They were, however, in the minority. "We finally agreed," my father told us, "to seek help from people engaged in organizing the needle trades." One man in particular by the name of Lapidus was of great help.

In the meantime, Reb Mendel Granatstein found out that his men were organizing. How he found out is a mystery to this very day. Whether any of the men actually broke the "Tkias Kaf " will never be known. Maybe Reb Mendel was actually never told by anybody. Maybe he came upon the truth by observing how differently his men were acting —as if they were hiding some secret. No one really knew.

The First Confrontation

One day Reb Mendel came up to the section where my father worked and addressed him directly. "So, Reb Michael (my father's name), I hear good things about you men holding secret meetings, organizing a union and I understand you are one of them, even a leader maybe." "Why the secrecy?"—Reb Mendel wanted to know—"if you have anything you want to talk about, why do you need secret meetings? Why don't you come to me and tell me what is bothering you? It's hard for me to believe that religious men of your type would do a thing like that."

It was an embarrassing moment. For a minute or so there was absolute silence. All the men kept their heads lowered looking at the rags on the table. "I confess I was at a loss what to do", my father remembered that moment of confrontation. "On the one hand we were sworn to absolute secrecy and yet how could we deny that we were having meetings once Reb Mendel knew about them. And how could we just stand there saying nothing in reply to him? Would that not be a sign of weakness on our part?"

"I finally stopped my work and looked up at Reb Mendel—and noticed, that all the other men also stopped their work and were looking at me. At that moment I felt I had no choice but to speak up and I did."

"It's true, Reb Mendel, the men get together, but that should be no surprise to you. We are lonely without our families and so we seek comfort of each other and exchange news from home and naturally when we do get together we also discuss our lot in this new land and our work, which is so new and so hard for us. And isn't it natural for people to want to better themselves. Really Reb Mendel, I cannot understand why you are so upset."

"Reb Mendel didn't say a thing. He just looked at me and the men and left. After he left we worked in silence for a long time. Then we began to discuss and evaluate what had happened. I was afraid I would be criticized for speaking up"—my father said—"but not even one of the men objected. On the contrary, all the men felt good about the confrontation. Our secret was out in the open. We were now able to discuss our work problems at work and not merely at secret meetings."

News of the confrontation with Reb Mendel rapidly spread to all other working sections in the building. After that Reb Mendel was a frequent visitor to the section where my father worked. He would come and talk about many things and would always manage to touch on the subject of organizing a union which was, in his opinion, totally unnecessary.

On one such visit Reb Mendel invited my father to come and have a talk with him about things that were bothering the men. My father told him that he would gladly do that, but since the men, as Reb Mendel well knows, do get together and discuss things, it would be much better if the men themselves would decide who should talk to him, and perhaps, too, it would be better if more than one person was involved in such a discussion with him.

As a result of this talk a committee of three was appointed to meet with Reb Mendel Granatstein and talk over matters. My father was one of the three.

The committee told Reb Mendel of the strong feeling among the men that the hours of work were far too long and the wages far too low. In particular the men wanted to do away with working "Shabeistzunacht" (Saturday night). There was much discussion back and forth and while Reb Mendel was prepared to make some concessions, they were far from satisfying to the men. An agreement was finally reached to go to arbitration and to accept the findings of the arbitration board as final. The men would appoint one arbitrator, Reb Mendel another and the two arbitrators would choose the third. . . .

After many meetings the men formulated the demands that were to be presented to the arbitration board of three. Their choice for the person to represent them was an active union man. The men consulted him on their demands, which were very simple: a) Abolish work on Saturday nights. b) a further reduction of hours in the work-week. c) a modest increase in pay.

I remember my father telling about the long discussions the men had as to whether to place emphasis in their demands on the reduction of hours or the increase in pay. "We decided to concentrate on the reduction of hours," father explained, "firstly because we felt this was the greatest evil and also because we felt that the work-week once reduced would be more permanent than a pay increase which can be first won and later on lost."

The arbitration board met at 350 Dundas street west, a hall used a lot in those days for meetings and social gatherings. Witnesses for both sides gave their opinions and answered questions. Many of the men attended the hearings, anxious to get first hand news on the progress of their case before the arbitration board. From time to time their representative would come out from the meeting room and give them a report on how things were going inside.

Once their representative came out and told them that things were not going very well. The arguments of the witnesses for Mr. Granatstein, were influencing the impartial chairman of the arbitration board. They were the same old arguments: that the men involved are all older than average, they are all religious and therefore must have special consideration such as leaving early on Friday before the Sabbath, not working on the Sabbath. They are new immigrants with no knowledge of English and Canadian customs. Because of all this, their chances of getting employment were limited. Such men, they kept repeating time and again, should feel fortunate they found employment and should not compare their conditions and standards to workers in other industries.

The union representative said he wished something would happen, some dramatic presentation on behalf of the men that would help get a favourable decision from the arbitration board.

It was then that my father asked the union representative if he could appear as a witness before the board.

The answer was yes, it could be arranged. But what can now be said that wasn't already said? the union representative wanted to know. My father told him that he knows this but what possible harm could there be in his appearing before the board? It was agreed that there could be no possible harm and father was called in to the board meeting.

"I don't know what came over me," father related this incident on many occasions, "I began to speak without any preparation and right from the heart. It was said here that we are all older and would find it hard to get other jobs. This is true, no one can deny it. But who, I ask, would take the kind of jobs we have? Who will work the hours we work at the low wages we work for and in the conditions of filth that we have to endure all the time? Who—but older men such as we and strangers in a new land? Do any of you realize the kind of dirt we wallow in all day and the things we take out of the bags when we open them and dump them on our tables? Why, only a week ago we opened a bag and among the rags that were spread on the table a new born infant was uncovered? Who are the men that will continue to work under such conditions? Where will you find others to replace us?"

"I observed," father told us, "that everyone in the room was very quiet. I could sense that my words were having the right effect. I then told them one more thing. A big case was made here of the fact that we leave early on Friday and don't have to work on the Sabbath. I say this is not true—all of us work on the Sabbath and thus commit a sin against God. Here I was immediately interrupted, and challenged"—father remembered. "Why? What are you saying, what kind of talk is this, everyone knows you don't work on the Sabbath! Please explain!"

"Oh yes, I know, formally we don't work on the Sabbath, we are in the synagogue saying our prayers. But do you know what really happens to us on the Sabbath? Why even as we sit in the synagogue saying our prayers, our thoughts are already somewhere else, in the shop where we have to go to the same evening. You call this resting on the Sabbath? To me this is the same as working. My lips are saying the prayers but my mind is already occupied with the work I will have to go to in a few hours. I say to you we have no Sabbath."

"I finished and waited for any questions but there weren't any. When I came out of the meeting room the union representative followed me. He came up to me and shook my hand." "You did very well," he said. "I feel what you said and especially how you said it influenced the impartial chairman."

The verdict was not long in coming. The men at Granatstein and Sons won their first victory. Saturday night work was abolished. The hours of the work-week were further reduced. And they also received a modest increase in pay.

WHEN TRUTH IS SEDITION: CAPE BRETON, 1924

The decade of the 1920s was a period of labour quiescence everywhere in Canada except Cape Breton Island. Over half the time lost in strikes and lockouts in the decade was in the Island's coal mines and steel mills. The leader of the famous BESCO strike, J. B. MacLachlan was imprisoned for 'seditious libel'. His crime? Criticizing the brutality of the Provincial Police!

In this article Woodsworth points out that under Canadian law, telling the truth is no defence.

J. S. Woodsworth, 'Besco', *The Canadian Forum*, vol. IV, no. 42 (March 1924), pp. 161-71. Reprinted by permission of The Canadian Forum.

What is the root of all this trouble in Nova Scotia? Bolshevism among the foreign miners? No, that is not an adequate answer, though an easy way of disposing of any industrial difficulty. The miners in Nova Scotia are chiefly of Scotch-Canadian stock and there was similar trouble long before Lenin came upon the international stage. No case can be summed in a word, yet there is one word that is much nearer than Bolshevism; that is 'Besco'—the common sobriquet of the British Empire Steel Corporation. . . .

Another Royal Commission has reported. It has been studying the miners; only incidentally has it studied Besco. Can its recommendation then prove other than futile? The Commission finds that the military were needed to cope with the situation at Sydney. Property rights were endangered and the Government had to step in. The papers feature this. But what of the primary human rights that have been disregarded until the men are rendered half desperate? On this point the report is couched in the most general terms. Certain obvious reforms are recommended, notably the abandonment of the eleven- and thirteen-hour shifts which involve, every fortnight, twenty-four hours continuous work.

But when the Commission reports to the Federal Government, the Federal Government disclaims any power to enact legislation along these lines, claiming that this is a provincial matter. Possibly growing public opinion may force the Nova Scotia Government to take action. A year ago Besco informed a delegation from a local ministerial association that Nova Scotia would not move until Judge Gary made the change!

Other investigators have reported on the situation but without bringing about material improvements. In 1920 the housing and sanitary conditions were described by a Royal Commission as being 'with few exceptions absolutely wretched.' Two years later a Board of Conciliation admitted that the company's houses were 'not in a satisfactory condition.' The minority report made went further describing the sanitary conditions as 'absolutely wretched.' Another two years and still no change in this or other conditions of life and labour.

In a series of articles which appeared a year ago in the *Toronto Daily Star*, Mr F. A. Carman puts his finger on one of the sore spots:

Fourteen companies of various grades of importance go to make up Besco. When the fourteen went into the cauldron they owned in stocks of various kinds a little under $83,000,000. When the merging process had been completed these $83,000,000 had been transmuted into just under $102,000,000. . . . To pay dividends on nearly $102,000,000 of stocks should be a sufficient task for the men who have to manage an industry which must meet the world competition in the steel and coal trade. But before they can begin to do this they have to meet prior charges of over $31,000,000 of mortgages of various sorts.... In the Besco process common stocks were reduced from 63 to 24 million while preferred stocks rose from 19 to 77 million.... The result of this transformation process has been the addition of charges of over $4,000,000 to the annual liabilities of the industry.... The recent watering down of the stock of these companies was not the first operation of the kind.... This original $15,000,000 of common 'watered' stock is represented in the existing issues of Besco stock by $6,000,000 of common stock and by $13,500,000 of 7% second preference on which the dividends are a cumulative liability. Which shows us in epitome how what was originally merely a speculative 'flyer' may by skilful financing be transmogrified into the next thing to a bond.

'Skilful financing'—aye, and unscrupulous financing. One transaction has recently been dragged to the light of day. At a time when important negotiations were in progress between the Newfoundland Government and the Compay, ex-Premier Squires received $46,000 from funds of the Dominion Steel Co. This action according to the evidence was approved by Roy Wolvin and other high officials (See *Montreal Star*, Jan. 31st, 1924). Such is Besco!

In vain have the workers appealed to Provincial and Federal Parliaments for legal redress or assistance. Besco was well represented in the Government councils. A year ago, when a deputation asked Mr Mackenzie King for the provision of pension for worn-out miners—a part of the pre-election programme of the Liberal party—all they received from the Prime Minister was a copy of his book *Industry and Humanity*!

In vain have the workers appealed to Provincial authorities to obtain representation in Parliament; constituencies were gerrymandered, an industrial county being united with a county peopled largely by farmers and fishermen with a two-member constituency. Then on the eve of the election 'roorbacks' were issued—'false tales' concerning the candidate J. B. MacLachlan who went down to defeat.

When two years ago, the miners resorted to the 'strike on the job', the Press entirely misrepresented the situation. Even Mr Meighen recognized the merits of their policy:

What have these men done? They have been requested, we will put it, to accept a wage reduction of 32-1/2 per cent. They have declined to do it. They say, 'No it is not a living wage, we cannot support our families, we cannot send our children to school, we do not want to go on strike or go out.' ... They say 'Here you are giving us two-thirds of a day's pay and we will give you two-thirds of a day's work, and only that; we don't pretend to give you any more.' (*Hansard*, March 30th, 1922)

At that time, the Government refused the Royal Commission asked for by the Mayors of the mining towns, but a little later sent down troops notwithstanding the protests of the local authorities that there was no need. So the struggle has gone on with growing bitterness. Last summer driven back to work by starvation, the steel-workers in a notable statement declared that every man's hand was against them. Within the last few weeks the coal miners have been forced into the pits, against their will, by the reactionary American officials at the head of their own union. But that is too long and too complicated a story to be even outlined here.

In the meantime the miners' leader is serving a two-year sentence in Dorchester penitentiary convicted of seditious libel. What had he done? In a circular letter he staged that the Provincial Police had brutally ridden down men, women, and children on a Sunday night when most of them were coming from church.

One old woman over 70 years of age was beaten into insensibility and may die. A boy of nine years old was trampled under the horses' feet and had his breast bone crushed in. One woman beaten over the head with a police club gave premature birth to a child. The child is dead and the woman's life is despaired of.

The coal operators gave this letter to the papers. Then MacLachlan was arrested and taken to Halifax charged with unlawfully publishing a false tale and also with seditious libel. The charge of publishing a false tale was withdrawn; the tale was all too true. MacLachlan's letter is substantially corroborated by statutory declaration and by the evidence given before the Royal Commission. But in the case of seditious libel, as the Attorney-General pointed out, the truer the statement the worse the libel. So J. B. MacLachlan is behind the bars because he dared to criticize the brutality of the Provincial Police of Nova Scotia.

That is technically true. But under this obsolete and discredited law of seditions any of us might be convicted. Mr Meighen might be sent to the penitentiary for criticizing the Liberal administrations. Why then was MacLachlan the victim? Because in fighting in the cause of the men he had incurred the enmity of the powerful British Empire Steel Corporation. They were out to 'get' him, and since he was irreproachable in his personal character and well within the law in his official activities, they invoked this old law that dates back to witch-burning days.

Even then MacLachlan did not get the fair play of those early times. He was not allowed a trial in his home county but was taken to Halifax where for years the minds of the people have been poisoned against the miners.

When an appeal was taken for another trial, the trial judge was a member of the Court of Appeal. Of the six judges on the Bench, four, before the time of their elevation to the bench, had been connected with the steel or coal companies subsidiary to Besco.

UNIONS, UNEMPLOYMENT, AND RELIEF IN THE 1920s

Rising costs and widespread unemployment added to the already precarious existence of the Canadian worker. Members of this Commons Committee pressed a reluctant government to alleviate the life of the worker. By 1927 mothers' allowances and old-age pensions had been won—though on a very limited basis. The Committee was now beginning to investigate the possibility of instituting a system of unemployment insurance. Twelve years later, the Unemployment Insurance Commission was finally established by a reluctant government.

House of Commons, Committee on Industrial and International Relations, *Proceedings* (Ottawa, 1928), pp. 25-126.

WITNESS: PIERRE BEAULÉ, President of the Canadian and Catholic Confederation of Labour.

Q. Have the Catholic syndicates any provision for sickness insurance, within their own organization?—A. I would qualify that by saying that there are special funds to cover sickness, and all labour liabilities.

Q. Are those funds made up by contributions from the employers and employees?—A. The only contributors to such sickness funds are the labour people themselves.

Q. Those funds would not be adequate as an insurance scheme? It is a mere matter of charity, and is not an adequate insurance scheme?—A. It is a philanthropic question. .

Q. Could you tell us something about the wages paid to the skilled workers in the industries you represent?—A. Here is a list of a few of the trades. Helpers, 40 cents per hour for a nine hour day; painters, 47 cents per hour for a nine hour day; carpenters, 55 cents per hour for a nine hour day; plasterers, 85 cents per hour for a nine hour day; bricklayers,

90 cents per hour for a nine hour day; and plumbers, 55 cents per hour for a nine hour day.

Q. What about the boot and shoe industry?—A. The men employed in the boot and shoe factories all work on piece work.

Q. What is the average wage per day?—A. In many factories, where the syndicates are represented, men on piece work make, on an average, between $1,000 and $1,200 per year. The men that are not organized, working on piece work, average from $12 to $20 per week.

Q. How many hours per day, or how many hours per week do they work?—A. In the summer time they work ten hours per day.

Q. Six days per week?—A. No, Saturday afternoon is taken off.

Q. Are the girls and women in the textile factories, and other trades, organized under the Catholic syndicates?

The WITNESS: The girls and women, working in the cotton factories, are not organized. . . .

Q. Can you give us any idea of the wages, and hours, with regard to the girls in the cotton factories?—A. They do not work more than forty-eight hours per week.

Q. What are the wages?—A. I cannot say precisely, but I do not think that those girls get more than $8 per week, the year round.

Q. $8 per week?

Mr. ST. PÈRE: $8. According to the statistics of the Labour Department, the average wage for men working in the cotton mills, is $666 per year. I got that information myself.

By Mr. Woodsworth:

Q. How do you propose that the people working on that low wage will be able to contribute to an insurance fund?—A. I would consider it very difficult for them to contribute to such an insurance fund.

Q. What percentage of the employees in the textile industry is women, or young girls?—A. I cannot say precisely, but I think that about two-thirds of them are women. In the shoe industry, it would be about fifty per cent.

Q. Fifty per cent of married women?—A. Young women.

Q. Girls and women?—A. Yes.

Q. Is it the practice for these girls, after they are married, to return to work in the factories?—A. There is a very small proportion. As far as I know, in Quebec, only a few of them go back to work after they are married. In Quebec practically no woman goes back to work after she is married except in needful cases. Where the husband is out of work, a woman goes back to her old job to help him along.

Q. Is it the practice of the employers to give a large wage or more steady work to married men?—A. From what I know of what happened during the last Quebec strike in the shoe industry—

Q. When was that strike?—A. In 1926. During that strike I heard some of these employers in the boot and shoe industry say that they would prefer girls and unmarried people, to get rid of the unionized workers.

Q. So far as you know are any of the employers opposed to Roman Catholic syndicates as such, or to all unionized industry?—A. About one-third of the employers are dealing with unionized labour.

Mr. ST. PÈRE: The witness said in the boot and shoe industry, those doing piece work get from $1,000 to $1,200 a year, and all the other workers from $12 to $20 per week.

The WITNESS: Girls working in the boot and shoe industry either in Quebec or Montreal draw from $300 to $360 per year salary, either for piece work or ordinary work.

Q. Nine hours a day?—A. Ten hours a day.

Q. Does the minimum wage law cover any of these industries in Quebec?—A. No, not in the boot and shoe industry.... Only girls working in the laundries and the printing industry have a minimum wage law covering their salaries....

Q. What would she make in a week? You mentioned $8 at one time. Is that about the average?—A. Yes. Ladies doing piece work have to work at the factories. They have to be there, waiting for work. Sometimes poor organization in the business does not supply them with ready work, and they have to stay there and wait for work.

Q. They do not get paid for the waiting time?—A. No.

Q. But they may have to be there for twelve months in the year, even though they are working only three-quarters of the time?—A. Most of the time they have to be there. The same system should prevail, so far as the men were concerned. In the boot and shoe industry the employers wanted the men to be there all the time, waiting for work.

Q. Even if they had no work for them?—A. Yes. That is why the boot and shoe industry threatened to quit. These fellows who were working there, when they found themselves out of a job, out of work, told the employers that they had to go somewhere else to work. The employers retorted and said, "If you go away, and we have to start over again, you will lose your jobs."

Q. Do you know that the same system prevailed with some other employers?—A. No, I do not know that, but as far as the shoe business is concerned, that is the system which presently prevails. I know men who stay there half a day in order to earn 60 cents in wages.

The CHAIRMAN: Are there any other questions? I think we have covered the ground fairly well.

Mr. ST. PÈRE: As far as I am concerned, I have only one question. He says that to summarize his evidence the Catholic Syndicates are in favour of having the federal authorities, the employers and the employees contribute to such an insurance fund.

WITNESS: Of course this may be outside the question, but as far as we are concerned we are of the opinion that the Federal Government should deal directly with organized labour, as far as all these social questions are concerned, without bothering at all to get into connection with the provinces, or trying to induce them to take the same view as that of the federal authorities.

Q. Have they more confidence in the Federal Government than they have in the provincial governments?—A. Truly, we have more confidence in the Federal Government than in the provinces.

The CHAIRMAN: He knows a good thing when he sees it.

WITNESS: Yes.

Witness retired.

Mrs. EDITH ROGERS, M.L.A., called and sworn.

By the Chairman:

Q. Now, Mrs. Rogers, you might just unfold to the Committee the views of the Committee of which you are a member, and which was appointed by the Manitoba Legislative Assembly to investigate the question of unemployment in the Province of Manitoba. Perhaps you might say something about the report you brought in, and anything else pertaining to the question of unemployment in Manitoba, as we are investigating here the question of insurance against unemployment, invalidity, and sickness?—A. Mr. Chairman, and gentlemen: Seasonal unemployment has been very great ever since the war. Last year it was less than this year. This year the conditions were very bad, from the early fall, on account of the crops being a failure in Manitoba, and in other parts of the country. The City of Winnipeg, of course, did what it could to help, and the unemployment Committee started their work in December. The Legislature met in December, which was a month earlier than usual, and then the Government participated, until about the end of January. But, as you know, and as they have done in former years, they gave out just sufficient groceries, the bare necessities of life, and for that the men had to work in the wood-yard. They tried to give work in the breaking of stones, and similar work, and they paid the men for that; but of course, as Mr. Heaps knows so well, it is terrible to think of our people having to come down to the dole system, year in and year out. As the years go on, it is seen that the men who are relieved are the same class, and almost the same men who are coming in for assistance. Naturally, their health is injured and their resistance to sickness is depleted, because they do not get the proper food during the winter months when they are unemployed. A regular system is adhered to which gives them a certain amount of food, which does not include very much meat, and in a country like ours, they need meat; and the amount of food they get is just enough to keep body and soul together. I have said this very often in Winnipeg, but they do not agree with me there. . . .

Then there is the subject of unemployed single men. We get such a cry from single men. For two years it has been the policy of the city not to help the single men. They say that single men can get work, if they will go to the bush; or if they go to the farms on a wage of $10 or $15 a month, where they will get their board anyway and their washing done. But there were a great many more single men than there was work for, even on the farms, and these men were not altogether floaters. They were single men, many of them returned soldiers, who were in Winnipeg, and it did not matter what their age was, young or old, if they went to the Social Service Department, they could not get any assistance at all. Naturally, these men were picked up on the streets as vagrants. A particular case was brought up on the floor of the House, and a Committee appointed to investigate the conditions of the single men. We found that during the past few months, there were 1,700 single men committed to the jails, just picked up because they could not get employment. They are given a bed for one or two nights, and then on the third night if found on the streets, are taken up as vagrants. . . . We had several conferences with the Chief of Police, and he said that on the whole these men are men who would like to get employment, but cannot. Our Committee brought in a small report, that was tabled, suggesting that something should be done for the single men. Why should the stigma of a jail sentence be imposed upon them? Any one knows how much harder it is for them to get employment if they have to say they have been in jail. . . .

Q. These 1,700 men you spoke of, Mrs. Rogers, who could not get a job, were they mostly men born outside of Manitoba, who came from abroad?—A. Not from abroad. They were not only from the Province of Manitoba but from all over Canada, men who came out to the harvest. There were a great many from Winnipeg.

Mr. HEAPS: They were nearly all Britishers.

By the Chairman:

Q. Do you think, Mrs. Rogers, that they were nearly all anxious to work, but could not get it?—A. They were anxious for work.

Q. But they were not suited for work on the farm?—A. There was not enough work on the farms. . . .

Q. But these men did get $4 to $5 a day in the harvest; could they not get back to Ontario? I think they could, surely, if they worked for three or four months at the rate?—A. A man goes out to the harvest fields, from the East; when he gets there, it rains, and the farmer will not pay him; he has to go to the nearest place and wait until the farmer needs him. He pays his own board, at a boarding house, until he is taken back. Some farmers in the House said they did not do that, when this was spoken about, but they do not think of the hundreds and hundreds of cases where farmers do it. You can get statistics from the employment offices in Canada, only they do not give them to the public. Very often the weather is bad, it rains three or four days, and they have to go to the nearest boarding house to live, and pay their own board and lodgings....

Q. They get $3.50 to $4 a day when they work?—A. Yes.

Q. Very often they will have but two or three days a week?—A. Only two or three days a week.

Q. They are hired by the day, or rather by the month?—A. Now they are hired by the day.

Q. Mrs. Rogers, you have not mentioned the unemployment that exists among the skilled men; there is always a certain amount of employment among people who work in iron works, railway shops, and in the building industry; have you considered the question of unemployment insurance for that type of worker; have you any opinion upon that, or have you given it any thought?—A. No, I have not really given it any thought. I had to leave the meeting downstairs, and that question was just being brought up, about getting a list of the unemployed through the Trades Unions. They could to a certain extent get a report of how many unemployed there are through the Unions, and perhaps that is the best way of getting at it. I have never considered it but you know there are a great many skilled mechanics laid off during the winter. There is no doubt about that.

Q. You think if these men who are laid off from industry were able to draw from some fund certain weekly benefits in the form of unemployment insurance, it would be beneficial to those men when they are out of work?—A. I certainly do....

I have not spoken about the women's work at all. There is nothing for the women at all, except the usual scrub work, house work, and things like that.

There is a type of man that has been very hard to get placed, that is the office man and the girls who want work there. We might say—perhaps I had better not.

By the Chairman:

Q. First impressions are sometimes the most lasting, Mrs. Rogers?—A. I know what causes that too. It is very sad to see that type of man, with a large family, not employed. Those men do not come to the Social Welfare; they would starve, some of them, before they would, and I do not blame them.

By Mr. McMillan:

Q. Have you a solution, Mrs. Rogers?—A. Work.

Q. Where are you going to get it?—A. I think that we have discussed this for many years past. Mr. Moore will remember when they said that governments, both provincial and federal, should not do all their building in the summer time, but should keep a great deal of it for the winter time. I think that all industries should try and do as much as they can to spread out their work, so that we would not have that vacuum in the winter. That is the only thing that will help out—work—and that is what men and women want. . . .

TOM MOORE, President of the Dominion Trades and Labour Congress (AFL affiliate)

Q. Mr. Moore, do you believe that immigration may have a tendency to induce unemployment?—A. Undoubtedly it accentuates unemployment and is responsible for a lot of it to-day. We had Mrs. Rogers speaking of the farm situation. I would just like to show a little of how that works out. Men go to a farm. This is not as immigrants. They make good. There is no housing accommodation for them; it does not matter what the farmer would like to do, but they simply have to go back to the city for the winter season. During the winter they are living on a little surplus if they have it, or, they are accepting charity while trying to get some kind of job in the city, and intending to go back to the same farm in the spring. But, before they get a chance to go back and notwithstanding our Provincial and Federal employment service, the railway agent—it has been said, but I have not proof of it, that he gets a commission—sees the farmer when he comes in to sell produce, and asks him to sign an appointment for another immigrant, and the result is that this man is left stranded in the city as a common labourer again, to bid for a job, or to go back to his trade, if he has one, and the result is he is competing for a job while another immigrant on an assisted passage is coming to assured employment on the farm, and the railway agent gets a dollar for his services. I am told that. I do not know it for sure, and so perhaps I should not assert it; but anyway, they get these nominative passages, and their employment for the season. Take the case of the Hollinger or one of the mines in the Porcupine district, about three years ago, or more. They brought out a number of Cornish miners. I was in London at the time, and I remember issuing a protest. The condition was that there were men registered in the employment service offices of Toronto, more than the numbers required. But the mining authorities said, they did not want those in Canada because they would be liable to leave and go back to the places they came from when trade opened up. They wanted people who had no other home in Canada, in order that they would stay where they were put. So they were bringing in immigrants by consent of the Government, whilst there were still unemployed men waiting for jobs, who were qualified miners. They had to issue notices warning miners to keep away from Hollinger because there were men sufficient for the jobs.

Q. From your experience, are there many firms who give the employees a hand in the management?—A. There are various experiments where some of them think they give them a hand. The Canadian National are developing quite a good system, and they have done much to stabilize employment, by budgeting their work annually through joint committees with the men. Instead of hiring a great number of men just a few months prior to the harvest to get their equipment ready, and then lay them off afterwards, they now budget the number of cars, and allocate them to the different shops, and that has to some extent stabilized employment on the railways, although it has reduced the amount of employment. I do not know of any industry that has gone to the same extent in bringing men into conference regularly for the budgeting of work, although we believe much might be done. And, we believe that if the employers are to contribute the major amount of unemployment insurance, they would do it, because it would be an advantage to them. Just as when compensation was put on, they started to get safety appliances because it reduced the cost of accidents. And if unemployment was charged on industry, it would have the same effect, we are sure. They would try to reduce the rush period in order to give employment in the dull period. On that point may I just mention, with all due respect, an advertisement that appeared the other day with regard to Simpson's in Toronto. They say they are going to put up a four million dollar addition to their store and open it by Christmas. I suppose the Committee knows what that means? It means that every year, the building industry is always busy about the same time as the harvest season, because the small firms want to get their roofs on, and get their work ready so that the employer and one or two assistants can go on through the winter. That is in the height of the season they will be complaining of a labour shortage, and that will be used for immigration advertising to get immigrants to come in. They will get a few weeks work on the Toronto building, and for the rest of the time be unemployed, instead of spreading that work over a year, which we think ought to be done. If the building industry had to bear the cost of unemployment, the work would be spread. Now, they will bid as to who can get the building done in the shortest time, so that there is a rush of work in the building industry at times, and then a long period of unemployment.

Q. Have you knowledge of cases where work has been offered to unemployed men and they have refused it?—A. Not personally, but I have seen records, in the employment service records, where men have been offered work on farms on no wage whatsoever, merely board and washing, and men have refused to take it, because they had families in the city, and they could not pay rent out of that.

Q. In other words, would you say that the conditions offered were the cause of the refusal?—A. Yes, there is often farm work refused by industrial workers, because if you offer a married man even $20 a month in winter, he may be a bricklayer, or a plasterer, and he is hoping that to-morrow he may get a job at his own trade; but to-morrow may be three or six months in the future. If he goes on the farm at $10 a month, who will keep his family in the interim? And if he has an accident on a farm, there is no compensation, and who will keep him then? Therefore, he refuses the job. So there are plenty of farm jobs refused by industrial workers, because of their responsibilities and commitments in the city, that they cannot afford to take it.

Q. Have you been to a number of the European cities in connection with labour conditions?—A. Yes.

Q. Has unemployment been discussed there and insurance against it?— A. Yes, in its broadest sense. . . . [U]nemployment insurance has the effect of creating a reserve in good times in order that it may be expended during bad times. If there is little unemployment, you would build the fund up, and then when a greater number comes on it, they would go into the labour market and by their buying, create labour, reducing the amount of unemployment, and thus stabilizing employment by stabilizing purchasing power to a great degree, by removing the fear of those who, because of that fear, restrict their purchasing power. . . .

Q. One other question Mr. Moore. This Committee has not yet discussed the question of unemployment. We have just touched on it in the early part, with reference to a scheme of this nature, and its relation to Provincial rights. We have had to overcome that difficulty in reference to the Old Age Pension scheme, which affects the provinces. My own view is that the Dominion and the provinces will have to join in something on the same lines as they did in the Old Age Pension scheme, in order to overcome any difficulty that may exist. Have you given any thought to that?—A. Yes, in regard to unemployment insurance, we are firmly convinced that the Federal Government must be the responsible factor. We cannot even go as far as we did on Old Age Pensions in this matter in making it contingent on the consent of the provinces; because the needs of Canada demand that men be transient. We are a new country. The trend of the employment service of Canada is to find employment for unemployed men, and that I agree with Mrs. Rogers, is the best remedy for unemployment if it can be found. They must, therefore, transfer men from province to province. They have a reduced rate on the railways to permit them to do that. There are new parts of Canada where, perhaps, no government exists; for instance up in the Flin Flon, and other mining districts, where there is as yet no development, or perhaps very little. Now, if you have a water-tight compartment of provincial qualification as you have in the Old Age Pensions' scheme, a five-years' qualification, labour could not be transferred.

Q. I do not know that we see your view point there. Will you explain? —A. The province sets up some qualifications as to when it shall be responsible. In the Old Age Pensions' scheme, it says, "there shall be not less than five years' residence." In the Mothers' Allowance, it says the husband must have died within the province, and the widow be resident there for at least two years before she is entitled to an allowance. In all these measures you have some provincial qualification, usually based on residence. Then, in the case of temporary relief, you have cities like Toronto, refusing to give jobs on relief work to men, unless they have been tax-payers for so many months or years previously. You have all these qualifications set up. Now, in unemployment, we say that if Canada is to be developed, we must have the utmost flexibility of labour, so that labour will move to where the employment is, and not remain unemployed in one province, with workmen needed in another province. So that, if you do not make it a nation-wide law, without provincial rights interfering, you will add to your volume of unemployment, and the amount of money to be expended on it rather than relieving the men in the primary case of unemployment, and enabling them to get unemployment....

HOWARD T. FALK called and sworn.
By the Chairman:
Q. First of all, what is your position, what position do you hold?—A. I am Secretary of the Financial Federation of the Montreal Council of Social Agencies.
...The next bit of evidence I would like to submit is this, which I think is significant, in this way, that it has to do with the employment of children. Since March, 1920, a little over eight years, 19,113 work permits have been granted to children in Montreal.
By Miss Macphail:
Q. What do you mean by that?—A. This means that they must be under fourteen years, unless it is the exceptional child over fourteen. There is no compulsory Education Act. The law says that a child must be able to read and write in order to work. I suppose 99 per cent of these are under fourteen years of age. It is simply the economic pressure that necessitates that.
Q. What class of work do they do?—A. Anything that they can do; they work in stores, they work as messenger boys. It applies to any kind of work.
By the Acting Chairman:
Q. Are they permitted to work in factories?—A. Not under the Factory Act, although in the rural districts there has been a good deal of work done by children on permits, because of the tremendous economic pressure in large families. The Dominion Textile Company have had great difficulty; they do not want to do it, but their managers have had tremendous pressure put upon them.
By Miss Macphail:
Q. It is terrible to have them go out to work at that early age. It is very significant but I think it is bad to see children almost grown up playing around; they would be better off if they were doing something. I would

sooner see them working than playing around?—A. I think if we could make the compulsory school age sixteen years we would solve a number of our industrial problems. If we raised the school age to sixteen, there would be more chance for all. That is one of the troubles of the whole situation.

The next thing I want to deal with is, the relation of unemployment to sickness dependency. It is obvious that unless we can carry on research work, except at very great cost, it is impossible to get exact figures, and our Council had no money to spend on expensive research work, but I can say this, out of an experience of ten years in Winnipeg directly in charge of relief work, because I held the position Miss Childs holds at the present time, and ten years in Montreal, where I have been close to the situation although not administering relief, that sickness, which is the greatest single cause of dependency in families, in a very large number of instances can be traced to unemployment at a previous stage. It is only natural that that should be so, because whilst we are perhaps inclined to think that the unemployed man is quick to seek relief, that is not our experience except—I am ashamed to say this in respect of my own countrymen (Englishmen) who have become demoralized before they came out here; but with the ordinary man it means that he does not seek relief until he is down and out, having burned up his furniture to supply heat, and has gone without food for himself and his wife. In dozens and hundreds of instances, where we get sickness in the winter, the history of that family in the previous winter has been one of unemployment.

In considering the whole question of unemployment and unemployment insurance, which I believe is in the back of the minds of some of this Committee, that feature ought to be considered. I would like to suggest this, that in industry, the owner of the physical machinery of industry, wood, steel, iron, or whatever it is, is extraordinarily careful that when a machine is not in use it is kept adequately cared for, oiled and so on; if not, it goes on the scrap heap, because when he wants to use it again it is no good. With human beings, who are first employed and then are unemployed, they do not receive the same attention, that is to say, they have not an income to enable them to keep themselves in repair, consequently your human machinery, your unskilled labourers in particular, are actually deteriorating in value. . . .

THE WORKERS' UNITY LEAGUE IN QUEBEC

Wage cuts were typical of the early 1930s. Strikes were few and usually hopeless. But what strikes there were, were almost always organized and led by the Workers' Unity League. Fred Rose was later to become the only Communist ever elected to Parliament, and the only M.P. in Canadian history ever to be convicted of espionage. Here he details the difficulties confronting WUL organizers in Quebec.

Fred Rose, 'Report of the Cowansville Strike 1930', Attorney-General's Papers, Public Archives of Ontario. Courtesy of Andrée Lévesque.

Cowansville is situated in the Eastern townships. The towns around that district are being rapidly industrialised. In that vicinity of Cowansville are found St. Hyacinthe, Drummondville, Windsor Mills, Farnham, St. John's, etc. ... where there are found textile mills as well as larger plants.

The Eastern Townships have always boasted about the fact that strikes are unknown in their district. In January, 120 textile workers of St. Hyacinthe went on strike for nine days and won some conditions. The news of this strike has come to our attention through the *Labour Gazette*.

A few weeks before the strike, the Company was running the night shift full speed and the workers had the feeling (those who were in previous strikes) that something was going to happen. On Wednesday, February 25th, the workers were laid off for the end of the week and on Saturday the 28th when they came for the pay, they found the notice that the wages of the weavers would be cut 25% and the wages of the warpers—spinners and winders—16½%. A few of the weavers who had been in strikes in the USA and who hold cards of the United Textile Workers of America got together and decided on a strike. They got in touch with the other weavers and all agreed on a strike. Seeing that the weavers went out, the warpers who had gone in on Monday morning also went out while the spinners and winders remained. The latter were later sent down by the boss as he closed all departments except the dyeing and printing departments. Altogether there were 200 on strike out of 300 workers.

Those who were out on strike elected a committee of 7 and picketed the factory and the railroad station. The leadership however felt that they were lacking the experience and one of them notified a fellow (a peddler from Montreal) that when he gets to Montreal he should notify the trade unions about the Cowansville strike. This fellow knowing Henry Segal got in touch with him and Segal notified us. On Tuesday morning, Tom Miller went down to Cowansville to find out whether the strike is still on, and he was instructed to get in touch with me if I'm to go there. Miller phoned before noon that they had arranged a meeting of the strike committee for the evening and that I must leave immediately. I met the strike committee at the station and from there we went to a meeting place. At this meeting we worked out five demands, decided to bring those to the strikers, decided on the first big meeting of the strikers in the theater, decided on broadening the strike committee as well as add girls to it and to elect a committee to bring our demands before the boss. The five demands worked out were: 1—Not a cent off the wages. 2—No fines for damages in silk. 3—No discrimination against active strike workers. 4 —Firing of scabs. 5—Recognition of Union. . . .

In addressing the strikers on Wednesday, I explained that I was a representative of the *Workers' Unity League* and showed the difference between our unions and the AF of L, ACCL, and Catholic Unions. The fact that I attacked the Catholic unions immediately resulted in the grouping of a bunch of strikers in the back of the hall who demanded that I produce a credential to show that I'm really a representative of a Union and which Union I come from. I explained that if they would look back to the *La Presse* they would find that both I and Tom Miller who was with me, were awaiting two trials for organising the unemployed, and further emphasized the difference between the WUL and the other unions also in connection with the question of unemployment. We then proceeded to enlarge the strike committee to 20 but none of the girls wanted to accept. This committee was also given the task to see the superintendent and present the demands. A phone call was sent in to the superintendent and he stated that he cannot accept a committee of 20 but only three. We decided that three can go in while the rest stay in the front of the office while all workers present march down and also stay outside of the factory. This was done and was very effective. Another meeting was called for the afternoon to report of the visit to the superintendent. The committee reported that they were told that not a cent more will be paid and that even if they would be willing to go back to work, the factory will be closed till Monday March 9th. I spoke on the attempt of the boss to demoralise the strikers, warned them against rumors (some were being told that the company has plenty of stock to keep closed for months) and stated that in spite of the closing of the factory picketing must be kept up and started agitation for mass picketing for Monday morning. At this meeting the workers started to demand union cards. At night Miller and I went to Montreal, we arranged for a meeting and together with us travelled the fellow who was sympathetic to the Party, I spoke to him on the importance of his activisation, the line which he should follow in case we were attacked as red if another union comes in, and asked him to keep his ears open as to what is being said about us while we're not around. This was to be the beginning of picking up a little group to support us.

At the meeting in Montreal it was decided to continue the formation

of a small group around us and to form a union using the WUL cards.
... At the strike committee meeting we discussed the issuance of a leaflet
to the surrounding towns where there are textile mills telling them that
there is a strike in Cowansville and appealing to them for financial aid.
The chairman of the strike committee then asked if issuing a leaflet is a
communistic act, and if it is, no leaflet should be printed. We were able
to put this through with the aid of the committee who on the other hand
started to talk about the enslavement of the workers in Russia etc.

During Friday and Saturday, a number of the strikers left town going
to their homes on farms in surrounding district. The main thing taken up
on Friday at the meeting was the fact that every striker going for the pay
was presented with the following statement for signature:

Receipt and Waiver

Cowansville, Quebec

I, the undersigned .... hereby acknowledge to have received this day
from the Bruck Silk Mills, Limited the sum of $ ..... in full payment
and settlement of all claims for wages, salaries, bonuses or expenses
due to me and in consideration hereof I do waive and renounce to any
and all rights of action whatsoever which I may have against the said
company.

And I have signed

_____

Witness

_____

It was decided that none of the workers should sign this statement. At
this meeting... I explained that the strike will sharpen during the next
week and that the workers will have to be prepared. I also spoke on the
news in the *Sherbrooke Record* where it was mentioned that a small
strike against a minor wage cut was taking place in Cowansville and that
unless the few workers return to work soon, they will be easily replaced,
and stressed the fact how the press was used against the workers.

On Sunday, the priest told the strikers that they can stay out on strike
but that they should make no trouble and shouldn't interfere with those
going in to work as they have a right to do so. This was a change in the
policy of the priest who on the first Sunday spoke altogether against a
strike. The members of the strike Comm. seemed satisfied with the
sermon and didn't mention to us that they were visited by the Sheriff
who warned them against disorder. On Saturday morning the Company
did not present those "Receipt and Waiver" to the workers but 7 of the
leading members had this printed on the back of the cheques. Demers,
one of the leading members on the strike committee who was chairman
of nearly all meetings of the strikers due to the fact that he was a fairly
good speaker, did not receive notice of firing and some members of the

strike committee charged him with backing out from active strike activity. On Sunday when we could not get a hall for the meeting of the strikers in Cowansville, we got a hall in the next town and all were transported with automobiles to the meeting place. We had a fairly good meeting. Demers again was chairman and he refuted all charges that he was dropping out. Following some speeches we had signing as at some of the previous meetings, and in the meantime the chairman went down drinking. He came back a little bit and he started again about the slave labour in the USSR and quoted figures from the paper. I then got up and refuted his statements, saying that I was working in Russia and compared the lies about the Soviet Union to the lies about the strike. After the meeting Demers started to use all kinds of arguments against us and was backed by a few. At this meeting we therefore for the first time came out against Demers who was kind of monopolizing the meeting and the defence of the USSR was to be followed by the winning of the elements who came out against Demers while speaking to us. In the evening we were met by some of the other leading members of the strike committee who said that they were with us and further stated that Demers was being considered by most of the strikers as a wind-bag.

On Monday morning we had a splendid picket line. For the first time the girls were out and did some good work. They were able to hold back some of the scabs from going both by talking to them and when it was necessary used force. Only about 9 scabs went in and amongst them were two good weavers while the rest were learners. During that morning there were already extra constables from the surrounding towns. Seeing the solid front of the strikers, the priest, some people who he got in touch with, including strikers, parents of some of the strikers, and all started to suggest to the strikers the sending of a committee to the boss which should put before him the demand of a 12½% cut. On my arrival to the theatre where the meeting was to take place a number of the strike committee approached me and talked to me about this proposition and at the same time showed willingness to accept such terms. Before the meeting started, I spoke to some of the leading members and while the meeting was going on I was trying to convince them of the harm which such a move may bring. Slowly some of them started to change their minds and the chairman stated that he is against it while all those who are for it should speak up at the meeting, rather they do all the talking outside. There then came a demand that I should speak. I spoke pointing to the good picketing of the morning, the possibility of taking down those who had gone in to work and the sending of a committee with a demand for a 12½% wage cut would show weakness, etc. Some of the strikers then followed me using a similar line.... We took a vote and nobody was then for the sending of the comm. Later in the day a warrant was issued against 4 of the girls for attacking a scab. The forces which worked against us in the morning got still busier and although not mentioning it to us after the strike I was told that the main arguments used were that the members of the strike committee were mostly people who could go out of town if they lost their jobs while the workers who have their families in Cowansville couldn't do so why not take a half loaf rather than no loaf at all. Another argument was "Are you going to allow yourselves to be led by the reds?" At Monday's meeting the cards were handed out.

On Tuesday morning, very few were present at the picket line and those who were there disgusted with the poor attendance, 11 scabs went in on that morning and some of these who had gone in on Monday stayed out after having been visited by strikers. On that morning two of the girls arrested were fined $7.50 each. We got in touch with some members of the strike committee, arranged for a meeting for 11 A.M. but none showed up. About 1 P.M., an hour before the meeting of the strikers was to take place we met some of the active fellows and we were told that the sentiment was for going in to work and that some members of the strike committee left town. Only about 30 showed up at the meeting while on Monday about 100 were present. One of the strike leaders came in and reported that the priest had been up to the boss and that the boss stated that he will cut wages of the day workers 25% but the night workers 20%, that [he] will not deduct any money for damages and none of the strikers will be blacklisted. We decided not to accept this report and sent a committee from the floor to get the conditions from the boss. The committee brought back a similar report, the only difference being that certain single people will be sent away to make place for the married workers. There was resentment amongst some of the strikers against the action of the priest, statements such as "The priest had no right to interfere; he doesn't work in the mill" etc. were expressed. However they all felt that there is no use staying out as the majority didn't even come to the meeting but accepted the report of the priest as final. We took a vote of those who are ready to stay out and only five voted (five who were fired). The only thing we could do was to send them back to work giving the lessons of the strike, pointing to the action of the police, the press, the member of parliament, and priest. Stress was laid on the necessity of organization for further struggles. . . .

THE ANYOX STRIKE IN BRITISH COLUMBIA, 1933

This strike in the hard-rock mining industry in British Columbia is typical of the WUL fight against huge odds. In 1935 the WUL was disbanded by the Communist Party and its organizers soon moved en masse into the newly created CIO. By 1937 auto, steel, mine and rubber workers in Ontario were organizing in five-man cells to foil company and police spies. They called it the 'Anyox system'.

Pete Loudon, *The Town That Got Lost* (Sydney, B.C., 1973), pp. 86-96. Reprinted by permission of Gray's Publishing Ltd.

Probably the greatest story the *Herald* ever printed was the account of the strike at Anyox. It was our biggest adventure and the one major occasion of violence. It scared us. It even got good mileage in the Vancouver papers and it became a political issue in Victoria long after it was all over in Anyox. It was one of the events that gave the dirty thirties their name. It was one of the many black events which old trade unionists refer to when they start to explain how unions developed the solidarity which many people today can't understand.

The strike was essentially a miners' uprising although it involved the men who worked in the crusher, concentrator, smelter and the various shops before it ended. Perhaps because it began with the miners, those of us who lived at the "beach" were kept in the dark when it was all getting organized. Anyox was really two communities. The plant workers, office workers and people involved with the business section lived and worked in the waterfront area while the mine people lived almost two miles away at the head of the valley. They had their own bunk houses and mess house as well as a number of private homes. . . .

For most of us, about all we knew about the miners was that they wore hard hats with a clamp on the front which was used to hold a carbide lamp when they were underground. I worked briefly in mines in Northern Ontario in later years, during school vacations, but there we had battery operated lamps. They weren't nearly as exciting as the carbide lamps. . . .

Anyway, carbide lamps were about all we knew about until miners one sunny morning in early February 1933.

We were all milling about in the schoolyard waiting the bell which would line us up to march into classes. Suddenly all the fooling around stopped and there was a strange silence. All the kids were looking up the plank road to the mine. All our lives previously that road had been barren of anything or anyone because only the jitneys appeared to use it and that was later in the day. But the road was filled with men, hundreds of men. They were wearing their hard hats and walking purposefully in a tight body. They weren't talking but you could hear their feet pounding the boards. You could smell their determination as they headed past us toward the beach. None of us had seen anything like it. It was so ominous that some of the kids verged on tears, scared without knowing why. At that moment everything changed for us in Anyox.

That night at home we found out more about it from our parents. They had read in the *Herald* that a union had been formed and what we had seen was a demonstration of strength aimed really at impressing the bosses at the company offices.

The *Herald* noted that a labour union was organized among workers at both the mine and the beach on January 29. A union organizer named Tom Bradley had addressed meetings of workers and also had met with company officials. He said he represented the Mine Workers of Canada, affiliated with the Workers Unity League of Canada and the Red International of Labour.

The newly-formed union let it be known that it wanted 50 cents-per-day increase in wages and a 20 per cent reduction in board and similar reductions in bunk house and home rents and if these things were not forthcoming, there would be a strike.

Later, in the British Columbia Legislature at Victoria, Atlin M.L.A. H. F. Kergin, a Liberal from Alice Arm, said the company employees had taken three pay cuts in the previous year. At the time the union was organized they were working 20 to 22 shifts a month for $2.25 to $2.40 per day. Out of this a single miner was charged $1.10 per day, every day of the month, for board.

One can't compare dollar values of 1933 and today but the figures indicate it was costing the miner more than half his earnings just to eat. The M.L.A., in any event, told the House that the men had a real grievance—and it was the way the company and the province of British Columbia replied to it, which drew his bitter criticism and led to more labour voilence in later months in Vancouver and Prince Rupert.

The *Herald* quoted the company as stating that it was impossible to accede to the union demands due to the low prices of copper. The company said it was hard enough to keep the plant going as it was. The upshot was that a strike was called at the mine on February 1 when all operations ceased. The same thing happened at the beach where the smelter, concentrator, crushers and all the maintenance shops shut down on February 3. . . .

The union held several meetings during the week after the strike began. It was reported that many of the beach workers, most of whom had families in town, were willing to go back to their jobs. The miners, however, most of whom were single, were adamant. They felt that if the wages couldn't be improved the plant might as well be closed. . . .

So the miners took up their picket signs. There were no incidents however, and those of us who lived in family surroundings at the beach didn't really expect trouble. We were a civilized community, we felt. And to ensure we stayed that way a company policeman always met every boat. Anyone arriving without a pre-arranged job or other good reason was quite likely to be speedily sent back aboard.

The lone British Columbia police constable at Anyox and the company policeman, Joe Shields, may not have shared our faith. They suspected the strike might lead to trouble. So by their arrangement, the Tuesday following the start of the strike a police launch arrived from Prince Rupert bringing a Staff Sergeant McNeill and seven additional constables.

This seemed a bit much at the time. After all, we had all been brought up on stories of how the lone constable of the Royal North-West Mounted would ride into a hostile Indian encampment, kick down the centre pole in the chief's teepee and with the dignity of his red coat, bring immediate order to the plains. Maybe if the policemen had worn red felts rather than the khaki uniforms of the provincial police, everything would have been different. But the pickets stayed put. The police avoided any confrontation. But then, two days later, ten more officers arrived from Vancouver under command of an Inspector J. Sherass. It was at this point the strikers decided to make a show of force too.

The men left the mine, perhaps 200 of them, with intention of showing their solidarity before the company offices at the beach. According to my memory picture and the memories of other, older witnesses I have talked to since, they were unarmed, although I think it likely that in such a situation some would have tucked a piece of hose or a section of pipe or some form of club in their belts. In the thirties labour demonstrators expected violence.

I don't know where the march began but it came down the plank road from the mine, the men seven or eight abreast. It was when they reached the bridge at the mine end of the valley, where Hidden Creek pierced a deep gully, that they saw the first police. The records suggest that there were only five or six officers at the bridge. You've got to give them credit for courage because they ordered the marchers to halt and disperse.

What happened then can only be pieced together from later newspaper accounts of trial evidence. A constable named Smith testified that the marchers refused to halt and stated they were going through to the beach. He said some of the men carried weapons and shown at the trial were sections of hose pipe, iron bars and some pick handles. (Still later in the British Columbia Legislature at Victoria, a huge bundle of such weaponry was displayed in the House and charges were made that the collection had miraculously multiplied while in custody like rabbits at a fall fair.)

Constable Smith told the court that he and his companions tried to hold the front rank of the marchers from advancing, but this proved impossible so the police drew their revolvers and fired several shots into the air. That apparently blew it. The men rushed the policemen.

Smith's testimony said that at this point two other policemen approached the marchers from the rear and they were immediately set upon. He said they were badly beaten and one "had the boots put to him."

A Constable Weir gave evidence that he was kicked and beaten and that someone had even tried to gouge out one of his eyes. His revolver was taken away from him and he was later sent to hospital for treatment.

A Constable Roberts showed his hat in court and indicated where it had been damaged by a blow to his head. He said his revolver, baton and watch had been stolen and efforts were made to throw him off the bridge.

At this point in the melee the police gave way to the miners. They testified later that they then permitted the march and preceded the men in their walk to the beach. A good many people in Anyox said later that the police should have done that in the first place. Men don't charge with fist or club against firearms if there is any way to reach a compromise, the community seemed to feel.

Bert Kergin, the Liberal M.L.A. for Atlin, spoke for a great many Anyox residents when he broached the whole matter in the British Columbia Legislature the following month. He attacked both the company and the government. He said this "foreign-controlled" company was landlord, employer and merchant at Anyox. He cited the three pay cuts the men had taken in the past year and he cited their wages and board charges. These things added up to a real grievance in his opinion. Kergin said the union gave the company advance warning of its intentions and when a strike was called the company asked for an additional two days of grace and it was agreed to by the workers. He intimated that the company used this time to ask the provincial government to send in police and within 24 hours, they were on their way.

The M.L.A. described the fight on the mine road and said that despite there being no further trouble police continued to arrive by plane until there were more than 100 on hand. He said that a dominion government vessel also arrived and sat in harbour and played a searchlight on the town all night. He said the police placed a machine gun outside the bunk house and suddenly the people of Anyox found themselves living in a huge armed camp. And in his mind, it was all unnecessary. . . .

The army of police were busy meantime. They arrested all those men who were thought to have been involved in the fight on the mine road and they singled out a large additional group of men and ordered them to leave town. A good many left with them of their own free will.

Then on February 6, Granby Company ordered notices to be posted saying they had received orders from company headquarters to close the camp permanently. Granby general manager Charles Bocking said in the statement however, that if sufficient men showed a willingness to return to their jobs, he would ask the directors to reconsider the matter.

The following day there was a mass meeting at the beach gymnasium and of .he 350 men in attendance, only seven voted to continue the strike. It was obvious that in the face of the company's unwillingness to even negotiate and with the power of expulsion the company had from the police, many men didn't even bother to vote. About 320 left town on the *Prince Rupert* or the *Prince George*, most of them single men who had been in the mine crew.

The union organizer Bradley was arrested by police at Prince Rupert and he and a John Rodoman were charged with unlawful assembly. They were freed later for lack of evidence. Five other men, Joe Servitch, Ken Montgomery, Nat Ugervitch, W. R. McIver and George Sampion were charged with taking part in an affray but when they came to court in Prince Rupert they were all acquitted in a jury trial.

Back at Anyox, with all the trouble makers disposed of, the police took their leave, the company agreed to re-open the mine and the miners were back underground February 20. Only one concession apparently was won by the strike—board at the mess houses was reduced from $1.10 to $1 per day. Rent on the cabins dropped from $10 to $8.50 There was a $2 rent reduction for homes in the $10-$20 class and $3 for those in the over $30 class.

Soon there were new men arriving in town, depression-hungry men who had been riding the rods and the box cars across Canada while we had lived in comfort if not luxury in Anyox. They came to take the places of the miners who had been deported or who had left on their own in disgust. Some of them arrived with bruises and there were news stories in the Vancouver papers to show that the struggle in Anyox was being backed up by trade unionists in other places....

Atlin M.L.A. Kergin drew attention to all these troubles in his speech in the British Columbia House and he was especially critical of the "deportation" of those miners who were felt to be troublemakers.

"If they call that British justice, then I'm a Red," he said. He asked for a legislative investigation to see that rental charges were fair and that a living wage was paid at Anyox. But his motion was voted down by the whole Conservative majority. Mines Minister W. A. McKenzie said a mines department official would make an enquiry as he was bound to do when complaints are made about safety conditions in a mine. A lack of safety was another of the beefs of the miners. About one man a month died in the mines at Anyox, old timers have claimed.

T. D. "Duff" Pattullo, the Opposition Leader, continued with the attack. Whether this publicity had anything to do with it or not, Anyox workers did finally obtain a 10 per cent increase in wages and salaries on July 1 "due to a rise in copper prices." For most of the workers the raise amounted to 20 to 24 cents per day.

A Canadian Press story dated April 5 told how Attorney-General Pooley displayed in the legislature dozens of lengths of weighted rubber hose and a couple of steel drills as samples of weapons carried by the Anyox strikers as they marched to town. He said there were 400 armed miners, mostly foreigners, and that foreigners must obey Canadian laws.

Atlin M.L.A. Kergin replied that corporations had invited Southern Europeans and other foreigners to come into Canada, given them jobs in preference to English-speaking workmen because they thought they were more docile and would work for lower wages. Several opposition members told the House that such firms must shoulder the responsibility themselves.

Pooley apparently ignored Kergin's statement that more than 100 police had attended. The Attorney-General lauded the efficiency of the small force of 18 men for dealing with the armed miners. He then produced the weapons which Anyox people claimed never to have seen. Pooley said the miners were also equipped with miner's helmets, better than the steel helmets used during the war and had planned to march to the town and take control.

Pooley also said that had the miners applied to the minister of labour they might have secured a peaceful settlement of their dispute. But, he said, secret organization was carried on. And when Bradley arrived—one of the worst agitators in the country—it only needed a spark to create trouble.

Years later I was to be told by a former provincial policeman that many of the officers who arrived in Anyox on the occasion of the strike were not trained constables. He claimed that a large number of them were recruited from the ranks of the unemployed, put into uniform and sent to Anyox to put down the troubles which might erupt there, with a firm hand. There were many Anyox people who observed how they herded the unwanted young men along the docks, made them open their suitcases and parcels and searched their possessions with the toes of their high leather boots, who could well believe this was a private army of the company. Such incidents probably did more to create political dissidents, agitators and outright Communists than all the writings of Karl Marx, so far as Anyox was concerned.

COMPANY 'STOOL PIGEONS' IN ONTARIO, 1936

Among the many tactics available to management in its bitter struggle to destroy the CIO was the use of labour spies. This pamphlet by Fred Rose describes one company's attempts to rid itself of its unions. This was only one of many such campaigns by big business.

Fred Rose, *Spying on Labour* (Toronto, 1938), pp. 5-8, 10, 12, 15-19.

It is common knowledge in the ranks of the Canadian labour movement that Canadian employers stoop to the use of informers in shops, mines, mills and trade unions. Such informers are referred to as "stool pigeons", the name of shame given to the lowest type of police agents planted in criminal circles. These informers work either directly for the employer or for private detective agencies.

But not generally realized is the extent to which this degrading aspect of the relationship between employer and employees has developed. And still less is it appreciated that this activity has grown to the point where it is a country wide network, illegal in many of its aspects, using the co-operation of municipal, provincial and federal police to spy on legal and constitutional activities of Canadian citizens and assumes the form of a dangerous threat to Canadian democracy.

Employers hire stool pigeons for the simple purpose of preventing the organization of trade unions or demoralization of labour unions already in existence. This is clearly revealed in a letter from the Foster Service, a private detective agency in the United States to a prospective client. In the letter we find the following claim.

"First I will say that if we are employed before any union is formed by the employees there will be no strikes and no disturbance. This does not say there will be no union formed. But it does say that we will control the activities of the union and direct its policies provided we are allowed a free hand by our clients.

"Second, if a union is already formed, and no strike is on or expected to be declared within 30 to 60 days although we are not in the same position as we would be in the above case, we could—and I believe with success—carry on an intrigue which would result in factions, disagreement, resignations of officers and general decrease of membership."

Recently, the General Investigations of Canada Limited, 36 Toronto, sent out the following letter to a number of manufacturers:—

March 29, 1939.

Dear Mr....

A recent survey indicates that manufacturers and business men in general, are alive to the necessity of protecting their business and their employees from sabotage and vicious distorted propaganda growing out of the present disturbed international situation. For this reason we are writing you to call attention again to the services rendered by this Company.

Our confidential representatives have been very successful in eliminating trouble of this sort by discovering plots, plans and unrest before serious action occurs.

Many of our clients tell us that the daily reports our operatives submit as to radical and illegal activities are by no means the only benefit derived from our work. They feel that the constructive leadership and propaganda which emanates from our representatives is worth, in itself, more than the modest charge for our service.

An executive of one of the largest manufacturers, writes us in part, "We have carried your service for a number of years and have found it very beneficial and that it is a money saving and money earning proposition instead of an overhead expense."

We have served leading manufacturers throughout Canada and the States for over thirty years and can give highest references. With your large investment, surely any proven protection is worth considering.

Will you not have your Secretary communicate with us, naming a time when it will be convenient for you to discuss this particular matter?

Very sincerely yours,

A. P. Cumming, Manager.

In 1936, the Toronto branch of this agency was known as The Auxilliary Co. of Canada Limited, with offices at 159 Bay St. That same year, the activities of this spy organization on behalf of the International Nickel Co. of Canada were exposed by the leaders of local 239, Mines and Smelter Workers Union. Mr. X. an employee of this stool-pigeon agency made the following Statutory Delcaration:

I, X...of the City of Toronto of the County of York, do solemnly declare that:

1. I saw an advertisement in the male help wanted section of the Toronto Evening Telegram of June 20th, 1936, asking for a Ukrainian interpreter willing to do factory work.

2. Being unemployed at the time, I answered the advertisement, sending my application to an address in the Telegram office.

3. That when I answered the advertisement, I had no idea the position was anything else but that of interpreter.

4. That about seventeen days later, I called at the office of the Auxilliary Co. of Canada Ltd., Room 905, 159 Bay Street, Toronto. This was on July 7th, 1936, and I was interviewed by Mr. Paul L. Keller, and then I learned for the first time that they wanted me to do some sort of detective work among labor unions and organizations.

5. That on July 17th, 1936, Mr. Keller gave me $45.00 for expenses and told me to go to Sudbury and check upon the Sudbury Mine and Smelter Workers Union, local 239, and other labor organizations, and do this work under the supervision of Mr. Keller.

6. That on my departure, Mr. Keller instructed me to secure a salesman's position in Sudbury to enable me to canvass from house to house and listen to what people, and in particular employees of the International Nickel Co. of Canada, might say about unions and about conditions in the mines and smelter, and to report everything to the Auxilliary Co. of Canada Ltd.

7. That Mr. Keller instructed me to seek an opportunity to get into trade unions, particularly the afore-mentioned Miner's Union, with a view of securing the membership lists and the plans of these unions, and to report everything to the Auxilliary Co. of Canada.

8. For this work I was promised the sum of $20.00 per week and some money for expenses.

And I make this solemn declaration conscientiously believing it to be true, and knowing that it is of the same force and effect as if made under oath, and by virtue of "The Canada Evidence Act."

Paul L. Keller at all times tried to impress the officials in INCO with the extent of the "red plots" against the company, and with the difficulties that his men are confronted with. Thus in August 13th, 1936, he sent a letter to his agents, of which no doubt he sent a copy to the Company, telling his men that: the "Intelligence Division of the Communist Party is going to unusual lengths to uncover confidential informers," and that, "a very attractive woman known as Number 5, is at present touring the North Country who with the aid of four or five women and girls are peddling perfume and posing as newspaper agents" in order "to gain the confidence of men who may be functioning as industrial spies."

The task of these women, who existed only in the perverted mind of Mr. Paul L. Keller, was "to gain the confidence of men who may be functioning as industrial spies and to attempt to entice men in the North Country who might later be found to be secret agents of some sort." Now, what would these women do with stool pigeons whom they would entice? Mr. Keller leaves this to the imagination of the Company officials and hopes to impress them with the dangerous work that his men are doing, as a means of getting more money from employers who prefer to be cheated by unscrupulous liars than to allow trade unions in their establishments. In fact the fantastic plots invented by stool-pigeons are used by the employers to justify their refusal to deal with unions. . . .

Following the exposure of the Auxilliary Co. activities in the nickel region, a resident of Toronto, W. R. Lucrow, wrote a letter to the Daily Clarion, relating his experience with the same spy agency. Mr. Lucrow wrote: "I believe it was at the end of April—about the 30th—that I answered an ad in the Toronto Telegram, under the same conditions as did Mr. X. . . . A few days later they sent me the enclosed telegram asking me to phone Mr. Keller immediately at Elgin 5833. . . .

"Mr. Keller introduced himself, and so did I. He told me to sit down and asked me if I smoked. I said I did, so he offered me a Lucky Strike, an American cigarette; I took it and he lighted it for me with an expensive lighter . . . I gathered the impression that this Mr. Keller was an American—and he talked like one at that . . .

"In my interview he told me that "these reds were ruining the country". I nodded in agreement, since if I was to get a job I'd have to agree with the boss. Right? Right. Even though I didn't know what kind of a job I was going to get. Well, he kept on the subject for about ten minutes and then he asked my life history. I told him part of it.

"In a little while he told me the job I was to get would be in Welland, to work in a factory—a mill factory. What kind of a mill I don't know. He told me that all I had to do was to go there (Welland) and mix with the Slavic workers . . . so as to get to know them. Later on I would then enter the factory and begin working, getting extra pay for the factory work . . . After working a few weeks in the factory getting acquainted with all the workers, including conversations I'd overhear purposely in the factory from the workers, I was to send in daily reports with the names or numbers of these workers, etc. At night, after factory work, I was supposed to attend all workers functions and meetings and get every bit of information I could obtain and write a report about it—every night.

"After a little more information this Mr. Keller told me to go home and write a sample report about our interview—and told me to meet him that night at a certain place with the report and my worst clothes, to be ready to leave . . .

"I wasn't going to turn traitor after all the years in the workers' movement—even though I was going to lose a pay envelope of thirty-two dollars a week—so that I was still unemployed that night—and the next—and the next—and I'm still unemployed because I'm a worker at heart and all over". . . .

FARM BOYS AND RADICALS: ORGANIZERS OF THE 1930s

This is a series of interviews with labour leaders about their lives as farm boys, bush farmers, and migrants in the 1920s, and their gradual change of attitude during the depression. It illustrates the different ways in which workers arrived at a radical position. These interviews should be read with some caution. The men being interviewed were all ideologues and are recalling events that took place 30 or 40 years before.

Both Mitch Sago and Nick Hrynchyshyn were leading members of the Ukrainian Farmer-Labour Temple Association, and active members of the Communist Party.

Bert Gargrave was a prominent CCF organizer in British Columbia.

Mike Fenwick was a CIO organizer in the packinghouse and steel industries, and son of a Winnipeg striker.

These interviews are part of the York University Oral History Project and were taped in the period from 1971 to 1974. The interviewers were Irving Abella, David Chud, and Steve Penner, and the tapes were edited by Irving Abella.

Mitch Sago
...We lived in an Anglo-Saxon area of Winnipeg. I found when I went to school a tremendous hostility towards me. I was called all the appellations that were used against foreigners and particularly Ukrainians, such as Bohunks, Galicians, and names of this order. Nobody ever called me by my name. And there were gang-ups on myself. I used to have to confront four, five, or six boys, and finally it reached the point where I raised the matter with my parents. I told them that I couldn't continue to go to school under these circumstances and that was when my father told me that there's no point in him going down. I think the very idea of having to speak to someone in English at the school intimidated him, but he said you do exactly what they do, fight back, and the next day I became involved in one hell of a battle with a couple of the boys—one of them was the son of the chief of police in East Kildonan—who came after supper to visit my father and asked if I was his son. He said, 'Your son beat my boy up' and he turned to me and asked me if it was so, and I said, 'Yes, I did.' 'Well, why'd you do it? And I told him. 'Well,' he said, 'good, do it again if it happens', and he left. Here I thought I was on the verge of beginning my jail career. Things were bad as more and more Ukrainians moved into the area. For example, when a Ukrainian kid raised his or her hand and wanted to leave the room for the obvious reason, they were turned down. If moments later one of the English boys would do it, they were told to go right ahead, and on the slightest provocation kids got the strap and so on. Finally it came to a point

where the brother of one of the Ukrainian boys on our street complained of being mistreated and abused and the older brother came down and really beat up the principal. He figured that was the only language that seemed to be understandable at the time; that's how bad things were.…

This was part of a much wider kind of campaign against the Ukrainian immigrant worker. We were treated as second-class citizens. The feeling was that we were brought to this country because of our brawn and muscle, not because of our intelligence—some lower grade of animal or beast of burden, and this attitude spilled over in many ways, on the job, in the legislatures, in various ways, and I think this had a great deal to do with the way in which the Ukrainian immigrant community very, very quickly solidarized itself, created those organizations that were able to provide for a great part of their life-cycle, to respond to the needs of everyday living other than the market place where they had to mingle with other people of other origins. But there was a tremendous sense of discrimination and it wasn't taken passively. It was dealt with physically. Later on it was dealt with in an organized fashion and representations were made and so on.

So it was in this context that organizations like the Ukrainian Labour Temple developed. A number of cultural organizations were established, many localities for purposes of conducting literary, cultural, and theatrical work. There was a very extensive Ukrainian theatre. I remember that well. Many of the plays that were put on by that theatre were written in Canada, based on the experience of the Ukrainian immigrant worker. If you take into account that at that time, there was no radio and no television, entertainment was hard to come by, and I guess one of the basic forms of entertainment were the concerts that were held. I remember the packed halls where there'd be repeat performances on Sunday night, and as a matter of fact, when I finally did join the Ukrainian Farmer-Labour Temple Association in 1921, it was as a result of my interest in theatrical work, concert work, and so on. This is how I came in.…

I joined the Young Communist League in January 1930. I was fifteen. At that time I was foot-loose. Unemployment was already making itself felt. I became extremely active. I didn't know much about it. I liked the people, I liked their thinking, I liked what they were doing. I'm talking about the younger crowd, and I became part of it and because there was such a desperate need for cadre, I found myself very quickly with all kinds of assignments, some of which I couldn't comprehend at the time but tried to carry out, and one of the things that I did do as the result of coming into the Young Communist League was the assignment of going out and organizing some of the factory workers in the city.…

We first organized the Wellwood workers. We received a complaint from a number of them. I don't know how they came to us, but additional wage cuts were being planned. At that time they were getting 15¢

an hour and I think the wage cut would have reduced their hourly rate to something like 12¢, and these boys wanted to do something about it. The peculiar thing about this assignment was that when we began to come around at lunch-time—you'd talk to the boys, become acquainted to see if it was possible to organize them—old man Wellwood who owned the factory, he was a member of the Independent Labour party, he very quickly made himself known to me and to my buddy and said, 'There's no reason for you to have to talk to the boys here you know. You can use the lunch-room upstairs for the task of organizing them', which I thought was rather strange, coming from a man who was going to implement a series of wage cuts and telling me that I can organize my boys on his premises. As it turned out, a strike was finally called. It lasted seven weeks. There was quite a bit of shooting. I think it was the shootingest strike at that time. . . .

I forget how many rounds of bullets were fired by the police. The argument was that it was done to scare us, to intimidate us. See, attempts were being made to take out excelsior, one of the things that was produced at this factory, by scabs. It began by Wellwood using his own son and we had a tremendous picket line. Sometimes the picket line was as large as 1200-1500 people, maintained 24 hours a day. The pickets were fed at the Ukrainian Labour Temple on East Kildonan.

As one of the organizers of that strike I found myself in the position where, for the first time in my life, at about ten paces I was fired on point blank, in this case by Mr. Wellwood himself. That's the closest I've ever come to the business end of a rifle. The matter was raised in court later because quite a few of the strikers and pickets were arrested, brought to trial before Lewis St. George Stubbs, who threw the whole damn thing out of court. This too was rather strange because the complaint laid by the police was, and it was typical, that the unemployed had no business participating in a strike action. It wasn't their concern. Secondly, they were the real troublemakers and they dumped literally sacks of rocks as exhibits on the table in court, and I remember sitting there listening to Stubbs quite calmly tell the crown prosecutor and the police that any damn fool can walk outside this court room and come back with three or four sacks of rocks, so he said it doesn't prove anything. At that time already he was beginning to show a bias for the underdog, the underprivileged and so on, which led finally to his removal from the Bench.

I believe what it did was to serve notice on the people of Winnipeg that there was somebody in jurisprudence that was prepared to be fair and just in assessing a case such as this, that the courts wouldn't be used merely to intimidate as was the case in other instances. And secondly it was regarded as a victory by the strikers and by the people who participated with them and solidarized themselves with them. You know, the fact that some 20-30 men *don't* go to jail for an action of this kind, which today is accepted, at that time it was challenged by authority....

There were other workers who came down, not systematically you know, but from time to time, but you had the unemployed who participated, manned the picket lines. As a matter the *Winnipeg Free Press* called it the 'picnic line' because thousands of people would come from all parts of the city at nights. We had huge bonfires in an open area around the plant....

It was rather unusual in the period when more and more people were being kicked out of jobs you know, when there was a labour surplus on the market, to have people who dared to put their jobs on the line by taking strike action. In other words, this was a period when for every job that was pre-empted either by strike action or by a firing, there were a hundred guys ready to take it. The trade union movement as such, took an attitude that it was impossible to win strikes and all you could do by strike action was to endanger the jobs of the very few people that still had them, and it would be best to try and negotiate some kind of a compromise, so that the strike became a kind of focal point. The factory itself wasn't that important to the economy of the city but what suddenly became extremely important was what these men were doing about a situation that faced hundreds and thousands of other people in other jobs in Winnipeg. In other words, they were demonstrating that you don't have to take it lying down. That there is something you can do about it.

There were thousands of unemployed, young and old. There was no place to go, no place to turn. After months and months of running down to employment officers and trying to follow ads for whatever kind of job and getting no place, you finally had to make up your mind that this was it. The doors were closed, it was a dead end, and there was no place to go from where you were, you see in terms of getting a job, getting employment, so that's when I began to get totally and completely immersed in some of the organizing campaigns....

A number of miners from Flin Flon sent a letter to the Workers' Unity League and said, 'Is there anybody who can come down and help us to organize this place?' And Eddy Edwardson and I were asked if we'd care to go down. The undertaking from the man that wrote the letter was that we'd live at his place. He'd see that we were at least fed while we continued to work and he would assist in any way he could. It was a company town, a great deal of intimidation in it. There was absolutely no organization, so Edwardson and I went down.

When we came there, the fellow who wrote offered to acquaint us with some of the people who were interested in unions, but it was a company town; there was a high degree of intimidation, people were afraid to even breathe the word union. We organized at first a number of social gatherings in an old abandoned Chinese restaurant, began to collect money at these social dos once a week, and later we organized a branch of the Canadian Labour Defence League. Meanwhile we adopted a system of organizing groups of five into the union. Only one person in the five knew the five. The others didn't know each other in order to minimize the possibility of discrimination or some company stool getting in and squealing.

By that time it became very evident to the company that we were there to organize a union. We received threats on our lives—some quiet night when we would be crossing Ross Lake, we wouldn't make it across the lake. By then we had moved to a small, knock-down shack that was the home of a shoemaker, and in those 35 below and 40 below winter nights it was pretty tough. One of us always stayed awake to keep the fire going or nobody would wake up in the morning. We lived for a long time on a diet of rabbit stew, rabbit steak, rabbit soup, you name it, the basic ingredient was rabbit, which we trapped.

Later, after this place was bust up by some of these company goons in order to intimidate us and to get us to leave town, we moved in with a trapper, a giant of a man, a beautiful man, and here we continued to exist on rabbit and then something much classier, ptarmigan. It was the first time I became acquainted with ptarmigan. In this period we organized something like 700 miners into these groups. We were also placed in a position where if we wanted to talk to anybody we had to talk to them in some of the bootleg joints or in the red-light district. These fellows would go and you would happen to be there, and the girls who operated the red-light district were extremely sympathetic to the miners and when the strike broke, they voluntarily shut down the district. They were being encouraged to keep it open, to see that the guys got so heavily and deeply in debt that they'd be most anxious to get back to work rather than continue with the strike. In any event things became untenable for us. It was becoming obvious that the company had us under constant surveillance, that anybody caught talking to us was in imminent danger of losing his job, and so we left. . . .

There was a high degree of solidarity in these strike struggles. Every so often, of course, you'd find types that became scabs, strike breakers, but that was not characteristic of the unemployed. The other side of that coin was that scabs were taken care of. A lot of scabs couldn't show up at work the next day. This was how they handled that situation. If they couldn't enlighten them on what was involved, they would seek other means. The unemployed became highly organized in two divisions. You had the residential unemployed and the unemployed single men, the transients. In each case they had their own organizations, and in addition to the Unemployed Single Men's Association, as a corollary to it, there was the Relief Camp Workers' Union that eventually came up once slave camps, as they were called, were introduced. The residential unemployed in that period had neighbourhood councils with block committees as the basic unit of organization. These served as neighbourhood grievance committees, they were rooted in the neighbourhoods. Everybody knew everybody else and the state of life, the conditions in the various homes, but what was important about these block committees and these neighbourhood councils was the capacity for swift mobilization. All you had to do was tell the block committee chairman and the neighbourhood council chairman, and in short order you could call a public protest meeting. The Unemployed Single Men were also structured on a group basis and also for the same reasons, and I was the organizer of the Unemployed Single Men.

A bit later the neighbourhood councils became inoperative for a variety of reasons. What happened was they were transformed into ward associations or suburban associations. These associations, together with the Unemployed Single Men's Associations, formed the Manitoba Conference on Unemployment, a sort of a central body for co-ordinating their activities and their interests. . . .

In terms of activities, we began with market-square meetings, and soup-kitchen meetings. These were the order of the day, and these would range in size from a few hundred, if what was involved was small grievances, to ten and fifteen thousand on a larger issue, and on one occasion it was estimated we had 30,000 people on that square. There was no P.A. system you could use. We had something like 9 or 10 speakers' stands going simultaneously in order to get at the crowd. Some of the larger campaigns were involved with such issues as a works program with full wages, work and wages was the way that the demand was put; an end to means tests for people on relief where one day a month they would be required to cut wood at the city woodyard to prove that they were willing to work; liens against working-class homes in return for city relief, which led to the loss of quite a few homes; free and adequate medical care; cash relief instead of vouchers, and soup kitchens; and quite a number of campaigns against unproductive jobs in such projects as pulling up the dandelions on boulevards and parks and even such a ridiculous exercise as digging and filling in holes for no rhyme or reason, but just to keep you occupied and to make it clear to you that you weren't getting the relief as an acknowledged social responsibility by the authorities but because they were charitable. There was also the tough struggle in many neighbourhoods against evictions and the tax sale of working-class homes and the struggle against Bennett's slave camps.

During this period too, the Unemployed Association put out a daily mimeographed bulletin for sale on the streets in downtown Winnipeg and in the north end. The daily sales, depending on the issues that were dealt with ranged from a minimum run of 3000 to 7000 copies. In the beginning it sold for a cent a copy. I was one of the reporters when it first came out. The man who became the editor was a reporter on the *New York Times* and because of his addiction to alcohol he lost his job; he moved through many Canadian centres and finally stopped in Winnipeg and became our editor. I always remember him, typical caricature of the reporter with the cigarette on the lip and the bottle on the floor, knocking off these gems of his. One of his most popular features was the social column. You can imagine in that day and age having a social column in an unemployed paper in which some of the local socialites would be reported from the daily press as having worn this or that or having travelled to this or that resort town and in the next column, by contrast, he would carry a story about this unemployed woman who'd just been cut off relief or that woman who was refused clothing or whatever, so that this was one of the features that gained a great deal of attention and had much comment. . . .

There was confrontation on the streets and picket lines that led to numerous arrests and jailings throughout these years and throughout these activities and there was a need for an alert and active defence organization. This was the Canadian Labor Defence League. The CLDL, as it was popularly known, arranged bail, obtained legal counsel in all cases of arrest, and organized protest actions against the campaign of arrests and jailings in cases where there was absolutely no justification.

I was arrested in the course of the picket-line battles and the unemployed demonstrations a total of 19 times, and I was convicted 17 times over the course of these years. Actually the sentences and the charges had a greater nuisance value than they had of demobilizing value. They were obstructing a police officer in performance of his duty. This simply meant that when a police officer ordered me to order the unemployed off the picket line immediately, this happened so often, and when I refused, I told him, 'You want to order them, there they are, I'm not giving them that order', that would bring forth a charge. Well, the first arrest that was ever made that involved me was at the Manitoba Cold Storage Plant. I remember how mortified my mother was when I came home. She told me that she could never face her neighbours now that her son had his picture in the paper and it was blared all over, but here I'd jumped on the running board of a truck and told the guy there was a strike on and 'What the hell do you think you're doing man, you know better than this,' because he bowled right through the picket line and when the truck stopped there were six or seven police officers. When I was taken into custody, bail was refused. I don't know what the chief of police or anybody else was planning, but in consequence of the fact that bail was refused, a big demonstration was called across the Rupert Street Police Station. I recall hearing the shouts and voices and wondering what it was. After two hours of speech-making at this meeting and a delegation to police chief Newton, I was allowed out on my own recognizance. The situation in terms of these arrests involving myself became so ludicrous that Magistrate Graham on one occasion when I showed up for another of these trials said, 'My God, not you again.' He was just fed up seeing me in his court room. . . .

The forms of protest and mass action were varied. There were demonstrations in the market square, the soup kitchens, but there was a great deal of leafleteering to inform the public at large of the issues. And in the relief crisis that developed in 1934 when thousands were threatened by city hall with being cut off wholesale in order to bring pressure on the provincial and federal governments to assume a greater part of the financial load, there was a big sit-in organized of mothers and children at city hall. There were numerous parades and snake parades, a technique that was developed on the west coast and very hurriedly adopted by the unemployed single men in Winnipeg. We had a column of three abreast or four abreast, and we would start on one side of the street and cross over to the other and cross back so that the snake was developed in order to exert pressure on the authorities. It was a form of disruption of the traffic of the city; it had tremendous nuisance value in the sense that it did bring pressures to bear on the authorities. You had situations where for blocks and blocks on Main Street, traffic was paralyzed for an hour, an hour and a half, because by the time they got through snaking from one curb to the other it was just one huge moving mass of people.

Some of the other techniques were such things as 'visits' en masse to the department stores and other nuisance campaigns of a similar nature to exert pressure on the authorities. You had 1500 guys walk into the T. Eaton Company, touch nothing. There was tremendous discipline in the ranks all the time, otherwise these things could have got out of hand; they'd simply examine goods and ogle goods and look at them, goods they could never hope to buy, but again it was a nuisance value; you had other cases where men, say 100 men, 200 men cut off relief would be brought together and they would be divided among 8 or 10 restaurants, have a meal and then tell the guy, 'Phone the police'. So that the police weren't confronted with making one arrest, they were confronted with arresting them in substantial numbers. There was also the seizure of the Princess Street Soup Kitchen by the On-to-Ottawa Trekkers in Winnipeg on July 1st, 1935 as a form of pressure to establish a tent city on the old exhibition grounds, and also in order to relieve RCMP pressure on the On-to-Ottawa Trekkers who were in Regina. And finally there were tag days, street-signature campaigns and the like, too numerous to go into. There were delegations to the Relief Committee at city hall, to City Council, to the provincial government, and other such representations to the authorities that became frequent occurrences and which were usually backed up by demonstrations by thousands of the unemployed.

We had a ridiculous situation for the unemployed single men at the

Princess Street Soup Kitchen. The doctor came there and he held court once a week. He would be seated behind his desk, you would stand 10 paces away and he'd say, 'What do you want?' You'd tell him you'd got an ache or a pain or something. He'd say, 'You look pretty good to me.' They began to use this doctor for the purpose of cutting men off relief as pressure to get them moved to some of the camps. You were cut off relief. What was your choice? Bumming off the streets wasn't that rewarding any more, there were so many doing it. Another thing that happened in the soup kitchens was that the Brown Shirts were organized with the co-operation of some of those who were operating the so-called dining hall for unemployed single men—Whittaker's Brown Shirts, and they began to become quite arrogant. They served notice that no demonstrations would be tolerated on the Market Square, that they would break them up. It attracted some dim-wits because they were given brown shirts and belts. I don't know who put the money up. The big chief was Whittaker, and they were continuing to have military drills and formations on the Market Square as sort of spectacles of intimidation. We informed the press and the city at large that we would not tolerate any further gatherings of the Brown Shirts. We served notice that there would be a confrontation the next time they appeared on the market square and that we would not permit it to continue. This was also at the time of Hitler's rise to power; the struggle against Fascism had developed quite widely and here you had the same type of breed developing right before your eyes. They called a big demonstration on the market square as a challenge to us, and one of the bloodiest battles that ever took place on the market square took place here. They had a truck pull in towards our ranks. We surrounded them completely. They stood in military formation. They were being exhorted and so on. The big chief sat in the Leyland Hotel beer parlour waiting to be called when it was safe to come, and in came this truck with a tarpaulin over it. We expected something like this and it was loaded with sawed-off pipes of every description. On the market square at that time there were market gardeners from truck gardens in suburban Winnipeg and adjoining areas, and many of these Brown Shirts went home with their heads sticking out of a box of plants. Shirts were torn off, some of them were stripped bare and herded down William Avenue away from the market square. Quite a few lost their teeth. That was the end of the Brown Shirts; they could never re-group after that. . . .

There was a genuine concern with the human conditions of the times, which were bad and intolerable and something that a man couldn't live with if he was a thinking and reasoning person. There was my own feeling, which strengthened and grew the more I learned not only from experience but from reading and from listening, that things didn't have to be this way, that there were alternatives that could be found so that people didn't have to go through this periodically. You're completely disoriented. It's forgotten sometimes that during the 30s, people got down to some basic values, which is incomprehensible today when you talk to some people. At the bottom of everything was the struggle to survive. This was number one and you didn't have to be a politically developed person to understand that, it was a gut feeling and it motivated you, but in the course of fighting to survive, people grew. They grew ideologically, they grew in the methods of organizing their ranks and acting together and so on, and the goals became something larger than just a question of survival. I think many of the social ideas of fundamental change from the kind of society that we have in Canada to the kind of society where people can share the good things of life and the good things which they produce began to develop. But the one thing that the struggles of the 30s did, in a situation where there was a little hope, where all you could see was a sort of dead end towards any changes year after year, where people were physically demobilized, where their hands and their minds were idled, the organization of the unemployed created a feeling of optimism, it provided certain goals that projected beyond the immediate question of what do we eat today, what do we eat tomorrow. There was a radicalization that took place, both in terms of the intellectuals of the time and the broad mass of people that were activists in these groups and organizations. But to me one of the things that I always look back on was the simplicity of getting at the basic values that counted with people, and it wasn't very difficult for you to take sides on an issue. The issue was relatively simple. You know, are you going to eat tomorrow or aren't you? Are you going to have a place to sleep tomorrow or aren't you? Is your family going to be taken care of and clothed and hospitalized where this need arises or aren't they? It's not as complicated as life is today. . . .

Nick Hrynchyshyn
The biggest mistake my dad made, I think, looking back on it now because he had a good job, he had security and living in a city, but he listened to his friends and left the job and bought a farm in Prince Albert, Saskatchewan and that farming didn't go. No experience and it just didn't work out at all, and he realised he'd made a very bad mistake. After two years he was losing the little bit of savings he had and he realised that there was no future in that farm in Prince Albert. The land was poor, sandy and so on and he couldn't get his job back, though he tried, so they moved to Winnipeg and here, he couldn't get a job. It was the post-war period, difficulties, the economic depression set in there after the first war and what happened is he had some friends up north of Winnipeg in the Arborg district, and he went up there to see these friends of his and there another chance to buy a farm came up. Though

he wasn't too keen on it, there wasn't anything more to do. Couldn't get a job and there were three children in the family. He bought another farm out in Arborg, Manitoba, about 75 miles north of Winnipeg and started to farm again in 1921.

With the experience he had and having learned something about farming, it was a little better but certainly not anything too good. The farmers were in pretty difficult conditions there at that time and the farms were poor because it's bush land, swampy land, and required a lot of real hard work. That's where a lot of the Ukrainian people had settled.... You had to clear the bush and the stones and we didn't have the machinery we have now. A lot of it had to be done by hand, with horses or oxen and with the children working and the women working. Then my dad, having the trade of a carpenter and a car-repair man, would go out working during the summer and it became a way of living there for us. He was able to get some jobs building elevators and other construction work someplace, and we would be on the farm working with my mother. She was running the farm or looking after the farm. He'd make enough money during the summer to buy clothes and pay the taxes and other necessities, the bare necessities, and that's how we were able to make a go of it. And then as the 30s approached, the real hard times came to farms generally in Canada but to that poor district in particular, where the prices for farm produce were very low. I can recall that wheat sold for 25¢ and 35¢ a bushel. Eggs sold for 5¢ a dozen. It was very hard and the way the people there were able to keep alive was by cutting wood. There was a lot of bush in that area and they used to cut the cord wood for fire-wood in Winnipeg and haul it into town and get groceries for it, mostly barter. So there were farmers that hauled wood in ten miles, fifteen miles. It would be a whole day to bring that wood into town. You'd have to start out early in the morning and get home late at night and the wood sold for $1.25 a cord, so you could get a cord and a half on the sleigh, haul it in, and the women and the children cut the wood in the bush, in the snow and in the cold and the men did the hauling....

When the crisis came in the 30s, when the farmers were really hard up, I actually saw people going in rags because you could still somehow get food on the farm, meat and so on, but as far as clothes were concerned, they were hard to get, and especially in the winter it was bad because in cold weather, children had to go two miles to school....

I began to think about these things and my dad was reading the Ukrainian progressive paper, the Ukrainian Labour News. I began to read this paper and to realise that there was no need for this hardship and these hard conditions, that Canada was a very rich country, that it could be developed and there could have been work and opportunities for everybody but there was something wrong with the system, and I became active in the farm movement in Manitoba. . . .

There was a branch of the Ukrainian Progressive Organization in town, just a hall where we came together and held our meetings, put on drama. This was my beginning in community work. In this work I participated in putting on plays and concerts and educational work, and of course everybody talked about the living conditions. We had to talk about that and we had meetings on questions of taxes, of the need for building roads, and other things that farmers were concerned with at that time. There was a great event that took place in Arborg, gaining international attention I think. In 1932 the farms were in a desperate situation. Prices were low and one of the big problems was payment of taxes, there wasn't the money to pay taxes so the municipality decided to hold a tax sale. If you were three years in arrears, they could put your farm up for sale. So they declared a tax sale in Arborg in November 1932 and the farmers were very worked up about it because it meant, if they were gonna sell the farms, where were you gonna go? And the organization, the Ukrainian Progressive Organization and also the Farmers' Unity League, set up a farmers' organization of all farmers and organized the protest meeting to stop that sale. The farmers responded terrifically to that call, in defence of their farms and livelihood. Around 600 farmers came into that little town of Arborg beyond all expectations of the committee. I was on the committee at that time and we had a big, big meeting there. That was the first speech I made. I talked to the farmers, that we had to protest and we had to stop this sale because we had no place to go and we put so much work there, cleared the land and a lot of toil went into it by the men, the women, and the children, so they just couldn't sell it away from them. So we elected a delegation of five people to go see the Municipal Council who were present to hold the sale. And there was such a crowd, it was hard to control, but it was a very orderly crowd, well behaved though it was a cold frosty day. Some of the farmers had started to come in, to drive in at five or six o'clock to be there at noon, when the demonstration or the sale would take place, so the delegation entered. They were let in to go see the Council, and as the five members of the delegation went in, everybody wanted to come in too and before you knew it, they just couldn't keep the door closed, the few mounted policemen. They were not able to stop it and everybody just went in. In a few minutes the place was just packed, everything was full and they'd quite a crowd outside. So the delegation presented its demand that the sale be stopped, a moratorium declared on that sale. The reeve of the council, Mr. Sigwalison said, 'Sorry, I can't do anything about this. We have to have this sale, have to follow the rules and there's nothing we can do about it.' So we argued with him and he said, 'No, you just can't stop it.' So the demands came that if he can't stop it, he should resign and then he would not be responsible for it, so he said, 'Well, I can't resign either.' Some people were getting very impatient and I don't blame them for they were hungry, they were cold, they were worried about their farms. Mr. Sigwalison was pushed on to the table. It was so crowded that the next thing he knew, he was standing on the table and refusing to resign and refusing to stop the sale, so a few of the women were pushed on to the table there with him and started to argue with him more strongly and shake him up. He had just one arm and as the commotion developed his jacket came off, fell off and his trousers fell off, so next thing you saw, he was there in his underwear and he said, 'I resign, I resign.' Hooray, hooray! Everybody welcomed that, and we said, 'We want you to sign', and he signed. It was a great victory. There was no sale and everybody was very happy about it and went home. The next day we hear that a special train came into Arborg of Royal Canadian Mounted Police from Winnipeg and they were starting to search for people who were at the demonstration and the committee. There was no radio at that time in our house. Farmers who went into town came with this news and they brought us this bad news. So next day the police came along to our house. I remember that well and they questioned my dad and then they questioned me whether we were at the demonstration or not, and they took my dad, they arrested him. I was pretty young and my mother and the other brothers and sisters, they were very upset, and anyways I wasn't taken but my dad, they took him and he was arrested, 23 farmers were arrested, and then they were taken to Winnipeg and released on bail and we had a new situation. Protest meetings were organized again in the district but people were pretty terrified by this action and wondering just what would happen. Well we mobilized a defence movement and the workers in Winnipeg came to defend the arrested farmers. After a few weeks a preliminary hearing was held in Arborg. There were about 600 farmers at this hearing and there was another demonstration, another protest, very orderly, and the preliminary hearing decided to have the trial in Winnipeg later on.

They were charged with creating a disturbance, and in the *Free Press* and others there were headlines that the farmers have taken over the Council, that there was a revolutionary situation and all kinds of statements like that. The result of the hearing was that of the 23, 14 were charged and had to go on trial and at the trial 12 were sentenced to two years suspended sentence and my dad was one of them. The great thing about it was the defence was organized on the farms and in Winnipeg by the workers in the labour movement who came to the defence of the farmers.... Saul Greenberg was their lawyer, a prominent lawyer at the time. He did a marvellous job. It was a tremendous victory because the sale never took place. Those farms were never sold and the government had to make concessions and things were put off. It had a tremendous impact. It showed what the people could do. Another wonderful thing about it was the unity because the people there were from many political views and religions and they were divided often, quarreling amongst themselves, but on this issue there was real unity. 600 farmers came in and they were all together and they felt what power they had. . . .

Bert Gargrave

In the 1930s I was President of the Young Socialist League of British Columbia. We had a real, live-wire group. As a matter of fact, the youth movements were a lot stronger then than they were for any period afterwards. The Young Liberals and the Young Conservatives had groups and we had Sunday night debates in the Colonial Theatre. We used to pack the place but the collection would only just about pay the rent, but things became interesting. There wasn't much work to do and the result was you got together and then we studied as much as anything else. We had study groups. There were lots of kindred organizations in existence at that time. I was a member of the old Wobblies for a short while, had the little red card; they were quite powerful in the North-West, particularly in the woods. They had a pretty interesting tradition. They developed techniques of strike I don't think have ever been equalled. In the woods, for instance, particularly in the North-West as much in Washington and Oregon as in British Columbia, when things were pretty tough, there was no point in striking. You had no strike pay or anything else, so in many cases what the IWW tried to organize was three groupings. They tried to organize a group that were working, then they'd organize a group that was coming in, and then they'd organize an in-between group, so instead of striking, everyone would quit and then a new crew would move in and the old crew would move out and maybe go somewhere else and this was quite an economic strength. You could use your economic power without having picket lines and policemen harrassing you. You just quit and moved in and out. Now the Wobblies developed that technique excellently in many areas. They developed techniques in the railroads when they were trying to organize. Some of them were freight handlers and they would change the destination of freight. There's an interesting story of the middle-west where farmers, instead of getting a combine got a truck-load of coffins; these techniques were developed because there wasn't the normal, orthodox method of striking. Another interesting group that were quite strong at that time was the Socialist Labour Party and they, of course, believed in the industrialization of the state. They had the great wheel that they called it in which the industries were divided up into segments on the wheel and industry would control itself and there would be a council from the various industries which would, in effect, become the government. But a lot of out time was spent in debating and listening to lectures. I listened to a lecturer who came up with the Wobblies from Seattle. He didn't have too much of a formal education. I remember his name was Frank Roberts, and he would give five or six lectures on Marxism a week, every one of them different, which fascinated the younger people and gave us, I think, a greater insight into economies, particularly from the Marxian point of view, than you could get anywhere else, because you were living the life of a restricted economy. You knew very well what it meant when the supply and demand wasn't there, it was no longer a theory—it was a fact. As a result of that, we developed in British Columbia a pretty strong labour movement. It had been strong on and off for a long time. So there was a tradition of working-class activity in the political field that followed over to a great extent into the trade union movement. Now the trade union movement began to develop a little and things were pretty tough, there was a limited amount of work and those of us that were interested tried to keep the trade union movement intact. It was pretty difficult. It was more difficult in the trades in the AF of L because dues were the number one consideration at that time, and if you were three months in arrears, you were suspended. The industrial set-up that we had made provision for unemployed members. There was no provision at all in the constitution of the old AF of L craft unions. Then of course, the mutterings of the CIO were apparent at that time. There was a need for industrial organization because the crafts were fairly well organized but the major industries, of course, weren't. . . .

But the depression was getting stronger of course, and unemployment was very bad. Perhaps it was most visible in British Columbia because workers, and young workers in particular, would go to British Columbia from the east because it's easier to winter out there, and the conditions were a little better except as far as welfare or relief payments. They faced the same situation as they did in the east, and labour camps being set up for single unemployed at 20¢ a day. They were not too successful. There was this militancy in the west because of the fact that radicals tend to go west. There were demonstrations held almost daily on the streets, not only by single unemployed but by married people too. The relief payments were absolutely niggardly and you had the food hand-outs more than anything else. I've taken a sack of potatoes home. You'd get a sack of potatoes and a streetcar ticket. It was usual to see dozens of people struggling on to the street-car with all sorts of produce which they handed out instead of money. Now in 1935 I became Secretary of the CCF in British Columbia, and we were actively engaged in supporting the struggle of the single unemployed and the married people. I find it rather amusing now when I hear about the new politics of confrontation. We had those politics of confrontation in 1935. I can remember the police saying that there'd be no more tin canning on the street. The unemployed used to go around with a tin can. They weren't begging. If you wanted to put anything in, then fine. So then we organized a tin-can day for a Saturday and we got outside all the major stores, hoping that we would get arrested as well as some of the single unemployed, but it was the most lucrative day the tin-can has ever had. There were no arrests, but the single unemployed organized demonstrations in camps and it finally culminated in the Post Office Riots when they sat down in the Post Office in the Art Gallery. Things were still pretty tough and the single unemployed decided they were going to bring it pretty drastically to the attention of the government, so they sat down in the main Post Office and in the main Art Gallery in Vancouver. There would be I suppose about 500 single unemployed sitting down in the main Post Office. They had them beautifully policed. You would go and buy your stamps between these fellows sitting down on the floor. They sat down there for a good couple of weeks. This was getting to be a real problem. The authorities didn't know what to do about it. The fellows were getting fed. We'd organized a pretty fair support in the way of food and the fellows were being fed in there, but we knew that sooner or later they were going to have to be moved and it was rather interesting. I got a phone call about 2 o'clock on a Sunday morning from Harold Winch, who was leader of the opposition in British Columbia at that time, and he said, "The Mounties are going to turn out the boys from the Post Office and the Art Gallery around five or six o'clock in the morning and you ought to go down to one of them and I'll go down to the other." So I went down to the Post Office I got there about 5 o'clock. It was obvious what was doing. There was nobody on the streets except policemen and a few odd persons like myself. I'd gone down there to see what was going to happen and there must have been 50 to 100 policemen and they moved into the Post Office, everything was so quiet, Sunday morning 5 o'clock and out the guys came. They tossed in a little tear gas. As they came out, they had their clubs and they were giving these guys a real going over. Now there was a leader of the group named Steve Brodie and Steve was well known for his orange sweater and I saw the police beat the hell out of Steve right in the gutter outside the Post Office. He was the one they wanted to get. I guess they figured if they could immobilize him, they would take a lot of the strength away, but they didn't. He was pretty badly bashed and the whole group of the unemployed went down Hastings Street, smashing every shop window en route. There must have been 600 of them and then it swelled as the word got around as it does, to the different flop-houses and they all came pouring out as reinforcements, and the same thing happened in the Art Gallery. I wasn't there. I was at the Post Office. First Aid stations were set up in the Ukrainian Labour Temple and another big hall on Pender Street and a lot of women out to try and clean up the wounds of these guys. Some of them pretty badly smashed up.

Negotiations had been going on for a while but they said, "We want something more than relief camps at 20¢ a day", which was beyond the power of local authorities of course, but they weren't going to move. They were going to be put out and they were put out pretty ruthlessly. Now there were a lot of injuries. Several of them went to hospital, a lot of them went to hospital because they'd smashed glass on the way down but the whole place was a shambles around 6 o'clock on Sunday morning. I'll never forget it as long as I live. Well, we got busy and that afternoon, we organized a meeting, and it wouldn't be any exaggeration to say that there were 10 to 12 thousand people there, the biggest meeting I ever spoke to. I introduced the speakers. All you could see was a ring of mounted policemen all around outside of the crowd and it was quite a tense situation because the grounds were only a matter of 4 blocks from the city jail and there was a demand on the part of some of the more radical that they should go down there and get the guys out of jail. Had that happened, I don't think bloodshed could possibly have been avoided in large quantity because the police would never have allowed them to break into jail, the bastion of security, but the crowd disappeared after they had heard the speakers. Campaigns were organized all over the city and all over British Columbia, and it was shortly after this that the Regina Trek took place and a lot of the single unemployed, of course, went down with that and some of them finished up in Regina where the Regina Riot took place. . . .

Mike Fenwick

I was in quite a number of camps because every time you complained about conditions, the camp administration called the RCMP in and they would take you out and put you on the highway and say "Walk", so you walked as far as the next camp. Maybe in one case 5 miles and in another case 20 miles. The pay was 20¢ a day and we worked, from 7 to 5 on, clearing the brush and so on and preparing it for the highway, which then of course, they'd get machinery to grade. This is where actually a lot of the people who were employed got their organizing experience, so that when things improved, and plants began opening, in the mid-30s, when John L. Lewis of the United Mine Workers announced the formation of the Committee for Industrial Organization or CIO, these people responded very readily to organize the industrial plants here which were essentially unorganized. Labour organization in those days was confined primarily to crafts, the trades like the electrical, sheet metal, plumbing and so on, mainly in the building trades, which of course were also affected pretty badly by the depression. There wasn't too much work. I remember when I came to Toronto from the Lakehead in 1935, one of the unions, the Electrical Workers Union, was charging an initiation fee of $250.00 for electrical linemen, because they didn't want too many members because the work was so scarce. . . .

Just getting back for a moment to the work camps—the conditions in the camps were fairly primitive as far as living conditions were concerned. The men had no control over it and if the cooks wanted to make bootleg whiskey out of prunes then we wouldn't get any dessert for a week. So then the only answer was to have a meeting. Well, we'd call a meeting in the camp and send a delegation to the camp supervisor. The camp manager'd immediately say "You bunch of agitators and Communists," and he'd call the RCMP and they would merely take the group that he'd pointed out as the leaders of this alleged agitation and they'd take you in the car and drive you out a few miles and say "Walk". So we'd walk to the next camp and say "We're unemployed. We'd like to get on the camp staff," so they'd say "Okay" and it'd be the same conditions, the same pay, 20¢ a day which was minimal so you could buy some smokes. I don't think you could buy much clothes out of the $5.00 a month but we got food and bunk-house lodging. . . .

The first project I was sent to was Grassmere Ditch, which was a sort of canal-like proposition north of Winnipeg. We were digging a ditch, we didn't know why and in fact, 30 years later, the Roblin government filled it in. It was just a make-work thing so that I suppose the people with the strong work ethic would be satisfied that we did something for our 3 soup-kitchen meals a day and a room.

One year, they had a farm work scheme where they paid a farmer $5.00 a month and you got $5.00 for working for him which wasn't such a hot thing because the farmer of course, could keep you forever. If you quit and came back, you couldn't get back on the relief because the farmer had to vouch that he didn't need you any more and of course, having such cheap labour, why should the farmer say he didn't need you any more, especially since he got $5.00 bonus for it. There was quite a lot of opposition to this from the single unemployed. In addition there were thousands of people roaming the country on the freight trains, so in 1932 the R. B. Bennett federal government ordered the RCMP to comb all the freight trains and get the men into camps wherever they were stopped. They were sent to the nearest camp, nearest to the community in which they were stopped. Whenever we complained about something, we'd be picked up and evicted and taken to another camp. Once there were some people who were arrested by the RCMP because they had objected to something and the RCMP pushed them around. There was a fight so they arrested them, and I was asked if I would go to court and talk to the magistrate at Kenora about the boys, tell him what the story was. In this case the provincial policeman was the prosecutor, and the judge, of course, was presiding and he asked if these men had a spokesman, so I got up and said "I'm here to speak for them." So he said "Well you're one of the relief camp people," and he said, "All right, give me your story." Well, after he heard the case, of course he dismissed the whole thing and let the boys go. He said he'd had lots of experiences like this between Kenora and the Lakehead, and he'd like, if I could, to come any time he had a case so at least there'd be some sort of gesture of someone speaking on behalf of anyone who was arrested and felt he couldn't handle his own case. So I had a deal with this man that any time there were any arrests, he was going to handle, he'd wire me and I'd go up and find out what the score was and then I'd get up and tell the judge what happened for the record.

I'd been spokesman at some of the camps for the delegations that went to see the camp administrations and fellows usually said, "Go ahead. You're the guy to talk to them." In the absence of anybody else, I'd just have to go, and despite the fact that I never had any speaking experience or my knees were pretty wobbly. Well at that stage, some of the fellows said, "Well, gee we should organize a union." So we sent word round to all the camps. By then I estimate that throughout Ontario from at least the Lakehead to way up to Red Lake and Kenora and that area, up to Sudbury, there were about 300 camps. So we sent fellows who hopped the freights. It was pretty easy to get on. We made some collections at the Lakehead amongst the community and printed up a card. There was a fellow who had some space over his hardware store in Port Arthur and he told us we could use the place for our office if we wanted to, so we were in business.

Our mail was always intercepted if it wasn't in camouflage. What we eventually started doing was that when we'd send the guys leaflets, we'd wrap them up in all kinds of coloured paper, pink and so on, and throw some tonic on it so it would smell and it went through. Otherwise, if you just sent straight mail, the camp authorities used to open it and censor it. Well, there was a lot of unnecessary fear on the part of the authorities. I think R. B. Bennett himself must have felt that he was facing a revolution because Canada never faced such a depression before, and of course there were thousands of unemployed just roaming the country on the freight trains. You'd have 600 or 700 people on a human freight train, thousands of them, and of course everybody went from east to west in quest of the same non-existent job. It was just a case of moving and asking, hoping that there was a job....

After we organized the Relief Camp Workers we decided to try and get relief in the town and see if we can't have some sort of an office to run the administration of the union and send delegations to the government. We had several delegations to Premier Henry [of Ontario]. His only offer was to give us some land in Kapuskasing to grow potatoes, and if you've ever visited Kapuskasing, see if you could ever grow potatoes in that muskeg. Apparently he hadn't. . . .

In Sioux Lookout, Ontario, I had a memorable experience. There were a few of the fellows arrested and I had gone there to see if we couldn't get them out from jail, then I was picked up and arrested. I had a leaflet made in Port Arthur asking the fellows in the camp nearby to stop work that day, to strike when the boys were going to go on trial. When I got to the post office, there was a man lurking there. I asked the fellow at the wicket if there was any mail for me and he says yes, so he gave me a bundle and I had it in my hand and as I was leaving the door of the post office, the hand descends on my shoulder and he says, "Come with me." The provincial jail was just across the street. I said, "What for?" Well, he said, "We're charging you with having seditious literature." I says, "Well, how do you know I've got it in my hands?" He didn't say anything so I assumed that they checked out the post office which had shown them the leaflet. I was charged with possessing seditious literature. Well, at that stage, I got a wire from Reverend A. E. Smith, of the Canadian Labor Defence League, and I thought that was very nice of the old gentleman to send me a wire. They're ready to defend me. I was in jail for about 8 days when a fellow came in and said he was from Toronto. He was a lawyer. He was going to Kenora. These fellows who were arrested were taken to Kenora for trial and he was going there but he thought he would stop over and get me out before going to the other one, so we had a trial that night. The magistrate was a surveyor and part-time magistrate for cases like mine. The provincial policeman was the prosecutor and he pulled out the leaflet and read the call to down tools in sympathy with our brothers who were arrested and said that's sedition. So Brown said, "Under what section of the Criminal Code is it sedition?" The policeman pulled out a clipping from one of the Winnipeg papers quoting R. B. Bennett as there'd been a lot of seditious talk all over the place. Something's got to be done about it. So the lawyer said to the magistrate, "Well I don't think my friend's got much of a case. The fact that a prime minister makes a statement in parliament and it's quoted in the papers is not the Criminal Code. I suggest that you let my client off with an apology." I guess the magistrate thought he'd better let me out, so he let me out. Well, then the Canadian Labor Defence League sent a girl who was their representative at the Lakehead to go to Kenora about arrangements for the trial of those fellows who were arrested. Before going on trial in Kenora, and she stopped over to talk to me about the background of it and so on. Well, that stage, I had really nothing to do in the area. I was out of the relief camp, so I decided to go to the Lakehead and that's when I met these young people from the Young Communist League and so on and I joined the Young Communist League.

As far as my experience went, they were the only ones who were vocal on our behalf. I didn't hear anybody else. Now whatever motive they had is something else, but the fact remains that to me, an unemployed person, the only people I heard who were interested in our situation, and in our welfare, were those people, so I felt that I'd like to help other people too and this is the attraction they had at that stage. Mr. Bennett may have railed against them that they were scoundrels and that they were Moscow agents and all that, but as far as Moscow agents, to me that had no relevance because I didn't see any Moscow agents except this girl, and she didn't look like a Moscow agent to me. A lot of people joined at that stage. You know, they went out to organized unemployed. They promoted sympathy in the community for the unemployed, then they tried to organize unions where established unions didn't want to go in, like lumbering and mining. So these people went in and did the work and they certainly in that particular period had a lot of spark and a lot of following. Finally in 1935 I left the camps and came to Toronto and I was unemployed and took part in the single, unemployed demonstrations.

In 1936, the CIO started organizing in the United States, and in 1937 the Oshawa General Motors people organized. That was the first big move of the mass-production industries to organize, and shortly after that, while still unemployed, I was helping to organize the Packing House Workers. Canada Packers here and Swifts and in 1940, I went to work for the United Steel Workers in Oshawa, where they had several plants and the area covered also Bowmanville, Port Hope and Whitby, then of course, the war broke out and things picked up and everybody was working. A lot of the unemployed went and joined the army. That eliminated the surplus labour. . . .

'FOR SOME, NOTHING CHANGES'

This final excerpt from a hard-hitting study done for the Ontario Federation of Labour is concerned with agricultural workers in Canada in the 1970s. It is clear that the working conditions of these men and women—and boys and girls—differ very little from those faced by unorganized workers of 40 or 50 years ago. For most Canadian workers—those covered by minimum standards laws, or the 35 per cent in unions—conditions over these years have improved drastically. For those not protected by legislation— most women, many immigrants, all agricultural workers—nothing has changed.

Bob Ward, *Harvest of Concern*, Ontario Federation of Labour, 1974, pp. 5-15, 25-33, 54-66. Reprinted by permission of Bob Ward and the Ontario Federation of Labour.

Agribusiness and the Farmworker
On many family farms, particularly the 29,000 reporting less than $2,500 income in 1971, the farmer barely survives at a poverty level.... At the outset the OFL wishes to make it clear that our sympathy is with the farmworker and the working family farm unit. The family farm has always had an uphill fight and has been caught in a constant rip-saw between the agricultural implement, fuel, and chemical companies, on the one hand, who exploit and grossly overcharge farmers for basic farm needs, and the big processors and wholesalers on the other who set down the prices.... Very few family farms employ any help, and where seasonal labour is hired, most reports indicate that workers are treated with some decency and respect, unlike the reports emanating from larger corporate farm operations and agribusiness concerns.

The farming community in Ontario consisted of 94,722 census farms in 1971. Only 38 per cent of these hired paid labour....

The major area of this study is field crops, fruits and vegetables, grown and harvested in Southern Ontario south of the line between Sarnia and Niagara Falls, Ontario. Farms in this area employ about half of all seasonal or part time labour used in Ontario. In 1970, a total of 800,426 weeks of temporary paid work were reported, the equivalent of 50,000 workers over a four-month period.

The farm labour force in Ontario is made up of local residents, our native people, youth, migratory workers who traditionally come from other parts of Ontario, Quebec and the Maritimes, and 'offshore workers', chiefly from four Caribbean islands, Mexico and Portugal. The local workforce is drawn mainly from housewives, students and others available in the area. The Caribbean seasonal workers are brought to Canada as part of a negotiated agreement [of 1966] between Canada, Jamaica, the Barbados, Trinidad and Tobago.... In Ontario we have several categories of 'migrants', and the definition used in this study is "a farmworker who travels beyond ordinary commuting distances and is employed in agriculture."

Traditionally there has been an annual exodus of families from Northern Ontario, Quebec, and the Maritimes to Southern Ontario under private arrangements between the grower and these families ... the families are usually large and all but the youngest children work in the fields with their parents, contributing towards total family income.

It is an anachronism that firm agreements between Canada and the Caribbean Islands (and now [in 1974] Mexico) that provide a $2 an hour minimum wage and decent living and working conditions do not apply to

Canadian citizens. Canadian farmworkers are not covered by minimum wage laws. Minimum conditions of work and sanitation are denied Canadian farmworkers. The exclusion of farmworkers from the Ontario Labour Relations Act and Canada Labour Code denies them the right to organize and win union recognition in order to struggle collectively for decent wages and conditions. The Employment Standards Act of Ontario specifically excludes farmworkers from its provisions denying them even this minimal protection.

The farmworker is little known to the bulk of the population. Most toil at the back-breaking task of 'stoop labour' remote from major highways and well-beaten paths. Much of the work demands constant bending, or working on hands and knees. This point is made by Stompin' Tom Connors in his song dedicated to a season worked at Tillsonburg, Ontario —which sings out "Tillsonburg—my back begins to ache when I hear that word...."

Harvest of Shame
In August, 1973, instances of feudal practices in Ontario's rich farmlands broke onto the public scene with the scathing report of the Task Force appointed by the Ministry of Manpower and Immigration. It had been publicly charged that "crops were rotting in the fields in Southwestern Ontario" with the Manpower Ministry singled out as the culprit for not having an available workforce on hand. Charges were also made by some growers that Canadians, including students, wouldn't take off the crops, that they were lazy, indolent, or overly dependent on government "hand-outs", welfare and unemployment benefits.

Striking back at the critics, the Task Force report said: "The Department of Manpower and Immigration has been taking it on the chin for all the ills said to be plaguing agriculture, including labour shortages caused by reasons over which we have no control...." The Task Force called for an end to the exploitation of... defenceless workers and their families from remote areas in Canada and from other countries, particularly Mexico and Portugal. It said the use of child labour, and in some instances sick, pregnant or otherwise physically unfit adults to a considerable extent helped underwrite growers' costs. "This reference is not only to Mexican families, but also to families—for the most part uneducated and unused to any other way of life—from other parts of Canada.... Until measures of elementary social justice such as minimum wages in agriculture, regulations concerning child labour, and better health inspection services are introduced, this unsavoury condition could continue."

Among the most victimized of all migrants are Mexicans, mainly of the Mennonite faith, who left Canada at the turn of the century and migrated to northern provinces of Mexico. Most of these migrants are in the country illegally. This occurs when the grower invites the father to

Ontario for a 'visit'. The 'visit' quickly turns into a summer-long job, and the father is then joined by his wife and family—often 12 to 15 children—who all work in the fields with their parents. It is customary that only adult family members draw wages....

Exploitation of our native people in farm work has long been practiced. A representative of the United Church Social Services reports visiting an Indian farm worker employed in the Beamsville area where due to inclement weather this "full-time" farmworker had only made $29 for an entire week's work. The family of six children had been without milk for four months and were destitute when the church worker visited them. The 'house' provided for the worker and his family was far below any acceptable standard of decency. The oldest boy, 15 years of age, had to sleep in a make-shift hammock suspended above bunkbeds occupied by the other five children. Another of our native people described being housed on one farm where "we had to move the bed several times in the night every time it rained".

In the Chatham area this season a grower said he didn't want French-Canadian workers because "they all stink". A prosperous tomato and cucumber grower in Southwestern Ontario referred to the accommodation provided for Mexicans on his farm, "They live like pigs in Mexico. If we gave them anything better here, they would feel uncomfortable." This chorus has sounded down through all time and has been used against all exploited peoples especially the blacks, or those of foreign extraction. In earlier days on this continent the same put-downs were hurled at Irish workers, driven from their own land by potato famines. The Toronto *Star* editorially put the matter in proper perspective when it said: "There is no room here for the mentality that says it is permissible to treat migrant workers like cattle because they are used to no better at home.... This is Ontario," it said, "and the conditions that apply here are the point at issue."

[By contrast, the Caribbean Agreement of 1966] provides that a farmer applying to Canada Manpower for seasonal workers must guarantee a minimum of six weeks' work at an average of $80 a week, guarantee return air fare with a maximum deduction of no more than $66 and assure decent living accommodation. To see these conditions are complied with, each island government has a liaison officer who has authority to inspect and certify living quarters and act as ombudsman for the workers in labour disputes or other problems.

Contractors Exploit Farmworkers
On May 30, 1973 a van carrying 22 migrant workers to hopyards near Chilliwack, British Columbia blew a tire and overturned. One of the migrants was killed, several seriously injured.

The van, now a twisted wreck in a scrapyard, had been fitted with planks to jam 22 persons into an area, which, police said, had a normal capacity of 10.

The driver of the van was a labour contractor, a growing breed in the country, who ship migrant workers to the fields like cattle. One of the injured women said that the overloading of vans was so bad "that it was common practice to drape all window areas so nobody could see how many people were crowded inside".

For delivering these exploited East Indian workers to the grower, the contractor received 75¢ an hour for each worker. That's $16.50 an hour! For a 10-hour day, common in the fields, it's $165 a day extracted from the pitiful pay of workers, who through normal channels. They thus become victims of unscrupulous individuals of their own tongue who 'contract' their labour for the growers.

The *Vancouver Province* report [June 12, 1974] said there is difficulty obtaining seasonal help and that "Middlemen have jumped into the void by placing advertisements in East Indian language programs...the advertisements tell people in Vancouver that jobs are available in the fields and that transportation will be provided...."

Farm labour contractors are also gouging their pound of flesh in the Chinese community in Vancouver, supplying elderly workers for as little as $1.40 an hour take-home pay....

As reported by the Manpower Task Force there are numbers of Montreal and Toronto-based Portuguese 'contractors'. These body peddlers recruit fellow Portuguese from the most impoverished sector of Portugal, contract them out to Ontario farmers and extract a flat fee of $500, plus air passage return. On the $500 fee alone, the 'contractor' picks up the entire amount earned by the Portuguese worker for at least seven or eight weeks hard labour in the fields. The government is aware of this nefarious practice and seemingly it is viewed as fair play within the context of the free enterprise system.

An arrangement is also reported in the movement of farmworkers from the Caribbean islands where, at least in Jamaica, the selection of those coming to Canada is part of a patronage system with Jamaican political bosses in on the action.

Sweatshops in the Sun
One hundred and fifty years after Charles Dickens and others campaigned for an end to child labour in industry in Great Britain, the United Nations reports that over 40 million children are still employed in agriculture throughout the world. Sadly enough, 'enlightened' nations such as Canada and USA have their fair quota of this world-wide exploitation of young children. In Dickens' era it is recorded he was castigated in the House of Lords for 'seeking to take away from British children their inherent right to work'.

Today when protest is voiced about child labour in agriculture the echo from the British House of Lords still resounds. Agriculture Minister Whelan stated [Aug. 18, 1973]—"It's part of the farm heritage for children to work. We'd pay a hell of a lot more for food if it wasn't. Child labour is a fact of life"....

It should be noted that being the child of the owner of the farm and doing ordinary chores is an entirely different matter from being the child of a farmworker, toiling day-long in the field, contributing almost from infancy to family income, and being destined to a lifetime of rural poverty.

What the [big Ontario] farmers' representatives want most is to be able to hire Mexican workers on employment visas so that their families can accompany them and work in the fields as they have done for many years in Southern Ontario....

The *Ottawa Citizen* [Feb. 18, 1974] reported that the Department of Manpower and Immigration, based on the report of their Task Force, wants to stamp out child labour in the fields. The OFL wholeheartedly endorses this endeavour of the Manpower Ministry....

The Manpower Task Force uncovered a French-Canadian family of 11, nine of them children, living in a "filthy drafty barn". The grower argued vociferously that the accommodation was one "where you or I would be proud to live". Members of the Task Force didn't agree.

They described another 'home' visited in this way. "The shack consists of an entrance-way and one room, where the family cooks and eats and the parents sleep.... There are no toilet facilities, apart from the natural ones outside...Unconnected is another shack where all eight children— aged 4 to 17—sleep, four boys and four girls, in one room". The owner claimed this family could easily earn "up to $150 a day" picking cucumbers and tomatoes. The Task Force report said that the father of the family advised them the entire family, including all children except the four-year-old earns between $50 and $60 a week.

A Mexican family of 15 persons, father and mother and 13 children, said they had come to Canada in April, would work to November, and in "a good year the entire family would net maybe $2,000, and in a not so good year, maybe $1,500".

Another ramshackle building was described in which a Mexican family resided and for which they pay $30 a month rent. "We were taken through this 'house' and found a scene of almost indescribable squalor. ...A stove pipe led from the stove through the roof. Wrapped around the pipe at the roof intersection were layers of cardboards and newspaper to keep the rain out. The place was literally a death trap if a fire ever broke out...and there is only one door."

This story would likely have never been reported but the family had come to the attention of a minister and local health authorities when the mother was admitted to hospital for caesarian section childbirth. The baby girl was kept in hospital, but the mother was back in the fields two weeks after her operation.

It was learned that each of the seven children, ranging in age from 8 down to 2 years, had at least one hernia, that they were ruptured when they came to Canada illegally and would continue to work despite this disability. Primitive toilet facilities for this family were situated beside a corn crib.

"Without trying to lose our objectivity," the report concluded, "this one scene appalled and sickened us more than any other on this assignment.

One spokesman told the seminar that a main problem in establishing decent wage scales on the farm had been that the farmers tended to base wages paid on what they make themselves. He suggested that attractive wages, even in excess of what the farmer made, was one possible solution to the farm labour shortage. He argued that farmers, unlike the hired help, have the security of owning the land, a position of status in the community, and the assurance of being able to sell their land, if need be, to live well in their old age. The farmworker, he said, should have a higher disposable income than the farmer if there is a serious desire to overcome the chronic labour shortage.

In Southern Ontario the urban areas grow at an ever accelerating rate, sprawling into the neighbouring farm areas and offering much more attractive work at substantially higher pay rates, a 40-hour work week, minimum standards on the job, fringe benefits including paid holidays, vacations, health coverage and pensions. Southern Ontario factories at Windsor, London, Kitchener, St. Catharines and other centres offer job inducements, so favourable by comparison with those on the farm, that large numbers of farmers' sons are lured off the farm and into the factory. . . .

Reports keep cropping up to show why Canadian workers are not enchanted and enamoured with life down on the farm. A [July 24, 1974] Globe and Mail article reported a farmer's complaint that "no one wants to work on their knees anymore." The article described work in the Holland Marsh lettuce patches where the workers get up before 5 a.m. and spend the 10 to 12 hour day working on hands and knees. For this back-breaking work the hourly rate is $2.25 an hour. The farmer conceded that this is possibly why farmers can't get labourers to commute 40 miles from Toronto, and also admitted that farmers who paid $3.25 an hour had no trouble getting workers.

Farms in the Holland Marsh area employ about 100 West Indian labourers. One worker said that in a good year he might take $600 back to Trinidad after five months work.

Typical of conditions and attitudes is the comment of the grower:

"After all, we are not overseers, they can go out in the evening." After 10 to 12 hours on hands and knees in the fields at a rate of $2.25 an hour how many of these farmworkers take advantage of this particular bit of freedom?

On the tomato farms of Southwestern Ontario the picker's rate in 1973 was 22¢ for a 35 lb. hamper of tomatoes. At this pay rate a worker had to stoop and pick a ton of tomatoes to make $13.35. A day's pay of $26.70 meant picking two tons, an almost impossible task.

Always, however, in the farm scene, the basic problem comes back to economics. The Ontario government knows this well. In August, 1969 it conducted a survey of its own. The 87-page study was to ascertain the feasibility of extending the minimum wage and other minimum employment standards to farmworkers.

The report, presented to both the Minister of Labour and of Agriculture in November 1970, was never acted upon. When this document finally came to light, the Toronto *Star* asked government spokesmen what action would be taken. The answer: "No legislation to improve farm wages is planned."

The report showed that 42 per cent of agricultural workers in Ontario received less than the minimum wage of $1.60 an hour. The top 54 per cent received an average of $1.71 an hour. Some 19,500 farmworkers made less than $1.60 and 13,480 made less than $1.30; 94.3 per cent of fruit and vegetable workers made less than $1.60 an hour. Yet in 1970 the average wage for industrial workers was $3.17 an hour.

The Summer of '74
Already, the construction and lumber industries are looking into the possibility of hiring from the pool of servile off-shore workers who accept wages below those required to provide a decent Canadian standard of living. Just recently we received reports that Canadian Canners Ltd. is bringing in 270 Caribbean workers to work in their canning plants. Libby's is also bringing in a hundred off-shore workers for the same purpose. This may be the thin edge of the wedge to undermine whatever standards we have in these factories. Organized labour is concerned.

Just what is going on 'down on the farm' in the season of '74? In Hamilton, Ontario, two French-Canadian youths, Jean, 17 and Richard 19, were found sleeping in a shack in a vacated construction site. They had come to Ontario to pluck the promised easy money in the tobacco fields. "We have no money and there is no place to go. Either we sleep here, or we sleep in the streets," Jean told a *Hamilton Spectator* reporter. They said as many as six youths slept in the 12 × 8' shack that had neither floor nor ventilation. The young men had fruitlessly searched for work in the Tillsonburg-Delhi area, but a late crop meant no work for these young Canadians.

A Hamilton youth hostel staff member said the story of Jean and Richard was not unique. "Tobacco workers will sleep anywhere or eat anything until they get work".... A major hostel in Tillsonburg, that accommodated 100 last season, was closed by government edict and hostel officials worked desperately to find alternate accommodation in a local church.

Migrant workers in the Chatham area, directed to work on fruit farms, found no living accommodation and picketed the home of Mayor Doug Allin, to publicize their plight. The Migrant Farm Workers Association, which organized the demonstration, had tried unsuccessfully to have a hostel constructed in Chatham. "Transients have been legislated out of Tecumseh Park at night and insurance companies are clamping down on churches that provide overnight accommodation," a Chatham United Church minister said. "Where are they to go?"

At Leamington tragedy struck a Mexican Mennonite family when their pick-up truck collided with another vehicle. H. Klassen, the father, and two children, eight and nine years of age, were killed. Four other members of the family are in serious condition in hospital. The family was here from Mexico to work in the fields. Authorities had no record of the family even being in Canada, not uncommon when it is recalled that the second Task Force report in 1973 found that of 471 foreign-based farmworkers interviewed, 145, an amazing 30.8 per cent, were in Canada illegally.... Even with the attempt to clamp down on the uncontrolled movement of Mexican families, it is possible that the 'male over 18 years of age' is duly cleared and airborne to Canada, only to be joined later in the fields by wife and 10-12 children who 'find' their way illegally into Canada. The great tragedy of the Henry Klassens is that they became identifiable statistics only at the cost of family tragedy.

Just south of Waterford [a Canadian] family of 11 worked in the fields throughout the season on the back-breaking cucumber and tomato crops. The family comes from northern New Brunswick where unemployment runs substantially above the national average and where available work draws low wages.

The father, mother and nine children, ages 3 to 18, have been migrating to Ontario for a number of years to earn a stake during the summer to supplement the $90 a week the father is able to make in New Brunswick. For much of the season the entire family lived in a large tent pitched on the farmer's property. No conveniences, other than the natural ones in the countryside, were provided.

Disdaining welfare, the family works ten hours a day for four months, in conditions of severe privation, to earn enough money to supplement the father's meagre income. Even with rigorous budgeting, the family must deprive themselves of basic essentials in order to make the money stretch throughout the year.

The children suffer the many afflictions that derive from malnutrition, from never having had an adequate income to provide nutritious food. Yet the pride of the family, their determination to cope, their belief that their eagerness to work will ultimately achieve security and 'a better life for the kids than the parents had', defies description. Like the great majority of Canadians they despise welfare of any kind and the stigma attached to it. . . .

Last year this family made a little more than $4,000 for the entire season. They should have made more, but were cheated out of a portion of their earnings by the grower who had agreed on a 50-50 split on cucumbers marketed, but subtracted from the family's share his own costs of trucking the crop. Like most such deals between grower and farmworker, the arrangement had been a 'gentleman's agreement', and in this instance the grower proved to be far from a gentleman.

One point that most rankles Canadian farmworkers is holding back or 'banking' monies earned until the end of the harvesting season. The rationale for this widespread policy, that would never be tolerated in other sectors of the economy, is supposedly to ensure that the workers will stay on the job until the crops are picked. What is not considered is the well established fact that farmworkers are impoverished and without funds of any kind when they are employed and desperately need monies earned on a regular weekly basis. It is widely held that many farmworkers never receive wages banked for them it they leave the job for any reason.

Government can no longer permit growers to bank farmworkers' earnings, except under a legal contract requesting such a procedure. Such long needed action would only bring Canadian farmworkers into line with policies already in effect with offshore workers. The agreement between Canada and Mexico, for example, states categorically that "the worker shall be paid weekly wages at his place of employment in lawful money of Canada . . . that the wages so paid shall not be less than the amount he would receive had he been paid an hourly rate of $2.00 . . . that the average income paid to him over the period of employment is not less than $80 a week . . . " The Mexico-Canada agreement further sets out that even when no work is done, for any reason whatsoever, the grower must pay the worker "a reasonable sum of money to cover his personal expenses . . . " Holding back any portion of Canadian farmworkers' wages is a feudal practice that can no longer be tolerated.

Another technique in withholding pay is reported from the St Catharines area where growers hire children who are told they'll be paid the following week. They're then advised to be at the Manpower office at a given time to be paid and the grower doesn't show. When the Community Counselling Service called the grower on behalf of the youngsters, he said they could come out to his farm to collect. This meant travelling 15 or more miles to get money owing to them by one of the Niagara Peninsula's most affluent corporate farmers. CCS also reported two teen-age boys fired by a strawberry grower and cheated out of $32 and $42 owing. The grower claimed he had not kept records of work done and refused to pay. An employer is responsible for keeping work records according to the Employment Standards Act.

"For throwing a strawberry at another boy," a teenager got fired by this same grower, and in another complaint he refused to pay a picker any wages until the end of the strawberry season. This, too, is contrary to the Employment Standards Act and practice established for off-shore workers that sets out that wages cannot be held back in seasonal employ-ment unless an agreement exists between employer and employee.

Dale O'Dell, CCS director, said that for every incident brought to their attention "There must be hundreds of victimized farmworkers who have no organization of their own to turn to for assistance that we don't hear about. It's criminal", he said, "that in cases where we have represented farmworkers to try to secure some justice we are compelled to use the Master-Servant Act, which as the name implies dates back to the days of complete servitude of the worker, making it almost legally impossible to secure a conviction against the Master." CCS is also highly disatisfied with complaints registered through Employment Standards.

The attitude of some growers towards farmworkers was frankly put in a series of articles in *The London Free Press* (Aug. 28, 29, 30, 31, 1974). The tomato grower interviewed by staff writer Julian Hayashi said: "Let's face it. Some are like pigs..." Eight members of a French-Canadian family from Gaspé area have worked summer-long for the grower but when asked what the family's name was he replied, "It's a hard name to say. Duchart, Dupart, DuChamp? I don't know. I think the father's name is Roland, though I'm not sure."

A Trinidadian worker told the reporter that he'd worked 86 hours at $2 an hour, a gross of $172., but when he was paid, with no explanation or statement, he only got $96 net pay. When asked how much money he thought he might take back to Trinidad the reply was, "Maybe I'll just take back my body. Up here a dollar is a dollar and it doesn't go far..." This worker and 20 of his fellow-countrymen work from 7:30 a.m. to 7:30 p.m. six days a week. No overtime is paid. A shower at their living quarters has been inoperative since mid-August necessitating arising at 5 o'clock each morning to get water from a neighboring farm.

The articles noted that severe as conditions were for Caribbean and Mexican workers, they get a better deal than Canadian workers. The off-shore farmworkers are guaranteed a minimum of $80 a week and tolera-ble living conditions. Canadians get no such guarantees, and the grower is able to hire employees without using the Canadian Farm Labour Pools. Thus even the minimal standards of CFLP have no bearing.

Hayashi reported that, "Canadian workers are not guaranteed housing and what housing there is, even though approved by the CFLP and the provincial health ministry, suffers badly in comparison with housing for foreign workers. . . . "

It is ironical that some in the farming community most critical of Canadian workers and who use terms such as "welfare bums", "government handouts", etc. are the same ones who for many years have received lucrative cheques and other government assistance in the way of subsidies and support programs. Some have been heavily subsidized "not to grow" various farm products. The Ontario Minister of Agriculture doesn't frown on 'handouts' passed by his own department, from which he got $1,000 to improve his barn and $2,000 for a new concrete silo. The minister saw no conflict in this.

The facts are that there is no loss of work ethic among Canadians. At a time when the average wage in industry is $171 a week, when the necessary income for a minimal standard of health and decency as set by the Canadian Council on Social Development for a family of four is $6,020 per annum, sub-standard wages of less than half the industrial average wage offered for much of the back-breaking jobs on the farms hold no incentive. They only condemn those working at these rates to a niggardly existence at poverty levels.

Today the farmworker is in similar straits to those of industrial workers in 1937. . . .

Bibliographical Note

After countless years of no activity the writing of working-class history has, over the past decade, become a veritable industry. Monographs, autobiographies, anthologies, and articles are appearing at an almost dizzying pace.

Much of the new important material may be found in various academic periodicals, the most significant of which is *Labour/Le Travailleur: The Journal of Canadian Labour History*. However, other key articles have appeared in the following: *The Canadian Historical Review, Historical Papers* of the Canadian Historical Association, *Acadiensis, Alberta History, B.C. Studies,* the *Dalhousie Review,* the *Journal of Canadian Studies,* the *Labour Gazette, Nova Scotia Historical Review, Ontario History, Histoire sociale/Social History, Industrial Relations,* and *Canada: A Historical Magazine.*

Despite the flood of publications there is still no comprehensive history of the trade-union movement in Canada. But both Irving Abella, *The Canadian Labour Movement* (Ottawa, 1975) and Jack Williams, *The Story of Canada's Unions,* are short, useful introductions. Much longer—and duller—are Harold Logan's *Trade Unions in Canada* (Toronto, 1948) and *Trade Union Movement of Canada* by Charles Lipton (Toronto, 1967). A good study of labour development is Stuart Jamieson's *Industrial Relations in Canada* (Toronto, 1973), while *Essays in Canadian Working Class History* edited by Gregory Kealey and Peter Warrian (Toronto, 1975) is a scholarly anthology with an excellent bibliography. Two interesting collections are *Canadian Labour in Transition* edited by R. Miller and F. Isbester (Toronto, 1971), and S. D. Clark's *Prophecy and Protest* (Toronto, 1975). Also helpful are *The Tyranny of Work* by James Rinehart (Toronto, 1975), Victor Levant's *Capital and Labour: Partners?* (Toronto, 1977), and Robert Laxer's attack on international unions, *Canada's Unions* (Toronto, 1976). For an earlier period the best books are

Robert Babcock's *Gompers in Canada* (Toronto, 1974) and *Canada: A Nation Transformed* by R. C. Brown and G. R. Cook (Toronto, 1974).

On industrial strife the two indispensable studies are Stuart Jamieson's *Times of Trouble: Labour Unrest and Industrial Conflict in Canada 1900-1966* (Ottawa, 1971), and *On Strike: Six Key Labour Struggles in Canada* edited by Irving Abella (Toronto, 1974). Of much less value is Walter Stewart's *Strike* (Toronto, 1975). On specific conflicts the best books on the Winnipeg Strike are *The Winnipeg Strike: 1919* edited by K. W. McNaught and David Bercuson (Toronto, 1974) and Bercuson's own *Confrontation at Winnipeg* (Montreal, 1974). Important as well, are *Winnipeg 1919* edited by Norman Penner (Toronto, 1975) and D. C. Masters' dated *Winnipeg General Strike* (Toronto, 1950). On the Asbestos Strike, Pierre Elliott Trudeau's *Asbestos Strike* (Toronto, 1974) is still the standard text, though for readers of French *En Grève* edited by J. P. Lefebvre is also useful.

For organized labour's relationship with the CCF, Communist, and other left-wing parties the three key books are Irving Abella's *Nationalism, Communism and Canadian Labour* (Toronto, 1973), Gad Horowitz's *Canadian Labour in Politics* (Toronto, 1968), and Martin Robin's *Radical Politics and Canadian Labour* (Kingston, 1966). Also informative are Norman Penner's provocative *The Canadian Left* (Toronto, 1976), Ivan Avakumovic's flawed *The Communist Party in Canada* (Toronto, 1975) and his *Socialism in Canada* (Toronto, 1978), William Rodney's *Soldiers of the International* (Toronto, 1968), Walter Young's authoritative *Anatomy of a Party: The National CCF* (Toronto, 1969), and Desmond Morton's *NDP: The Dream of Power* (Toronto, 1974). As well, David Kwavnick's *Organized Labour and Pressure Politics* (Montreal, 1972) is quite enlightening.

The regional studies of the Canadian labour movement are, except for Western Canada, quite spotty. For the West however two excellent works are David Bercuson's study of the One Big Union, *Fools and Wise Men* (Toronto, 1978), and A. Ross McCormack's *Reformers, Rebels and Revolutionaries* (Toronto, 1977). Others of some value are Paul Phillips' *No Power Greater: A Century of Labour in British Columbia* (Vancouver, 1967), and Jack Scott's history of the IWW, *Plunderbund and Proletariat* (Vancouver, 1976). For the Maritime Provinces both *Miners and Steelworkers* by Paul MacEwan (Toronto, 1976) and *Essays in Cape Breton History* edited by Brian Tennyson (Halifax, 1973) are useful. For Quebec, in English a most informative book is *The Bitter Thirties in Quebec* by Evelyn Dumas (Montreal, 1975). In French, worth reading are Jacques Rouillard, *Les Travailleurs du Coton au Québec* (Montreal, 1974), *Aspects Historiques du Mouvement Ouvriére au Québec* edited by Fernand Harvey, and *Le Travailleur Québécois et le Syndicalism* by Richard Desrosiers and D. Heroux (Montreal 1973).

Memoirs and autobiographies are also becoming a valuable source of information for students of Canadian social and labour history. The following are amongst the most useful: Steve Brodie, *Bloody Sunday* (Vancouver, 1975); Tim Buck, *Yours in the Struggle*, edited by Bill Becching and Phyllis Clarke (Toronto, 1977); Alfred Charpentier, *Cinquante Ans d'action Ouvrière* (Quebec, 1971); Silver Donald Cameron, *Everett Richardson* (Toronto, 1977); Hugh Garner, *One Damn Thing After Another* (Toronto, 1973); Sydney Hutcheson, *Depression Stories* (Vancouver, 1976); Mary Jordan's biography of R. B. Russell, *Survival* (Toronto, 1975); Ronald Liversedge, *Recollections of the On-to-Ottawa Trek* (Toronto, 1970); Dorothy Livesay, *Left Hand Right Hand* (Toronto, 1977); Tom McEwen, *The Forge Glows Red* (Toronto, 1974); K. W. McNaught's biography of J. S. Woodsworth, *A Prophet in Politics* (Toronto, 1959); and Dorothy Steeves' biography of Ernie Winch, *Compassionate Rebel* (Vancouver, 1960).

For aspects of the history of working women in this country the best ongoing source is the *Canadian Newsletter of Research on Women* published monthly by the Ontario Institute for Studies in Education. Important secondary material may also be found in the excellent *Women at Work: Ontario 1850-1930* edited by Janice Acton et al. (Toronto, 1974), Pat and Hugh Armstrong's *The Double Ghetto: Women and Their Work in Canada* (Toronto, 1978), Gail Cook's key study *Opportunity for Choice, A Goal for Women in Canada* (Montreal, 1976), Wayne Roberts' *Honest Womanhood* (Toronto, 1976), *A Harvest Yet to Reap* edited by Laura Salverson (Toronto, 1976), Veronica Strong-Boag's *A Parliament of Women* (Ottawa, 1976), and *The Neglected Majority: Essays in Canadian Women's History* edited by Susan Trofimenkoff and Alison Prentice (Toronto, 1977).

For social and immigration history there is no better place to start than the invaluable Social History Reprint Series published by the University of Toronto Press under the general editorship of Michael Bliss, which includes some thirty titles. In addition there are several crucial articles in the periodical *Canadian Ethnic Studies*. The best anthologies are *The Dirty Thirties* edited by Michiel Horn (Toronto, 1973), *Studies in Canadian Social History* edited by Michiel Horn and Ronald Sabourin (Toronto, 1974), and *Immigration and the Rise of Multiculturalism* edited by Howard Palmer (Toronto, 1976).

The following is, of necessity, a short list of what we consider to be some of the most useful social history books: Grace Anderson, *Networks of Contact: The Portuguese in Toronto* (Waterloo, 1974); M. Bergren, *Tough Timber: The Loggers of British Columbia* (Toronto, 1966); Barry Broadfoot, *Ten Lost Years* (Toronto, 1973); and *Six War Years* (Toronto, 1974); Terry Copp, *Anatomy of Poverty: The Condition of the Working Class in Montreal 1897-1929* (Toronto, 1974); James Gray, *Booze*

(Toronto, 1972); *Red Lights on the Prairies* (Toronto, 1972); *Roar of the Twenties* (Toronto, 1974); *The Winter Years* (Toronto, 1966); Robert Harney and Harold Troper, *Immigrants* (Toronto, 1975); Walter Johnson (ed.), *Working in Canada* (Montreal, 1975); Myrna Kostash, *All of Baba's Children* (Edmonton, 1977); Rolf Knight, *A Very Ordinary Life* (Vancouver, 1974); Elliot Leyton, *The Ravages of Industrial Carnage* (Toronto, 1975); Rex Lucas, *Mine Town, Mill Town, Rail Town* (Toronto, 1971); Vera Lysenko, *Men in Sheepskin Coats* (Toronto, 1947); *Man Along the Shore, Longshoreman's Oral History* (Vancouver, 1975); Gloria Montero, *The Immigrants* (Toronto, 1977); Joy Parr, *Barnardo Children* (Ottawa, 1976); Helen Potrebenko, *No Streets of Gold: A Social History of Ukrainians in Alberta* (Vancouver, 1977); Daphne Read (ed.), *The Great War and Canadian Society* (Toronto, 1978); Heather Robertson, *Grass Roots* (Toronto, 1976); Paul Rutherford (ed.), *Saving the Canadian City* (Toronto, 1974); Susan Trofimenkoff (ed.), *The Twenties in Western Canada* (Ottawa, 1972); and G. H. Westbury, *Misadventures of a Working Hobo in Canada* (Toronto, 1930).

Two other sources of great value are the many studies published by the Task Force on Labour Relations (Ottawa, 1968) and the superb series of slides in *Canada's Visual History* issued by the National Museum of Man (Ottawa).

Finally, an unequalled source of material on the history of the Canadian worker are the various Royal Commissions set up by both the Federal and Provincial governments. Their reports, and often the evidence on which these reports were based, can be found in the government document sections of most reference libraries. For the student of social history, the most helpful of the Federal commissions are the 1903 study of the strike of railway workers, the 1904 investigation of Italian immigration, the 1907 Toronto telephone strike, the 1913 examination of technical education, the 1919 survey of industrial unrest, the 1934 investigation on price spreads, and the 1935 study of relief camps. There are of course many others. In addition, the dozens of Royal Commissions appointed by each of the provinces also contain invaluable information.